Contents

BARRON'S

Regents Exams and Answers

Global History and Geography 2020

MICHAEL J. ROMANO, Ph.D.
Former District Chairperson, Northport School District, Northport, New York

WILLIAM STREITWIESER, B.A., M.A.
Former Social Studies Teacher, Northport High School, Northport, New York

KRISTEN THONE, B.A., M.A.T.
Social Studies Teacher, Smithtown High School East, Smithtown, New York

Glossary by
MARY MARTIN
Social Studies Teacher, Greene Central School, Greene, New York

Published by Kaplan, Inc., d/b/a Barron's Educational Series
750 Third Avenue
New York, NY 10017
www.barronseduc.com

ISBN: 978-1-5062-5407-4
Printed in Canada

10 9 8 7 6 5 4 3 2 1

Introduction

THE GLOBAL HISTORY AND GEOGRAPHY COURSE AND REGENTS EXAM

Upon completion of your Global History and Geography course in New York State, you will be required to take the Global History and Geography Regents exam. Since June 2019, two versions of this Regents exam have been available: the "Transition Exam in Global History and Geography" and the "Global History and Geography II Exam." The first version of this exam is referred to as the "Transition Exam in Global History and Geography" because it follows a similar format to the one used for previous administrations of this test, but there are fewer multiple-choice questions as well as a significant change in the content that is tested. This exam tests your knowledge of all major world events, key nations, and noteworthy individuals from 1750 to the present and your understanding of how the events that take place in one country often affect several other countries around the world. For this exam, you will be expected to recall information about significant moments in global history in order to answer multiple-choice questions; analyze passages, maps, and political cartoons; write a thematic essay based on a central theme and prompt; respond to several document-based questions; and write a document-based essay that addresses a given task. The second version of this exam, the "Global History and Geography II Exam," which will replace the "Transition Exam" in the near future, has a different format and method of testing your knowledge of all key Global History and Geography topics. While this book will focus primarily on preparing you for the "Transition Exam," you can go online at *bit.ly/Barrons-Regents-Global-2020* to prepare yourself for what to expect if you are taking the "Global History and Geography II Exam."

This book will provide you with all the tools you need to excel on every section of the "Transition Exam." First, review the format of this exam. Next, learn how to use this book, and practice the steps for success on this test. From there, study a series of test-taking tips that can be applied to all sections of the exam. Then, review the Glossary to familiarize yourself with important terms, international organizations and agreements, and important people who made a global impact from 1750 to the present. Next, complete the Practice Section of this book. It provides additional examples of the various question types that you will see on test day. Check the answer explanations when you are finished. Finally, take the June 2018, August 2018, June 2019, and August 2019 Regents exams. These exams will show you exactly how this exam is formatted, what types of questions are asked, and what topics, events, and key individuals are typically covered. Be sure to review all of the answer explanations, especially for any questions that you had difficulty with or did not answer correctly. These answer explanations will clarify why each answer choice is correct or incorrect, and sample high-scoring responses for the essays and each document-based question are included. After working your way through the test overview, the tips and strategies, and all of the practice material enclosed in this book, you should be more than prepared to achieve success on the Regents exam.

WHAT IS THE FORMAT OF THE TRANSITION EXAM IN GLOBAL HISTORY AND GEOGRAPHY?

The Transition Exam in Global History and Geography is a three-hour test that contains questions on topics, concepts, skills, and themes from 1750 to the present. Each examination will include:

Part	Question/Item Type	Number of Questions/Items	Percentage of the Total Exam
I	Multiple-Choice Questions	30	55%
II	Thematic Essay	1	15%
IIIA	Document-Based Questions	6–9	15%
IIIB	Document-Based Essay Question (DBQ)	1	15%

Each multiple-choice question will have four possible answer choices, only one of which is correct. Choose the best possible answer of those provided, and use the process of elimination to help you arrive at the correct answer. Refer to the “Specific Helpful Hints for Answering Multiple-Choice Questions,” beginning on page 9, for additional advice for answering these questions.

The thematic essay will be based on a specific theme, concept, or issue that you will need to respond to. For example, you may need to discuss historical themes involving belief systems, human rights, or political systems; geographical concepts involving specific places and regions or the environment and society; or major world issues such as war and peace, hunger and poverty, or economic growth and development. Review the "Strategies for Answering the Thematic Essay Question," beginning on page 23, for more details.

The document-based questions will ask you to review several documents and then answer questions based on the information presented in those documents. The documents may consist of written items (such as speeches, letters, diaries, or news articles) or non-written items (such as maps, cartoons, photographs, paintings, tables, or graphs). Pay attention to these documents and remember your responses to the questions, as these same documents and questions will help you as you work on the document-based essay. This essay will require you to write a response to a task using evidence from the documents that you reviewed to answer the document-based questions. You will also need to demonstrate some of the knowledge that you learned from your Global History and Geography course. Be prepared to make comparisons and contrasts or to draw connections between global events over time, if the task requires it. Familiarize yourself with the "Strategies for Answering the Document-Based Essay Question (DBQ)," beginning on page 30, in order to learn the steps necessary to score high on this section of the exam.

How to Use This Book to Study

This book contains various features that will enable you to get the most out of your review and help you score well on the Regents exam. The book is divided into the following sections:

- **Test-Taking Tips**
- **Glossary (of Important Terms, International Organizations and Agreements, and Important People)**
- **Practice Section and Answers**
- **Regents Examinations, Answers, and Self-Analysis Charts**

Read each of these sections carefully, and you will be on the road to success.

TEST-TAKING TIPS

These hints, suggestions, and practice questions will help you become a better test taker and enable you to develop the skills that will lead to success on the Regents exam. The sample multiple-choice questions, the thematic essay, and the document-based essay question will provide you with specific strategies for how to answer these question types. Read this section before you start your review and then again after you have taken two or three practice Regents exams. This step will help you realize how these hints have improved your score.

GLOSSARY

The Glossary contains important terms, international organizations and agreements, and important people that are part of the Global History and Geography course of study. The Glossary should be used as a study guide to help you focus on the key terms, turning points, and people in Global History.

PRACTICE SECTION AND ANSWERS

This section of the book provides an additional opportunity to prepare and practice for the Regents exam. Sixty multiple-choice questions have been selected that contain material from old Regents exams along with some new questions that cover Global History and Geography from 1750 to the present. In addition, practice document-based questions are provided along with two practice thematic essays and two practice DBQ essays. Answer all questions to the best of your ability. As with the previous Regents exams, carefully review the answer explanations provided and read the model answers for the document-based questions as well as the essays. The more you practice, the better you will become at taking the Regents exam!

REGENTS EXAMINATIONS AND ANSWERS

The final section of this book contains previous Transition Exams in Global History and Geography with an analysis of the right and wrong answers. These Regents exams are an excellent study guide because they focus on the key content areas of the course. Answer the multiple-choice questions first. This step will provide you with an overview of your strengths and weaknesses. Review the answers because they will provide you with additional information about a particular question.

Carefully read the model answers for the thematic essay and the DBQ. This step will help you to understand how the scoring rubric is used to determine the essay score on a scale of 1–5.

SELF-ANALYSIS CHARTS

The self-analysis chart following the Answers Explained section for each Regents exam has been designed to help you note the number of questions and the frequency of the questions in each of the five social studies standards. You should use the chart to analyze your strengths and deficiencies in each of the historical periods.

STEPS FOR SUCCESS

1. Read your notes, review packets, and material on the topics in the course.
2. Read the test-taking tips.
3. Check the Glossary to make sure that you are familiar with the information that it contains.
4. Look over the practice section and past examinations to become familiar with the format of the test.
5. Take the most recent Regents exam and try to complete it within the specified time period.
6. Check all your answers in Part I, and carefully read all explanations for the correct and incorrect answers, especially for the questions you were unable to answer.

7. Complete the self-analysis chart; this will help you focus on the areas in which you need more review.
8. Read your essay responses for Parts II and III, and compare your responses with the ones given in the book; check the rubric to determine how you would have scored on these parts of the exam.
9. Recheck your notes, review the test-taking tips, and continue to take more practice Regents exams.
10. Always think positive—you will succeed!

Test-Taking Tips

HELPFUL HINTS FOR ALL TESTS

TIP 1

Be prepared and have an optimistic approach.

- Organize/review your notes.
- Don't cram; develop good study habits throughout the year.
- Complete all your written and reading assignments on time.
- Be familiar with the format of the test.
- Review past exams under test conditions (no headphones, tablets, etc.).
- Visit *barronsregents.com* for the latest information on the Regents exams.
- Come prepared for the test; bring pens.
- Focus on the test.
- Relax and be positive.

TIP 2

Carefully read the directions and questions.

- Be familiar with the test directions before you take the exam.
- Become familiar with the grading of the test and which questions are worth more points.
- Circle or highlight important terms or phrases.
- Answer all questions on each part of the test.
- Ask for assistance from the proctor if the directions are unclear.

TIP 3

Budget your time.

- Make a note of when the test began and when it will end.
- Wear a watch or make sure that the clock in the room is working, so that you can keep track of the time.
- Quickly look over the entire exam first before you begin to answer any questions.
- Spend an appropriate amount of time developing the thematic essay and the DBQ essay thoroughly. A good guide would be to spend forty minutes on the multiple-choice questions and two hours and twenty minutes on the two essays (plus the document-based questions).
- Answer the easy questions first. Don't get stuck on one question. Move on to the next questions; you might find a clue or hint in other questions on the test.
- Don't leave early if you finish before the three-hour limit. Recheck your answers; you may want to add information, or you may have omitted something asked for in the question.

TIP 4

Don't give up on your reasoning abilities.

- Don't leave out any questions.
- Restate the question in your own words so that you understand it.
- Try to connect the question with some ideas or topics that you have covered in class.
- Check the whole test to determine if you can use any information from one part to help you answer a question on another part.
- Make a list of the Global History Connections: cultural diffusion, migration, regional empires, belief systems, trade/conflict, etc. See if any of these topics can help you answer a question.

TIP 5

When in doubt, guess.

- Answer all questions. Remember that an unanswered question receives no credit; there is no penalty for guessing.
- Go with your first choice.
- Eliminate the least likely answer choices by drawing a line through them. Try to leave only two possible correct answers, and then make an educated guess.

Let's review the helpful hints for all tests:

1. Be prepared and have an optimistic approach.
2. Carefully read the directions and questions.
3. Budget your time.
4. Don't give up on your reasoning abilities.
5. When in doubt, guess.

SPECIFIC HELPFUL HINTS FOR ANSWERING MULTIPLE-CHOICE QUESTIONS

The Transition Exam in Global History and Geography has many kinds of multiple-choice questions. They require knowledge of some basic facts and analysis or application of the facts.

TIP 1

Read the questions carefully and underline the key words.

WHY WILL THIS TIP HELP YOU?

- It helps you avoid making careless mistakes.
- It focuses on the key ideas.
- It directs your answer to what is being tested.

WHEN SHOULD YOU UTILIZE THIS TIP?

- Use this tip whenever taking a multiple-choice test.

The example that follows shows the importance of key words. The key words provide the specific meaning of the question and point you to the correct response.

Example

The purpose of Mohandas Gandhi's actions such as the Salt March and the textile boycott was to

(1) begin a cycle of armed revolution
(2) draw attention to critical issues
(3) increase the strength of the military
(4) resist the power of religious leaders

(from an actual Regents exam)

By underlining *Mohandas Gandhi*, *Salt March*, and *textile boycott*, you are focusing on the key points of the question. You are being asked to show the connection between Mohandas Gandhi and the purpose of his actions that resulted in the Salt March and the textile boycott. The correct answer is choice 2. The purpose of Mohandas Gandhi's nonviolent actions, such as the Salt March and the textile boycott, was to draw attention to critical issues. Gandhi was a pacifist who believed in the principle of satyagraha, which in English means passive resistance or civil disobedience. Gandhi believed that one perfect civil resister was enough to win the battle of right and wrong.

Practice

Underline the key words in the following question:

- The popularity of English as a foreign language spread to various parts of the world in the 20th and 21st centuries.
- Bollywood movies, created in India, grew in popularity with westerners in the 20th century.
- Muslim merchants continued to spread Islam into western China in the 19th and 20th centuries.

Which term is used to describe the historical process mentioned in the events above?

(1) ethnocentrism
(2) isolation
(3) imperialism
(4) cultural diffusion

You should have underlined *English*, *spread*, *India*, *westerners*, *Islam*, and *western China* because they are important terms in the question. The correct answer is choice 4 because *cultural diffusion* is a term used to describe the spread of ideas and cultural characteristics to different societies. The other terms are not related to the spread of culture.

TIP 2

Answer the easy questions first and leave the difficult questions for later.

WHY USE THIS TIP?

- It instills confidence.
- It enables you to use your time more efficiently.
- It provides an opportunity to find clues/ideas in other questions that can be useful in answering the ones left blank.

WHEN DO YOU USE THIS TIP?

- This tip is helpful whenever you take a test that contains difficult or unfamiliar questions.

Easy questions are those that contain limited vocabulary and short statements and are readily answered from the given information.

Example

Which aspect of a nation's culture is most directly influenced by the physical geography of that nation?

(1) form of government
(2) religious belief
(3) population distribution
(4) social class system

(from an actual Regents exam)

Choice 3 is the obvious answer; it is the only choice that is connected to physical geography. The other choices are not related to the main idea of the question and have little to do with a nation's geography.

Practice

An aspect of society that an economist would study in depth would be the

(1) development of self-image and causes of mental illness
(2) problem of scarcity of resources
(3) origins of religion, legends, and festivals
(4) migratory patterns of animals

(taken from a Test Sampler Draft)

The correct answer is choice 2. Economics is the only social science that deals with scarcity of resources.

TIP 3
Read all choices. Look out for decoys.

WHY USE THIS TIP?

- It encourages you to read all possible answers before making a selection.
- It makes you aware that initial choices may seem correct but sometimes are not.

WHEN DO YOU USE THIS TIP?

- Use this tip when taking a multiple-choice test.

Be a patient test taker. Very often, the decoy precedes the correct choice, and the careless student will choose the incorrect answer.

Example

Which slogan expressed the ideals of the Bolshevik Revolution of 1917?

(1) Liberty, Equality, and Fraternity
(2) Bread, Land, and Peace
(3) Land and Liberty
(4) Nationalism, Democracy, and the People's Livelihood

(from an actual Regents exam)

The correct answer is choice 2. It is the only choice that applies specifically to the Bolshevik Revolution. However, all three other choices are historical slogans and represent other revolutions that occurred in history.

Practice

One reason for both the French Revolution (1789) and the Cuban Revolution (1959) was that

(1) people often rebel when they are governed by a foreign power
(2) the monarchs did not meet the needs of culturally diverse populations
(3) the writings of Karl Marx encouraged workers and the industrialists to unite
(4) existing governments failed to address the major economic differences between social classes

(from an actual Regents exam)

Did you select choice 3? It is an attractive choice, but the French Revolution took place *before* Karl Marx wrote and indicated that the workers would revolt against the industrialists. However, choice 4 is correct because revolutions take place when governments ignore the needs of the people.

TIP 4
Use your understanding of chronology to help eliminate decoys and incorrect responses.

WHY USE THIS TIP?

- It enables you to use your understanding of the order in which historical events occurred to answer the questions correctly.
- It helps you to utilize the test as an educational tool. The questions are sometimes asked in a relatively chronological order!
- It allows you to use your "process of elimination" skills better to eliminate incorrect responses.

WHEN DO YOU USE THIS TIP?

- You should typically use this tip for the first 25–28 questions. The exceptions are sometimes the first few questions, which often ask you to use historical thinking skills to interpret maps or reading passages, and the last few questions, which are often cross-topical and cover multiple topics and time periods.

Often, you can use your knowledge of chronology, or the order in which events occurred, to help you eliminate decoys and incorrect responses. Although the first few questions will often ask you to demonstrate your historical thinking skills and the last few questions will often be cross-topical, the majority of the questions will be asked in the order in which the events occurred. Look at the number of the question as well as the questions asked before and after to help you eliminate incorrect responses.

Example

25. The primary goal of Mikhail Gorbachev's policy of perestroika for the Soviet Union was the

(1) restriction of trade
(2) censorship of the press
(3) restructuring of the economy
(4) establishment of five-year plans

(from an actual Regents exam)

The correct response is choice 3. Even if you don't remember Mikhail Gorbachev or the policy of perestroika, this question is number 25 and appears toward the end of the exam. If you remember that five-year plans happened very early in Soviet history, you can eliminate choice 4. If you remember that toward the end of the history of the Soviet Union the goal was to have more openness in society, then you can eliminate choice 2.

Practice

14. First they came for the Communists, but I was not a Communist so I did not speak out. Then they came for the Socialists and the Trade Unionists, but I was neither, so I did not speak out. Then they came for the Jews, but I was not a Jew so I did not speak out. And when they came for me there was no one left to speak out for me.

—Martin Niemoller

Which event is Martin Niemoller referring to in this passage?

(1) Ukrainian Famine
(2) World War I
(3) Breakup of Yugoslavia
(4) Holocaust

(from an actual Regents exam)

The correct response is choice 4. Even if you had trouble interpreting the passage, this question appears in the middle of the test as question 14. That should help you eliminate choice 3 because you know that the breakup of Yugoslavia did not occur until the 20th century and would therefore not likely appear in the middle of the test. If you looked at questions 12 and 13 from this Regents exam, you would have seen that both questions were about World War II; therefore, it would be unlikely that question 14 would ask questions from before World War II. Understanding chronology will help you eliminate choices 1 and 2 because both occurred before World War II.

TIP 5
Use the process of elimination.

WHY USE THIS TIP?

- It helps you discard the wrong choices.
- It narrows down the possible correct choices and increases the possibility of getting the right answer.

WHEN DO YOU USE THIS TIP?

- Use this tip whenever you face a tough question and are unsure about the correct response.

Always use the process of elimination to arrive at a conclusion when you are uncertain about the answer. Look at the example that follows and begin using this process.

Example

"Archduke Franz Ferdinand Assassinated!"
"Germany declares war on Russia and France!"
"Peace Treaty signed at Versailles!"

Which event is referred to in these headlines?

(1) Franco-Prussian War
(2) Crimean War
(3) World War I
(4) Cold War

(from an actual Regents exam)

You may not be familiar with all the headlines, but you can eliminate choice 4 because Russia and the United States opposed each other in the Cold War. If you know that Archduke Ferdinand was from Austria, you can rule out the Franco-Prussian War. You can eliminate choice 2 if you remember that England and Russia fought in the Crimean War. Thus, you have arrived at your answer—choice 3.

Practice

One way in which Soviet leader Mikhail Gorbachev and Chinese leader Deng Xiaoping are similar is that both

(1) granted autonomy to satellite countries
(2) promoted a multi-party political system
(3) encouraged religious dissenters to seek freedom
(4) incorporated capitalist ideas into communist societies

(from an actual Regents exam)

Questions that ask for similarities between people or groups are good because if you know a fact about one, you know that it is the same for all. For this question, the best course of action would be to eliminate some of the answer choices. You may remember that Communist countries do not promote a multi-party political system or encourage religious freedom. You may also recall that the Soviet Union did not grant autonomy to its satellite states. The only correct answer is choice 4. One way in which Soviet leader Mikhail Gorbachev and Chinese leader Deng Xiaoping are similar is that both incorporated capitalist ideas into communist societies. In 1981, Deng Xiaoping introduced his goals for more economic freedom that became known as the Four Modernizations. Four years later, in 1985, Mikhail Gorbachev introduced the idea of perestroika.

TIP 6

Identify differences among the choices.

WHY USE THIS TIP?

- It helps you decide between general and specific answers.
- It helps you identify decoys.

WHEN DO YOU USE THIS TIP?

- Use this tip when several choices seem correct.
- Use this tip when you have reduced the answer down to two potential choices.

How do you answer a question when several choices seem to be correct? Tip 6 provides you with a way to recognize the differences among these choices. Try the following example.

Example

The Armenian massacre (1910s) and the forced famine in Ukraine (1930s) are examples of

(1) international terrorism
(2) religious conflicts
(3) guerrilla warfare
(4) human rights violations

(from an actual Regents exam)

This is a difficult question because it mainly implies that to some extent more than one of these choices is correct. Choices 1 and 3 do not fit. The Armenian massacre resulted in the deaths of 1.5 million people, while 2.4 to 7.5 million people died as a result of the Ukraine famine. Neither of these two events were the result of international terrorism or guerrilla warfare. Choice 2 may explain the conflict between the Christian Armenians and the Muslim Turks, but it does not fit the forced famine in Ukraine. The Armenian massacre (1910s) and the forced famine in Ukraine (1930s) are examples of human rights violations. Human rights are the freedoms and rights that all people enjoy as members of society. Some of these rights include freedom of expression, life, religion, and equal protection under the law. Choice 4 is the best answer.

Practice

The strong showing by the Communist Party in the Russian Presidential election of 1996 suggests that large numbers of Russian people

(1) favored a return to Stalin's policy of imprisoning dissidents
(2) feared continuing economic instability and high inflation
(3) wanted the Russian Orthodox Church to play a larger role in government
(4) supported a return to isolationist policies

(from an actual Regents exam)

This, again, is a difficult question because two of the wrong choices have elements of truth. While some people did want a return to stability, as stated in choice 1, they rejected Stalin's strict policies. Choice 3 is a possible option because the Russian people resumed worshiping in the Russian Orthodox Church; however, there is no evidence to suggest an end to separation of church and state. Choice 4 is incorrect because Russian leaders wanted to reject isolationism and play a greater role in world politics. Therefore, this leaves choice 2 as the correct answer because many Russian people did indeed fear inflation and instability.

TIP 7
Don't select an answer that is correct in itself but is wrong as it relates to the question.

WHY USE THIS TIP?

- It assists you in relating answer choices to the question.
- It guides you in focusing on the question and its connection to the answer.

WHEN DO YOU USE THIS TIP?

- Use this tip whenever answering a multiple-choice question.

Quite often one or more of the options are accurate but are the wrong answer for that question. Always keep in mind which choices best relate to the specific question. Try the following.

Example

Which economic policy of the Soviet Union in the 1980s was the most different from the economic policies of Stalin?

(1) government ownership of the means of production
(2) the development of heavy industry
(3) central planning of basic economic decisions
(4) private management

(from an actual Regents exam)

All of the choices describe the Soviet economy in the 1980s; however, choice 4 is the one that best answers the question. Gorbachev's policy of perestroika was a direct rejection of Stalin's command economy.

Practice

The amount of carbon dioxide in the atmosphere has increased in recent years. Environmentalists suggest this change is a direct result of the

(1) improper storage of solid and nuclear wastes
(2) overcutting of forests and the increased use of fossil fuels
(3) dumping of inorganic material into lakes and rivers
(4) use of herbicides and toxic substances such as asbestos and DDT

(from an actual Regents exam)

Choices 1, 3, and 4 are all regarded as environmental hazards that reduce the quality of life and may cause death. However, they do not contribute to the increase in the level of carbon dioxide. Choice 2 is the correct statement for this question because the overcutting of forests leads to global warming.

TIP 8
Always pick the broader encompassing option.

WHY USE THIS TIP?

- It is helpful when two choices are accurate but one choice more fully answers the question.

WHEN DO YOU USE THIS TIP?

- Use this tip when two or more choices are correct but one of the choices includes the other.

This is a valuable tool when answering questions that call for inclusive answers. Below is a sample of this type of question.

Example

People in both Japan and India eat very little meat. A study of these cultures would show that

(1) although these cultures have similar practices, the reasons for these practices differ
(2) the raising of cattle in both nations is very different due to the extreme climate
(3) neither culture is concerned with health issues
(4) the governments of both nations enforce strict dietary laws

(from an actual Regents exam)

Use the process of elimination when answering the question (Tip 5). You could have eliminated choice 2 because you know that Indians do not eat meat because of religious reasons. You can cross out choices 3 and 4 because both of these governments are secular democratic governments. They would not ignore health issues nor impose dietary laws. The most general answer is choice 1 and is likely to be true of both countries.

Practice

Which factor is the best indicator of the wealth of a nation?

(1) Gross National Product (GNP)
(2) Prime Interest Rate
(3) Number of millionaires
(4) Defense spending

(from an actual Regents exam)

Choices 2, 3, and 4 have some validity since they indicate certain characteristics of an economy. However, choice 1 is a broader statement and a more accurate way to measure the total economic activity during a set time period.

TIP 9

Have an idea about the answer before looking at the answer choices.

WHY USE THIS TIP?

- It helps you to recall an idea or term associated with the question.
- It helps you to stimulate your memory.

WHEN DO YOU USE THIS TIP?

- Use this tip whenever you answer a multiple-choice question.
- Use this tip when interpreting cartoons.

When you read a question, you should put it in the context of the time period and associate the important events in that era. Try the following example.

Example

Which statement about the Soviet economy under Joseph Stalin is accurate?

(1) The Soviet Union increased its power by developing heavy industry.
(2) The government reduced its role in planning industrial production.
(3) Farmers were encouraged to compete in a free market.
(4) A large selection of consumer goods became available in the Soviet Union.

(from an actual Regents exam)

As you read this question, you should associate Joseph Stalin with the progression of communism in the Soviet Union and, more specifically, his five-year plans. These were implemented in 1928 and 1932, and they focused on heavy industry. Therefore, choice 1 is correct.

Try this tip when you look at a cartoon. Interpret the meaning of the cartoon before looking at the choices.

Practice

Base your answer to this question on the cartoon below and on your knowledge of social studies.

What is the main idea of this 1994 cartoon?

(1) Haiti's lack of industrialization has led to economic stagnation.
(2) Haiti's limited experience with democracy has made it difficult to establish this form of government.
(3) The desire for democracy has led Haiti to neglect its development of modern technology.
(4) The presence of American industry has failed to improve Haiti's economy.

(from an actual Regents exam)

The cartoon suggests that Haiti has to put many parts together to develop a democracy. The words "Some assembly required" provide the focus of the cartoon. Focusing on these words will enable you to select choice 2 as the correct answer.

TIP 10
Make educated guesses.

WHY USE THIS TIP?

- There is no penalty for guessing.
- Any answer is better than no answer.
- Using the process of elimination helps you to arrive at the right answer.

WHEN DO YOU USE THIS TIP?

- Use this tip when there is no penalty for guessing.
- Use this tip when there is nothing to lose; a blank answer is wrong anyway.

Remember, you should use guessing as a last resort! The question below will give you an opportunity to use the technique of intelligent guessing to arrive at the correct answer.

Example

In the 1930s and 1940s, Japan expanded its borders to include parts of

(1) eastern Europe and southwest Asia
(2) China and southeast Asia
(3) Turkey and the Soviet Union
(4) Australia and Latin America

(from an actual Regents exam)

Even if you are not certain of the choices, you can make an informed guess that choice 2 is the correct answer. You probably realize that Japan, like China, is in east Asia and is in close proximity to Southeast Asia. Logically, Japan would extend its borders into those regions closest to it.

Practice

Which practice was similar under the rule of the Bolsheviks in Russia and of the Nazi Party in Germany?

(1) establishing communism in their respective nations
(2) permitting a series of multi-party elections
(3) increasing the power of the middle class
(4) limiting government opposition through intimidation and fear

(from an actual Regents exam)

Choice 4 is the correct answer. It contains the key words—*limiting*, *intimidation*, and *fear*—all essential features of the two ideologies. Communism and Fascism are opposed to each other, and thus choice 1 is eliminated. A series of multi-party elections would not exist in a dictatorship, so you can rule out choice 3.

CHECKLIST FOR ANSWERING THE MULTIPLE-CHOICE QUESTIONS

1. Read the questions carefully and underline the key words.
2. Answer the easy questions first and leave the difficult questions for later.
3. Read all choices. Look out for decoys.
4. Use your understanding of chronology to help eliminate decoys and incorrect responses.
5. Use the process of elimination.
6. Identify differences among the choices.
7. Don't select an answer that is correct in itself but is wrong as it relates to the question.
8. Always pick the broader encompassing option.
9. Have an idea about the answer before looking at the answer choices.
10. Make educated guesses.

STRATEGIES FOR ANSWERING THE THEMATIC ESSAY QUESTION

There will be one thematic essay on the Transition Exam. It will count for 15 percent of the exam. The thematic essay requires you to **interpret, understand, and explain key concepts that link several events in Global History**.

THEMES	EXAMPLES
Major Belief Systems	Judaism, Confucianism
Turning Points in History	Fall of Rome, French Revolution, Birth of Islam
Forms of Government (Political System)	Monarchy, Democracy
Economic Systems	Communism, Capitalism
Geography and the Environment	Early River Civilizations
Justice/Human Rights	Code of Hammurabi, Justinian Code, Violations (i.e., Holocaust, Apartheid)
Science/Technology	Invention of Printing Press
Movement of People/Goods (Cultural Diffusion)	Crusades, Silk Road
Nationalism	Italian/German Unification, Zionism
Imperialism	British in India, European Partition of Africa
Conflicts	Political (World War I, World War II) Religious (Northern Ireland, Middle East, India)
Culture/Intellectual Life	Roman Civilization, Gupta Civilizations, Renaissance

Most thematic essays will have the following parts:

THE THEME: Identifies the broad concept that will be the topic of the essay. Usually, there is a general explanation statement that provides more focus to the question.

THE TASK: Provides the instruction for what you will need to write about your topic or concept.

SUGGESTIONS: Provide you with a specific area that you might choose to discuss in your essay. **Note:** These are only suggestions, and you are not limited to these examples. Despite the fact that this test focuses on content from 1750 to the present, you can choose content from prior to 1750 as your topic. **Beware:** *Do not* choose the United States as your topic. Students will lose credit if they do not follow the directions.

Thematic Essay Question

Directions: Write a well-organized essay that includes an introduction, several paragraphs addressing the task below, and a conclusion.

Theme: Justice and Human Rights

> Throughout history, the human rights of certain groups of people have been violated. Efforts have been made to address these violations.

Task:

- Define the term "human rights"
- Identify *two* examples of human rights violations that have occurred in a specific time and place
- Describe the causes of these human rights violations
- For *one* of the violations identified, discuss *one* specific effort that was made or is being made to deal with the violation

You may use any example from your study of global history and geography. Some suggestions you might wish to consider include untouchables in India, Black South Africans, Jewish people in Nazi Germany, Chinese people under Japanese occupation in Nanjing, Muslims in Bosnia, Tutsis in Rwanda, Kurds in Iraq or Turkey, Tibetans in China, or the Rohingya people in Myanmar.

You are *not* limited to these suggestions.
Do *not* use an example from the United States in your answer.

STEP 1
Read the entire question first.

This will help you focus on what is expected of you in the essay.

STEP 2
Analyze the task.

Review key phrases and words in the task directions that you must include in your essay. In the sample thematic essay question on page 24, taken from an actual Regents exam, you should underline the key words in the directions:

- *Define* human rights.
- *Identify* two examples of violations in different time periods.
- *Describe* the causes of these violations.
- *Discuss* one specific effort to deal with the violations.

By underlining the key words and/or listing these items, you can begin to organize your outline.

STEP 3

Check the suggestions.

This will help you recall the importance of themes in different places and time periods.

STEP 4

Organize the information.

Begin to outline the information you could include in your essay. In the sample thematic essay question on page 24, you might include:

- Definition of human rights: rights and liberties guaranteed by birth, freedom of religion, right to vote
- Identify two human rights violations: Apartheid (South Africa), Holocaust (Germany)
- Causes: White minority control, but black majority, separation of races, Hitler's extermination of Jews, Nuremberg Laws, Kristallnacht
- Effort to deal with violations: Roles of Nelson Mandela and Bishop Tutu, economic boycott in South Africa

STEP 5

Identify the main ideas of the essay.

Use the theme or the task of the thematic essay question to create your topic or thesis statement. An example of a thesis statement might be as follows:

> Throughout history, the human rights of certain groups, such as Black South Africans and Jewish people in Nazi Germany, have been violated.

STEP 6

Write the introductory paragraph.

The introductory paragraph should connect the thesis or topic to the main idea of the essay. You might include in your paragraph a definition of human rights and two examples, such as Black South Africans and the Jewish people in Nazi Germany. Below is an example of an introductory paragraph:

> Human rights are those rights and liberties that are guaranteed to everyone from birth by virtue of belonging to a civil society. These rights include freedom of religion, the right to vote, and freedom of expression without fear of abuse by government officials. In 1948, the United Nations adopted a Universal Declaration of Human Rights, which set forth those basic liberties and freedoms to which all people are entitled. Throughout history, the human rights of certain groups, such as Black South Africans and Jewish people in Nazi Germany, have been violated. (**Note:** The introductory paragraph concludes with the thesis statement.)

STEP 7

Write the supporting paragraphs.

Each of these paragraphs should deal with one aspect or part of the task. These paragraphs should explain your answer with facts, details, and examples. Check the facts from the outline as you are writing. Remember the following:

1. Develop your essay logically.
2. Do not list facts. Analyze, evaluate, compare, or contrast various aspects.
3. Do not use meaningless facts unrelated to the theme.
4. Use concrete examples to support your ideas.
5. Make sure that you have completed all the assigned tasks listed in the question.

STEP 8

Write the concluding paragraph.

Restate or rewrite the thesis summarizing the essay. Make sure that your essay has both a strong introduction and a strong conclusion. You will not receive full credit if either of these pieces is missing or weak. A good concluding paragraph would be as follows:

> Human rights violations, such as those in South Africa and Nazi Germany, have existed throughout history. It is important to be aware of these violations and for society to make an effort to ensure that they never happen again. History has shown that the global community does not benefit when any group of people become victims of intolerance or injustice.

STEP 9

Keep in mind the generic scoring rubric.

Depending on time, reread your essay to check for errors of facts, spelling, or grammar. Check to see if the essay is organized, reads clearly, and makes sense. The following scoring rubric shows exactly what an essay must contain to receive a particular score. For example, in order to obtain a score of 4, the rubric indicates your essay must contain relevant facts and examples. If, while reviewing your essay, you discover you've neglected to include relevant facts, you can add them at this time.

THEMATIC ESSAY: GENERIC SCORING RUBRIC

Score of 5:
- Shows a thorough understanding of the theme or problem
- Addresses all aspects of the task
- Shows an ability to analyze, evaluate, compare and/or contrast issues and events
- Richly supports the theme or problem with relevant facts, examples, and details
- Is a well-developed essay, consistently demonstrating a logical and clear plan of organization
- Introduces the theme or problem by establishing a framework that is beyond a simple restatement of the task and concludes with a summation of the theme or problem

Score of 4:
- Shows a good understanding of the theme or problem
- Addresses all aspects of the task

- Shows an ability to analyze, evaluate, compare and/or contrast issues and events
- Includes relevant facts, examples, and details, but may not support all aspects of the theme or problem evenly
- Is a well-developed essay, demonstrating a logical and clear plan of organization
- Introduces the theme or problem by establishing a framework that is beyond a simple restatement of the task and concludes with a summation of the theme or problem

Score of 3:
- Shows a satisfactory understanding of the theme or problem
- Addresses most aspects of the task or addresses all aspects of the task in a limited way
- Shows an ability to analyze or evaluate issues and events, but not in any depth
- Includes some facts, examples, and details
- Is a satisfactorily developed essay, demonstrating a general plan of organization
- Introduces the theme or problem by repeating the task and concludes by repeating the theme or problem

Score of 2:
- Shows limited understanding of the theme or problem
- Attempts to address the task
- Develops a faulty analysis or evaluation of issues and events
- Includes few facts, examples, and details, and may include information that contains inaccuracies
- Is a poorly organized essay, lacking focus
- Fails to introduce or summarize the theme or problem

Score of 1:
- Shows very limited understanding of the theme or problem
- Lacks an analysis or evaluation of the issues and events
- Includes little or no accurate or relevant facts, examples, or details
- Attempts to complete the task, but demonstrates a major weakness in organization
- Fails to introduce or summarize the theme or problem

Score of 0: Fails to address the task, is illegible, or is a blank paper

CHECKLIST FOR WRITING THE THEMATIC ESSAY

1. Read the entire question first.
2. Analyze the task.
3. Check the suggestions.
4. Organize the information.
5. Identify the main ideas of the essay.
6. Write the introductory paragraph.
7. Write the supporting paragraphs.
8. Write the concluding paragraph.
9. Keep in mind the generic scoring rubric.

Here is your task: Use these steps to answer the following thematic essay question from a past Test Sampler Draft. Use the thematic essay rubric (pages 27–28) to evaluate your answer.

Thematic Essay Question

Directions: Write a well-organized essay that includes an introduction, several paragraphs addressing the task below, and a conclusion.

Theme: Change—Challenges to Tradition or Authority

Throughout history, individuals have challenged established traditions and authorities. Their efforts have inspired or influenced change and have met with varying degrees of success.

Task:

Select ***two*** individuals who have challenged tradition or authority and for ***each***

- Describe the established tradition or authority as it existed before it was challenged by the individual
- Discuss how the individual challenged established tradition or authority
- Discuss the extent to which change was achieved as a result of this challenge

You may use any individuals from your study of global history and geography. Some suggestions you might wish to consider include Mary Wollstonecraft, Toussaint L'Ouverture, Charles Darwin, Vladimir Lenin, Emiliano Zapata, Mohandas Gandhi, Ho Chi Minh, Nelson Mandela, Mikhail Gorbachev, Aung San Suu Kyi, and Wangari Maathai.

You are *not* limited to these suggestions.
Do *not* write about an individuals from the United States.

STRATEGIES FOR ANSWERING THE DOCUMENT-BASED ESSAY QUESTION (DBQ)

There will be one document-based essay question on the Transition Exam. It will count for 30 percent of the exam, because your responses to the 6–9 document-based questions count for 15% of this score while your response to the essay prompt counts for the other 15% of this score. The document-based essay question requires you to write an essay incorporating information from several documents. The documents may consist of both primary and secondary sources, including maps, charts, political cartoons, graphs, or photographs. Remember, the documents may look different, but they are all related to a single subject or theme. The DBQ tests your ability to **interpret and draw conclusions from historical documents**.

Most DBQs will have the following parts:

GENERAL DIRECTIONS: The directions tell you what to do for each part of the question.

HISTORICAL CONTEXT: This is the theme of the question. Read the historical context before you start to answer the question. Each document is related to or takes a position on that theme.

TASK: This statement defines what you must do as you examine the documents, as well as what you are being asked to write about in your essay response. Be sure your response answers all parts of the task.

PART A—SHORT-ANSWER QUESTIONS: In this part, you study between six and nine documents. Each document will be followed by one or more possible questions to which you will provide a short response. This portion of the test is worth 15 percent of the exam grade.

PART B—ESSAY: In this part, you will write an essay response to the task, which focuses on the same topic as the documents. This portion of the test is worth 15 percent of the exam grade.

STEP 1
Read the historical context carefully.

Determine what you must do. Underline or box the main topic of the historical context.

Historical Context:

Economic systems attempt to meet the needs of the people. Capitalism and communism represent two different ways to meet people's economic needs.

(from an actual Regents exam)

The key words to underline would be: *economic systems, capitalism, communism, different ways, economic needs*.

STEP 2

Read the task.

As you read, circle key words and phrases and try to identify the theme or issue.

Task:

- Describe how these two economic systems attempt to meet the needs of the people.
- Evaluate how successful each system has been at meeting the economic needs of the people.

(from an actual Regents exam)

You should have circled the following: *describe, two economic systems, evaluate, successful.*

Write down any information that you know about the theme, task, or issue.

STEP 3

Read and analyze each document.

Circle key words and phrases. Take note of the author, date of the document, and the place. When reviewing each document, assess "How is the document related to the theme?" "How does Document 1 compare with or contrast to ideas in Document 4?"

Document 1

Capitalists are rich people who own factories and have lots of money and workers.... A factory can belong to one person in Capitalism but in [Communism] it belongs to the government.... I am for the idea of [Communism]. It seems to me that you have more of an opportunity to live well. You won't lose your job in [Communism]... I've heard about the unemployment problem in America. People can't find any kind of job.... That's the way we heard about it—that [in] the West, unemployment, everything there is bad, a real mess.

—"Katia," a 16-year-old ninth grader from Moscow, 1980s

(from an actual Regents exam)

Document 4

Andrei, his wife, his father, and [his] elder son all have to work on the collective farmlands... He is not stupid and sees that almost all the produce ends up in the hands of the Government. The local Communist party boss is always coming back... for more and more. Andrei and his family know ahead of time that they are going to get [a] very small return for working on the collectivized fields. Naturally this condition [changes] their attitudes. They are constantly on a sort of slow-down strike...

—T. P. Whitney, "The Russian Peasant Wars on the Kremlin," 1954

(from an actual Regents exam)

In Document 1, you should have noted that it was written by a 16-year-old ninth grader from Moscow in the 1980s. Compare the statement with Document 4, which was written in the 1950s. How are they different? What other outside information can be applied to them?

STEP 4

Begin to answer Part A.

Summarize the main viewpoints expressed in each document and answer the question or questions following each document. These short-answer questions are called **scaffolding**, because scaffolding provides the foundation for answering the essay portion (Part B).

Note: Answers to the scaffolding questions should be *concise* and *straightforward*—one or two sentences are sufficient. Answer the questions in complete sentences. See sample Document 3 and sample questions 3a and 3b that follow

Document 3

> Above all, [the government]... will have to take the control of industry and of all branches of production out of the hands of... competing individuals, and instead institute a system as a whole, that is for the common account [good], according to a common plan, and with the participation of all members of society. It will... abolish [eliminate] competition.... Private property must therefore be abolished.
>
> —Friedrich Engels, *Principles of Communism*

(from an actual Regents exam)

3*a* Who controls the means of production and all property in a Communist system?

You would receive the point if you stated the following: *Government, not the individual, controls the means of production and all property.*

3*b* What happens to competition in a Communist system?

You would receive the point if you stated the following: *Competition is abolished.*

STEP 5

Begin to organize your essay for Part B.

Make an outline or chart of key ideas from each document, separating them to reflect both sides of the task. Following is a summary of the key ideas from the documents of the Regents exam the preceding documents were taken from.

Capitalism

Unemployment—Document 1
Supply and demand—Document 2
Rewards talent—Document 2
Laissez-faire—Documents 2 and 5
Private ownership—Document 3
Economic class distinction—Document 6
Negative aspects of factory system—Document 6
Free enterprise—Document 7

Communism

Classless society—Documents 1 and 6
Concept of common good—Document 3
Government control of industry—Document 3
Elimination of private property—Document 3
Collectivization—Document 4
Exploitation by leadership—Document 4
Five-year plan—Document 7
Free social and medical services—Document 8
No unemployment—Document 8

STEP 6

Begin to write your essay for Part B.

You can approach this part as you would a thematic essay, but you should try to incorporate outside information from your Global History and Geography course. Write an introductory paragraph in which you state your position (if necessary) and the varying issues that your essay will discuss. Following is an example of an introductory paragraph that you might use when answering a DBQ that contains these points:

> Capitalism and communism are two types of economic systems that have attempted to meet the needs of the people. Each of these economic systems must address the following three questions: What goods and services should be produced? How should these goods and services be produced? Who should consume these goods and services?

STEP 7

Write the body of your essay.

Include specific historical examples and refer to the documents you analyzed in Part A to either provide conflicting viewpoints or to support your position or thesis. **Do not merely copy the documents or use long passages from them.** Try to summarize the documents in your own words in one or two sentences. Cite the documents as needed.

Document 5

The Wealth of Nations carries the important message of *laissez-faire*, which means that the government should intervene as little as possible in economic affairs and leave the market to its own devices. It advocates the liberation of economic production from all limiting regulation in order to benefit the people…

—Adam Smith, *The Wealth of Nations*

A good way to summarize this document is to refer to Part A, in which your response included the idea that government should leave business alone (laissez-faire).

STEP 8

Evaluate/analyze the different viewpoints expressed in the documents.

Note that the documents contain a variety of ideas on the topic, in this case, capitalism and communism. Some documents are contradictory. This is not done to confuse you but rather to assess how you will analyze different points of view. In your answer, you should explain how the documents support/oppose your thesis or viewpoints.

Remember, you must use as many documents as are stated in the directions to receive full credit.

STEP 9

Write your conclusion.

Restate or rewrite the thesis summarizing the essay. Make sure that you have responded to all parts of the task, check for a strong introduction, and include a judgment in your conclusion, if the question warrants it. Following is a conclusion that you might use when answering the DBQ.

Capitalism has become the dominant economic system in the world today because it has been successful in providing a stable economic environment that gives society basic needs as well as allowing freedom for each individual. However, there are concerns that capitalism has resulted in widening the gap between the rich and the poor in our industrial society and between the developed and developing nations of Africa and Latin America. Pope John Paul II applauded the fall of communism and the freedom associated with capitalism. However, he also reminded all capitalistic countries that we must ensure that capitalism meets the social needs of the people.

STEP 10

Keep in mind the generic scoring rubric.

Proofread your essay to see if it is clear and logical and to confirm that the facts are accurate. The following scoring rubric will help you decide if your essay has enough detail, relevant outside information, and facts to receive a score with which you will be satisfied. Notice that to receive a score of 4 or 5 you must correctly analyze and interpret at least **four** documents. Comparing your essay to the rubric will make sure you have included four documents in your essay.

DOCUMENT-BASED QUESTION: GENERIC SCORING RUBRIC

Score of 5:

- Thoroughly addresses all aspects of the *Task* by accurately analyzing and interpreting at least **four** documents
- Incorporates information from the documents in the body of the essay
- Incorporates relevant outside information
- Richly supports the theme or problem with relevant facts, examples, and details
- Is a well-developed essay, consistently demonstrating a logical and clear plan of organization
- Introduces the theme or problem by establishing a framework that is beyond a simple restatement of the *Task* or *Historical Context* and concludes with a summation of the theme or problem

Score of 4:

- Addresses all aspects of the *Task* by accurately analyzing and interpreting at least **four** documents
- Incorporates information from the documents in the body of the essay
- Incorporates relevant outside information
- Includes relevant facts, examples, and details, but discussion may be more descriptive than analytical
- Is a well-developed essay, demonstrating a logical and clear plan of organization
- Introduces the theme or problem by establishing a framework that is beyond a simple restatement of the *Task* or *Historical Context* and concludes with a summation of the theme or problem

Score of 3:
- Addresses most aspects of the *Task* or addresses all aspects of the *Task* in a limited way, using some of the documents
- Incorporates some information from the documents in the body of the essay
- Incorporates limited or no relevant outside information
- Includes some facts, examples, and details, but discussion is more descriptive than analytical
- Is a satisfactorily developed essay, demonstrating a general plan of organization
- Introduces the theme or problem by repeating the *Task* or *Historical Context* and concludes by simply repeating the theme or problem

Score of 2:
- Attempts to address some aspects of the *Task*, making limited use of the documents
- Presents no relevant outside information
- Includes few facts, examples, and details; discussion restates contents of the documents
- Is a poorly organized essay, lacking focus
- Fails to introduce or summarize the theme or problem

Score of 1:
- Shows limited understanding of the *Task* with vague, unclear references to the documents
- Presents no relevant outside information
- Includes little or no accurate or relevant facts, details, or examples
- Attempts to complete the *Task*, but demonstrates a major weakness in organization
- Fails to introduce or summarize the theme or problem

Score of 0: Fails to address the *Task*, is illegible, or is a blank paper

CHECKLIST FOR WRITING THE DOCUMENT-BASED ESSAY QUESTION (DBQ)

1. Read the historical context carefully.
2. Read the task.
3. Read and analyze each document.
4. Begin to answer Part A.
5. Begin to organize your essay for Part B.
6. Begin to write your essay for Part B.
7. Write the body of your essay.
8. Evaluate/analyze the different viewpoints expressed in the documents.

9. Write your conclusion.
10. Keep in mind the generic scoring rubric.

Here is your task. Use these steps to answer the following document-based essay question taken from a past Transition Exam. Use the document-based essay specific rubric (pages 49–50) to evaluate your answer.

Document-Based Essay

This question is based on the accompanying documents. The question is designed to test your ability to work with historical documents. Some of these documents have been edited for the purposes of this question. As you analyze the documents, take into account the source of each document and any point of view that may be presented in the document. Keep in mind that the language used in a document may reflect the historical context of the time in which it was written.

Historical Context:

Throughout history, people have revolted in response to a number of problems in their countries. Political revolutions such as the ***French Revolution***, the ***Bolshevik Revolution***, and the ***Chinese Communist Revolution*** attempted to address these problems with varying degrees of success.

Task:

Using the information from the documents and your knowledge of global history and geography, answer the questions that follow each document in Part A. Your answers to the questions will help you write the Part B essay in which you will be asked to

Select ***two*** revolutions mentioned in the historical context and for ***each***

- Discuss problems that led the people to revolt
- Discuss how a revolutionary and/or post-revolutionary government attempted to address the problems

Part A: Short-Answer Questions

Directions: Analyze the documents and answer the short-answer questions that follow each document in the space provided.

Document 1

Source: Greg Hetherton, *Revolutionary France: Liberty, tyranny, and terror*, Cambridge University Press.

1 Based on this document, what were ***two*** problems faced by the people of France on the eve of the French Revolution? [2]

(1) ____

____

(2) ____

____

Document 2

	Ruling Body	Chief Characteristics of the Period
1789 ↓ 1791	National Assembly	Abolition of the abuses of the Old Régime
1791 ↓ 1792	Legislative Assembly	Drift toward greater radicalism—beginning of foreign wars
1792 ↓ 1795	Convention	Success in foreign wars—Radicalism Reign of terror
1792 ↓ 1799	Directory	Period of reaction Rise of Napoleon

Source: Philip Dorf, *Visualized Modern History*, Oxford Book Company (adapted)

2 Based on this chart, what was ***one*** change made to the government of France during the French Revolution between 1789 and 1799? [1]

____

____

Document 3

Consulate Reforms (1799–1804) under Napoleon

. . . Another deep demand of the French people, deeper than the demand for the vote, was for more reason, order, and economy in public finance and taxation. The Consulate gave these also. There were no tax exemptions because of birth, status, or special arrangement. Everyone was supposed to pay, so that no disgrace attached to payment, and there was less evasion. In principle these changes had been introduced in 1789; after 1799 they began to work. For the first time in 10 years the government really collected the taxes that it levied and so could rationally plan its financial affairs. Order was introduced also into expenditure, and accounting methods were improved. There was no longer a haphazard assortment of different "funds" on which various officials drew independently and confidentially as they needed money, but a concentration of financial management in the treasury and even in a kind of budget. The revolutionary uncertainties over the value of money were also ended. Because the Directory had shouldered the odium [shame] of repudiating [abandoning] the paper money and government debt, the Consulate was able to establish a sound currency and public credit. To assist in government financing, one of the banks of the Old Regime was revived and established as the Bank of France. . . .

Source: R. R. Palmer et al., *A History of the Modern World*,
McGraw Hill, 2002 (adapted)

3 According to R. R. Palmer et al., what was ***one*** change made under Napoleon in order to fix the economy of France? [1]

____

____

Document 4

22 January 1905
The Czar's troops shoot dead more than 500 strikers on "Bloody Sunday".

28 May 1905
The Japanese annihilate the Russian fleet in the strait of Tsushima.

3 April 1907
Twenty million people are threatened with starvation in the worst famine on record.

1 August 1914
Germany declares war on Russia.

30 August 1915
The great Russian fortress of Brest-Litovsk falls to the Germans.

7 November 1917
Kerensky and the provisional government are ousted in a Bolshevik coup.

Source: Konecky & Konecky, trans., *Chronicle of World History*, Grange Books (adapted)

4 Based on the information on this time line, what were ***two*** complaints the people of Russia had with the Russian government? [2]

(1) ____

____

(2) ____

____

Document 5a

Russian Production Statistics 1913 and 1921

	1913 Czarist Russia Pre–World War I	1921 Communist Russia at the end of the Civil War
Grain	85 million metric tons	23.7 million metric tons
Coal	29 million metric tons	9.5 million metric tons
Pig Iron	4.2 million metric tons	1.2 million metric tons
Oil	9.2 million metric tons	3.8 million metric tons

Source: B. R. Mitchell, *European Historical Statistics 1750–1975*, Second Revised Edition, Facts on File (adapted)

Document 5b

War Communism was an emergency programme established by Lenin during the civil war [1918–1921]. War Communism included forced seizure of grain, nationalization of all trade and industry and strict control of labour. As a result of this program and of the ravages of the war, industrial and agricultural production declined sharply, and the population suffered severe hardship. It caused a famine that led to the death of an estimated 5 million people. . . .

Source: Stephen Tonge, "Russia 1917–1924," *A Web of English History online*

5 Based on this statistical information and this excerpt by Stephen Tonge, what was ***one*** way that Lenin's policy of War Communism and the civil war affected Russia? [1]

____

____

Document 6

. . . Drought had drastically reduced crop output. Under communism, all land was owned by the state. The crops belonged to the state, which seized them. The peasants could not sell them. As a result, they had no incentive to grow more food than they could eat. A famine developed in the land. People starved to death.

In 1921, Lenin had instituted the New Economic Policy (NEP) to deal with this situation. When Stalin took over in 1924, the NEP was firmly in place. It was a retreat from communism, "a partial return to private enterprise." The peasants no longer had to turn over their crops to the government. Instead, they paid a tax on what they produced, and were allowed to sell it at a profit. Although private property had technically been abolished, they could now own and run small farms. They could hire labor. Citizens could start new businesses. Badly managed industrial plants were returned to their former owners. The entire Communist financial system was reorganized along semicapitalist lines. Foreign capitalists were invited to invest in state-owned businesses. The response was limited. . . .

Source: Ted Gottfried, *The Stalinist Empire: The Rise and Fall of the Soviet Union*, Twenty-First Century Books, 2002 (adapted)

6 According to Ted Gottfried, what was ***one*** effect of Lenin's New Economic Policy on Russian society? [1]

____

____

Document 7

... The peasant was China's "forgotten man." Probably the most serious problem that faced the Kuomintang [Nationalists] was the extreme poverty that China's people had suffered for centuries. In the 1900's they continued to be desperately poor. In a year the average Chinese peasant perhaps earned as much as an American worker made in a week. If drought or floods destroyed his crops, the Chinese peasant went hungry or even starved. The payment of even the smallest taxes was a heavy burden for millions of Chinese farmers. Yet most of the government's income came from taxes on the land. Thus, painful sacrifices were demanded from people who already had suffered too much. From the record of Chinese history, it could have been predicted that the Nanking government was headed for trouble unless it could provide relief for the peasants....

The Nationalists' failure to solve the farm problem had unfortunate results. China urgently needed foodstuffs to feed its growing population. The inability of the peasants to increase crop production meant hunger throughout the land. Lack of farm surpluses to use in trade limited China's ability to purchase machinery abroad. Furthermore, the suffering of the peasants furnished the Communists with a powerful weapon to use against the Nanking government [under Chiang Kai-shek]. The Kuomintang was blamed for all of China's troubles....

Source: Hyman Kublin, *China*, Houghton Mifflin Company, 1968

7 According to Hyman Kublin, what were ***two*** problems facing China under the Nationalists? [2]

(1) ______________________________

____

(2) ______________________________

____

Document 8

. . . The first years of the Communist regime [under Mao Zedong] were devoted to emergency work and drastic social change. In the countryside land previously owned by wealthy landlords was claimed by the government and divided among the peasants. Dams were reconstructed and canals dredged. Railroads were repaired and new ones built.

There was a nation-wide drive to wipe out all the opposition to the new regime. Counter- revolutionaries (people who were opposed to the regime) were rounded up, tried at mass public trials, and executed. These trials were public spectacles where thousands of people confessed their "political sins," and hysterical mobs decided their death. . . .

Source: Earl Swisher, *China*, Ginn and Company, 1964

8 According to Earl Swisher, what was ***one*** way the Chinese Communist regime attempted to bring about change? [1]

____

____

Document 9

> ...But the Chinese Communists also placed stress on persuasion—through thought control, propaganda, and group pressures—to force individuals to conform. The object was to develop a new sort of person in China, obedient to the state and dedicated to serving the new Chinese society....
>
> Drastic measures were ordered. Factories and mines were given high production schedules. This meant that workers had to work harder and put in longer hours. Farming communes were formed in the countryside. Families were often broken up (husbands and wives living in separate dormitories and children living in nurseries). Farmers ate in commune dining halls and marched to work in military formations. Their work day was from dawn to dusk, with breaks only for military drills and propaganda lectures....

Source: Daniel Chu, *Scholastic World Cultures: China*, Scholastic Book Services, 1980 (adapted)

9 According to Daniel Chu, what was ***one*** method used by the Chinese government to force the Chinese people to conform? [1]

____

____

Part B: Essay

Directions: Write a well-organized essay that includes an introduction, several paragraphs, and a conclusion. Use evidence from *at least* ***four*** documents in your essay. Support your response with relevant facts, examples, and details. Include additional outside information.

Historical Context:

Throughout history, people have revolted in response to a number of problems in their countries. Political revolutions such as the ***French Revolution***, the ***Bolshevik Revolution***, and the ***Chinese Communist Revolution*** attempted to address these problems with varying degrees of success.

Task:

Using the information from the documents and your knowledge of global history and geography, write an essay in which you

Select ***two*** revolutions mentioned in the historical context and for ***each***

- Discuss problems that led the people to revolt
- Discuss how a revolutionary and/or post-revolutionary government attempted to address the problems

DOCUMENT-BASED ESSAY SPECIFIC RUBRIC

Score of 5:

- Thoroughly develops ***all*** aspects of the *Task* evenly and in depth, by discussing at least ***two*** problems that led people to revolt in ***each*** of ***two*** revolutions and discussing how a revolutionary and/or post-revolutionary government attempted to address the problems
- Is more analytical than descriptive (analyzes, evaluates, and/or creates information); for example: *French Revolution*: connects abuses of power under the Old Regime and economic disparities within the society to efforts by succeeding governments to expand political equality and develop a national financial plan to reform the political and economic systems of France; *Bolshevik Revolution*: connects the unwillingness of czars to address the concerns of the peasant and working classes and Russian defeats in international conflicts to Lenin's coup and his efforts to reform and improve the economy through War Communism and the introduction of the New Economic Policy (NEP)
- Incorporates relevant information from at *least* ***four*** documents
- Incorporates substantial relevant outside information related to political revolutions
- Richly supports the theme with many relevant facts, examples, and details; for example: *French Revolution*: National Assembly, Louis XVI, Marie Antoinette, the Estate System, *Declaration of the Rights of Man and of the Citizen*, government bankruptcy
- Demonstrates a logical and clear plan of organization; includes an introduction and a conclusion that are beyond a restatement of the theme

Score of 4:

- Develops ***all*** aspects of the *Task* but may do so somewhat unevenly by discussing one revolution more thoroughly than the other or by developing one aspect of the *Task* less thoroughly than the other aspect
- Is both descriptive and analytical (applies, analyzes, evaluates, and/or creates information); for example: *French Revolution*: discusses King Louis XVI's inequitable policies, the privileges of the upper classes, and government bankruptcy as causes of the revolution and the efforts of Napoleon to reorganize the government and establish fairer economic policies; *Bolshevik Revolution*: discusses Russian defeats and famine under the czarist government as the basis for Lenin's rise to power and his attempted economic reforms and his retreat from some Communist policies
- Incorporates relevant information from at *least* ***four*** documents
- Incorporates relevant outside information
- Supports the theme with relevant facts, examples, and details
- Demonstrates a logical and clear plan of organization; includes an introduction and a conclusion that are beyond a restatement of the theme

Score of 3:

- Develops ***all*** aspects of the *Task* with little depth or develops at *least* ***one*** aspect of the *Task* in some depth
- Is more descriptive than analytical (applies, may analyze and/or evaluate information)
- Incorporates some relevant information from some of the documents
- Incorporates limited relevant outside information
- Includes some relevant facts, examples, and details; may include some minor inaccuracies
- Demonstrates a satisfactory plan of organization; includes an introduction and a conclusion that may be a restatement of the theme

Score of 2:

- Minimally develops ***all*** aspects of the *Task* ***or*** develops at *least* ***one*** aspect of the *Task* in some depth
- Is primarily descriptive; may include faulty, weak, or isolated application or analysis
- Incorporates limited relevant information from the documents or consists primarily of relevant information copied from the documents
- Presents little or no relevant outside information
- Includes few relevant facts, examples, and details; may include some inaccuracies
- Demonstrates a general plan of organization; may lack focus; may contain digressions; may not clearly identify which aspect of the *Task* is being addressed; may lack an introduction and/or a conclusion

Score of 1:

- Minimally develops some aspects of the *Task*
- Is descriptive; may lack understanding, application, and/or analysis
- Makes vague, unclear references to the documents or consists primarily of relevant and irrelevant information copied from the documents
- Presents no relevant outside information
- Includes few relevant facts, examples, and details; may include inaccuracies
- May demonstrate a weakness in organization; may lack focus; may contain digressions; may not clearly identify which aspect of the *Task* is being addressed; may lack an introduction and/or a conclusion

Score of 0:

- Fails to develop the *Task* or may only refer to the theme in a general way; *OR* includes no relevant facts, examples, and details; *OR* includes only the *Historical Context* and/or *Task* as copied from the test booklet; *OR* includes only entire documents copied from the test booklet; *OR* is illegible; *OR* is a blank paper

Glossary

The Glossary that follows contains a list of important terms, international organizations and agreements, and important people that are an integral part of the Global History and Geography course of study. The Glossary should be used as a device to help you recall some significant terms, concepts, and people in Global History and Geography. It is not all-inclusive but is one study tool to prepare you for the Regents exam.

IMPORTANT TERMS

absolute monarchy system in which a ruler (king or queen) has complete authority over the government without limits on his/her powers.

absolutism political system in which the monarch has supreme power and control over the lives of the people in the country.

acid rain toxic pollution that is produced by the burning of fossil fuels. It affects plants, animals, and people who have a respiratory illness.

African National Congress (ANC) group formed in 1912 to work for Black South Africans' rights. This group led the fight against apartheid and continues to encourage independence for the black majority.

agrarian economy economic system that centers on agriculture as the chief source of wealth.

alliance agreement between two or more countries that provides for their mutual defense or protection.

animism traditional African religion; a belief that the spirit dwells in all living and nonliving things.

annexation the process by which territory is seized by and added to a nation.

anti-Semitism prejudice against the Jewish people.

apartheid (Afrikaans word—apartness) an official policy of strict segregation of the races; practiced in South Africa from 1945 until it was repealed in 1991.

appeasement policy of giving in to the demands of the aggressor to avoid war; policy used by England and France to satisfy Hitler's demands for land during the 1930s.
archipelago chain or group of islands.
aristocracy government ruled by nobles or the upper class.
armistice temporary agreement to stop fighting.

balance of power distribution of military and economic powers among rival nations so that one nation does not have more power than its neighbors or other nations.
balance of trade difference in value between a nation's imports and exports over a period of time.
Bolsheviks left-wing majority group of the Russian Socialist Democratic Party under the leadership of Vladimir Lenin, which seized control of the government by revolution in November 1917; the group was later called Communists.
bourgeoisie middle class between aristocrats and workers. This term was used by Marx and Engels in the *Communist Manifesto* to describe the capitalists, or factory owners, who exploit the worker, or the proletariat. In the Middle Ages, the bourgeoisie were members of the merchant class or the townspeople of the city.
Buddhism major religion of eastern and central Asia founded in 6th century B.C. and based on the teaching of Siddhartha Gautama, who believed people must reject the material world and follow a philosophy of self-denial and meditation.
Bushido traditional code of the Japanese warrior class (the samurai) during the feudal period; emphasizes loyalty and honor to the local warlord over allegiance to the emperor.

capitalism economic system in which the means of production and the distribution of goods and wealth are controlled by individuals and operated for profit. Consumers have freedom of choice to buy or not buy goods.
caste system division of society into four major groups based on occupation or birth; a rigid social system that was characteristic of traditional Hindu Indian society.
Christianity belief system based on the teachings of Jesus Christ that began in the Middle East about 2,000 years ago and was rooted in the monotheistic religion of Judaism.
citizen member of a state or country.
civil disobedience nonviolent or passive resistance; refusal to obey unjust laws that are morally wrong.

civilization advanced form of society characterized by a complex social system, some form of writing, and advances in science and technology.
clan extended family unit or groups of families that have a common ancestor or family ties.
class system social division of society based on wealth, birth, education, occupation, or race.
codified law organized and written set of rules or laws.
Cold War period of tension and hostility between the United States and the Soviet Union after 1945 because of their different political and economic systems; worldwide struggle without actual fighting between the two powers; ended in 1991 with the collapse of the Soviet Union.
collectivization system under communism in which many small farms were combined into large farms owned and operated by the government and worked by the peasants; started by Stalin in the late 1920s.
command economy economic system in which the central authority makes all the production decisions on what and how to produce goods.
communism form of socialism proposed by Karl Marx and Friedrich Engels; characterized by a classless society that supports a common ownership of the means of production and equal distribution of the products of society; no class struggle and the government will wither away.
Confucianism belief system based on the teaching of the Chinese philosopher Confucius, also known as Kung Fu Zi; emphasizes traditional values such as obedience, knowing each person's role in society, and respect for education, elders, and leaders.
Congress of Vienna an assembly of powers to reorganize Europe, in particular the German states; occurred from 1814 to 1815 following the Napoleonic wars to prevent future aggression from France.
Constitutional Monarchy system of government in which the power of the king or queen is limited or defined by the legislature or parliamentary body.
consumer goods tangible economic products used to satisfy the wants and needs of a society.
containment policy of the United States toward the Soviet Union during the Cold War to prevent the spread of communism in the world.
coup d'état (French term) swift overthrow of the government by force or by a small group of people.
cultural diffusion spread of ideas, customs, and technology from one group or region to another culture.
Cultural Revolution program organized by Mao Zedong in China in the 1960s against those who opposed the Communist government. Mao used the Red Guards (Chinese Youths) to purge China of anyone who disagreed with his ideas or policies.

culture people's way of life, which includes language, customs, religion, traditions, and institutions.

czar title of the Russian emperor; also spelled tsar.

decolonization process by which European colonies in Africa and Asia became independent countries after World War II ended.

deforestation destruction of a forest, especially the tropical rainforest, to clear the land to raise food or sell the lumber. The remaining soil is of poor quality because heavy rains wash away the nutrients; the land becomes barren.

democracy system of government in which the people rule.

demographic pattern population distribution.

depression period of drastic economic decline, characterized by a large increase in unemployment, falling prices, and wages.

desalination process of removing salt from seawater in order to make it drinkable.

desertification process by which fertile land becomes a desert due to natural causes or sometimes by man's destructive use of the land.

détente relaxation of tension between the United States and the Soviet Union during the 1970s. The policy was developed by U.S. President Richard Nixon and Soviet leader Leonid Brezhnev.

developed countries highly industrialized nations that have advanced technology.

developing countries countries that are in the process of industrializing, have limited resources, and poor educational and health systems; mainly located in Africa, Asia, and Latin America.

dictatorship system of government in which one person or one party rules the government with absolute control.

disarmament reduction or limiting weapons and military forces as outlined in a treaty.

dissident a person who openly disagrees with the policies or methods of a political party or government, such as those who disagree with the policies of the Communist Party in China or Cuba.

divine right belief that the king or queen was God's earthly representative and received all power directly from God.

domestic system system of manufacturing prior to the Industrial Revolution in which weavers and craftsmen produced goods at home.

dynasty series of rulers from the same family or line of descent.

economics study of how people make a living; how goods and services are produced and distributed to satisfy people's needs.

embargo government order restricting the selling of a particular product to or trading with another nation.

empire groups of territories controlled by one ruler or government.
encomienda system established by the Spanish government in the Americas that enabled the colonists to tax or get labor from the Native Americans.
enlightened despot absolute ruler who bases decisions on the Enlightenment ideas; uses absolute power to begin social changes.
Enlightenment period known as the Age of Reason in 18th-century Europe. Enlightenment thinkers believed that one could use reason to understand the universe; they rejected traditional ideas based on authority.
Estates-General legislative assembly of France composed of clergy, nobles, and commoners.
ethics standards or rules that guide human behavior.
ethnic cleansing term used to describe the forcible removal or murder of Muslims from former Yugoslav provinces of Bosnia and Herzegovina by the Serbian Christian majority during the years 1992–1995; similar policy used by Serbs in Kosovo against the Muslims in 1998.
ethnic group group of people sharing a common language, religion, history, and cultural heritage.
ethnocentrism prejudicial belief that one's culture or standards are superior to those of other societies.
Eurodollar uniform currency introduced in Europe in 1999.
expansionism policy of increasing a nation's territory at the expense of another nation.
exploitation term used to describe how the mother countries took advantage of their colonies to ensure that their own economies grew.
extended family family made up of grandparents, parents, children, aunts, uncles, and cousins whose members may live in the same household or area; this type of family structure exists primarily in a traditional society.
extraterritorality special right of citizens of a foreign country to be tried for a crime by the laws and courts of their own nation; applied to Westerners in China during the 19th and 20th centuries.

factory system system that brought workers and machines together to produce goods in large quantities; began in the British textile industry during the Industrial Revolution.
famine drastic shortage of food that results in severe starvation and hunger.
fascism political philosophy that glorifies the nation over the individual. A dictator has complete control, suppresses all opposition, promotes a policy of extreme nationalism and racism, and has no regard for democracy.
Five Pillars of Wisdom basic beliefs of Islam that include: one God, Allah, praying five times a day, fasting during the month of Ramadan, making a pilgrimage to Mecca, and giving alms to the poor.

five-year plan series of economic goals set by the government in either a Communist or Socialist system; instituted by Joseph Stalin in Russia in 1927 to build up industry and improve farm production.
fossil fuels fuel such as oil, coal, wood, and natural gas.
free enterprise economic system in which individuals and businesses have the freedom to operate for profit with little or no government interference.
free trade removal of trade restrictions among nations.

genocide deliberate effort to kill all members of an ethnic or religious group.
geography one of the social sciences that studies the people, the environment, and the resources of an area.
glasnost Russian term for "openness"; refers to Mikhail Gorbachev's effort in the 1980s to introduce political reform in the Soviet Union by providing freedom of speech and press.
globalization integration of capital, technology, and information across national borders, creating a single global market and, to some degree, a global village.
Great Depression worldwide economic decline that began in 1929 and ended in 1940; businesses and banks failed, and there was widespread joblessness.
Great Leap Forward five-year economic program introduced by Mao Zedong in China in 1958; designed to improve China's agricultural and industrial production.
greenhouse effect rise in the global temperature due to excessive carbon dioxide and pollutants that create a layer in the atmosphere that traps the heat.
Green Revolution 20th-century technological advances in agriculture that have led to increased food production on a limited parcel of land.
gross national product (GNP) total value of goods and services produced in one year; indicator of a country's standard of living.

heavy industry industries requiring complex machinery in the production of iron, steel, and coal.
hierarchy group of people or things arranged or organized by rank or level of importance.
Hinduism major religion of India based on a rigid caste system containing rules for proper behavior. Karma, or a person's behavior, influences his or her reincarnation after death into a higher or lower caste. An endless cycle of rebirth is created for each soul.
Holocaust Nazi genocide against Jews and other minorities during World War II, resulting in the death of millions of people.
Holy Land sacred Israel/Palestine area where Christian, Islamic, and Judaic shrines are located commemorating the birth of their religions.

human rights freedom and rights that all people belonging to a society are entitled to, such as freedom of expression, life, religion, right to vote, and equal protection before the law.

ideology system of beliefs and ideas that guide a nation or group of people.

illiteracy inability to read or write; one measure of a country's industrial development and standard of living.

imperialism policy whereby one nation dominates by direct or indirect rule the political, economic, and social life of a foreign country, region, or area.

indemnity payment of damages or losses suffered in war.

Industrial Revolution historical event that began in the textile industry in England in the 18th century resulting in the shift from the manufacturing of goods by hand to the use of machinery, along with social and economic changes accompanying this change.

inflation economic cycle resulting in a general rise in prices and a decline in the purchasing power of money.

interdependence mutual way in which the economies of countries are dependent on the goods, resources, and knowledge from other parts of the world.

Internet global computer connection using telephone lines or modems providing online contact with people and information on most subjects.

intifada Palestinian uprising against the territory held by Israel that lasted from 1987 until 1988.

Iron Curtain term coined by Winston Churchill in 1946 to describe an imaginary line dividing Soviet Communist-dominated Eastern Europe and the democracies of Western Europe.

Islam name that means submission to the will of God; major religion of the Middle East founded in the 7th century A.D. by the prophet Muhammad whose teachings include belief in one God—Allah.

Islamic Fundamentalists Muslims who believe that public and private behavior should be guided by the principles and values in the Koran. They are against the materialism of Western society.

isolationism policy of avoiding or limiting involvement in the affairs or conflicts of other nations.

Judaism monotheistic religion of the Hebrews whose spiritual and ethical principles are rooted in the Old Testament of the Bible and in the Talmud.

junta group of military officers who rule a country after seizing power.

kaiser German word for emperor used in the 1870s and early 1900s.

kibbutz collective farms established by Jewish settlers in Israel that are based on socialist principles of shared ownership and communal living.

Koran sacred book of Islam containing the revelations made by Allah to Muhammad.

kulak group of wealthy peasants in the Soviet Union who opposed the collectivization of agriculture in the 1920s and 1930s.

labor union an association of workers of a particular trade or craft, formed to further the interests of its members.

laissez-faire economic policy stating that there should be a "hands off" or limited government involvement with private business.

liberalism political philosophy supporting social changes, democracy, and personal freedom.

liberation theology movement in the Catholic Church in Latin America in the late 1970s and 1980s urging the clergy to take an active role in changing the social conditions of the poor.

limited monarchy system of government in which the king's powers are not absolute but specifically guided by a constitution or legislative body.

literacy rate percentage of people in a country with the ability to read and write; method used to measure the standard of living of a country.

market economy economic system in which the laws of supply and demand and the price system influence the decisions of the consumers and the producers of goods.

Marshall Plan formally known as the European Recovery Act; American economic aid package proposed by Secretary of State George Marshall in 1947 to assist European countries in rebuilding after World War II as a way to strengthen democratic governments against communism. The United States gave $17 billion in aid from 1947 to 1951.

Marxism political and economic theory developed by Karl Marx and Friedrich Engels in support of an economic interpretation of history that contributed to a class struggle between the haves and have nots; belief that private ownership must be abolished in favor of collective ownership.

matriarchy system in which ancestry is traced through the mother and her descendants.

Meiji Restoration period lasting from 1868 to 1912 when Japan adopted Western ways in order to become a modern and industrialized nation.

mercantilism economic theory developed during the 17th and 18th centuries in which the colonies existed for the benefit of the mother country; wealth and power of a country was based on exporting more than it imported through strict regulation of colonial trade.

mestizo people of mixed European and Native American ancestry in the Spanish colonies of Latin America.

militarism policy in support of aggressive military preparedness.

mixed economy economic system combining government regulation of industries with private enterprise or capitalistic characteristics.

modernization change in a nation from a traditional economy or way of life to modern ideas, methods, and technology.

monopoly complete control by one person or group over a particular product or market resulting in the ability to set or fix market prices.

monotheism belief in one God.

monsoons seasonal winds from the Indian Ocean that bring heavy rain. They dominate the climate of South Asia, the Middle East, and East Africa.

Mosque Muslim house of worship.

multinational corporation large business enterprises such as Coca-Cola and McDonald's that have branches in many countries.

Muslim follower of the Islamic religion.

nationalism feeling of pride in and loyalty to one's nation or group and its traditions; belief that each group is entitled to its own nation or government.

nationalization government seizure of private businesses or industries.

nation-state political state that developed in Western Europe at the end of the Middle Ages with the decline of feudalism. At that time, the strong monarchs of England and France united people of a common nationality who began to transfer their loyalty from the local lord to the monarch who molded a unified national state. Today it refers to a country with a strong central government and a common history and culture.

natural laws rules of human behavior based on reason and an inborn sense of morality. Enlightenment philosophers thought these laws were universal.

Nazism policies associated with German dictator Adolf Hitler of the National Socialist Party stressing militarism, racism, and extreme nationalism.

neutrality policy of not supporting any one side in a conflict.

New Economic Policy (NEP) policy introduced by Lenin in 1921 in the Soviet Union providing for some restoration of private enterprise and capitalism in order to ease the economic crisis created by the civil war in Russia (1918–1921).

nomad person who has no fixed home and travels from place to place in search of food and other necessities of life.

nonaggression pact agreement between two nations to not attack each other.

nonalignment policy that some Third World nations followed during the Cold War of not supporting either the United States or the Soviet Union.

nuclear family family structure usually found in industrial societies consisting of only parents and their children.

oligarchy form of government in which a small group or elite has power.

overpopulation condition in many developing countries where the population is too large to be supported by the available resources of the region.

Palestine Liberation Organization (PLO) group formed in 1964 and led by Yasir Arafat whose goal was to establish a Palestinian homeland by the use of terrorist tactics in the lands occupied by Israel. The PLO later renounced terrorism and became the official organization to negotiate with Israel over the creation of a Palestinian state.

Pan-Africanism nationalist movement that began in the early 1900s encouraging unification and cooperation among all African nations.

Pan-Arabism mid-20th-century movement promoting the unification of all Arab countries based on cultural and political ties.

Pan-Slavism nationalist movement promoting the cultural and political unification of Slavic people.

parliamentary system type of government in which representatives to the legislative branch of government (Parliament) are democratically elected by the people and the majority party in Parliament selects a prime minister from their ranks. Parliament has supreme legislative powers.

passive resistance form of civil disobedience using nonviolent methods; technique used by Indian leader Mohandas Gandhi, included the boycott of British goods and refusal to pay taxes or serve in the army as a way to promote Indian independence. A similar approach was adopted by Dr. Martin Luther King, Jr., in the civil rights movement in the United States during the 1960s.

patriarchy family organization in which the father or eldest son heads the household.

peaceful coexistence Soviet policy adopted by Nikita Khrushchev in the 1950s, believing that communism and democracy could exist with each other peacefully and avoid hostility.

peasants small farmers or laborers who work the land.

peninsular person born in Spain or Portugal who was eligible for the highest position in the Latin American colonies.

per capita income average income per person of all the citizens in a country; one way to measure the standard of living of a country.

perestroika Russian term for reconstructing; Gobachev's economic policy of the 1980s promoting private enterprise and the free market system instead of a strict government-planned economy.

planned economy system in which the government determines what, how much, and who is allowed to receive the goods that are produced; used by the Soviet Union starting in 1927 and lasting until the 1980s.

pogroms organized attacks or persecutions against a minority group, particularly the Jews in czarist Russia.
polytheism worship or belief in many gods.
population distribution average number of people in a particular area or region.
population explosion large increase in the world's population due to the availability of better medical technology contributing to a longer life expectancy for children and adults.
primary source eyewitness account or firsthand information about people or events; examples include diaries or legal documents.
privatization returning or selling of government facilities to private individuals or investors.
proletariat term used by Marx and Engels to describe the industrial working class in capitalist countries.
propaganda spreading of ideas, information, and rumors to promote a cause or damage an opposing cause.
protectorate form of imperial control in which the foreign country allows the local ruler to remain in power but controls affairs behind the scenes.

racism prejudice and discrimination based on the premise that one group is superior to another because of race.
reactionary political leader who is opposed to change or wants to restore the old order such as those leaders at the Congress of Vienna in the 1800s.
recession decline in economic activities that lasts for a limited amount of time.
reform to try to make things better by change.
reincarnation Hindu belief that the soul is reborn in different forms that indicate whether a person led a good or bad life.
reparation payment for war damages.
republic form of government in which the people choose their officials.
revolution sudden and drastic change resulting in the overthrow of the existing government or political system by force, as in the Russian Revolution; changes in cultural systems, as in the Industrial or Computer Revolution.
Russification policy adopted by Russian czar Alexander III in 1882. Its purpose was to unite the empire's many provinces. It became an official policy of intolerance and persecution of non-Russian people. Jews were singled out in particular for persecution.

samurai members of the Japanese warrior class during the medieval period.
sanctions penalties or actions imposed on a nation by other countries for breaking international laws in order to end its illegal activity.

satellite countries countries politically and economically controlled by a nearby country such as the Eastern European countries that were dominated by the Soviet Union after World War II.

savanna broad grassy plain with few trees in a tropical or subtropical region that has an irregular rain pattern.

scapegoats people who are made to bear the blame for the actions of others; technique used by the Nazi Party in Germany against the Jews for problems confronting the country in the 1920s and 1930s.

scarcity fundamental economic problem describing limited resources combined with unlimited wants and needs.

scramble for Africa time period from 1890 to 1914 when European imperialistic countries divided up the continent for markets and raw materials.

secondary source information about past historical events based on the knowledge collected from several sources.

secularism rejection of the importance of religion in favor of worldly matters.

self-determination right of the people to make their own decisions about their political and economic development.

Shintoism native Japanese religion stressing the connection between people and the forces of nature. In the 18th century, it became the national religion of Japan extolling nationalism, ancestor worship, and divinity of the emperor.

shoguns military generals who ruled Japan from the 12th century to the 1800s.

social contract political theory of 17th- and 18th-century Europe stating that there is an agreement between the people and the government, with people giving up power to their leader in return for life, liberty, and property; governments that fail to fulfill their agreement can be changed.

socialism system in which the government owns and operates all the essential means of production, distribution, and exchange of goods; society as a whole, not the individuals, owns all the property.

social mobility ability to move from one social class to another through education or improvement in income or occupation.

Solidarity independent trade union movement led by Lech Walesa of Poland contributing to the demise of communism.

Soviet bloc countries in the Cold War that were allied with or supported the Soviet Union.

sphere of influence area or region of a country in which a foreign country had exclusive trading privileges such as the right to build railroads and factories; special regions along the coast of China in the 19th century controlled by European imperial countries.

standard of living measure of how well people are living based upon the availability of resources and wealth.

status quo describes a state of affairs existing as they are at the present time.
subsistence agriculture type of farming in which the farmer and his or her family can barely make a living.
suffrage the right to vote.
superpowers the United States and the Soviet Union, which dominated world politics from the end of World War II until the late 1980s.
supply and demand economic theory (of a market economy) that prices reflect the demand for a product and its availability.

tariff tax on goods coming into the country usually to protect industries from foreign competition.
technology use of science and inventions to help society achieve its basic needs or improve a way of living.
terrorism deliberate use of force or violence by an organized group to achieve its political goals.
theocracy nation ruled by religious leaders who base their power on the divine right.
Third World term used to describe the developing nations of Africa, Asia, and Latin America.
totalitarianism government in which one person or group controls all aspects of the political, economic, social, religious, educational, and cultural life of the nation with no regard for individual rights.
total war commitment of a nation's entire military and civilian resources to the war effort.
trade deficit excess of imports over exports.
traditional economy economic system that meets the basic needs of its people through fishing, hunting, and gathering; basic economic decisions are made according to customs or habits.

untouchable (harijan) name derived from the ideas that others would be made dirty and impure from touching them; social group belonging to the lowest caste in Hinduism who do all the undesirable work; outlawed by the Indian Constitution but still prevalent in some communities.
urbanization development of cities due to the movement of people from rural areas in search of jobs and better opportunities.
utopian 19th-century socialist who believed in the ideal society in which all members of society worked for the common good and shared equally in the economic success of the group.

vernacular language of the people in a country.

war crimes atrocities committed by the military or the government against the civilian population during armed conflicts; they include mass murders, genocide, rape, or persecution of religious or racial groups. Since World War II, war crime tribunals such as Nuremburg and The Hague have been set up to deal with these crimes against humanity.

welfare state system under which the government assumes responsibility for the people's social and economic well-being.

Westernization process of adapting Western culture and technology; adapted by Peter the Great of Russia in the 18th century and during the Meiji Restoration of Japan in the 19th century.

Young Turks members of the Turkish Nationalist Party who favored the replacement of the Ottoman Empire's absolute monarchy with a constitutional government and who led the revolution of 1908.

zero population growth situation in which the birth rate of a country equals the death rate.

Zionism worldwide organized movement to build or gain support for a Jewish homeland in Palestine.

INTERNATIONAL ORGANIZATIONS AND AGREEMENTS

Antarctic Treaty treaty signed in 1959 by the United States, the Soviet Union, and ten other nations forbidding the building of military bases, testing of nuclear weapons, or disposing of radioactive wastes by these nations in the area near the Antarctic. It was meant to foster cooperation among scientists from all nations who conduct research on the continent; other nations later signed this treaty.

ANZUS Pact mutual defense agreement among Australia, New Zealand, and the United States, signed in 1951 to contain communism; each nation considered an attack upon one of the others as dangerous to its own safety.

Arab League organization founded by Arab nationalists in 1945 to promote Arab unity during times of crisis; worked jointly for common economic, political, and social goals.

Asia-Pacific Economic Cooperation (APEC) group formed by the nations of the Pacific Rim including countries in Southeast Asia, East Asia, and the Americas that border the Pacific Ocean; goal is to promote trade and investment across the Pacific region and the world.

Association of Southeast Asian Nations (ASEAN) organization consisting of members that are archipelago nations in Southeast Asia and nations on the Indochina peninsula; seeks to promote economic and cultural cooperation as well as solve regional disputes.

Camp David Accords agreement negotiated by President Jimmy Carter between Prime Minister Menachem Begin of Israel and President Anwar Sadat of Egypt; later became the basis of the peace treaty in 1979 calling for diplomatic recognition of Israel by Egypt and normalization of relations, the return of the Sinai Peninsula to Egypt in exchange for the opening of the Suez Canal to Israel, and discussion on Palestinian self-rule in the West Bank and the Gaza Strip.

Caribbean Community and Common Market (CARICOM) formed in 1973 to promote cooperation in the areas of economics and foreign policy among the 13 Caribbean countries.

Commonwealth of Independent States (CIS) association created in December 1991 to replace the government when the Soviet Union collapsed; consisted of 12 of the 15 independent republics including Russia, Ukraine, and Belarus, whose city of Minsk became CIS headquarters; designed to promote economy and political cooperation among the former Communist republics.

Commonwealth of Nations (originally known as the British Commonwealth of Nations established by the Statute of Westminster enacted in 1931); voluntary association linking Great Britain and its former colonies on an equal basis; members try to coordinate economic, political, social, and military matters.

Council of Europe old European organization established by the Treaty of London; an international organization in Strasbourg comprised of 47 democratic countries of Europe. Its purpose is to promote democratic stability and economic and social progress for Europe; composed of a committee of ministers, a secretariat, selected for five years, and an assembly of delegates; council advises on social, political, and economic matters but has no power of enforcement. It is an influential organization because all European nations are members and participate in activities.

Dayton Accords agreement negotiated to end the conflict in Bosnia-Herzegovina in November 1995 in Dayton, Ohio by three presidents: Slobodan Milosevic of Serbia, Aliza Izetbegovic of Bosnia-Herzegovina, and Franjo Tudjman of Croatia, with strong diplomatic assistance from U.S. President Bill Clinton; signed in December; provided for the partition of Bosnia and Herzegovina into two distinct areas—a Serb republic and a Muslim-Croat Federation; 60,000 multinational forces were provided to safeguard the peace.

European Economic Community (EEC) organization established in 1958 by Belgium, Luxembourg, France, Italy, the Netherlands, and West

Germany, which agreed to form a Common Market to expand free trade by eliminating internal tariff barriers and allowing labor and capital to move freely among member nations. Now called the European Union, it includes Great Britain, Ireland, Spain, Portugal, Greece, and Denmark; by the 1990s, membership increased to 15 countries with the addition of Finland, Sweden, and Austria.

European Parliament legislative branch of the European Union founded in 1958; composed of representatives elected by the votes of member nations for five years; powers are advisory with all final decisions requiring approval of the ministers of the Council of Europe.

European Union group that includes the countries that were members of the European Coal and Steel Community, European Atomic Energy Commission, and the European Economic Community (Common Market); official name since 1967 after the merger of these three organizations into one governing unit.

General Agreement on Tariffs and Trade (GATT) agreement signed in 1947 to provide for free trade among member nations and to settle trading disputes. In 1995, the World Trade Organization (WTO) was formed as the successor to GATT.

Helsinki Accords major diplomatic nonbinding agreement signed on August 1, 1975, in Helsinki, Finland, among the United States, Canada, the Soviet Union, and 32 European nations except Albania; agreed to legitimize the USSR's World War II territorial gains (status quo in Europe), agreed to respect human rights, and agreed to promote scientific and cultural exchanges with each other.

International Court of Justice agency of the United Nations consisting of 15 judges; power to settle disputes among nations by majority vote; nations that submit disputes must agree in advance to accept all decisions.

International Monetary Fund (IMF) financial agency of the United Nations established after World War II to promote international trade, help developing nations with troubled economies, and provide balance for currencies of member nations.

Israeli-PLO Accord (The Oslo Accord) agreement negotiated by Israeli Prime Minister Yitzhak Rabin and Palestinian Yasir Arafat in September 1993; provided for Israel and PLO recognition of each other, eventual Palestinian self-government in the West Bank and Gaza Strip, and the gradual withdrawal of Israeli troops from these areas; implemented in May 1994 in the West Bank city of Jericho and the Gaza Strip. In 1995, following difficult negotiations with the PLO, Israel agreed to the removal of forces from other Palestinian areas and the establishment of a Palestinian police force to govern these regions.

League of Nations world peace organization with headquarters in Geneva, Switzerland, created by the Versailles Treaty at the end of World War I. Failure of the United States to join and the lack of power to enforce decisions contributed to its demise as a peacekeeping organization; precursor of the UN, which replaced the League at the end of World War II.

Montreal Protocol agreement signed in 1987 in Montreal, Canada, by 46 nations; urged that the world's nations reduce the use of chemicals that were damaging the earth's ozone layers.

North American Free Trade Agreement (NAFTA) agreement signed by the United States, Canada, and Mexico in 1991 and implemented in 1993; designed to remove all tariffs, quotas, and trade barriers among the three nations over a 15-year period.

North Atlantic Treaty Organization (NATO) defensive alliance formed in 1949 as a way to contain communism in Europe; members Britain, France, Belgium, the Netherlands, Luxembourg, Denmark, Iceland, Italy, Norway, Portugal, Canada, and the United States agreed that an attack on one was an attack on all and they would assist each other; Greece, Turkey, West Germany, and Spain later became members; extended membership to Poland, Hungary, and Czech Republic in 1997.

Northern Ireland Peace Accord agreement reached on April 10, 1998 (Good Friday) to bring peace to Northern Ireland; representatives of United Kingdom, Republic of Ireland, and leaders of Protestants and Catholics of Northern Ireland participated in the negotiations; agreed to a 108-member Northern Ireland Assembly in which Protestants and Catholics would share power, ending 26 years of direct rule from London; encouraged cooperation between Northern Ireland and the Republic of Ireland on issues of agriculture and tourism; renunciation of the Irish Republic to territorial claims in Northern Ireland; accord approved in May in a referendum by 71 percent of voters in Northern Ireland and 94 percent of voters in the Republic of Ireland.

Nuclear Test Ban Treaty signed in 1963 by Great Britain, the Soviet Union, and the United States prohibiting the testing of nuclear weapons in the atmosphere; underground testing was still permitted; nations could withdraw from the treaty if the test ban jeopardized national interest; the United Nations voted in 1996 to prohibit all future nuclear testing; only Pakistan and India failed to agree to it.

Organization of African Unity founded in 1963 by Kwame Nkrumah of Ghana to promote African unity, end colonialism, and foster cooperative approaches in foreign policies, economics, education, and defense; by 1994, with the end of white dominance in South Africa, there were 53 members with the admission of South Africa into the group.

Organization of American States (OAS) regional organization set up in 1948 to promote common defense of Western Hemisphere, democracy, economic cooperation, and human rights; headquarters in Washington, D.C.; members include the United States and many South American, Central American, and Caribbean countries; pressure by the United States led to the expulsion of Cuba, an original member, in 1962.

Organization of Petroleum Exporting Countries (OPEC) organization founded in 1960 by Iran, Iraq, Kuwait, Saudi Arabia, and Venezuela to control production and price of oil; membership expanded to include Algeria, Ecuador, Gabon, Indonesia, Iraq, Libya, Nigeria, Qatar, and United Arab Emirates.

Paris Climate Accord (The Paris Agreement) signed by 195 member countries of the United Nations in 2015; the first-ever universal global climate deal that encourages initiatives, such as a reduction in greenhouse gas emissions, to limit temperature increases in the 21st century to below 2 degrees Celsius; the accord replaces the Kyoto Protocol, which was signed in 1997; the United States withdrew from the accord in 2017.

SALT I and SALT II (Strategic Arms Limitations) agreements signed in 1972 and 1979; designed to limit the spread of nuclear weapons and reduction of specific types of new missile systems such as ICBM and SLBM; limits set on the number of heavy bombers carrying nuclear weapons and air-to-surface ballistic missiles with ranges of more than 375 miles.

START I (Strategic Arms Reduction Treaty) treaty signed by President George Bush and Soviet leader Mikhail Gorbachev on July 31, 1991, to reduce their strategic nuclear forces over a seven-year period by 25 to 35 percent; agreed to destroy their nuclear arsenals; ratified by the United States and Russia in 1992. Later, the former Republics of the Soviet Union Belarus, Kazakhstan, and Ukraine agreed to transfer their nuclear forces to Russia.

START II treaty signed by Presidents George Bush and Boris Yeltsin in January 1993; called for reduction of Russian nuclear warheads to 3,000 and those of the United States to 3,500 by the year 2003 or by the end of 2000, if the United States agreed to finance the dismantling of weapons in Russia; ratified by the United States in 1996; rejected by the Russian Parliament in 1997.

United Nations (UN) world peace organization established in 1945; included six major components: General Assembly, Secretariat, Economic and Social Council, International Court of Justice, Trusteeship Council (largely inactive with the end of colonialism), and Security Council. The Security Council keeps world peace and has five permanent members: China, France, former USSR, United Kingdom, and the United States, with ten rotating members. It has many specialized and autonomous agencies such as the World Bank, World Health Organization, and World Trade Organization.

Universal Declaration of Human Rights adopted by the United Nations General Assembly on December 10, 1948; outlined the basic rights of all individuals without regard to race, color, sex, or nationality.

Warsaw Pact mutual defense alliance formed in 1955 by Russia and its satellite nations of Eastern Europe; agreed to assist each other if attacked by Western powers; Cold War answer to NATO. The treaty is no longer operational since the collapse of communism in 1991.

World Bank specialized agency of the UN (International Bank for Reconstruction and Development) established in 1944; created to provide economic and technical help for developing nations to improve their condition; single most lending agency in international development.

World Court (International Court of Justice) court consisting of 15 judges who meet in The Hague, Netherlands, and decide cases by majority votes; judges settle disputes between nations according to the principles of international law; nations submitting disputes to the court agree in advance to accept its decisions.

World Health Organization (WHO) UN agency whose main activities include setting of international health standards. It provides information on fighting infectious diseases such as AIDS.

World Trade Organization (WTO) successor to GATT; purpose is to make global trade free for all; this agency monitors trade agreements so that a trade benefit granted to one member must be extended to all other members; tries to settle disputes and foster the development of prospering economies by keeping tariffs low and promoting fair competition.

IMPORTANT PEOPLE

Annan, Kofi (1938–2018) elected UN Secretary-General in 1997 for a five-year term of office; first Secretary-General to rise through the ranks of the organization; first black African from sub-Saharan area (Ghana) to serve as head of the United Nations; educated in the United States; proposed UN reform such as consolidation of offices and revision of the UN charter to improve efficiency.

Arafat, Yasir (1929–2004) chief spokesman and leader of the Palestine Liberation Organization (PLO) beginning in 1969; chief goal—destruction of the state of Israel. In 1974, he was the first representative of a non-governmental agency to address the UN General Assembly; in 1988, he renounced terrorism; supported UN-sponsored resolution for a peaceful resolution of the Arab-Israeli crisis; formally recognized Israel's right to exist in 1993 and negotiated an accord with Israeli Prime Minister Rabin, providing for gradual implementation of Palestinian self-rule in the West Bank and Gaza Strip (over the next five years). In 1996, he was elected president of Palestinian-controlled areas of Gaza and the West Bank. The peace process has stalled over the issue of control of Jerusalem. Arafat promised to proclaim a Palestinian State in the West Bank by September 2000.

Assad, Hafez-al (1928–2000) president of Syria from 1971 to 2000; defense minister and leader of nationalist Ba'ath Party who led a successful coup after Syria's loss of the Golan Heights to Israel in the 1967 Six-Day War; domestic popularity rose after the 1973 Arab-Israeli war in which Syria failed to gain the Golan Heights but the army performed creditably; authoritarian ruler who faced opposition at home from Muslim fundamentalists; supported the United States in the Gulf War of 1990; prior to his death expressed a willingness to negotiate with Israel over the Golan Heights.

Atatürk, Kemal (1881–1938) means Father of Turks; military officer who led the revolution in 1923 to overthrow the sultan; first president of Turkey from 1923 to 1938; introduced reform to create a secular state based on Western customs; Islamic law and Arabic script replaced by Western laws and alphabet; women were given the right to vote; separation of church/public schools; encouraged Western dress.

Begin, Menachem (1913–1992) Israeli prime minister from 1977 to 1983; signed Camp David Accords with Egypt calling for recognition of Israel, discussion of self-rule for Palestine, and withdrawal of Israeli troops from Sinai Peninsula; shared the Nobel Peace Prize in 1978 with Egyptian President Anwar Sadat.

Bismarck, Otto von (1815–1898) Prussian-born landowner known as the Iron Chancellor; responsible for unifying the German state into the German Empire in 1871 by a policy of Blood and Iron; dominated central Europe; upset the balance of power leading to an alliance between England and France in 1904.

Bolívar, Simón (1783–1830) Creole leader of the South American independence movement against Spanish rule; liberator of South America; led a series of campaigns resulting in independence for Venezuela, Colombia, Ecuador, Peru, and Bolivia.

Bonaparte, Napoleon (1769–1821) general and emperor of France; called "Son of Revolution"; gained control of France by a coup d'état in 1799; crowned emperor in 1801; very popular due to his reform of the French legal system (Napoleonic Code) and educational system (state-controlled education); improved finance system; conquered and dominated most of Europe except England; defeated by Allied forces of Prussia, Russia, and England; exiled to Elba; returned and defeated at Waterloo; exiled to Saint Helena. He influenced the growth of nationalism in Europe.

Boutros-Ghali Boutros (1922–2016) first African and Arab to serve as Secretary-General of United Nations; served from 1992 to 1997; member of Egyptian delegation that helped to negotiate Camp David Accords in 1978.

Brezhnev, Leonid (1906–1982) Soviet leader from 1964 to 1982 who succeeded Nikita Khrushchev; longest-ruling Communist leader after Stalin; followed the policy of détente; signed SALT, Helsinki Accords; harsh policy toward dissidents; invaded Czechoslovakia (1968) and Afghanistan (1980) to protect Soviet interests.

Castro, Fidel (1927–2016) Cuban revolutionary leader; became the premier in 1959 when he overthrew the Fulgencio Batista dictatorship; established Communist state; one of the last Communist leaders in the world; aided Communist movements in Africa and Latin America; his brother Raúl was named his successor.

Catherine the Great (1729–1796) German-born empress of Russia who ruled from 1792 to 1796; extended Russia's border to the south against Ottoman Turks by securing a warm water port on the Black Sea; in the West took part in the partition of Poland; efficient ruler who codified laws; began state-sponsored education for boys and girls; ruthless toward serfs; last of the great absolute monarchs of the 1700s.

Cavour, Camillo di (1810–1861) Italian political leader of Piedmont Sardinia from 1852 to 1859 and 1860 to 1861; considered the "Brains of Italian unification."

Chamberlain, Neville (1869–1940) Prime Minister of the United Kingdom from 1937 to 1940; known for his policy of *appeasement*, in which he allowed Adolf Hitler to claim the Sudetenland in 1938.

Chiang Kai-shek (1888–1975) also known as Jiang Jieshi; military leader of Chinese Nationalist Party (Kuomintang) after the death of Sun Yat-sen in 1925; involved in a civil war with Communist forces of Mao Zedong from 1927 to 1949; exiled to Taiwan after being defeated by Communists in 1949; strongly supported by the United States during his presidency of the Nationalist government of Taiwan from 1950 to 1975.

Churchill, Winston (1874–1965) prime minister of England during World War II; strongly condemned England's policy of appeasement toward Germany prior to World War II; coined the term "Iron Curtain" describing Eastern European countries under communism after 1945.

Darwin, Charles (1809–1882) British naturalist; wrote *On the Origin of Species*, stating the theory of evolution that human beings are evolved by natural selection or survival of the fittest; theory used by Europeans to justify imperialism, "White Man's Burden," in the Scramble for Africa.

Deng Xiaoping (1904–1997) Chinese Communist political leader from 1976 to 1997; implemented economic reforms modernizing industry and allowing some privatizing of agriculture and consumer industries; allowed increased contact with the West; harsh treatment for the protest movement for political freedom at Tiananmen Square.

Díaz, Porfirio (1830–1915) Mexican dictator, or caudillo, from 1876 to 1880 and from 1884 to 1911; brought foreign investments and economic stability to Mexico; prosperity for the rich and poverty for the lower classes.

Engels, Friedrich (1820–1895) German philosopher, socialist, and associate of Karl Marx; wrote *The Communist Manifesto.*

Frederick the Great (1712–1786) king of Prussia; ruled from 1740 to 1786; doubled the size of his kingdom through foreign wars and converted the country into an important European power; enlightened despot who supported educational and legal reforms and religious freedom.

Gandhi, Mohandas (1869–1948) Hindu nationalist leader of India's independence movement from Great Britain; revered as a prophet; called *Mahatma* (saintly one); advocated civil disobedience and passive resistance to achieve his goals; against mistreatment of women and untouchables; assassinated in 1948 by a Hindu extremist.

Garibaldi, Giuseppe (1807–1882) Italian general and nationalist who led his volunteers (Red Shirts) in the capture of Naples and Sicily; the conquest led to the formation of a united Italy; known as the "Sword of Italian Unification."

Gorbachev, Mikhail (1931–) Soviet leader of Communist Party who ruled from 1986 to 1991; introduced liberal policies of glasnost, or openness, for more democracy, and perestroika, economic reforms encouraging more free-market activities; was awarded the Nobel Peace Prize in 1990 for permitting self-rule in Eastern Europe; resigned when Soviet Union collapsed in 1991.

Hitler, Adolf (1889–1945) German chancellor from 1933 to 1945; leader of the Nazi Party; brutal dictator whose policies led to the murder and persecution of Jews and other minorities and dissidents; promoted extreme nationalism contributing to World War II; conquered Europe except for England; defeated by Allied forces of United States, England, France, and Russia in 1945.

Ho Chi Minh (1890–1969) president of North Vietnam; founded Vietnamese Communist Party; Nationalist leader against France and United States in the Vietnam War.

Hussein, ibn Talal (King Hussein) (1935–1999) called Father of Modern Jordan, he ruled from 1955–1999; instrumental in drafting UN Resolution 242 in 1967 calling for Israel to withdraw from all occupied lands; resolution served as a benchmark for future negotiations; a shrewd political leader who survived the demands of Arab neighbors, Israel and Palestinian refugees, who are a majority in his country; in 1994, signed a peace treaty with Israel, becoming the second Arab leader to end a state of war with Israel that had technically existed since 1945.

Hussein, Saddam (1937–2006) president and dictator of Iraq from 1979–2003; expansion policies led to war against Iran and the United States (Persian Gulf War 1990); despite disastrous defeat in both wars, maintained power by destroying all opposition, especially Kurd minority; development of chemical weapons led to problems with the United Nations and war with the United States starting in 2003.

Jinping, Xi (1953–) president of China since 2013.

Kenyatta, Jomo (1891–1978) prime minister of Kenya from 1963 to 1964 and then president from 1964 to 1978; was notable for anti-colonial activism; played a significant role in the transition of Kenya from a colony of the British Empire to an independent nation.

Khomeini, Ayatollah (1902–1989) Islamic Fundamentalist who returned from exile in 1978 to lead a revolution resulting in the overthrow of the Shah of Iran; established an Islamic republic based on ideas contained in the Koran; rejected westernization, particularly the United States, which he called "The Great Satan"; supported militants who held 52 American hostages for 444 days.

Khrushchev, Nikita (1894–1971) Stalin's successor, who became the first secretary of the Communist Party after Stalin's death in 1953; eliminated all opposition in a power struggle to become preeminent leader of the country; began the process of de-Stalinization in 1956; tried to increase agricultural production; supported peaceful coexistence but suppressed the Hungarian Revolution and constructed the Berlin Wall.

Klerk, Frederik Willem de (1936–) former president of South Africa; released Nelson Mandela from prison in 1990; repealed the apartheid law; negotiated a plan to end white minority rule; shared the Nobel Peace Prize with Mandela in 1993; became a member of Mandela's government in 1994.

Lenin, Vladimir Ilyich (1870–1924) also known as Nikolai; founder of Bolshevik Party in Russia; set up Communist government in 1917; created Union of Soviet Socialist Republics in 1922 after defeating anticommunist forces of the czar and foreign nations; his death in 1924 led to a power struggle between Stalin and Trotsky.

Leopold II of Belgium (1835–1909) king of Belgium from 1865 to 1909; acquired lands in the Congo through treaties; licensed companies that harshly exploited and abused Africans, leading to the deaths of over 10 million Congolese.

L'Ouverture, François Toussaint (1743–1803) revolutionary leader of Haiti; led struggle for independence from Napoleon; ruled from 1798 to 1802; his success ended Napoleon's dream of an empire in the Americas.

Malthus, Thomas (1766–1834) philosopher of industrialization; wrote *An Essay on the Principle of Population*, in which he argued that population increases occurred more rapidly than food supply and that without natural checks on population, the majority of people would be impoverished.

Mandela, Nelson (1918–2013) South African statesman; leader of the African National Congress; arrested in 1962 for his opposition to apartheid; spent 27 years in jail; became the international symbol for freedom against white minority rule in South Africa; released in 1990 and negotiated a plan with the white government to turn South Africa into a multiracial democracy; shared the Nobel Peace Prize with Frederik Willem de Klerk in 1993; elected first black president in a free election in 1994; served from 1995 to 1999.

Mao Zedong (also known as Mao Tse-tung) (1893–1976) Chinese Communist leader who led the struggle against Nationalists from 1927 to 1949; established his regime in 1948 and ruled the People's Republic of China from 1949 to 1976; introduced Great Leap Forward to industrialize China and compelling people to join communes; initiated the Cultural Revolution to diminish all opposition and strengthen his power; his book *Quotations of Chairman Mao* promoted terrorist tactics; became a cult symbol (Maoism).

Marx, Karl (1818–1883) German philosopher and founder of modern socialism; wrote *The Communist Manifesto* with Friedrich Engels (1820–1895), proposing an economic interpretation of history; wrote *Das Kapital*, an analysis of economic and political aspects of capitalism.

Mazzini, Giuseppe (1805–1872) Italian patriot and founder of Young Italy, a secret society to promote Italian unity; headed short-lived Republic of Rome in 1849; continued his efforts for independence from Austria from abroad; "Soul of Italian Unification."

Mussolini, Benito (1883–1945) Fascist dictator of Italy (1924–1945); called *Il Duce* (leader); ally of Germany (Rome-Berlin Axis) in World War II; shot by Italian partisans in 1945.

Nasser, Gamal Abdel (1918–1970) president of Egypt from 1956 to 1970; seized power with other military officers by overthrowing King Farouk in 1953; nationalized the Suez Canal, resulting in war with Britain, France, and Israel; promoted economic businesses and irrigation projects such as the Aswan High Dam; supported Pan-Arabism to encourage unity in Arab world.

Nehru, Jawaharlal (also known as Pandit Nehru) (1889–1964) first prime minister of independent India in 1947, serving until his death in 1964; supported Gandhi's policy of civil disobedience; imprisoned during the 1930s for his activities; rejected Gandhi's proposal for hand production; urged industrialization; set up mixed economy; leader of nonaligned nations in the Cold War; father of Indira Gandhi, India's prime minister from 1966 to 1977.

Netanyahu, Benjamin (1949–) conservative prime minister of Israel from 1996 to 1999; his party opposed additional concessions to the Palestinians on the issue of the West Bank and Gaza Strip; replaced as prime minister in 1999 by moderate leader Ehud Barak; re-elected as prime minister in 2009.

Nicholas II (1868–1918) last Romanov czar of Russia; ruled from 1894 to 1917; abdicated in the Russian Revolution of March 1917; killed with his entire family by Bolsheviks (Communists) in 1918.

Nkrumah, Kwame (1909–1972) African leader who became the first prime minister of Ghana; American-educated; promoted Pan-Africanism encouraging cooperation among African states; deposed in 1966 due to resentment created by his dictatorial policies.

O'Higgins, Bernardo (1778–1842) Chilean general who led a revolt against Spain in 1816; ruled Chile from 1817 to 1823.

Owen, Robert (1771–1858) English industrialist and socialist; established utopian communities in New Lanark, Scotland, and New Harmony, Indiana, both of which failed.

Pahlavi, Mohammad Reza Shah (1919–1980) last shah of Iran who ruled from 1941 to 1978; autocratic ruler; employed secret police (Savak) and permitted no political opposition; encouraged economic and social modernization, including land reforms, literacy, and women's rights; pro-Western foreign policy; special relationship with the United States; overthrown by Ayatollah Khomeini in 1978; workers protested the poor economic conditions; religious leaders opposed his modernization policies.

Perón, Juan (1895–1974) elected president of Argentina in 1946 with the support of the military; established a dictatorial government; widely popular due to his wife, Eva; instituted economic nationalization of many industries (public works program) and political and social reforms; opposed by the Catholic Church; the poor economic conditions led to his exile to Spain in 1955; returned in 1973 and was reelected president; died in 1974.

Perry, Matthew (1794–1858) U.S. Navy Commodore; led the fleet that sailed into Tokyo harbor in 1854 and negotiated the reopening of Japan to American trade, which led to the resignation of the Shogun and modernization (westernization) of Japan.

Rabin, Yitzhak (1922–1995) Israel's prime minister from 1974 to 1977 and 1992 to 1995; first prime minister to meet with Palestinian leader Yasir Arafat; agreed to set up Palestinian self-rule in the Gaza Strip, the city of Jericho, and the West Bank; negotiated a peace treaty with King Hussein of Jordan; awarded the Nobel Peace Prize in 1994; assassinated in 1995.

Rousseau, Jean-Jacques (1712–1778) French philosopher of the Enlightenment; wrote the *Social Contract*, claiming that "Man is born free and everywhere he is in chains" and that the people give power to the government (General Will) to act for the good of the people and also have the right to overthrow the government if it fails the people; his ideas were used to support democracy and justify dictatorship under the General Will.

Sadat, Anwar (1918–1981) Egyptian president from 1970 to 1981; directed nation's policy away from dependence on Soviet Union; promoted foreign investments, some privatization of businesses; first Arab leader to visit Israel; signed Camp David Accords with Israeli Prime Minister Menachem Begin in 1978; shared the Nobel Peace Prize with Begin; assassinated in 1981.

Smith, Adam (1723–1790) social philosopher and economist; founder of modern economics; authored *The Wealth of Nations*; believed in the doctrine of laissez-faire—government should keep a "hands-off" approach to business.

Stalin, Joseph (1878–1953) dictator of the Soviet Union from 1925 to 1953; used his position as general secretary of the Communist Party to gain absolute power; established a totalitarian state; crushed all opposition by terror and mass executions; introduced five-year plans to transform Russia into an industrial giant; allied with the West during World War II.

Sun Yat-sen (also known as Sun Yixian) (1866–1925) leader of the Chinese revolt against the Manchu dynasty in 1911; founded the Chinese Republic; briefly served as president; believed in three principles of democracy, nationalism, and people's livelihood to make China strong.

Teresa, Mother (1910–1997) Roman Catholic nun who founded a missionary order to provide food, shelter, and medical help for underprivileged people of India; won the Nobel Peace Prize in 1979 for her humanitarian efforts.

Trotsky, Leon (Lev Bronstein) (1879–1940) Russian revolutionary who worked with Lenin to overthrow the czar in November 1917; directed the Red Army in the civil war from 1917 to 1922; lost the power struggle with Stalin after Lenin's death; exiled and assassinated in Mexico by Stalin's order in 1940.

Tutu, Desmond (1931–) Anglican Archbishop in South Africa who won the Nobel Peace Prize in 1984 for his opposition to apartheid; his leadership created worldwide pressure on South Africa to end its repressive policies; appointed head of Truth and Reconciliation by Nelson Mandela to investigate the injustices of apartheid.

Voltaire (François-Marie Arouet) (1694–1778) French philosopher; major figure of the Enlightenment; supported control by enlightened absolute rulers and despots; his satirical works mocked the Church and royal authority; exiled to England for three years; praised Britain's limited monarchy; credited with the statement, "I disapprove of what you say, but I will defend to the death your right to say it."

Walesa, Lech (1943–) first democratically elected president of Poland, from 1990 to 1995, in the post-Soviet era; electrician in a Gdansk shipyard who led a strike for better wages and living conditions against the Communist government; formed Solidarity, an independent labor union; arrested for his activities and released; became an international hero; awarded the Nobel Peace Prize in 1983. In 1989, he helped to make Solidarity a legal political party and end Communist rule in Poland.

Yeltsin, Boris (1931–2007) rival of Gorbachev who opposed the slow pace of political and economic reform of the 1980s; elected president of the Russian Republic in 1991; led the resistance to the conservative coup to oust

Gorbachev; resigned from the Communist Party and became the first popularly elected president of Russia with the end of communism in 1991; elected in 1996 to a five-year term as president of the Russian federation. Unable to solve Russia's economic problems and ethnic tensions, his poor personal health caused him to resign the presidency in 1999 in favor of Vladimir Putin, his protégé.

Zapata, Emiliano (1879 [?]–1919) Mexican revolutionary who helped overthrow the dictator Porfirio Díaz; supported by peasants whose battle cry was "Land and liberty!"; assassinated in 1919.

Zemin, Jiang (1926–) former Communist leader of China; introduced economic reforms to increase private ownership; little toleration for political dissenters.

Practice Section

PART I: MULTIPLE CHOICE

Directions (1–60): For each statement or question, write in the space provided the *number* of the word or expression that, of those given, best completes the statement or answers the question.

1 Which pair correctly links the region where Enlightenment ideas first developed to a region to which those ideas spread?

(1) Asia → eastern Europe
(2) Africa → southeastern Asia
(3) western Europe → the Americas
(4) eastern Africa → India 1 ____

2 Which situation is a direct result of the Enlightenment in Europe in the 18th century?

(1) the rise of fascist leaders in Germany and Italy
(2) the outbreak of revolution in France
(3) the creation of Soviet satellite states in Eastern Europe
(4) the creation of an expansive British Empire 2 ____

Base your answer to question 3 on the passage below and on your knowledge of social studies.

> ...We must ask ourselves three questions.
>
> 1. What is the Third Estate? *Everything*.
> 2. What has it been until now in the political order? *Nothing*.
> 3. What does it want to be? *Something*....

—Abbé Sieyès, 1789 (adapted)

3 Based on this passage, what did the Third Estate want?

(1) independence from France
(2) more influence in the political system
(3) removal of the monarchy
(4) freedom of religion in France

3 ____

Base your answer to question 4 on the document excerpts below and on your knowledge of social studies.

Declaration of the Rights of Man and of the Citizen

1. Men are born and remain free and equal in rights. Social distinctions may be founded only upon the general good.
2. The aim of all political association is the preservation of the natural and imprescriptible [inalienable] rights of man. These rights are liberty, property, security, and resistance to oppression. . . .

— French National Assembly, 1789

Declaration of the Rights of Woman and Female Citizen

1. Woman is born free and remains equal to man in rights. Social distinctions can only be founded on common service.
2. The aim of all political associations is to preserve the natural and inalienable rights of Woman and Man: these are the rights to liberty, ownership, safety and, above all, resistance to oppression. . . .

— Olympe de Gouges, 1791

4 Based on these excerpts, which action would most likely be supported by Olympe de Gouges?

(1) executing the king
(2) restricting access to education
(3) creating more radical military strategies
(4) expanding the definition of equality 4 ____

---

5 Which of the following events led to the other three?

(1) the creation of the Napoleonic Code
(2) the Congress of Vienna
(3) Napoleon Bonaparte seizing political power in France
(4) the Battles of Trafalgar and Waterloo 5 ____

6 Simón Bolívar, Toussaint L'Ouverture, and José de San Martín are all associated with revolutions in

(1) Africa
(2) Europe
(3) South Asia
(4) Latin America

6 ____

7 Adam Smith's *Wealth of Nations* stressed the importance of

(1) tradition
(2) supply and demand
(3) large corporations
(4) government ownership

7 ____

8 Laissez-faire practices are most closely associated with a

(1) traditional economy
(2) market economy
(3) command economy
(4) mixed economy

8 ____

9 In the late 1700s, the Industrial Revolution developed in Britain because Britain

(1) possessed key factors of production
(2) excluded foreign investors
(3) suppressed the enclosure movement
(4) required a minimum wage be paid to workers

9 ____

10 Which of the following best describes the greatest social change to occur in Europe in the 18th century as a result of the Industrial Revolution?

(1) the establishment of Communist governments throughout Europe
(2) the rise of a new economic theory of mercantilism
(3) increased wealth for many European powers as new colonies were established
(4) a shift in population to cities and the rise of a working class

10 ____

Base your answer to question 11 on the passage below and on your knowledge of social studies.

> ...Economic reforms included a unified modern currency based on the yen, banking, commercial and tax laws, stock exchanges, and a communications network. Establishment of a modern institutional framework conducive to an advanced capitalist economy took time but was completed by the 1890s. By this time, the government had largely relinquished direct control of the modernization process, primarily for budgetary reasons. Many of the former *daimyo*, whose pensions had been paid in a lump sum, benefited greatly through investments they made in emerging industries. Those who had been informally involved in foreign trade before the Meiji Restoration also flourished. Old *bakufu*-serving firms that clung to their traditional ways failed in the new business environment...
>
> —*Japan: A Country Study*, Library of Congress

11 According to this passage, what was this country trying to do?

(1) provide benefits to the daimyo
(2) develop a safety net for traditional businesses
(3) become an industrialized nation-state
(4) relinquish control over foreign trade 11 ____

---

12 Which course of action does the theory of laissez-faire suggest a government should follow?

(1) providing help for people in need
(2) establishing businesses to create jobs
(3) letting natural laws regulate the economy
(4) controlling the mineral resources of a country 12 ____

13 One effect of the British landlord system in Ireland in the mid-1800s and in India in the early 1900s was that these landlord systems

(1) contributed to famine and suffering
(2) allowed local economies to prosper
(3) emphasized food crops over mining
(4) led to an agrarian revolution 13 ____

14 Which description of trade patterns best represents the relationship between Africa and Europe during the late 19th century?

(1) Trans-Saharan trade caravans led by Europeans were the most profitable.
(2) South Africa was of no interest to European traders.
(3) Raw materials were shipped from Africa to European industries.
(4) Rivers were the key highways connecting Europeans to much of the African interior. 14 ____

15 Which statement best reflects an effect of imperialism in Africa?

(1) Land was distributed equally between social classes.
(2) Territorial divisions were primarily established using tribal boundaries.
(3) Natural resources were exploited for the benefit of European powers.
(4) Timbuktu became the center of great learning. 15 ____

16 Commodore Matthew Perry is best known for taking which action?

(1) leading the British East India Company
(2) rescuing Europeans during the Boxer Rebellion
(3) justifying European spheres of influence in China
(4) opening Japan to American and European influences 16 ____

Base your answer to question 17 on the map below and on your knowledge of social studies.

China, 1895–1914

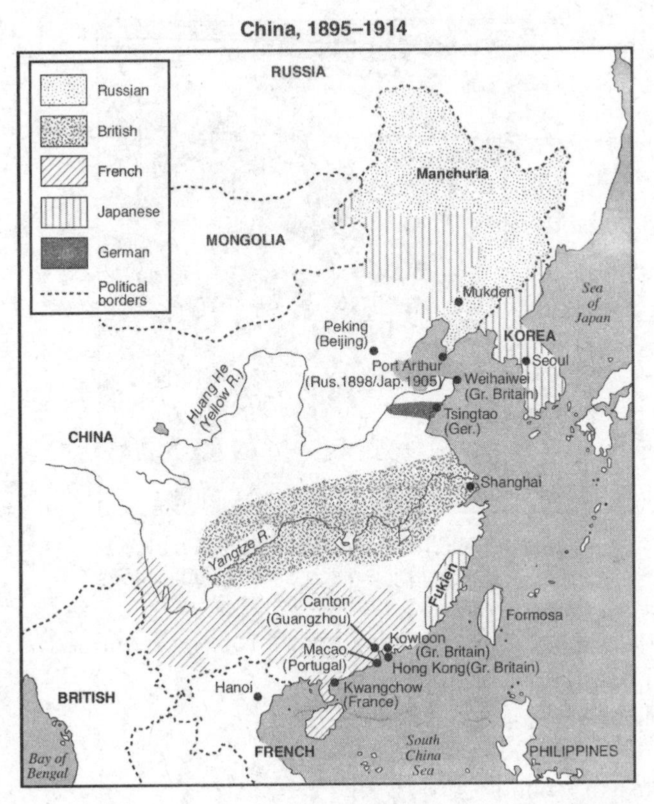

Source: Historical Maps on File (adapted)

17 What is the primary focus of this map?

(1) population density
(2) resource distribution
(3) imperialism
(4) urbanization

17 ____

---

18 During the 19th century in Latin America, the Catholic Church and the military generally supported the interests of

(1) wealthy landowners
(2) landless peasants
(3) democratic reformers
(4) indigenous peoples

18 ____

Base your answer to question 19 on the cartoon below and on your knowledge of social studies.

Source: Abraham and Pfeffer, *Enjoying World History*, Amsco School Publications

19 This cartoon suggests that political power is often acquired through

(1) the inheritance of land
(2) market demands
(3) religious conversion
(4) the use of technology

19 ____

---

20 Which heading best completes the partial outline below?

I. ______________________
A. "Blood and Iron"
B. Austro-Prussian War
C. Franco-Prussian War
D. Kaiser Wilhelm I

(1) Congress of Vienna
(2) Scramble for Africa
(3) Age of Absolutism
(4) Unification of Germany

20 ____

Base your answers to questions 21 and 22 on the maps below and on your knowledge of social studies.

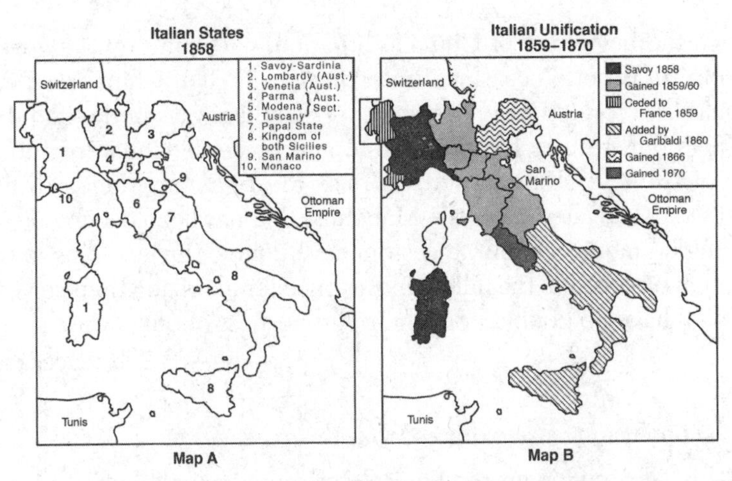

Source: Alexander Ganse, 2000 (adapted)

21 Which factor provided the motivation for the changes that took place between 1858 and 1870 as indicated on these maps?

(1) exploration
(2) appeasement
(3) religion
(4) nationalism

21 ____

22 Which pair of individuals played a direct role in the changes that took place between Map A and Map B?

(1) Otto von Bismarck and Wilhelm II
(2) Klemens von Metternich and Victor Emmanuel III
(3) Camillo di Cavour and Giuseppe Mazzini
(4) Alexander II and Frederick the Great

22 ____

---

23 Which of the following best describes the direct effect of nationalism in Europe during the 19th century?

(1) the unifications of Italy and of Germany
(2) the creation of the Austrian Empire
(3) an extended period of peace and lack of conflict
(4) the rise of absolute monarchies

23 ____

Base your answer to question 24 on the passage below and on your knowledge of social studies.

> ... Since the beginning of China as a nation, we Chinese have governed our own country despite occasional interruptions. When China was occasionally occupied by a foreign race, our ancestors could always in the end drive these foreigners out, restore the fatherland, and preserve China for future generations of Chinese. Today when we raise the righteous standard of revolt in order to expel an alien race [the Manchus] that has been occupying China, we are doing no more than our ancestors have done or expected us to do. Justice is so much on our side that all Chinese, once familiarizing themselves with our stand, will have no doubt about the righteousness of our cause....
>
> — "A Public Declaration," 1906

24 Which conclusion can be drawn from this passage?

(1) China can no longer remain isolated from its neighbors.
(2) The Chinese people are happy with the rule of the Manchu.
(3) The Chinese people wanted to end foreign occupation.
(4) China has prospered under the rule of foreign powers.

24 ____

---

25 One reason the Suez Canal has been of strategic importance to countries other than Egypt was that the canal

(1) allowed for faster movement between the North Atlantic Ocean and the Indian Ocean
(2) enabled Europeans to explore the Western Hemisphere
(3) made it easier for Russia to gain control of Afghanistan
(4) provided the Austro-Hungarian Empire with access to its colonies in South Asia

25 ____

26 A similarity between the Sepoy Rebellion in India and the Boxer Rebellion in China is that both were

(1) attempts to remove foreign influence
(2) movements to establish communist governments
(3) efforts to restore trade monopolies
(4) struggles to westernize cultures

26 ____

Base your answer to question 27 on the passage below and on your knowledge of social studies.

> . . . The Opium War of 1839–42 was short and one-sided due to the superiority of European weapons, which came as a complete surprise to the Chinese. In the first skirmish alone, in July 1839, two British warships defeated twenty-nine Chinese ships. On land, the Chinese and their medieval weapons were no match for British troops armed with state-of-the-art muskets. By the middle of 1842 British troops had seized Hong Kong, taken control of the key river deltas, and occupied Shanghai and several other cities. The Chinese were forced to sign a peace treaty that granted Hong Kong to the British, opened five ports for the free trade of all goods, and required the payment of reparations to the British in silver, including compensation for the opium that had been destroyed by Commissioner Lin. . . .
>
> —Tom Standage

27 What was an immediate result of the Opium War described in this passage?

(1) signing the Treaty of Nanking
(2) forming the Guomindang
(3) beginning the Boxer Rebellion
(4) organizing the Taiping Rebellion 27 ____

---

28 A key idea in the *Communist Manifesto* by Karl Marx and Friedrich Engels is that workers should support the

(1) overthrow of the capitalist system
(2) establishment of labor unions
(3) legislative regulation of wages and working conditions
(4) technological changes in production methods 28 ____

29 Which of the following factors contributed to the rise of Zionism in the late 19th century?

(1) the establishment of the State of Israel as an autonomous nation
(2) the expansion of Islam throughout Southwest Asia
(3) the defeat of Germany in World War I
(4) anti-Semitism and Jewish persecution throughout Europe 29 ____

30 Which action did Japan take during the Meiji Restoration?

(1) established a social system to benefit the samurai
(2) sent experts to learn from modern Western nations
(3) allowed communist ideas to dominate its government
(4) started an ambitious program to expel foreign manufacturers 30 ____

31 Which of these groups were the major supporters of 20th-century communist revolutions?

(1) priests and artisans
(2) bourgeoisie and nobility
(3) entrepreneurs and capitalists
(4) workers and peasants 31 ____

32 Which factor led to the rise of communist revolutions in Russia and in China?

(1) increase in agricultural production around the world
(2) onset of the global depression that restricted trade
(3) scarcity of workers for available jobs
(4) unequal distribution of wealth between social classes 32 ____

Base your answer to question 33 on the poster below and on your knowledge of social studies.

Source: A. Apsit, Coloured Lithograph, 1918 (adapted)

33 In early 20th-century Russia, which group may have gained support by circulating this poster?

(1) aristocracy
(2) Bolsheviks
(3) monarchists
(4) Orthodox clergy

33 ____

34 • Imperial troops fire on peaceful demonstrators in an event known as "Bloody Sunday."
• Vladimir Lenin stages a coup d'état against the Duma.
• Czar Nicholas II and the royal family are assassinated in Yekaterinburg.

These events led to which of the following?

(1) the Bolshevik Revolution
(2) the establishment of the Romanov dynasty
(3) the outbreak of World War II
(4) the collapse of the Soviet Union 34 _____

35 One way in which the government under Czar Nicholas II of Russia and the government under Benito Mussolini of Italy are similar is that both governments

(1) liberated the serfs and industrial workers
(2) reformed the executive branch by incorporating theocratic principles
(3) established policies of censorship and repression
(4) used televised propaganda to rally the masses 35 _____

36 A primary objective of the New Economic Policy (NEP) in the Soviet Union was to

(1) promote private ownership of heavy industry
(2) organize support for educational reforms to improve literacy
(3) coordinate efforts to end World War I
(4) gain stability by increasing production 36 _____

37 Which statement about the Soviet economy under Joseph Stalin is accurate?

(1) The Soviet Union increased its power by developing heavy industry.
(2) The government reduced its role in planning industrial production.
(3) Farmers were encouraged to compete in a free market economy.
(4) A large selection of consumer goods became available in the Soviet Union. 37 _____

38 During World War I, developments in military technology led to

(1) an early victory by the Allied powers
(2) the establishment of industrial capitalism
(3) the use of poisonous gas and submarine attacks
(4) an increase in ethnic tension in western Europe 38 _____

Base your answers to questions 39 and 40 on the passage below and on your knowledge of social studies.

> ... Gas travels quickly, so you must not lose any time; you generally have about eighteen or twenty seconds in which to adjust your gas helmet....
>
> For a minute, pandemonium [chaos] reigned in our trench,—Tommies adjusting their helmets, bombers running here and there, and men turning out of the dugouts with fixed bayonets, to man the fire step....
>
> Our gun's crew were busy mounting the machine gun on the parapet and bringing up extra ammunition from the dugout....
>
> —Arthur G. Empey, "*Over The Top*," G. P. Putnam's Sons

39 Which aspect of warfare is emphasized in this passage about World War I?

(1) importance of civilian support
(2) impact of government propaganda
(3) shortage of manpower on the battlefield
(4) role of military technology

39 ____

40 Which type of source does this passage best represent?

(1) census study
(2) government decree
(3) first person account
(4) encyclopedia article

40 ____

---

41 One reason the League of Nations failed as a world organization was that it

(1) supported the rise of fascist states
(2) lacked a military force to settle conflicts
(3) dealt with conflict by establishing naval blockades
(4) encouraged the annexation of territory by force

41 ____

42 Which event is considered an immediate cause of World War II?

(1) signing of the Treaty of Versailles
(2) Germany's invasion of Poland
(3) Japan's attack on Pearl Harbor
(4) the bombings of Hiroshima and Nagasaki

42 ____

43 Which headline is most closely associated with the cities of Hiroshima and Nagasaki?

(1) **"Japan Signs Treaty of Kanagawa"**
(2) **"Nuclear Bombs Dropped on Japan"**
(3) **"Japan Invades Korea"**
(4) **"Japan Hosts Discussion on Greenhouse Gases"** 43 ____

44 Which sequence of events is in the correct chronological order?

(1) rise of Nazism → Treaty of Versailles → German invasion of the Soviet Union
(2) Treaty of Versailles → rise of Nazism → German invasion of the Soviet Union
(3) German invasion of the Soviet Union → rise of Nazism → Treaty of Versailles
(4) Treaty of Versailles → German invasion of the Soviet Union → rise of Nazism 44 ____

45 During the Cold War, nations that adopted a policy of nonalignment believed they should

(1) be exempt from United Nations decisions
(2) restrict trade with neighboring countries
(3) reject international environmental treaties
(4) follow a course independent of the superpowers 45 ____

46 The Truman Doctrine and the Marshall Plan were similar in that

(1) both helped to spread communism to neighboring regions
(2) both shared the goal of containment
(3) both attempted to end the Cold War
(4) both sought to disarm the Soviet Union 46 ____

47 Which pair of countries that gained independence in the 20th century experienced the migration of millions of people across their shared borders due to religious tensions?

(1) Czech Republic and Slovakia
(2) Kazakhstan and Uzbekistan
(3) Egypt and Libya
(4) India and Pakistan 47 ____

48 Which reform is most closely associated with Turkish leader Kemal Atatürk?

(1) implementation of Sharia law
(2) introduction of Arabic script
(3) establishment of a communist government
(4) adoption of Western culture 48 ____

Base your answer to question 49 on the passage below and on your knowledge of social studies.

> ... There is no fundamental contradiction between socialism and a market economy. The problem is how to develop the productive forces more effectively. We used to have a planned economy, but our experience over the years has proved that having a totally planned economy hampers the development of the productive forces to a certain extent. If we combine a planned economy with a market economy, we shall be in a better position to liberate the productive forces and speed up economic growth....
>
> —Deng Xiaoping

49 According to Deng Xiaoping, what should be done to improve China's economy?

(1) restrict imports from competitive market economies
(2) incorporate economic principles of a market economy into a command economy
(3) become a Marxist socialist state
(4) implement the economic reforms of Mao Zedong 49 ____

---

50. The British reliance on India as a market for its manufactured goods caused Mohandas Gandhi to

(1) run for a seat in the British Parliament
(2) lead the Sepoy Rebellion
(3) support traditional caste divisions
(4) refuse to buy British textiles 50 ____

51. What was one social change Mao Zedong instituted in China after 1949?

(1) granting legal equality for men and women
(2) requiring arranged marriages
(3) adopting the practice of foot binding
(4) mandating Confucianism as the state philosophy 51 ____

52 During the Great Leap Forward, Chinese peasants were forced to

(1) join communes
(2) move to the cities
(3) convert to Christianity
(4) attack the Red Guards 52 ____

53 Japan's policy of expansion in the early 20th century was motivated by

(1) a lack of natural resources
(2) a plan to end unequal treaties
(3) the need to increase cultural diffusion
(4) the desire to spread communism 53 ____

Base your answer to question 54 on the map below and on your knowledge of social studies.

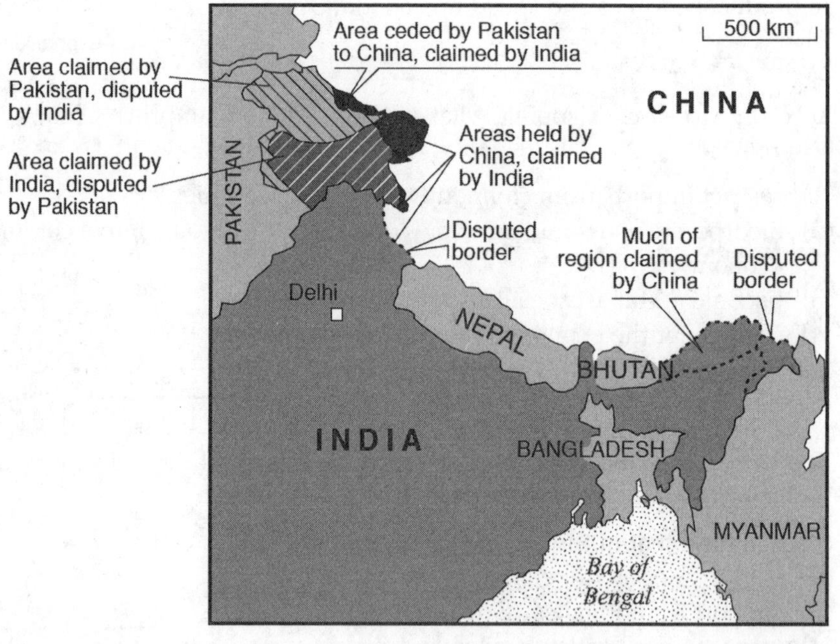

Source: *The Economist*, June 21, 2003 (adapted)

54 Which statement can best be supported by the information on this 2003 map?

(1) India and Pakistan have agreed on shared borders.
(2) Several borders are in dispute between India and China.
(3) India and Nepal are currently involved in border disputes with each other.
(4) The inhabitants of the territory claimed by both India and China have little voice in the conflict.

54 ____

---

55 Joseph Stalin, Benito Mussolini, and Saddam Hussein were similar in that

(1) all were totalitarian rulers who controlled all aspects of life within their nations
(2) all were mid-20th-century fascist dictators
(3) all were leaders who sought to "westernize" their nations
(4) all were nationalist leaders who led their countries to independence

55 ____

Base your answer to question 56 on the passage below and on your knowledge of social studies.

> ... More than 30 years after "Year Zero" and more than a decade after the "return to democracy," Cambodia remains in a league of its own—miserable, corrupt and compassionless. Only the toughest and the most unscrupulous can "make it" and get ahead. There is hardly any social net to speak of; the savage insanity of the Khmer Rouge has been replaced with savage capitalism, but often with the same people in charge....
>
> —Andre Vitchek, "A Tortured History and Unanswered Questions"

56 What does the author of this 2006 passage conclude?

(1) As democracy develops, circumstances will improve.
(2) Though governments change, circumstances often remain the same.
(3) New leadership is determined to replace the Khmer Rouge.
(4) Harsh living conditions have caused people to rely extensively on a social net.

56 ____

Base your answer to question 57 on the chart below and on your knowledge of social studies.

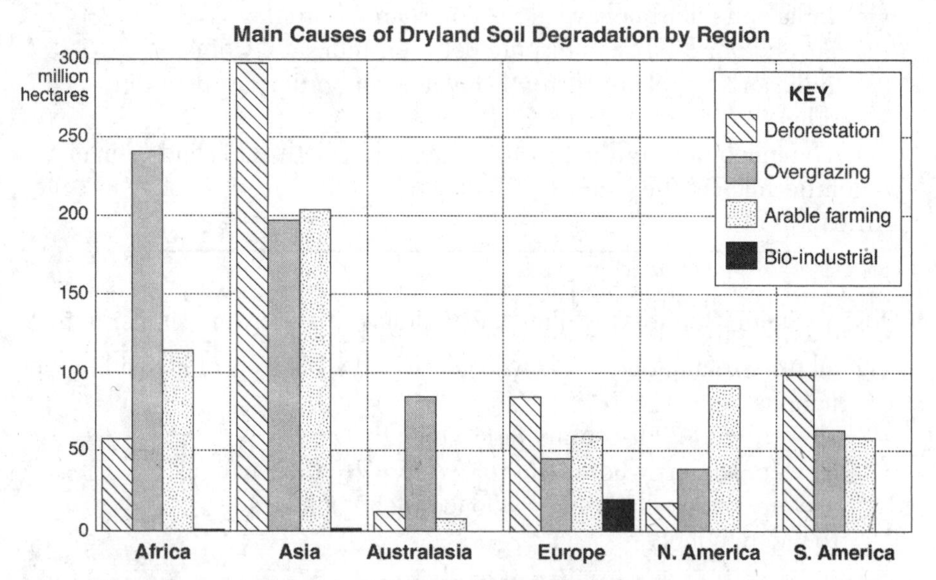

Desertification does not refer to the moving forward of existing deserts but to the formation, expansion or intensification of degraded patches of soil and vegetation cover.

Source: Food and Agricultural Organization of the United Nations (adapted)

57 What is a valid conclusion based on the information shown in this chart?

(1) The primary cause of soil degradation throughout the world is bio-industrial.
(2) Deforestation causes soil degradation to more hectares of land in South America than in Asia.
(3) The largest number of hectares affected by soil degradation due to overgrazing is located in Africa.
(4) The fewest number of hectares affected by soil degradation due to arable farming is located in North America. 57 ____

58 One way in which Miguel Hidalgo, Ho Chi Minh, and Jomo Kenyatta are similar is that they all were

(1) leaders of independence movements
(2) communist dictators
(3) enlightened despots
(4) advocates of liberation theology

58 ____

59 A goal of the Sepoy Rebellion in India and of the Zulu Resistance in South Africa was to

(1) divide their country
(2) establish theocratic governments
(3) oppose nationalist movements
(4) end foreign control

59 ____

60 Since the end of the Cold War, what has been the primary cause of conflicts in Chechnya, Azerbaijan, and Bosnia?

(1) religious and ethnic tensions
(2) adoption of capitalism
(3) poor health care and starvation
(4) efforts at Russification

60 ____

PART II: THEMATIC ESSAY QUESTIONS

Question 1

Directions: Write a well-organized essay that includes an introduction, several paragraphs addressing the task below, and a conclusion.

Theme: Change

> Nations throughout history have experienced rapid changes that upended their societies and economies.

Task:

> Choose ***two*** nations that have experienced rapid social and/or economic changes, and for ***each***
>
> - Explain the historical circumstances surrounding the social and/or economic changes
> - Evaluate whether the social/economic changes were positive or negative

You may use any example from your study of global history and geography. Some suggestions you might wish to consider include changes in France following the French Revolution, changes in Russia following the Bolshevik Revolution, or changes in China following the Communist Revolution.

You are *not* limited to these suggestions.
Do *not* use the United States as the focus of your response.

Guidelines:

In your essay, be sure to:

- Develop all aspects of the task
- Support the theme with relevant facts, examples, and details
- Use a logical and clear plan of organization, including an introduction and a conclusion that are beyond a restatement of the theme

Question 2

Directions: Write a well-organized essay that includes an introduction, several paragraphs addressing the task below, and a conclusion.

Theme: Technology

> Throughout history, existing technology has been modified or replaced by new technological innovations. These new technological innovations have had various effects on societies and the world.

Task:

> Select ***two*** technological innovations, and for ***each***
> - Describe the existing technology that was replaced by this new technological innovation ***and*** how this new innovation changed the existing technology
> - Discuss the effects this new technological innovation has had on a society or the world

You may use any technological innovation from your study of global history and geography. Some suggestions you might wish to consider include aqueducts, gunpowder, printing press, caravel, steam engine, factory system, nuclear power, and internet communications.

You are *not* limited to these suggestions.
Do *not* make the United States the focus of your response.

Guidelines:

In your essay, be sure to:
- Develop all aspects of the task
- Support the theme with relevant facts, examples, and details
- Use a logical and clear plan of organization, including an introduction and a conclusion that are beyond a restatement of the theme

PART IIIA: DOCUMENT-BASED QUESTIONS

Directions: Analyze the documents and answer the short-answer questions that follow each document in the space provided.

Set 1

Document 1

The power of the [Ottoman] Empire was waning [fading] by 1683 when the second and last attempt was made to conquer Vienna. It failed. Without the conquest of Europe and the acquisition of significant new wealth, the Empire lost momentum and went into a slow decline. Several other factors contributed to the [Ottoman] Empire's decline:

- Competition from trade from the Americas
- Competition from cheap products from India and the Far East
- Development of other trade routes
- Rising unemployment within the Empire
- Ottoman Empire became less centralised, and central control weakened
- Sultans being less severe in maintaining rigorous standards of integrity in the administration of the Empire
- Sultans becoming less sensitive to public opinion

Source: "Ottoman Empire (1301–1922)," BBC online, 2009 (adapted)

1*a* According to the BBC, what was ***one*** *economic* problem that contributed to the decline of the Ottoman Empire?

____

____

1*b* According to the BBC, what was ***one*** *political* problem that contributed to the decline of the Ottoman Empire?

____

____

Document 2

> . . . In 1875, the Slavic peoples living in the Ottoman provinces of Bosnia and Herzegovina (currently the state of Bosnia-Herzegovina), led an uprising against the Ottomans in order to gain their freedom. The general weakness of the Ottomans led two independent, neighbor Slavic states, Montenegro and Serbia, to aid the rebellion. Within a year, the rebellion spread to the Ottoman province of Bulgaria. The rebellion was part of a larger political movement called the Pan-Slavic movement, which had as its goal the unification of all Slavic peoples—most of whom were under the control of Austria, Germany, and the Ottoman Empire—into a single political unity under the protection of Russia. Anxious also to conquer the Ottomans themselves and seize Istanbul, the Russians allied with the rebels, Serbia, and Montenegro and declared war against the Ottomans. . . .

Source: Richard Hooker, "European Imperialism and the Balkan Crisis," *The Ottomans*, World Cultures

2 According to Richard Hooker, what was ***one*** role that nationalism played in the decline of the Ottoman Empire?

____

____

Document 3

> . . . Mustafa Kemal [Atatürk] was a secular nationalist who believed that all the inheritance of the Ottoman Empire should be abandoned and Turkey should be transformed into a modern European state. This involved less of a sudden break with the past than might appear. The Tanzimat reforms [between 1839 and 1876] had laid the foundations of a secular state, and the Young Turks, even while attempting to preserve the empire, had given a powerful impetus [motivation] to the cause of Turkish nationalism. During the war years [1914–1918], the secularization of education had proceeded and the universities and public positions had been opened to women. Certain of the law courts under the control of the religious authorities had been placed under the Ministry of Justice. A law in 1916 had reformed marriage and divorce. . . .

Source: Peter Mansfield, *A History of the Middle East*, Viking

3 According to Peter Mansfield, what was ***one*** change that occurred as the Ottoman Empire declined and a new state of Turkey began to take shape?

____

____

Document 4

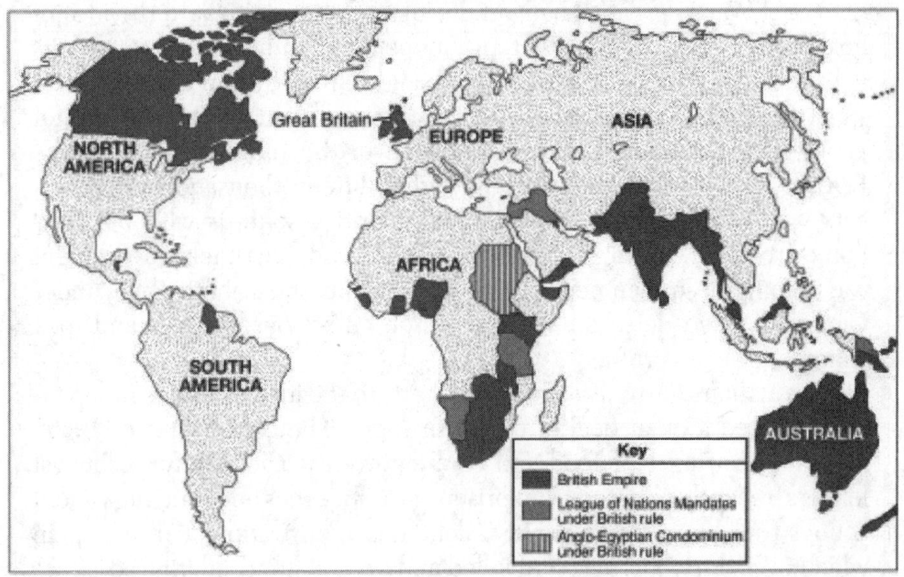

Source: Encyclopedia Britannica Kids (adapted)

4 Based on the information shown on this map, what was a problem the British faced that made it difficult to govern its empire?

____

____

Document 5

> . . . World War II greatly changed the British attitude toward the idea of India's freedom. The fear that an independent India would not pay its debt to Great Britain was no longer valid. Great Britain actually owed India over a billion pounds. Nor was the concern that there were not enough Indian military officers to take over the Indian army from the British. As a result of the war, more than fifteen thousand Indian officers were available. In addition, many British soldiers who returned home from serving in India realized how unpopular their government was among the Indian people. In Great Britain, the Labour Party under Clement Attlee defeated Winston Churchill's Conservatives and took charge of the government. . . .
>
> The Labour Party, already sympathetic to the idea of India's independence, faced a great deal of unrest in India. The cold winter of 1945–46 made shortages of food and clothing even worse. Many nationalist leaders, recently released from prison, gave speeches encouraging violent actions to achieve freedom. In Calcutta, demonstrations led to riots in which over thirty people were killed and several hundred injured. . . .

Source: *Indian Independence and the Question of Pakistan*, Choices Program, Watson Institute for International Studies, Brown University

5*a* Based on this excerpt from *Indian Independence and the Question of Pakistan*, what was ***one*** factor that made Great Britain more willing to grant India independence?

____

____

5*b* Based on this excerpt from *Indian Independence and the Question of Pakistan*, what was ***one*** feature of the independence movement in India in 1945?

____

____

Document 6

> ... During the last 60 years [since 1928], the British Empire has broken apart. Most of the nations that were in the empire demanded and got their independence. With the empire gone, Britain lost a major source of wealth. At the same time, it lost industrial advantages it had enjoyed for many years....

Source: Clare McHugh, *Scholastic World Cultures: Western Europe*, Scholastic, 1988

6 According to Clare McHugh, what was ***one*** change Great Britain faced with the breakup of its empire?

____

____

Set 2

Document 1

> ... Stalin came to power after Lenin's death in 1924, inheriting a government that was still struggling to control an unwieldy empire. The new premier [leader] soon turned his attention toward Ukraine, the largest and most troublesome of the non-Russian Soviet republics. The Ukrainians were a fiercely independent people, given to ignoring directives from Moscow and stubbornly maintaining their individualistic, agrarian way of life.
>
> That independent spirit made them a problem. At a time when Stalin wanted to build a strong industrial base, they clung to their rural peasant traditions. At a time when he wanted to abolish private ownership of land, they refused to surrender their farms. In short, the Ukrainians had become a threat to the revolution....

Source: Linda Jacobs Altman, *Genocide: The Systematic Killing of a People*, Enslow Publishers

1 What was ***one*** way in which the Ukrainian people were a threat to Stalin's power according to Linda Jacobs Altman?

____

____

Document 2

In 1929, Stalin's policy of all-out collectivization had disastrous effects on agricultural productivity. He increased the amount of grain to be exported from Ukraine. This action resulted in famine among the Ukrainian peasants and resistance among the landowners.

Addendum to the minutes of [December 6, 1932] Politburo [meeting] No. 93.

The Council of People's Commissars and the Central Committee resolve:

To place the following villages on the black list for overt disruption of the grain collection plan and for malicious sabotage, organized by kulak [wealthy Ukrainian farmers] and counterrevolutionary elements: …

The following measures should be undertaken with respect to these villages:

1. Immediate cessation [stoppage] of delivery of goods, complete suspension of cooperative and state trade in the villages, and removal of all available goods from cooperative and state stores. …

The Council of People's Commissars and the Central Committee call upon all collective and private farmers who are honest and dedicated to Soviet rule to organize all their efforts for a merciless struggle against kulaks and their accomplices in order to: defeat in their villages the kulak sabotage of grain collection; fulfill honestly and conscientiously their grain collection obligations to the Soviet authorities; and strengthen collective farms.

CHAIRMAN OF THE COUNCIL OF PEOPLE'S COMMISSARS OF THE UKRAINIAN SOVIET SOCIALIST REPUBLIC—V. CHUBAR.
SECRETARY OF THE CENTRAL COMMITTEE OF THE COMMUNIST PARTY (BOLSHEVIK) OF UKRAINE— S. KOSIOR.

6 December 1932.

Source: Soviet Archives Exhibit, Library of Congress (adapted)

2 According to this document, what was ***one*** action the Soviet government proposed to enforce its policies of collectivization and grain quotas?

____

____

Document 3

This is an excerpt from a speech given by Dr. Oleh W. Gerus in 2001 at the unveiling of a monument in Manitoba, Canada, to the victims of the famine-genocide in Ukraine.

> . . . What have been the historical consequences of the Great Famine-Genocide?
>
> By ravaging the country side, the famine not only destroyed millions of innocent human beings—estimates range from 4 to 10 million—but also retarded [slowed] by generations the natural evolution [development] of Ukrainian nationhood. The traditional Ukrainian values of hope, individualism and hard work disappeared. Fear, apathy and alcoholism became the hallmarks of the collective farm. Cities of Ukraine remained bastions [strongholds] of Russification. In general, the traumatized survivors found themselves voiceless cogs in the huge bureaucratic machine that the Soviet Union had become. . . .

Source: Dr. Oleh W. Gerus, "The Great Ukrainian Famine-Genocide," Centre for Ukrainian Canadian Studies, University of Manitoba, August 4, 2001 (adapted)

3 What were ***two*** consequences of the great famine-genocide in Ukraine according to Oleh W. Gerus?

(1) ______________________________

____

(2) ______________________________

____

Document 4

In 1970, Lon Nol overthrew Prince Norodom Sihanouk and became the leader of Cambodia. The Vietnam War had destabilized Cambodia's government and Lon Nol used this situation to gain power.

> . . . Richard Nixon's May 1970 invasion of Cambodia (undertaken without informing Lon Nol's new government) followed simultaneous invasions by Saigon and Vietnamese Communist forces. It created 130,000 new Khmer [Cambodian mountain people] refugees, according to the Pentagon. By 1971, 60 percent of refugees surveyed in Cambodia's towns gave U.S. bombing as the main cause of their displacement. The U.S. bombardment of the Cambodian countryside continued until 1973, when Congress imposed a halt. Nearly half of the 540,000 tons of bombs were dropped in the last six months.
>
> From the ashes of rural Cambodia arose Pol Pot's Communist Party of Kampuchea (CPK). It used the bombing's devastation and massacre of civilians as recruitment propaganda and as an excuse for its brutal, radical policies and its purge of moderate Communists and Sihanoukists. This is clear from contemporary U.S. government documents and from interviews in Cambodia with peasant survivors of the bombing. . . .

Source: Ben Kiernan, *The Pol Pot Regime: Race, Power, and Genocide in Cambodia under the Khmer Rouge, 1975-79,* Yale University Press (adapted)

4 According to Ben Kiernan, what were ***two*** problems Cambodia faced during Lon Nol's rule that enabled Pol Pot to rise to power?

(1) ____

____

(2) ____

____

Document 5

Pol Pot came to power in April 1975. He overthrew Lon Nol in a coup d'état and attempted to create a utopian agrarian society.

> . . . He [Pol Pot] began by declaring, "This is Year Zero," and that society was about to be "purified." Capitalism, Western culture, city life, religion, and all foreign influences were to be extinguished in favor of an extreme form of peasant Communism.
>
> All foreigners were thus expelled, embassies closed, and any foreign economic or medical assistance was refused. The use of foreign languages was banned. Newspapers and television stations were shut down, radios and bicycles confiscated, and mail and telephone usage curtailed. Money was forbidden. All businesses were shuttered, religion banned, education halted, health care eliminated, and parental authority revoked. Thus Cambodia was sealed off from the outside world.
>
> All of Cambodia's cities were then forcibly evacuated. At Phnom Penh, two million inhabitants were evacuated on foot into the countryside at gunpoint. As many as 20,000 died along the way. . . .

Source: "Genocide in the 20th Century: Pol Pot in Cambodia 1975-1979," *The History Place*

5 Based on this *History Place* article, what was ***one*** economic action taken by Pol Pot's government that contributed to human rights violations against the Cambodian people?

____

____

Document 6

In 1998, President Bill Clinton traveled to Rwanda to pay America's respects to those who suffered and died in the Rwandan genocide. During the visit, a panel discussion was held and later aired by *Frontline*. This is an excerpt from the transcript of that broadcast.

> ... **NARRATOR:** In 1993, Rwanda, one of Africa's smallest countries with just seven million citizens, was a deeply troubled country with a deeply troubled past. Decades earlier, under colonial rule, the Belgians had used the Tutsis, Rwanda's aristocracy, to enforce their rule over the Hutu majority, who were mostly poor farmers.
>
> **PHILIP GOUREVITCH, "The New Yorker":** The Belgians created an idea whereby the Tutsi were a master race, the Hutu an inferior race. And ethnic identity cards were issued. Much like in South Africa, an apartheid-like system was imposed. All privileges went to the Tutsi minority, and the Hutu majority was almost in bondage.
>
> At independence in the late '50s and early '60s, this system was reversed. The majority Hutu rebelled, seized power, in the name of majority rule imposed an apartheid-like system in reverse and oppressed the Tutsi bitterly.
>
> **NARRATOR:** Faced with discrimination and increasing Hutu violence, most Tutsis fled to neighboring countries, where they formed a guerrilla army, the Rwandan Patriotic Front.
>
> In 1990, the rebel Tutsis invaded Rwanda and forced peace talks with Juvenal Habyarimana, the Hutu president. Anxious to stay in power himself, Habyarimana signed a peace treaty agreeing to share power with the Tutsis....

Source: "The Triumph of Evil," *Frontline,* January 26, 1999

6 According to this *Frontline* transcript excerpt, what were ***two*** causes of conflict between the Hutus and the Tutsi in Rwanda?

(1) ____

____

(2) ____

____

Document 7

After the assassination of President Juvenal Habyarimana on April 6, 1994, radical Hutus attempted to exert control over Rwanda.

> ... The Hutu officials who took over the government organized the murders [of Tutsis] nationwide. They used the government-run radio and press to do this. They also used the private newspapers and a private radio station, known as Radio Television des Mille Collines (RTLM). RTLM told the population to look for the "enemies" and to kill them. Those Tutsi and Hutu [opposing the government] who could, fled to safety in neighboring countries, to Europe, or to Canada and the United States. Meanwhile, when the murders started, the RPF [Tutsi-led Rwandan Patriotic Front] in Uganda invaded Rwanda again. . . .

Source: Aimable Twagilimana, *Teenage Refugees from Rwanda Speak Out*, Globe Fearon Educational Publisher

7 According to Aimable Twagilimana, what was ***one*** method Hutu officials used to organize the murders of the Tutsis?

____

____

Document 8a

. . . Over the course of the genocide nearly one million people were killed, and more than three million fled to other countries, creating the world's worst ever refugee crisis. Only then did the West respond, launching the largest aid effort in human history, which finally concluded two years later in March of 1996. Soon after, war broke out in several neighboring countries causing almost all of the refugees to return home by 1997.

Post-genocide, a Unity government was formed [in Rwanda], and in 2000, Paul Kagame, former head of the RPF, was elected transition president. Kagame was then elected to a regular term in the country's first standard elections in 2003. The United Nations established the International Criminal Tribunal for Rwanda, which has been trying high-level Hutu officials for crimes against humanity, while local governments have resorted to tribal councils, called *gacaca*, to sanction the estimated 80,000 people involved in the genocide. . . .

Source: Terry George, ed., *Hotel Rwanda,* Newmarket Press

Document 8b

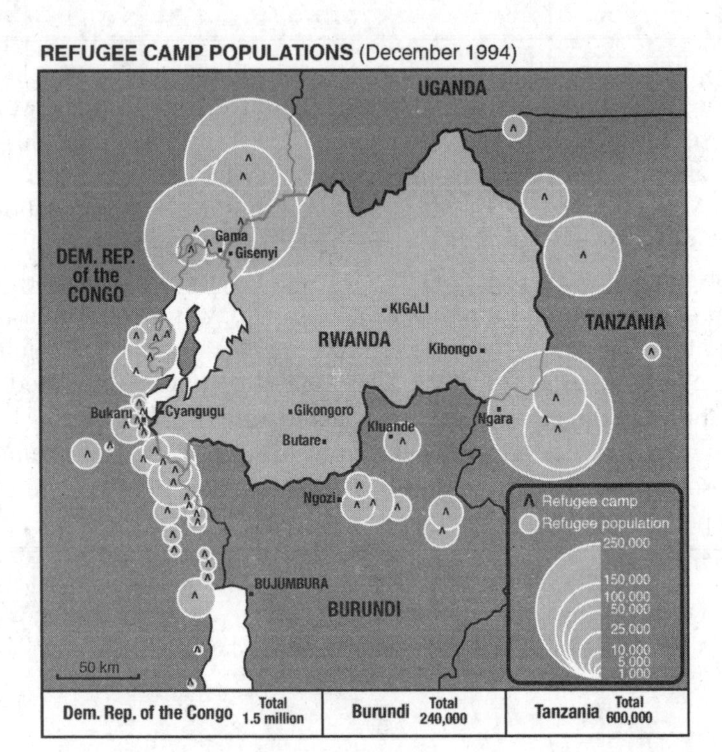

Source: UN High Commissioner for Refugees, December 1994 (adapted)

8 Based on these documents, state ***two*** effects of genocide on Rwanda.

(1) ____

____

(2) ____

____

PART IIIB: DOCUMENT-BASED ESSAY QUESTIONS

Question 1

Directions: Write a well-organized essay that includes an introduction, several paragraphs, and a conclusion. Use evidence from *at least* ***four*** documents in your essay. Support your response with relevant facts, examples, and details. Include additional outside information.

This question is based on the accompanying documents. The question is designed to test your ability to work with historical documents. Some of these documents have been edited for the purposes of this question. As you analyze the documents, take into account the source of each document and any point of view that may be presented in the document. Keep in mind that the language used in a document may reflect the historical context of the time in which it was written.

Historical Context:

Economic development in some countries has resulted in a variety of changes. These economic developments have affected the people and the country in positive and negative ways. Three countries experiencing economic development are ***China (1976–present)***, ***Mexico (1980–present)***, and ***Botswana (1966–present)***.

Task:

Using the information from the documents and your knowledge of global history and geography, write an essay in which you

Choose ***two*** of the countries mentioned in the historical context and for ***each***

- Describe a change that resulted from economic development within the country
- Discuss positive ***and/or*** negative effects this economic development has had on the people and/or the country

Guidelines:

In your essay, be sure to:

- Develop all aspects of the task
- Incorporate information from *at least* ***four*** documents
- Incorporate relevant outside information
- Support the theme with relevant facts, examples, and details
- Use a logical and clear plan of organization, including an introduction and a conclusion that are beyond a restatement of the theme

Document 1

China Rejoins the World Economy

. . . In China after Mao Zedong's death in 1976 the communist leadership introduced comprehensive economic reforms that relaxed state control of the economy, allowing more initiative and permitting individuals to accumulate wealth. Beginning in 1978 the Communist Party in Sichuan province freed more than six thousand firms to compete for business outside the state planning process. The results were remarkable. Under China's leader Deng Xiaoping these reforms were expanded across the nation. China also began to permit foreign investment for the first time since the communists came to power in 1949. Between 1978 and the end of the 1990s foreign investors committed more than $180 billion to the Chinese economy, and McDonald's, Coca-Cola, Airbus, and other foreign companies began doing business there. But more than 100 million workers were still employed in state-owned enterprises, and most foreign-owned companies were segregated in special economic zones. The result was a dual industrial sector—one modern, efficient, and connected to international markets, the other dominated by government and directed by political decisions. . . .

Source: Richard W. Bulliet, et al., *The Earth and Its People*, 3rd Edition, Houghton Mifflin, 2005 (adapted)

Document 2

. . . In China, where almost a quarter of the human race still lived under a communist regime, the economy was also changing with the times. China's leaders embraced the market, and instead of insisting on equality said that the Chinese should try to make themselves rich; individual enterprise and increased spending on consumer products was the only way China would be able to fulfill its 'Four Modernizations' policy and become a major economic power by the end of the [20th] century. While the Chinese came to resemble Western capitalists in the ways they acquired and spent money, with production soaring by some 10 per cent a year, their elderly leaders remained in unchanged political control, determined to stamp out any sign of dissent or desire for democracy.

China's economic growth depended on the manufacture of consumer goods for export to the rest of the world. By 1995 some 60 per cent of toys for the international market were made in southern China, where 3000 factories were staffed by more than a million workers, most of them young women. Their wages were lower than those that would have been paid to workers in most other countries, but they were for the first time earning money that enabled them to make consumer choices of their own. . . .

Source: Godfrey Hodgson, *People's Century*, Times Books, 1998 (adapted)

Document 3a

> Since China's reform and opening up started more than two decades ago, a special social group has come into being. Mostly coming from the countryside, they are mainly doing low-paying manual work in the fields of construction, commerce, service and so on. They become the floating population in big cities, called as migrant workers or peasant workers.
>
> China's floating population has increased from 70 million of 1993 to 140 million of 2003, exceeding 10 percent of the total population and accounting for about 30 percent of rural labor force.
>
> At present [2005], the general floating direction is from the countryside to cities, from underdeveloped regions to developed regions, and from central and western areas to eastern coastal areas. . . .

Source: *People's Daily Online*, July 27, 2005

Document 3b

> ...China's roaring industrial economy has been abruptly quieted by the effects of the global financial crisis [in 2008]. Rural provinces that supplied much of China's factory manpower [floating population] are watching the beginnings of a wave of reverse migration that has the potential to shake the stability of the world's most populous nation.
>
> Fast-rising unemployment has led to an unusual series of strikes and protests. Normally cautious government officials have offered quick concessions and talk openly of their worries about social unrest. Laid-off factory workers in Dongguan overturned patrol cars and clashed with police last Tuesday, and hundreds of taxis parked in front of a government office in nearby Chaozhou over the weekend, one of a series of driver protests....

Source: Shai Oster, *Wall Street Journal*, December 2, 2008

Document 4

...Mexico's trade policy following World War II through 1986, was essentially one of import substitution and closely regulated commercial ties with other countries, including the U.S. Behind a protective wall of tariffs, import licensing requirements, domestic-content provisions, and restrictive foreign investment policies, Mexico was one of the world's most closed economies.

Since joining the General Agreement on Tariffs and Trade (GATT) in 1986, Mexico has pursued a policy of economic liberalization, sharply reducing trade restrictions, promoting foreign investment, cutting domestic subsidies, and expanding the role of the private sector. NAFTA [North American Free Trade Agreement] gives formal recognition and permanence to the policy changes that are already taking place and which are critical to Mexico attracting the foreign investment and technology needed for its future economic growth....

Source: J. Michael Patrick, "U.S.–Mexico Trade Patterns Under NAFTA," Texas Center for Border Economic and Enterprise Development, March 1994

Document 5

Mexican governments had mixed results reforming the economy and reducing extreme poverty between 1980 and 2008.

Accomplishments	Ongoing Challenges Faced
• Expansion of competition through the implementation of privatization in the areas of: seaports, railroads, telecommunications, electricity generation, natural gas distribution, airports • Tripling of trade with the United States and Canada since the implementation of NAFTA (1994) • Establishment of 12 free trade agreements with over 40 countries	• Continuation of corruption • Uneven development in Mexican states; prosperity in north and center, economic lag in south • Mixture of modern and outmoded industry and agriculture

Document 6

> … NAFTA was supposed to bring economic prosperity to Mexico, but the poverty and human suffering along the border tell a different story. Mexico's more than 3,000 border *maquiladoras*—the mostly foreign-owned manufacturing and assembly plants—send about 90 percent of their products to the United States. The Spanish word "maquilar" means "to assemble," but it is also slang for "to do someone else's work for them." This is what's really going on; the maquiladora sector produced more than $100 billion in goods last year [2005], but the typical maquiladora worker earns between $1 and $3 per hour, including benefits and bonuses. Special tariff-free zones along the border mean that many maquiladoras pay low taxes, limiting the funds that could improve quality of life. . . .

Source: Oliver Bernstein, "Walking the Line," *Grist Magazine: Environmental News & Commentary,* March 7, 2006

Document 7

... In 1966 when Botswana became independent, it had one of the least promising economic outlooks of any emerging African country. That changed dramatically with the discovery of diamonds in 1967. Although it took four years before mining could start, the promise of considerable wealth gave the fledgling government a remarkable advantage in planning for the future. The intelligent use of resources to create the badly needed schools, roads, water systems, and electric power stands out as a testament to Botswana's leaders. Seretse Khama and his successor, Quett Masire, put Botswana's newfound wealth to work for all the people....

Source: Jason Lauré, *Botswana,* Childrens Press, 1994

Document 8a

Botswana—Diamond Facts from De Beers Diamond Company

- In Botswana, diamonds account for 76% of Botswana's export revenue, 45% of the government revenue, and 33% (approximately US $3 billion) of the gross domestic product
- Over the past 25 years, Botswana has had one of the fastest growing economies in the world
- Due to the revenues generated by diamonds, every child in Botswana receives free schooling to the age of 13
- In 1966 there were only three secondary schools in Botswana, now [2006] there are more than 300
- The diamond mining industry is the largest single employer in Botswana after the government

Source: De Beers Family of Companies (www.debeersgroup.com), January 11, 2006 (adapted)

Document 8b

. . . However, Jay Salkin, an economist at the Botswana Institute for Development Policy Analysis, warns that the country is still facing big challenges.

"The economy is diversifying but not rapidly enough," he says.

"The non-mining sectors are growing at 5% per annum at present, and while that's quite good by international standards, it's not good enough to absorb the growing labour force, and to move as many people out of poverty as the government is committed to doing." . . .

Source: Peter Biles, "Botswana: Africa's Success Story?," *BBC News*, March 7, 2005

Document 9

Botswana, the world's largest diamond producer by value, saw its diamond production fall by 3.6 percent in 2008 and is preparing for far steeper declines this year [2009]. Baledzi Gaolathe, the finance minister, said in his 2009 budget speech to the National Assembly on Monday that diamond production in 2008 was 32.6 million carats, compared with 33.8 million carats the previous year....

Gaolathe noted that the diamond market performed "exceptionally well" during the first three quarters of 2008—when prices rose by about 20 percent—but the global financial crisis caused a sharp decline in commodity prices during the final quarter. As the negative global trends continue, the minister said, he expects 2009 diamond sales revenue to decline by about 50 percent, as prices are projected to decrease by 15 percent from 2008 levels. Production is expected to fall by 35 percent this year, he added. Diamond mining company Debswana, in which the government and De Beers each own a 50 percent stake, has already said it would curb production in reaction to the slump in global demand for rough diamonds....

Earlier, Minister of Minerals, Energy and Water Resources, Ponatshego Kedikilwe, warned that Botswana's vast mineral resources may undo the country's strong economic growth of recent years if the proper survival measures are not put in place....

Source: Avi Krawitz, "Botswana 2008 Diamond Production –4%," *Rapaport*, February 3, 2009

Question 2

Directions: Write a well-organized essay that includes an introduction, several paragraphs, and a conclusion. Use evidence from *at least **four*** documents in your essay. Support your response with relevant facts, examples, and details. Include additional outside information.

This question is based on the accompanying documents. The question is designed to test your ability to work with historical documents. Some of these documents have been edited for the purposes of this question. As you analyze the documents, take into account the source of each document and any point of view that may be presented in the document. Keep in mind that the language used in a document may reflect the historical context of the time in which it was written.

Historical Context:

Armed conflict, ***disease***, and ***child labor*** have affected children throughout the world. Governments, groups, and individuals have attempted to reduce the effects of these global issues on children.

Task:

Using the information from the documents and your knowledge of global history and geography, write an essay in which you

Select ***two*** global issues mentioned in the historical context and for ***each***

- Describe the effects of the global issue on children
- Discuss how governments, groups, and/or individuals have attempted to reduce the effects of this global issue on children

Do *not* make the United States the focus of your essay.

Guidelines:

In your essay, be sure to:

- Develop all aspects of the task
- Incorporate information from *at least **four*** documents
- Incorporate relevant outside information
- Support the theme with relevant facts, examples, and details
- Use a logical and clear plan of organization, including an introduction and a conclusion that are beyond a restatement of the theme

Document 1

The Toll of War
(Child victims of armed conflicts, 1990s)

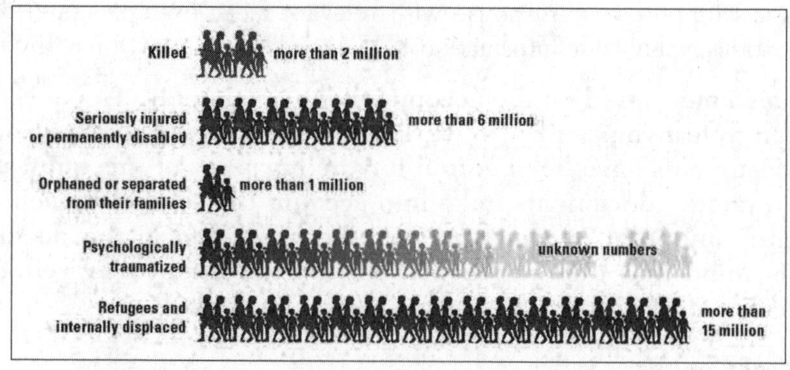

Source: *The State of the World's Children, 2000*, UNICEF (adapted)

Document 2

Child Soldiers

To commemorate our 25th anniversary, The Advocates for Human Rights would like to dedicate this issue of Rights Sites News to the abolition of one of the worst forms of child labor, child soldiers. When armed conflict exists, children will almost inevitably become involved as soldiers. In over twenty countries around the world, children are direct participants in war. Denied a childhood and often subjected to horrific violence, an estimated 200,000 to 300,000 children are serving as soldiers for both rebel groups and government forces in current armed conflicts. These young combatants participate in all aspects of contemporary warfare. They wield AK-47s and M-16s on the front lines of combat, serve as human mine detectors, participate in suicide missions, carry supplies, and act as spies, messengers or lookouts.

Physically vulnerable and easily intimidated, children typically make obedient soldiers. Many are abducted or recruited by force, and often compelled to follow orders under threat of death. Others join armed groups out of desperation. As society breaks down during conflict, leaving children no access to school, driving them from their homes, or separating them from family members, many children perceive armed groups as their best chance for survival. Others seek escape from poverty or join military forces to avenge family members who have been killed....

Despite progress achieved over the last decade in the global campaign to end the recruitment and use of child soldiers, large numbers of children continue to be exploited in war and placed in the line of fire. The international treaty on child soldiers, the *Optional Protocol to the Convention on the Rights of the Child on the involvement of children in armed conflict,* entered into force on February 12, 2002. With over 100 countries signed on, this treaty is a milestone in the campaign, strengthening the legal protection of children and helping to prevent their use in armed conflict....

Source: "Child Soldiers Edition," *Rights Sites News,*
The Advocates for Human Rights, Spring 2008

Document 3

NEW YORK, 4 April 2006—Ridding the world of landmines and other explosive remnants of war could be accomplished in years instead of decades, saving thousands of children from devastating injuries and death, UNICEF said today on the first International Day for Mine Awareness and Assistance in Mine Action....

Landmines are designed to disable, immobilize or kill people travelling by foot or in motor vehicles. Other explosive remnants of war include unexploded ordnance—weapons such as grenades and cluster bombs that did not explode on impact but can still detonate—and weapons that are discarded in civilian areas by combatants, known as abandoned ordnance. These munitions outlast the conflicts during which they were planted and become hazards for innocent civilians, particularly for unsuspecting children who often make the fatal mistake of playing with the unfamiliar objects....

Children suffer debilitating physical injuries from mine explosions, often losing fingers, toes and limbs. Some are left blind or deaf. An estimated 85 per cent of child victims die before they can get medical attention. Many disabled victims lose opportunities to go to school, and often cannot afford rehabilitative care. The persisting threat of mines takes its toll on entire societies, perpetuating poverty and underdevelopment....

More than three-quarters of the world's nations have ratified the Mine Ban Treaty since it came into force in 1999, outlawing the production, stockpiling and use of antipersonnel landmines. According to the International Campaign to Ban Landmines, the number of countries thought to be producing, stockpiling and using landmines has dropped significantly over the last decade....

UNICEF supports and implements mine action activities in over 30 countries, and believes that mine-risk education is key to preventing the death and disabling of children. Through programmes brought to their schools and communities, children are taught how to live safely in areas contaminated with landmines and other explosive remnants of war....

Source: "Saving Children from the Tragedy of Landmines,"
UNICEF Press Release, April 4, 2006

Document 4

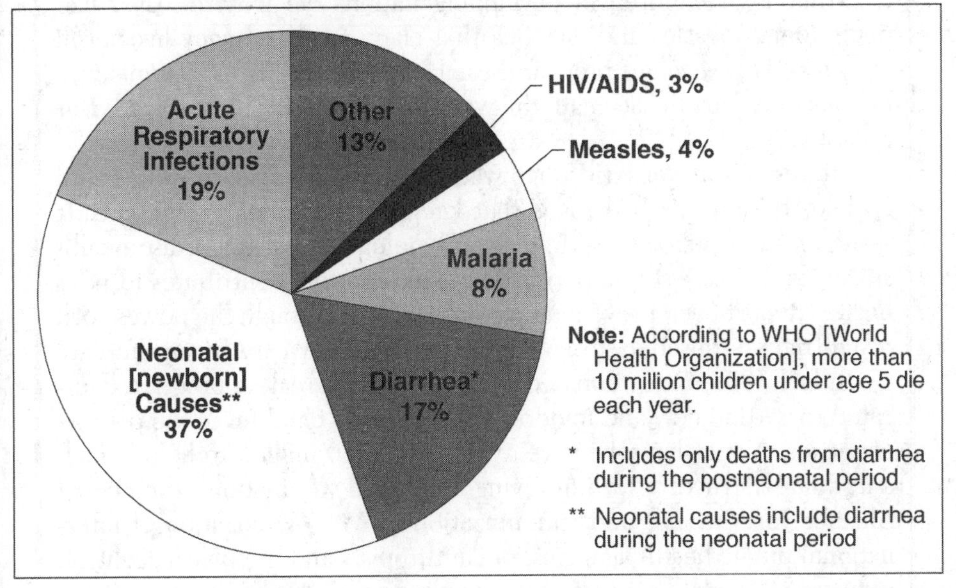

Source: *World Health Report*, World Health Organization, 2005 (adapted)

Document 5

... Millions of children in developing nations die from diseases like pneumonia, measles and diarrhea that claim twice as many lives each year as AIDS. Vaccines prevent these basic illnesses. Bill Gates pledges billions of dollars to vaccinate the world's children. Problem solved. But it's not that easy.

Money alone won't rid dirty water of parasites that can blind and cripple. It won't fix bad roads that keep people from getting care. It won't end the political corruption and violent unrest that erase health advances. It won't stop a population explosion that contributes to poor health. It can't even prevent a rat from gnawing through the power cord of a refrigerator used to store vaccines in a remote West African clinic....

In late 1998, Gates donated $100 million to create a program dedicated to getting new and underused vaccines to children in the poorest countries. A year later, he gave a stunning $750 million to help launch a new superstructure for improving childhood vaccinations, the Global Alliance for Vaccines and Immunization (GAVI)—a coalition of international public health agencies, philanthropists and the pharmaceutical industry....

Gates knows that vaccines can't do it all, not when a regional hospital in Nigeria draws its water from an open pit in the ground. Or where a 6-year-old Ivory Coast boy with a leg twisted by polio faces a life of begging because his mother couldn't afford a trip to a clinic for vaccines. Or where a broken board on a bridge can halt the shipment of medicine for days....

Source: Tom Paulson, "Bill Gates' war on disease, poverty is an uphill battle," *Seattle Post-Intelligencer,* March 21, 2001

Document 6

... Doctors Without Borders/Medecins Sans Frontieres (MSF) [a non-profit medical organization] has witnessed firsthand how a lack of medicine for treatable infectious disease destroys many lives in the developing world. In response, MSF has launched the Access to Essential Medicines Campaign. Introduced in November 1999, the MSF campaign has been working worldwide to find long-lasting solutions to this crisis. The campaign has four main goals: to increase access to certain medicines; to support high quality local manufacture and import of less expensive medicines; to implement and apply international trade rules regarding medicines; and to bring together governments, the pharmaceutical industry, and organizations to focus on investment in, research on, and development of essential medicines for neglected disease....

Source: Catherine Gevert, "A Lack of Medicine," *Faces,* March, 2005

Document 7

. . . "Tens of thousands of refugees have fled to urban areas in Pakistan since September 11, [2001], but almost all international assistance and protection efforts are focused on refugees in camps, and the situation for young Afghans in the cities is deteriorating seriously," said Jane Lowicki, Senior Coordinator, Children and Adolescents Project, who visited Pakistan in January. "Many of these refugees and the communities that are struggling to support them are wondering why help promised by the U.S. and other countries has not reached them."

With few alternatives for earning a livelihood, many Afghan refugee parents in urban areas are forcing their children to work in high-risk industries to support the household. "Thousands are carpet weavers, others are street children working as garbage pickers, beggars, brick makers, house servants and, in some cases, drug sellers," Lowicki said. "These young workers are the poorest and most desperate among the Afghan community. Their work exposes them to disease, physical and sexual abuse, and few have access to health services, education or recreation. Their situation has become even more difficult since Sept. 11 because many new young refugees have entered the competition for work, and resources are scarce."

Afghan refugee adolescents and children, some as young as five years old, are working harder than ever for less money. The formerly lucrative carpet weaving industry, for example, which relies heavily on cheap Afghan child labor, bottomed out after Sept. 11; young refugees are now being paid less than half of what they were making to weave carpets for markets around the world.

In many cases, children and adolescents are the primary wage earners for their families, and all of the young Afghan refugees interviewed for the report said they urgently need food, shelter and medical care. They are also eager for a chance to go to school and to learn skills and trades to support themselves through less hazardous work. . . .

Source: "Afghan Refugee Children and Adolescents in Pakistan's Cities Receive Minimal International Assistance," Women's Commission for Refugee Women and Children Press Release, May 30, 2002

Document 8a

This is an excerpt from a Web-only interview conducted as part of *Enterprising Ideas*, a project of *NOW on PBS*.

RugMark USA

Ten years ago [in 1994], RugMark USA was established to eradicate child labor in the handwoven rug industry. Using a unique "certification" method, RugMark USA has created a model that generates income to finance its programs for children and raises awareness among consumers about the prevalence of child labor. Nina Smith, RugMark USA's executive director, believes the RugMark model could be applied to other industries, including Brazil's shoe industry, India's silk weaving and embroidery sectors and the cocoa industry in West Africa. We talked with Smith about why the RugMark model works and what big challenges the organization is facing. . . .

NOW [host]: Describe RugMark's strategy to change the use of child labor in the industry.

Smith: Our goal is to change the market dynamics so that there is no longer a demand for child labor. If we can educate the marketplace—consumers, interior designers, architects, importers, retailers—about what they can do then ultimately the message is sent to the manufacturers that child labor won't be tolerated—in essence eliminating the demand.

The idea has three components: First, you have to raise awareness and educate people about the problem of child labor and to look for our independently certified child-labor-free rugs. On the ground in South Asia we have an inspection and monitoring system. Companies whose rugs receive the RugMark label agree to random, surprise inspections at their factories or village-based looms. . . .

Source: "RugMark USA," *NOW on PBS: Enterprising Ideas,* July 26, 2007

Document 8b

This is an advertisement RugMark used in its campaign to raise awareness about carpets and rugs made with child labor.

THE SINGLE MOST BEAUTIFUL THING ABOUT AN IMPORTED RUG.

Nearly 300,000 children are exploited as child labor in the carpet industry. This has to end, and it will. RugMark is the international organization devoted to building the schools, programs and opportunities that give children back their childhood. It's working, from Pakistan to India to Nepal, and you can help. Look for the certified and numbered RugMark label on the back of an imported rug. It's your best assurance that no children were exploited in the manufacture of the carpet you're buying. Because an imported rug that was made using child labor is ugly no matter what it looks like.

Source: www.rugmark.org (adapted)

Document 9

Give a "Red Card* to Child Labour"
in celebration of the World Day Against Child Labour 2006!

... The day, which is observed worldwide on the 12th of June, is intended to serve as a catalyst for the growing worldwide movement against child labour, as reflected in the 160 ratifications of Convention No. 182 on the worst forms of child labour and the 144 ratifications of Convention No. 138 on the minimum age for employment. The event on 12 June will be celebrated with the presence of football [soccer] stars that will "kick the ball" against child labour, in a match with girls from the Geneva International School and the Signal de Bernex Football Club. The idea behind the game is that girls and boys should be given the time to study and play, and that child labour and its worst forms symbolically get a "red card". This action is linked to the "Red card to child labour" campaign which since its inception in 2002 has reached thousands of people in all continents. The idea is that the values in football, such as, team spirit, youth empowerment, solidarity among countries, non-discrimination regarding religion, gender and race, are also shared by the ILO [International Labour Organization]. Using the symbol of the Red Card at International football competitions offers the opportunity to spread one simple, universal message over time and benefits from media coverage. Building this kind of strategic alliance is a very good way to reinforce the global movement against child labour.

Source: "Celebration of the World Day Against Child Labour," The International Programme on the Elimination of Child Labour of the International Labour Organization, June 2006

*A red card is issued to remove a player from a game for committing a serious violation.

Answers Practice Section

Global History and Geography

Answer Key

PART I: Multiple Choice

1. 3	**13.** 1	**25.** 1	**37.** 1	**49.** 2
2. 2	**14.** 3	**26.** 1	**38.** 3	**50.** 4
3. 2	**15.** 3	**27.** 1	**39.** 4	**51.** 1
4. 4	**16.** 4	**28.** 1	**40.** 3	**52.** 1
5. 3	**17.** 3	**29.** 4	**41.** 2	**53.** 1
6. 4	**18.** 1	**30.** 2	**42.** 2	**54.** 2
7. 2	**19.** 4	**31.** 4	**43.** 2	**55.** 1
8. 2	**20.** 4	**32.** 4	**44.** 2	**56.** 2
9. 1	**21.** 4	**33.** 2	**45.** 4	**57.** 3
10. 4	**22.** 3	**34.** 1	**46.** 2	**58.** 1
11. 3	**23.** 1	**35.** 3	**47.** 4	**59.** 4
12. 3	**24.** 3	**36.** 4	**48.** 4	**60.** 1

PART II: Thematic Essay Questions See Answers Explained section.

PART IIIA: Document-Based Questions See Answers Explained section.

PART IIIB: Document-Based Essay Questions See Answers Explained section.

Answers Explained

PART I: MULTIPLE CHOICE

1. **3** The pair that correctly links the region where Enlightenment ideas first developed to a region to which those ideas spread is western Europe and the Americas. In the 1700s, educated Creoles (natives of Spanish America of European descent) read the works of Voltaire, Rousseau, and Montesquieu. These Enlightenment writers supported the idea that people had the right to rebel against unjust rulers. Many of the Enlightenment ideas influenced the French Revolution. Some Creoles also traveled throughout Europe and were inspired by the ideas of the French Revolution. Simón Bolívar, who studied in Europe and witnessed the reforms of the French Revolution, was an important leader in the Latin-American independence movement in the 1800s. In North America, the ideas of John Locke and Baron de Montesquieu influenced the American Revolution and the writing of the Constitution. Many Creoles read the translation of the American Declaration of Independence, thus influencing their ideas of government. The Enlightenment ideas that arose in the western European countries of France and England directly impacted the Americas.

WRONG CHOICES EXPLAINED:

(1), (2), and (4) These areas were not affected by the spread of Enlightenment ideas. The Enlightenment did not develop in Asia, Africa, or eastern Africa.

2. **2** The outbreak of revolution in France is the correct answer because many of the revolutionary leaders, such as Maximilien Robespierre, were versed in the Enlightenment ideals of natural rights, shared power, freedom, and equality. These Enlightenment ideals influenced the revolutionary spirit in France by 1789. They also led to the creation of the *Declaration of the Rights of Man and of the Citizen*, which was passed by the National Assembly in 1789 at the start of the French Revolution.

WRONG CHOICES EXPLAINED:

(1) Fascist dictatorships arose in the 20th century in Germany and Italy. They were in direct contrast to the ideals of freedom and shared power that were emphasized during the Enlightenment.

(3) The Eastern European satellite states of the Soviet Union, such as East Germany, Hungary, and Romania, were created in the 20th century.

(4) The Enlightenment reduced the size of the British Empire as the American colonies led a revolution for independence from British rule, with these Enlightenment ideals in mind.

3. **2** Based on this passage, the Third Estate wanted more influence in the political system. In January 1789, Abbé Sieyès wrote a pamphlet entitled "What Is the Third Estate?" He argued that the Third Estate is everything in France but has no political power. France was divided into three social classes in 1789. The First Estate (Bishops of the Church) represented 1 percent of the population. They paid no taxes. The Second Estate was the nobles and landowners. They consisted of less than 2 percent of the population and owned about 20 percent of the land. Like the First Estate, they were exempt from paying taxes. The Third Estate consisted of the middle class, urban lower classes, and peasant farmers. They represented

97 percent of the population and owned about 40 percent of the land. Although the middle class had grown in France, the majority of the Third Estate consisted of the peasants who lived on the land.

The bulk of the taxes fell on the Third Estate. The bourgeoisie, the rising commercial and professional classes, paid fewer taxes than the peasants but felt unjustly treated. They were denied good jobs, wanted to reform a system that was outdated, and wanted political and social rights that were on par with their economic conditions. In May 1789, Louis XVI convened the Estates General to deal with the country's financial problems. Abbé Sieyès, who was chosen as a delegate, wanted to change the traditional way of voting in the Estates General. The Estates General voted as a unit and not by individual members. Each Estate had one vote. Therefore, the First and Second Estates combined could outvote the Third Estate that comprised a majority of the people. Sieyès wanted to abandon this system of voting. He was successful in getting the Third Estate to create a National Assembly that eventually adopted a constitution that created a limited monarchy and wrote the *Declaration of the Rights of Man and of the Citizen*. Sieyès's pamphlet was instrumental in dramatizing the importance of the Third Estate, which contributed to the French Revolution in 1789 that eventually led to the end of the absolute monarchy in 1793. These changes gave the Third Estate more power.

WRONG CHOICES EXPLAINED:

(1), (3), and (4) None of these ideas is contained in this passage. Sieyès did not write about independence, removal of the monarchy, or freedom of religion.

4. **4** Based on these excerpts, expanding the definition of equality is an action that would most likely be supported by Olympe de Gouges. Olympe de Gouges was a butcher's daughter who became a major radical during the French Revolution. She was disappointed with the *Declaration of the Rights of Man and of the Citizen* for its failure to grant equal rights for women. In her *Declaration of the Rights of Woman and Female Citizen*, which she addressed to Queen Marie Antoinette, she argued that women should be regarded as citizens, have the right to own property, and have equality of sexes in marriage. She also wanted improved education and the right to initiate divorce for women who are born free and have the same rights as men. De Gouges was guillotined in 1793 in part due to her criticism of Maximilien Robespierre, the leader of the Reign of Terror. The work of de Gouges marks the birth of the modern women's movement for equal rights.

WRONG CHOICES EXPLAINED:

(1), (2), and (3) None of these choices is supported by these excerpts. There is no reference to executing the king, restricting access to education, or creating more radical military strategies.

5. **3** Napoleon Bonaparte seized political power in France in 1799 and crowned himself emperor in 1804. Following his coup d'état of the sitting government in 1799, he created the legal system called the Napoleonic Code, which emphasized Enlightenment ideas and governed France throughout his reign. Napoleon also sought to expand France; this goal began the Napoleonic Wars. Two important battles during the Napoleonic Wars were the Battle of Trafalgar in Great Britain and the Battle of Waterloo in present-day Belgium. The Congress of Vienna met at the end of the Napoleonic Wars with the ultimate goal of limiting future French aggression.

WRONG CHOICES EXPLAINED:

(1), (2), and (4) These choices are all considered effects of the reign of Napoleon as opposed to causes of the other events listed.

6. **4** Simón Bolívar, Toussaint L'Ouverture, and José de San Martín are all associated with revolutions in Latin America. Simón Bolívar, who was born to a wealthy Venezuelan Creole family in 1783, always envisioned an independent and united Latin America, free from Spanish domination. As a young man, he studied in Europe. His love of freedom was strengthened by the ideas of the French Revolution. Before returning from Europe, Bolívar promised that he would not rest until he broke the chain put upon the people of Latin America by the Spanish. He became known as the "Liberator" for his role in the wars for independence against Spain. In 1819, he helped free Venezuela. By 1834, he had secured the freedom of Colombia, Ecuador, Peru, and Bolivia.

In 1791, Haitian slaves exploded in a revolt against French rule. Toussaint L'Ouverture, an ex-slave, emerged as the leader. It is said that he got the name L'Ouverture (which means "opening" in French) because he was so skilled at finding openings in the enemy's lines. Although untrained, Toussaint was a brilliant and inspiring commander. The struggle was long. By 1798, however, Toussaint and the rebels had achieved their goal. Enslaved Haitians had been freed. Although Haiti was still a French colony, Toussaint's forces controlled most of the island. In January 1802, Napoleon sent 16,000 men to reconquer Haiti. In May, Toussaint agreed to halt the revolution if the French would end slavery. Despite the agreement, the French soon accused him of planning another uprising. They seized him and sent him to prison in the French Alps. In 1803, he died in a cold mountain prison; however, Haiti's struggle for independence continued. In 1804, Haitian leaders declared independence. Haiti was the first black colony to free itself from European control.

José de San Martín was a Creole. He was born in Argentina, but he went to Europe for military training. In 1816, San Martín helped Argentina win freedom from Spain. He then joined the independence struggle in other areas. San Martín led an army across the Andes from Argentina to Chile. He defeated the Spanish in Chile before moving into Peru to strike further blows against colonial rule. Bolívar and San Martín tried to work together, but their views were too different. In 1822, San Martín stepped aside, letting Bolívar's forces win the final victories against Spain.

WRONG CHOICES EXPLAINED:

(1), (2), and (3) None of these men is associated with revolutions in Africa, Europe, or South Asia.

7. **2** Adam Smith's *Wealth of Nations* stressed the importance of supply and demand. In 1776, Adam Smith wrote the *Wealth of Nations*. Smith argued that the free market—the natural forces of supply and demand—should be allowed to operate and regulate business. The free market would produce more goods at lower prices and make them affordable to everyone. A growing economy would also encourage capitalists to reinvest new profits in new ventures. Smith and other capitalists argued that the marketplace was better off without any government regulation. Adam Smith's ideas illustrated the theory of laissez-faire capitalism. He argued that individuals should be allowed to pursue their self-interests in a free market. However, Smith did believe that the government had a duty to protect society and administer justice.

WRONG CHOICES EXPLAINED:

(1), (3), and (4) None of these choices is stressed in the *Wealth of Nations*. Smith rejected the traditional principle of regulation as outlined in the economic theory of mercantilism. Corporations did not become a major facet of capitalism until the 19th century. Smith rejected government ownership or regulation that would interfere with the production of wealth.

8. **2** Laissez-faire practices are most closely associated with a market economy. Price based on supply and demand is a characteristic associated with an economy based on the principles of laissez-faire. The economic ideas of laissez-faire were presented by Adam Smith in his book *Wealth of Nations*. Smith argued that the free market—the natural forces of supply and demand—should be allowed to operate and regulate business. The free market would produce more goods at lower prices and make them affordable to everyone. A growing economy would also encourage capitalists to reinvest new profits in new ventures. Smith and other capitalists argued that the marketplace was better off without any government regulation. However, Smith believed that the government had a duty to protect society and administer justice.

WRONG CHOICES EXPLAINED:

(1) A traditional economy is one in which the distribution of goods is determined by customs or traditions. In a traditional economy, the basic needs of the people are met through fishing, hunting, and gathering.

(3) A command economy is one in which production quotas are established by the central government. The Soviet Union followed a command economy.

(4) A mixed economy is an economic system that combines government regulation of industries with private enterprise or capitalist characteristics.

9. **1** In the late 1700s, the Industrial Revolution developed in Britain because Britain possessed key factors of production. A major reason why the Industrial Revolution began in England was because England possessed abundant coal and natural resources. Great Britain was rich in natural resources, including water power and coal to fuel steam power and iron ore to make machines, tools, and buildings. Great Britain was also blessed with an abundance of rivers for inland transportation and trading and good harbors for trade with the rest of the continent and the world. Its fleet of more than 6,000 merchant ships sailed to almost every part of the globe. This overseas trade gave Britain access to raw materials and markets.

Great Britain's greatest natural resource was its growing population of workers. Improvements in farming led to an increased availability of food. More nutritious foods allowed people to enjoy longer, healthier lives. In just one century, England's population nearly doubled from about 5 million in 1700 to about 9 million in 1800. The population boom swelled the available work force. Thus, by the middle of the 18th century, Great Britain was ripe for industrial development.

WRONG CHOICES EXPLAINED:

(2) and (4) Neither excluding foreign investors nor requiring minimum wages be paid to workers helped to promote the Industrial Revolution. The wealthy class in England had sufficient capital to invest in the economy. Workers in England were poorly paid, and the government did not support a minimum wage law.

(3) The British government did not suppress the enclosure movement. The government promoted these laws of private ownership of land to improve the agricultural production of food.

10. **4** A working class emerged in the late 18th and early 19th centuries as rural workers flocked to cities looking for new factory jobs that resulted from industrialization. Workers were in search of greater economic opportunities. However, many in the working class were exploited by factory owners and were forced to work in harsh and often dangerous conditions.

WRONG CHOICES EXPLAINED:

(1) Although the exploitation of workers during the Industrial Revolution led to the rise of Communist ideology, the establishment of Communist governments throughout Europe did not occur until the 20th century. Additionally, this was a political change, not a social change.

(2) Mercantilism resulted from the establishment of colonies following the discovery of the Americas in the 15th and 16th centuries.

(3) The Industrial Revolution did not directly lead to the establishment of colonies. The establishment of colonies and the raw materials extracted from those colonies helped spur the Industrial Revolution in Europe.

11. **3** According to this passage, this country was trying to become an industrialized nation-state. This passage describes periods in Japanese history, known as the Meiji Restoration, during which Japan focused on modernizing Japan's economy to compete with westernization. The Meiji Restoration, which began in 1862 and lasted until 1912, reversed the Japanese policy of isolation, ended feudalism, and began to modernize by borrowing from the Western powers. Although the Japanese had accomplished their goal by the 1890s, as stated in this passage, the Meiji Restoration continued until the early 20th century. Japanese leaders sent students abroad to Western countries to learn about their forms of government, a capitalist economy based on unified currency, stock exchanges, and technology. The Meiji emperor realized that the nation had to modernize to avoid becoming a victim of imperialism like China had in the late 19th century.

WRONG CHOICES EXPLAINED:

(1) The daimyo were samurai warriors under the Japanese feudal system. The country did not provide benefits to them. They only benefited if they invested their money in the new emerging industries created by the policy of modernization.

(2) There was no safety net for traditional businesses. These industries failed if they did not abandon their old ways of doing business.

(4) The passage does not indicate that the government relinquished control over foreign trade. The reading notes that the government gave over direct control of the modernization process for budgetary reasons but does not specifically mention foreign trade.

12. **3** Letting natural laws regulate the economy would be a course of action that the theory of laissez-faire suggests a government should follow. The economic theory of laissez-faire proposes that governments should not interfere with businesses. Laissez-faire stemmed from the economic philosophers of the 18th-century Enlightenment. They argued that government regulation only interfered with the production of wealth. The economy would prosper without government regulation. The economic ideas of laissez-faire were skillfully presented by Adam Smith in his book *Wealth of Nations*. Smith argued that the free market—the natural forces of supply and demand—should be allowed to operate and regulate business. The free market would produce more goods at lower prices making them affordable for everyone. A growing economy would also encourage capitalists to reinvest new profits in new ventures. Smith and other capitalists argued that the marketplace was better off without any government regulation. Smith argued for free trade in which the trade of goods and services between or within countries flows unhindered by government-imposed restrictions. Smith believed that government intervention generally increases costs of goods and services for both consumers and producers. Smith is considered the founder of the market economy. Adam Smith's idea of laissez-faire would gain increasing influence as the Industrial Revolution spread across Europe.

WRONG CHOICES EXPLAINED:

(1) The theory of laissez-faire would not support the government providing help for people in need. Laissez-faire promotes the belief that the individual, not the government, should take care of his or her needs.

(2) Laissez-faire supports the belief that the market economy, not the government, would lead to businesses creating jobs.

(4) The supporters of laissez-faire assert that private industries, not the government, should control the mineral resources of a country.

13. **1** One effect of the British landlord system in Ireland in the mid-1800s and in India in the early 1900s was that these landlord systems contributed to famine and suffering. Most of the Irish countryside was owned by the English who were absentee landlords, who visited their properties only a few times a year. Protestants held titles to enormous tracts of land that had been confiscated from native Irish Catholics by the British. The average tenant farmer lived at subsistence level, on less than ten acres. They rented land on the estates of the landlords. Many of the estates were deeply in debt, and the tenant landholdings were too small to support a family. Under the British rule, three-quarters of Irish farmland was used to grow crops that were exported to England. The potato introduced from the Americas was the main source of food for most of the Irish. In 1845, a blight or disease destroyed the potato crop, yet the British continued to require the Irish to ship their crops outside Ireland, leaving little for the Irish except the blighted potatoes. The result of the Great Hunger was that out of a population of 8 million about 1 million died from starvation and disease over the next few years.

After the Sepoy Rebellion in 1857, the British ended the rule of the East India Company and put India directly under the British crown. British rule brought about economic and social changes. They built railroads, telegraph systems, and modern forms of transportation. However, other changes destroyed the traditional Indian economy. The British transformed Indian agriculture. It encouraged nomadic herders to settle into farming and pushed farmers to grow cash crops such as cotton and jute that could be sold on the world market. The British also discouraged local industries and pushed for laws to limit British import of Indian-made goods. Thus, Indian industries declined, and they were forced to buy expensive British-made products. To pay for these imports, the Indians had to rely more and more on cash crops. As Indian farms grew less food, famine became widespread. In the late 1800s and early 20th century, terrible famines swept across India. It is estimated that under the period of British colonial rule from 1859 to 1914, major famines occurred in India on the average of every two years.

WRONG CHOICES EXPLAINED:

(2) Under British rule local economies were not allowed to prosper in Ireland and India. Ireland and India existed to ensure that the British industrial economy prospered at the expense of local industries.

(3) The landholding system in England was never concerned about the mining industries in Ireland or India. These countries were expected to grow products that would benefit the mother country.

(4) The agrarian revolution began in England in the 1770s and was not connected with the landholding system in Ireland and India.

14. **3** A description of trade patterns that best represents the relationship between Africa and Europe during the late 19th century is that raw materials were shipped from Africa to European industries. Economics was a major motive for this relationship between Africa and Europe. By the late 1800s, the nations of Western Europe had industrialized. They competed for control of raw materials for their factories. Africa was a source of palm oil for soaps, cotton for textiles, and gum for paper and fabrics. The rainforests provided rubber, ivory, and rare hardwoods. In addition, Europeans looked on African societies as possible markets for the goods produced by European factories. Only by directly controlling these regions in Africa could the industrial economy work effectively.

WRONG CHOICES EXPLAINED:

(1) The trans-Saharan trade between Mediterranean countries and sub-Saharan Africa existed between the 11th and 15th centuries. It was a major trading route exporting goods to Europe, Arabia, India, and China.

(2) The British ruled South Africa beginning in 1806, when they displaced Dutch rule.

(4) There are no major rivers connecting Europeans to much of the African interior. Africa was known as the Dark Continent and remained unknown to the outside world until the late 19th century because of its interior of mountains, deserts, and jungles that discouraged exploration.

15. **3** The statement that best reflects an effect of imperialism in Africa is that natural resources were exploited for the benefit of European powers. European countries engaged in a "Scramble for Africa" (1870–1890), during which most of the continent fell under their control except for Ethiopia and Liberia. The Industrial Revolution in Europe created the need for raw materials that spurred overseas expansion. European countries wanted the rubber and gold from Africa that contributed to the industrial economy. The imperialist countries profited by digging mines and starting plantations with little regard for the people or the environment. In 1877, King Leopold II of Belgium claimed the Congo as a private plantation. He enslaved the Congolese people, destroyed the forests for rubber, and killed elephants for ivory tusks. His brutal actions shocked the world. He was later forced to turn the Congo over to the Belgian government.

WRONG CHOICES EXPLAINED:

(1) European powers did not distribute land equally between social classes. European countries considered their colonial subjects inferior, and only a small minority of the African population received some benefits such as education or economic opportunities.

(2) European countries did not establish territorial divisions primarily along tribal boundaries. Europeans divided Africa artificially, ignoring tribal, ethnic, and cultural boundaries. Ethnic violence erupted in the 20th century in countries such as Nigeria and Rwanda because of the political boundaries drawn by European countries in the late 19th century.

(4) Mali's famous ruler, Mansa Musa, not European powers, turned the city of Timbuktu into a center of great learning in the 1300s.

16. **4** Commodore Matthew Perry is best known for opening Japan to American and European influences. After the visit of Commodore Perry in 1853, Japanese leaders opened more ports to trade. Until the middle of the 19th century, the Japanese had almost completely cut themselves off from European trade. Tokugawa shoguns, or rulers, allowed trade only with the Dutch at Nagasaki. In 1853, the United States sent Commodore Matthew Perry, with a naval squadron of four ships, to halt the mistreatment of shipwrecked American sailors. Perry also came to ask the Japanese to open their country to foreign trade. The United States also sought to develop new markets and to establish a port where Americans could obtain supplies on their way to China. The Japanese, who lived in what is now Tokyo Harbor, were astounded by ships made of iron and powered by steam. They were also shocked by the cannons and rifles that could easily destroy their samurai warriors. Fearing that they might become victims of imperialism like the Chinese, Japanese leaders signed a treaty that opened up their ports to trade. By 1860, Japan had negotiated trade agreements with the British, Russians, and Dutch.

WRONG CHOICES EXPLAINED:

(1) The British East India Company traded primarily with India and China. The joint stock company had little contact with Japan.

(2) and (3) Perry's expedition did not rescue Europeans during the Boxer Rebellion nor did it justify European spheres of influence in China. The Boxer Rebellion broke out in 1900, and Europeans began to penetrate China after the Opium War of 1839–1842.

17. **3** The primary focus of this map is imperialism. Imperialism refers to the policy whereby one nation or several nations dominate, by direct or indirect rule, the political, economic, and social life of a foreign country. This map shows how European countries dominated China between 1895 and 1914. Imperialism in China began with the Opium War in 1839 in which the British easily defeated and demonstrated the weaknesses of China. In 1842, England and China signed the Treaty of Nanking. For China, the treaty marked the beginning of a century of humiliation. The British annexed Hong Kong and won the right to trade at four Chinese ports besides Canton. In subsequent years, European countries carried China into spheres of influence or control in which outside powers claimed exclusive trading rights. France acquired territory in southwestern China. Germany gained the Shandong Peninsula in northern China. Russia obtained control of Manchuria and a leasehold over Port Arthur. The British took control of the Yangzi valley. In the Sino-Japanese War of 1894–1895, Japan defeated China and forced it to give up its claims in Korea. Japan also gained control of Formosa. Thus, by 1914, China had become a victim of imperialism.

WRONG CHOICES EXPLAINED:

(1), (2), and (4) None of these topics is a focus of this map. This map does not provide information about population density, resource distribution, or urbanization.

18. **1** During the 19th century in Latin America, the Catholic Church and the military generally supported the interests of wealthy landowners. Since the Spanish conquests of the Americas in the 16th century, those of pure European ancestry held the highest positions in the church, the government, and the military. The Peninsular and Creole classes were comprised with those with pure Spanish ancestry. Peninsulars and Creoles were the wealthy elite who ruled over those with native or African ancestry. Therefore, the Catholic Church and the military supported the wealthy elite's interests.

WRONG CHOICES EXPLAINED:

(2) The landless peasants were exploited by those in positions of authority. The Catholic Church and the military were in positions of authority and did not support the interests of the landless peasants.

(3) In the 19th century, the military supported the interests of the *caudillos*, or dictators, such as Juan Vicente Gómez. The newly independent nations in Latin America did not have experience with democratic reformers.

(4) Indigenous peoples were converted to Roman Catholicism by the Catholic Church, but the Catholic Church and the military did not support their socioeconomic interests.

19. **4** This cartoon suggests that political power is often acquired through the use of technology. The cartoon refers to the era of Western Imperialism from the mid-1800s to the early 20th century. Imperialism is the domination by one country of the political, economic, or cultural life of another country or region. Western countries like England, France, and Germany were able to dominate Asia, Africa, and the Middle East during the late 19th and early 20th centuries because of their superior technology. The combination of the steamboat, the telegraph, and the railroad as shown in the cartoon enabled Western powers to increase their mobility and quickly respond to any situation that threatened their dominance. The

rapid-firing machine guns and repeating rifles also gave them a military advantage and was helpful in convincing Africans and Asians to accept Western control. In the Opium War (1839–1842), the British gunboats equipped with the latest technology in firepower easily defeated the Chinese wooden-clad ships and the army with its outdated weapons and fighting methods.

WRONG CHOICES EXPLAINED:

(1), (2), and (3) None of these choices is represented or suggested in the cartoon.

20. **4** Unification of Germany is the heading that best completes the partial outline. Germany was the last of the great European powers to achieve complete political unity. Beginning in the early 19th century, some Germans began to think of a unified fatherland or country. This nationalist awakening reflected the efforts of German educators, poets, writers, historians, and philosophers. These individuals stressed the factors that unite Germans, such as customs, race, language, and historical tradition. Napoleon aroused nationalist feelings and reduced the number of small German states from 300 to 100. In 1819, Prussia formed the Zollverein, a German custom union. By the 1840s, it included most of the German states except Austria. The Zollverein ended trade barriers among states but maintained high tariffs against nonmembers. The Zollverein promoted economic unity but, more importantly, established Prussia as a leader among the states. In 1862, Otto von Bismarck was appointed Chancellor of Prussia. Over the next decade, he was the leading force behind the drive to unify Germany. Bismarck believed that the only way to unify Germany was through a policy of blood and iron. He believed that the only way to unite German states was through war. From 1864 to 1871, Bismarck led Prussia into three wars that united Germany. These three wars were the Danish War, the Austro-Prussian War, and the Franco-Prussian War. During the Danish War (1864), Prussia allied with Austria, seizing territory from Denmark. During the Austro-Prussian War (1866), Prussia turned against Austria. Within seven weeks, Austria had been defeated, and Bismarck had annexed the northern German states with Prussia. During the Franco-Prussian War (1870–1871), Bismarck used nationalism to rally the people against Napoleon III of France and easily defeat France. During this war, the southern German states united with Prussia. In 1871, Bismarck proclaimed William I as Emperor (Kaiser) of the German Empire.

WRONG CHOICES EXPLAINED:

(1) The Congress of Vienna convened in 1814–1815 to reorganize Europe after the Napoleonic Wars.

(2) The Scramble for Africa was the time period from 1881 to 1914, during the New Age of Imperialism. European imperialistic countries divided up the African continent for markets and raw materials.

(3) The Age of Absolutism refers to the time period in the 1500s–1600s when monarchies in Europe and Asia sought to centralize their complete authority over their governments and the lives of the people in their nation. Louis XIV in France, in the 17th century, and Akbar the Great in India, in the last half of the 1500s, represented the idea of the absolute ruler.

21. **4** As indicated on these maps, nationalism was the factor that provided the motivation for the changes that took place between 1858 and 1870. Nationalism is a belief that each group is entitled to its own nation. For many years, Italy was divided into a number of small states as reflected in Map A. It was considered a geographic expression rather than a united country. Between 1858 and 1870, the spirit of nationalism would lead to the creation of a united Italy.

WRONG CHOICES EXPLAINED:

(1) and (3) Neither of these choices provided the motivation for the changes that took place between 1858 and 1870. European exploration took place in the 16th century in Latin America and Asia. Religious leaders opposed the unification of Italy.

(2) Appeasement was a policy that European leaders adopted in the 1930s. England and France believed that if they gave in to the aggressive demands of Hitler or Mussolini, war could be averted.

22. **3** Camillo di Cavour and Giuseppe Mazzini played a direct role in the changes that took place between Map A and Map B. These leaders helped to create a united Italy. Much of Italy was united under either Austrian or Spanish colonies. Giuseppe Mazzini was a writer, orator, and founder of the Young Italy Society in 1831, a nonsecret society dedicated to the liberation of Italy. Mazzini is considered the soul of Italian unification. His speeches and pamphlets stirred up the passions of the people for a united Italy with a democratic republic. His most widely read book, *The Duties of Man,* placed a pure duty to the nation between duty to family and duty to God. The failure of the 1848 revolution forced him to flee from Italy. He continued his fight for freedom from abroad.

In 1852, Count Camillo di Cavour became prime minister of Piedmont (also known as the kingdom of Sardinia). He strengthened the country by promoting industry, enlarging the army, and improving agriculture. He was also successful in getting diplomatic assistance to free Italy from France if Austria attacked Sardinia. Cavour maneuvered Austria into war. With the help of France, he was successful in driving Austria out of northern Italy. Farther to the south, Giuseppe Garibaldi and his volunteer army of 1,000 Red Shirts gained control of Naples and the Two Sicilies. Cavour joined Naples to enlarge the kingdom of Piedmont. By 1860, Italy had become a united nation. Cavour died in 1861, and he is considered the "Brains of Italian Unification." Venice, and later Rome, joined Italy in 1866 and 1870, respectively, to complete the unification movement.

WRONG CHOICES EXPLAINED:

(1) Otto von Bismarck and Wilhelm II are associated with the unification of Germany in 1870.

(2) Klemens von Metternich was an Austrian diplomat who played a leading role at the Congress of Vienna in 1815. Victor Emmanuel III was the last king of Italy. He ruled from 1900 to 1946.

(4) Alexander II was the czar of Russia from 1865 until his assassination in 1881. Frederick the Great was the ruler of Prussia from 1740 to 1786.

23. **1** The single most significant force for Italian and for German self-determination and unification was nationalism in the 1800s. Nationalism led to the desire for different groups in these regions to be freed from rulers of empires, particularly Austria, and to form their own countries. Nationalist leaders like Camillo di Cavour in Italy and Otto von Bismarck in Germany led the unification efforts in their respective nations, resulting in the creation of new countries.

WRONG CHOICES EXPLAINED:

(2) Nationalist movements in the 19th century led to the breakup of the Austrian Empire in central Europe. Germany unified, and Hungary broke away by 1867.

(3) Nationalist movements led to hostilities throughout Europe as tensions rose in the late 19th and early 20th centuries. These hostilities eventually led to the outbreak of World War I.

(4) The power of monarchies began to decline as nationalism became the impetus for self-determination in various regions throughout Europe.

24. **3** The conclusion that can be drawn from this passage is that the Chinese people wanted to end foreign occupation. In 1644, the Manchus invaded China and ruled the country until 1911. The author is asserting that it was time to end the Manchu control of China. They had set up a new dynasty called the Qing, meaning pure. The Manchus did not want to be absorbed into Chinese civilization. To preserve their distinct identity, the Manchus barred intermarriage between Manchus and the Chinese. They also passed laws forbidding Manchus from wearing Chinese clothing. Women were also not allowed to follow the traditional Chinese practice of foot binding. Local government remained in the hands of the Chinese, but Manchu troops stationed across the empire ensured loyalty. In the first decade of the 1900s, Chinese nationalists called for a new government. Reformers like Sun Yat-sen led the movement to replace the Manchu (Qing) dynasty. In 1911, workers, peasants, students, and warlords overthrew the monarch. Sun Yat-sen became the president of the Chinese Republic and ended the ancient rule by the Qing (Manchu) dynasty.

WRONG CHOICES EXPLAINED:

(1), (2), and (4) None of these conclusions can be drawn from the passage. The declaration does not discuss isolation, the emotional status of the population, or the economy under the Manchu.

25. **1** One reason the Suez Canal has been of strategic importance to countries other than Egypt was that the canal allowed for faster movement between the North Atlantic Ocean and the Indian Ocean. The Suez Canal, which opened in November 1869, allowed water transportation between Europe and Asia without navigating around Africa. This would be especially beneficial to trade routes or during times of conflict, where a canal could maximize transportation efficiency.

WRONG CHOICES EXPLAINED:

(2) Europeans had explored the Western Hemisphere well before the Suez Canal was built, and its location is not relevant to travel in that hemisphere.

(3) Russian forces would not use the Suez Canal to gain control of Afghanistan.

(4) The Austro-Hungarian Empire had more efficient ways to access its colonies in South Asia.

26. **1** A similarity between the Sepoy Rebellion in India and the Boxer Rebellion in China is that both were attempts to remove foreign influence. They were responses to European imperialism. The Sepoys were Indian soldiers serving under British command. These soldiers were protesting the policies of the British East India Company. The British cartridges used by the Sepoys had to be bitten to remove the seal before inserting them into their guns. The coverings were said to be greased with pork and beef fat. In 1857, the Sepoy soldiers refused to accept these cartridges. Both Hindu soldiers, who considered the cow sacred, and Muslim soldiers, who did not eat pork, were angry. The Sepoy Mutiny (Rebellion) lasted more than a year. The British government sent troops to help the British East India Company. This was a turning point in Indian history. After 1858, the British government took direct control of India. Eventually, the British began educating and training Indians to take a role in their own Indian government. The Boxers were a secret society formed in 1899. Their goal was to drive out the foreigners who were destroying China with their Western technology. In 1900, the Boxers attacked foreign communities in China as well as foreign embassies in Beijing. In response, Western owners and Japan formed a multinational force of 25,000 troops. They crushed the Boxers and rescued the foreigners besieged in Beijing. Both of these rebellions were attacks against Western imperialism or foreign influence.

WRONG CHOICES EXPLAINED:

(2), (3), and (4) Neither the Sepoy Rebellion in India nor the Boxer Rebellion in China sought to establish a communist government, restore trade monopolies, or make any efforts to westernize cultures. Both of these movements were nationalist attempts to gain control of their country from imperialists.

27. **1** The signing of the Treaty of Nanking was an immediate result of the Opium War described in this passage. In the late 1700s, British merchants began to trade opium in China. The Chinese became addicted to the drug. In 1836, the Chinese government appealed to Queen Victoria to help them stop the opium trade. In 1839, when the Chinese tried to outlaw the drug, the British went to war. This conflict, which became known as the Opium War, demonstrated the weaknesses of the Chinese. British gunboats and troops equipped with the latest in fire power easily defeated the Chinese who fought with medieval weapons and fighting methods. Two British warships defeated 29 Chinese ships. In 1842, England and China signed the Treaty of Nanking. For China, the Treaty of Nanking marked the beginning of a century of humiliation. The British annexed Hong Kong and opened up five treaty ports to Western trade, including Canton, Amboy, Foochow, Shanghai, and Ningbo. China was required to pay a $100 million indemnity for the opium it had destroyed. The trade in opium continued. Britain received the privilege of extraterritoriality, which meant that the British did not have to obey Chinese laws and were subject only to British laws and courts. In subsequent years, other European countries established spheres of influence, or control, in China.

WRONG CHOICES EXPLAINED:

(2) The Guomindang Party was the Nationalist Party founded by Sun Yat-sen. He would become the first leader of the Republic of China in 1912.

(3) The Boxer Rebellion occurred in 1900. The Boxers were a secret society formed in 1899 to drive out foreigners who were destroying China with their Western technology. This rebellion was crushed by the Western countries.

(4) The Taiping Rebellion lasted from 1850 to 1864. It was a peasant revolt, and the leaders were inspired by religious visions. They wanted to establish a "Heavenly Kingdom of Peace."

28. **1** A key idea in the *Communist Manifesto* by Karl Marx and Friedrich Engels is that workers should support the overthrow of the capitalist system. In 1848, Karl Marx, in collaboration with Friedrich Engels, wrote this work in which he called for a worldwide revolution to end the abuses of capitalism created by the Industrial Revolution in Europe. Marx proposed a scientific theory of history in which economic conditions determined history. He wrote that history is a struggle between the haves and have-nots. In ancient times, the struggle occurred between the patricians and the plebeians. During the Middle Ages, the struggle was between the lords and serfs. In industrial society, it was between the capitalists (factory owners), who are the haves, and the proletariat (workers), who are the have-nots. Capitalists exploited the workers by paying them just enough to keep the workers alive. Marx believed that industrialization created prosperity for a few and poverty for many. Since class struggle was international, workers in each nation faced the same problems and the same capitalist oppressors. Marx predicted that a worldwide violent revolution by the workers would overthrow the capitalists in the industrial countries of the world.

WRONG CHOICES EXPLAINED:

(2) Marx and Engels rejected the establishment of labor unions. They believed in a classless society with the goal "from each according to his ability, to each according to his needs."

(3) Marx and Engels believed that the state would wither away under communism and there would be no need for governmental or legislative regulations of wages and working conditions.

(4) Marx and Engels opposed technological changes in production methods because these changes would enable the capitalists to exploit the workers further.

29. **4** Anti-Semitism and Jewish persecution throughout Europe were factors that contributed to the rise of Zionism in the late 19th century. Anti-Semitism in Western Europe was exemplified by the controversy over the Dreyfus affair, in which a Jewish officer in the French Army was accused of selling military secrets to Germany and was convicted. Although later evidence proved that he was framed and innocent, anti-Jewish groups refused to let the case be reopened. In Eastern Europe, Russian officials allowed pogroms, or campaigns of violence against the Jewish population, leading many to flee the region. This long history of anti-Semitism and Jewish persecution led Theodor Herzl to start the movement known as Zionism to work for the re-establishment of a Jewish homeland in Israel.

WRONG CHOICES EXPLAINED:

(1) The establishment of the State of Israel as an autonomous nation was the *goal* of Zionism, which was achieved in 1948. It was not a *contributing factor* for this movement.

(2) Islam expanded throughout Southwest Asia in the 7th century CE. This was not a contributing factor for the rise of Zionism.

(3) Germany was defeated in World War I in 1918. Zionism was a movement that began in the 1890s as a result of widespread anti-Semitism and Jewish persecution.

30. **2** During the Meiji Restoration, the Japanese took the action of sending experts to learn from modern Western nations. During the Meiji Restoration from 1862 to 1912, Japan reversed its policy of isolation, ended feudalism, and began to modernize by borrowing from the Western powers. The goal of the Meiji leader, or enlightened ruler, was to make Japan a strong military and industrial power. The Meiji emperor realized that the nation had to modernize to avoid becoming a victim of imperialism like China. Japanese leaders sent students and experts abroad to Western countries to learn about their form of government, economics, technology, and customs. The Japanese government also brought foreign experts to Japan to improve industry. The Japanese adopted a constitution based on the model of Prussia with the emperor as the head. The new government was not intended to bring democracy but to unite Japan and make it equal to Western powers. The Meiji government established a banking system, modern shipyards, and factories for producing cement, glass, and textiles. The leaders also built up a modern army based on a draft and constructed a fleet of steam-powered iron ships. By imitating the West, Japan remained independent but also became an imperial power.

WRONG CHOICES EXPLAINED:

(1) The samurai were members of the Japanese warrior class during their medieval period. The goal of the Meiji Restoration was to modernize Japan by destroying the power of samurai warriors, not to establish a social system to help the samurai.

(3) Communist ideas did not dominate the government during the Meiji Restoration of the 19th century.

(4) The Japanese government did not start an ambitious program to expel foreign manufacturers during the Meiji Restoration. No foreign businesses operated in Japan. In fact, the Japanese government encouraged the people to imitate Western technology and Western ways to help the Japanese establish a strong country.

31. **4** Workers and peasants were the major supporters of 20th-century communist revolutions. In Russia, Vladimir Lenin, the father of Russian communism, was successful because the Soviets (council of workers) supported the Bolsheviks or Communist Party. In the March Revolution of 1917, the moderate government of Alexander Kerensky was unsuccessful

because he did not understand the needs of the people. Lenin was successful because, unlike the government of Kerensky, he appealed to the peasants, the industrial workers, and the soldiers by using the slogan peace, land, and bread." The peasants supported the communists because of the promise of taking control of nobles' estates. The workers saw communism as an opportunity for them to gain control of the factories. The peasants in China supported communism because Mao Zedong, the leader of the Chinese Communist Party, promised to end years of oppression by landlords and government officials. His goal was to set up a dictatorship of the people and redistribute lands to the peasants. Mao, with the strong support of the peasants and the middle class who hoped that he would end years of foreign domination, established a communist state in China. As in Russia and China, peasants and workers in Cuba supported Fidel Castro because of his promise of land reforms and improving the economic life of the workers. The communist leadership of the Sandinistas in Nicaragua had similar appeal to the peasants and workers of the country. The communist revolutions of the 20th century were successful because of the support of the peasants and workers.

WRONG CHOICES EXPLAINED:

(1) The artisans or workers supported the communist revolutions. However, priests did not endorse the revolutions.

(2) The communists had some middle-class support. However, the nobility saw communists as a threat to their way of life.

(3) Entrepreneurs and capitalists opposed the communist revolutions of the 20th century. The communists promised to take over the factories and redistribute the wealth.

32. **4** The factor that led to the rise of communist revolutions in Russia and in China was the unequal distribution of wealth between social classes. At the end of the 19th century and the beginning of the 20th century, Russia underwent an industrial growth that enabled the nation to become one of the world's leading producers of steel. Rapid industrialization also stirred discontent among the people of Russia. The growth of factories brought new problems. Among these problems were grueling working conditions, low wages, and child labor. Workers were unhappy with their low standard of living. The gap between the rich and the poor was enormous. In 1914, Czar Nicholas II's mismanagement of World War I created further problems. Over 15 million men joined the army, which left an insufficient number of workers in the factories and on the farms. The result was widespread shortages of food and materials. Riots and strikes broke out as workers demanded higher wages and better working conditions. By March 1917, famine threatened many cities and workers continued to strike. Peasants, like factory workers, were also treated poorly. Under Czar Nicholas II, 85 percent of the Russian people were peasants, but they owned very little of the land.

Although the serfs or peasants had been liberated in 1861, half of the farmable land was in the hands of the nobles. The other half was given out to serfs who were required to pay the government for it. The land allotted to the peasants was too small to be efficient to support a family. As a result, the peasants remained poor, and discontent festered up until the early 1900s. When Russia entered World War I in 1914, it added to the social tension between the nobles and the peasants. By March 1917, the shortage of food for workers and peasants and the deaths of over 2 million soldiers in the war forced Nicholas II to abdicate. However, the new provisional government was unable to provide the cities with food and refused to approve land seizure by the peasants. Alexander Kerensky, the leader of the government, believed that confiscating the large estates of the nobles and giving them to the peasants would lead to the disintegration of Russia's social system.

Moreover, the government insisted on continuing the war. Thus, it began to lose support with the peasants and especially the Soviets, or council of workers and soldiers. In 1917, the Bolsheviks, under the leadership of Vladimir Lenin, were successful in organizing and controlling these Soviets. Lenin, who is considered the father of Russian communism, demanded "peace, land, and bread" for soldiers, city workers, and peasants. The Bolsheviks attracted the masses of people because they promised land to peasants, food for the people, and an end to the war. The majority of Russian people were not communists but were displeased with the government of Alexander Kerensky. On November 7, 1917, the Bolsheviks, or communists, overthrew the provisional government and seized power.

Chinese Communists were able to gain control of China primarily due to the peasants' support. The struggle for China began in the 1920s between the communists and the Nationalists. During the late 1920s and 1930s, Mao Zedong emerged as leader of the Chinese Communists. Mao believed that the Communists would succeed in China only by winning the support of the peasants. He insisted that the Communist forces treat the peasants fairly. Unlike the other Chinese armies, the Communists paid the peasants for the food their forces required. With the peasants' support, Mao's army grew. The civil war was halted during World War II as both forces joined together to fight the Japanese. After World War II ended, the civil war resumed. In 1949, Mao's Communists were victorious, and he established the People's Republic of China. Mao was successful because his peasant army was highly disciplined. He preached a philosophy that appealed to China's poor and promised to end years of oppression by the landlords and government officials and introduce land reform. Mao's pledge to end years of repression by the nobles and crushing taxes contributed to the success of the Communists in China. In Russia and in China, the inequities of the social structure led to revolutions that changed the government.

WRONG CHOICES EXPLAINED:

(1) The increase in agricultural production around the world did not contribute to the rise of communist revolutions in Russia and in China. It was the lack of food in Russia and poor conditions of peasants in China that led to revolutions.

(2) The onset of the global depression in the 1930s that restricted trade contributed to the rise of Nazism in Germany.

(3) The rise of communist revolutions in both of these countries was not the result of a scarcity of workers.

33. **2** In early 20th-century Russia, the Bolsheviks may have gained support by circulating this poster. In Russian, the word *Bolshevik* translates to "one of the majority." The Bolshevik political party was founded by Vladimir Lenin and had been part of the Marxists' Social Democratic Labor Party but split from that group in the early 20th century. The Bolsheviks were mainly workers and followed the philosophy of democratic centralism—all members of the party were encouraged and able to speak their minds about all issues, but once a majority vote was obtained about a particular issue, all members of the party were expected to support the decision of the majority regardless of their individual beliefs. Lenin himself said that the Bolshevik approach was "freedom of discussion, unity of action." The poster presented in this question illustrates the Bolshevik party's primary problem with Russia's political system—that those in power took advantage of and made their fortune on the backs of the workers who had no power or ability to contribute to the political process. The poster directly attacks the Tsar (who held all power in Russia), priests (who were seen as abusing their position to advance their own wealth), and the wealthy Russians (who took advantage of the working class). This poster was meant to be a rallying cry and to encourage the workers of Russia, who formed the Bolshevik party, to recognize that they were being taken advantage of under this system. The Bolsheviks successfully rose to power during the Russian Revolution, and in 1917, they founded what would eventually become the Soviet Union.

WRONG CHOICES EXPLAINED:

(1) and (4) The aristocracy ("Rich Man") and Orthodox clergy ("The Priest") are being directly attacked in this poster and would likely not want this poster circulated for fear of upsetting a system that enabled them to obtain wealth and maintain their privileged positions in society.

(3) Monarchists are those who support the rule of a monarchy rather than the rule of the people. They would not have gained support from this poster.

34. **1** Although the Bolshevik Revolution of 1917 in Russia had many causes, one of the first major events that demonstrated the czar's disregard for the "ordinary people" was Bloody Sunday in 1905. When protesters marched toward the Winter Palace, they believed the czar would listen to their grievances. However, Nicholas II was weak and responded with violence, which undermined his legitimacy. Unrest followed during the next decade. Vladimir Lenin, who promised the people "peace, land, and bread," gained increasing support, which led to an overthrow of the Duma, or parliament. The revolutionaries then ordered the assassination of the czar and his family while they were in exile in Yekaterinburg.

WRONG CHOICES EXPLAINED:

(2) The events listed led to the end of the Romanov dynasty since Czar Nicholas II was the last Romanov monarch.

(3) The outbreak of World War II occurred over two decades after the events listed. The Russian Revolution is more closely associated with World War I. Russian losses in World War I contributed to the unrest that helped fuel the Bolshevik Revolution.

(4) The events listed led to the establishment of the Soviet Union in 1922 as opposed to the collapse of the Soviet Union, which occurred in 1991.

35. **3** One way in which the government under Czar Nicholas II of Russia and the government under Benito Mussolini of Italy are similar is that both governments established policies of censorship and repression. Czar Nicholas II ruled Russia from 1884 to 1917. At the end of the 19th century, big changes were sweeping across the country. The Industrial Revolution was altering Russian society, different revolutionary groups were trying to turn Russia from an autocratic state into a constitutional monarchy, and some even called for an overthrow of the monarchy. Nicholas II considered these groups a threat to the Romanov dynasty. The czar's secret police, the "Okhrana," was used to disrupt these different groups and exiled many of them to Siberia. There was discontent among many groups, including peasants, national minorities, middle-class liberals, and factory workers. Nicholas II sent out Okhrana agents to root out revolutionaries and placed spies in the universities and coffeehouses. These agents also shut down printing presses or any newspapers that criticized the government.

Benito Mussolini became the Fascist leader of Italy in 1922. Under fascism, Mussolini or "Il Duce" exercised total control of the government. He permitted the existence of only one political party. He denied private ownership and strictly controlled the Italian workers. He suppressed all opposition and maintained strict control of the mass media. Mussolini enforced his power through the Black Shirts. The men in this unit were usually ex-soldiers whose job was to bring into line those who opposed Mussolini. Mussolini also used his secret police called the OVRA to suppress any opposition. Prisons were set up in remote Mediterranean islands for those who opposed his regime. Mussolini claimed the duty of everyone under fascism was "Believe, Fight, and Obey." Both Czar Nicholas II and Benito Mussolini used the secret police to punish anyone who disagreed with the government.

WRONG CHOICES EXPLAINED:

(1) Neither Nicholas II nor Benito Mussolini liberated the serfs and industrial workers. Alexander II of Russia liberated the serfs in 1861.

(2) Nicholas II and Benito Mussolini did not reform the executive branch by incorporating theocratic principles. Nicholas II was an autocratic ruler, and Benito Mussolini was a dictator.

(4) Czar Nicholas II ruled Russia prior to the invention of television. Benito Mussolini rose to power in 1922 and depended on the radio as a medium for political propaganda.

36. **4** A primary objective of the New Economic Policy (NEP) in the Soviet Union was to gain stability by increasing production. Lenin is considered the father of Russian communism. In November 1917, Lenin and communists known as the Bolsheviks seized control of the government and established the first communist nation in Europe. Lenin, who had gained popular support with the slogan "peace, land, and bread," began to change the government. Lenin ended private ownership of land and distributed land to the peasants. Workers gained control of the factories and mines. However, many Russian people were not communists, and a civil war between the followers of the czar and the communists broke out and lasted for three years. The civil war in Russia caused the deaths of millions and resulted in economic disaster. Lenin realized he had to readjust his economic policies. In 1921, he introduced the New Economic Policy. Under this system, peasants were allowed to sell surplus crops on the open market, and private owners were allowed to operate retail stores for profit. Lenin also allowed private ownership for small-scale manufacturing. However, the government still continued to control banks, large industries, and foreign trade. The NEP, which Lenin called a temporary retreat from communism, revived the economy. Lenin died in 1924, but by 1927 the NEP helped Russia to improve its agricultural and industrial production to the pre–World War I level. The NEP provided the economic stability that enabled communism to survive in Russia.

WRONG CHOICES EXPLAINED:

(1) Under the NEP, the government did not allow private ownership of heavy industry such as iron and steel.

(2) The NEP was an economic policy and did not address educational reforms.

(3) Russia did not make any effort to coordinate an end to World War I. In March 1918, Lenin withdrew from World War I by signing the Treaty of Brest-Litovsk.

37. **1** An accurate statement about the Soviet economy under Joseph Stalin is that the Soviet Union increased its power by developing heavy industry. In 1928, Joseph Stalin, who became leader of the Soviet Union after the death of Lenin in 1924, launched the first of a series of five-year plans to make Russia into an industrial giant. Stalin believed that the Soviet Union would be unable to stand up to the capitalist countries unless it modernized rapidly. Stalin established a command economy in which the government made all the economic decisions. Stalin poured resources into heavy industries like building steel mills, dams, and hydroelectric power. He set high goals for coal and oil production. New factories were built to produce chemicals, tractors, and other machines. By 1930, Soviet production in oil, coal, and steel had increased rapidly and helped create an industrial giant.

WRONG CHOICES EXPLAINED:

(2) Under the five-year plans, the government did not reduce its role in planning industrial production. Stalin established a command economy in which the government set production goals.

(3) Farmers were not encouraged to compete in a free market economy under Joseph Stalin. Stalin established collective farms. The state set all prices and controlled all access to farm supplies.

(4) A large selection of consumer goods was not available in the Soviet Union. Stalin emphasized heavy industry, and the Soviet Union did not produce many consumer goods.

38. **3** During World War I, developments in military technology led to the use of poisonous gas and submarine attacks. World War I is considered to be the first truly technological war. Poison gas, which destroyed the lungs of soldiers and left victims in agony for days and weeks, was probably the most fatal of all weapons used in World War I. The French were the first to use it in 1914 in their unsuccessful attempt to stop the German army advance through Belgium. However, it was at the Second Battle of Ypres in April 1915 that the Germans used poison gas on a large scale on the western front. Although the eventual use of the gas mask mitigated the effects of this deadly weapon, it showed how modern warfare had become deadly and inhuman. The Germans were the first to use submarines as serious fighting machines against merchant ships. German U-boats numbered only about 38 at the beginning of the war and achieved notable success against British ships, but because of the reactions of neutral countries (especially the United States), Germany was reluctant to adopt a policy of unrestricted submarine warfare against merchant ships. By 1916, Germany used unrestricted submarine warfare, which led to attacking merchant ships without warning as a way to break the British blockade against all German ports. The adoption of unrestricted submarine warfare would lead to the United States's entry in World War I in April 1917 against Germany.

WRONG CHOICES EXPLAINED:

(1) There was no early victory by the Allied powers. The lack of technology on the western front led to a stalemate. Europe's hope for a quick war deteriorated into trench warfare that lasted from 1914 until the armistice ending the war in 1918.

(2) Military technology did not lead to the establishment of industrial capitalism. The government's direction of the economy in the Allied countries (England, France, and the United States) contributed to the growth of industrial capitalism.

(4) There was no direct connection between the development of military technology and increased ethnic tension in western Europe.

39. **4** The role of military technology was an aspect of warfare that is emphasized in this passage about World War I. Modern weapons added to the destructiveness of the war. Rapid-fire machine guns, larger artillery, and armed tanks contributed to the numerous loss of lives. The use of poisonous gas added to the horrors of this war as described in this passage. In 1915, Germany began using poisonous gas that blinded or choked its victims or caused agonizing burns and blisters. Though soldiers were eventually given gas masks, poisonous gas remained one of the most dreaded hazards of the war.

WRONG CHOICES EXPLAINED:

(1), (2), and (3) None of these aspects is emphasized in this passage about World War I. There is no information about civilian support, government propaganda, or the shortage of manpower on the battlefield.

40. **3** First person account is the type of source that this passage best represents. A first person account is a primary source that provides a direct or eyewitness description of an event. The author, Arthur G. Empey, was an American soldier fighting in the British Army. His book, *Over the Top*, published in 1917, describes his experiences as a machine gunner, fighting in World War I, and how modern warfare affected the soldiers fighting in the trenches.

WRONG CHOICES EXPLAINED:

(1), (2), and (4) The passage is not a census study that provides details about the population, nor is it a government decree. It is also not an encyclopedia article, which is a type of reference source.

41. **2** One reason the League of Nations failed as a world organization was that it lacked a military force to settle conflicts. The League of Nations was created in 1919 to prevent war by collective security. More than 40 nations joined the League. The members of the League had promised a common action against any aggressor state. The problem was that the League had no army. The United States did not join, even though President Woodrow Wilson had the idea of setting up the international organization. England and France were not willing to support the League with military aid because they were still recovering from World War I. The League could only verbally warn a country against aggressive action or put sanctions on the country. However, sanctions did not prevent such a country from trading with nonmembers of the League, like the United States.

WRONG CHOICES EXPLAINED:

(1) The League of Nations opposed the rise of fascist states but had little power to prevent them from seizing power.

(3) The League had no power or authority to establish naval blockades to deal with conflicts.

(4) The League opposed the annexation of territory by force, but it was powerless to do anything. It condemned Japan's invasion of Manchuria in 1931 and Italy's attack on Ethiopia in 1935, but neither country withdrew its forces.

42. **2** Germany invaded Poland in 1939 in a surprise attack after signing a Nonaggression Pact with the Soviet Union. This prompted Great Britain and France to declare war on Germany. France and Great Britain began to mobilize their troops, leading to the outbreak of a full-scale military conflict in Europe.

WRONG CHOICES EXPLAINED:

(1) The signing of the Treaty of Versailles is a long-term, not an immediate, cause of World War II. The treaty, which ended World War I, placed sole responsibility for the war on Germany. The treaty punished Germany by demilitarizing the nation and forcing it to surrender territories like the Alsace-Lorraine to France, which led to resentment and bitterness within Germany. Some argue that this punishment led to Hitler's aggression and was a long-term cause of World War II.

(3) Although the Japanese attack on Pearl Harbor in 1941 brought the United States into the war, the conflict had already been occurring throughout Europe and East Asia for over two years.

(4) The bombings of Hiroshima and Nagasaki brought an end to the conflict in Japan and was not a cause of the war.

43. **2** "Nuclear Bombs Dropped on Japan" is the headline most closely associated with the cities of Hiroshima and Nagasaki. On August 6, 1945, an American Boeing B-29 plane, the *Enola Gay*, named for the mother of its pilot Paul Tibbets, dropped an atomic (or nuclear) bomb on the city of Hiroshima, a Japanese city of 365,000 people. The bomb, referred to as "Little Boy," flattened four square miles and instantly killed more than 70,000 people. Three days later, on August 9, a second bomb known as "Fat Man" was dropped on Nagasaki, a Japanese city of 200,000 people. It killed about 40,000 people. Dropping the atomic bombs brought a quick end to the war. On September 2, 1945, the Japanese officially surrendered, and World War II ended.

WRONG CHOICES EXPLAINED:

(1), (3), and (4) None of these choices is correct. These headlines are not associated with events in Hiroshima or Nagasaki.

44. **2** The sequence of events that is in the correct chronological order is Treaty of Versailles (1919) ⟶ rise of Nazism (1920–1933) ⟶ German invasion of the Soviet Union (1941).

WRONG CHOICES EXPLAINED:

(1) and (3) The Treaty of Versailles occurred before the rise of Nazism and before the German invasion of the Soviet Union.

(4) The rise of Nazism took place before the German invasion of the Soviet Union in 1941.

45. **4** During the Cold War, nations that adopted a policy of nonalignment believed they should follow a course independent of the superpowers. In 1947, Prime Minister Nehru of India announced a policy of nonalignment. He wanted India to remain neutral in the Cold War competition between the United States and the Soviet Union. He felt that India could ease international tensions by following an independent course. Under Nehru, India formed a bloc of nonaligned developing nations. In that role, India arranged a prisoner of war exchange after the Korean War. In 1955, Indonesia hosted the leaders of Asian and African countries in the Bandung Conference. They formed what they called a "third force" of independent or nonaligned countries. The policy of nonalignment ended with the collapse of the Soviet Union in 1991.

WRONG CHOICES EXPLAINED:

(1) Nonalignment did not exempt nations from UN decisions. The nonaligned nations were exempt from supporting either the United States or the Soviet Union during the Cold War but not from UN decisions.

(2) Nonalignment did not restrict nations from trading with neighboring countries.

(3) The nonaligned countries were concerned with reducing international tensions, not environmental treaties.

46. **2** The Truman Doctrine, adopted by President Harry Truman following the end of World War II, established a commitment to aiding and assisting democratic countries that rejected communism. The doctrine's ultimate goal was to prevent these countries from falling to communism. This policy was known as *containment*. Likewise, the Marshall Plan, which was adopted in 1948, provided aid, food, machinery, and other assistance to Western European countries that experienced economic turmoil following World War II to prevent communism from spreading.

WRONG CHOICES EXPLAINED:

(1) The goal of both the Truman Doctrine and the Marshall Plan was to stop communism from spreading (containment).

(3) Ending the Cold War was not a goal of either the Truman Doctrine or the Marshall Plan. In 1946, Stalin declared that communism and capitalism could not coexist together in the world. The Truman Doctrine and the Marshall Plan sought to prevent more countries from becoming communist. They didn't attempt to make amends with the Soviet Union.

(4) Both the Truman Doctrine and the Marshall Plan were aimed at containment and didn't seek to disarm the Soviet Union.

47. **4** The pair of countries that gained independence in the 20th century and experienced the migration of millions of people across their shared borders due to religious tensions are India and Pakistan. Hinduism is the major religion of India. The Muslims, a distinctive

minority, had invaded India in 700 and by 1200 had established a Muslim empire in northern India. However, unlike other invaders, the Muslims were never absorbed into Hindu society. The difference between the two religions was too great. The Hindus believed in many gods. Islam was based on the belief in one god. Islam taught that all Muslims were equal before God. Hinduism supported a caste system. Muslims were always a small percentage of the population. For example, in the 1940s, there were approximately 350 million Hindus and about 100 million Muslims. Initially, the Muslims and Hindus cooperated in their campaign for independence from Great Britain. However, Muslims grew distrustful of the Indian National Congress, which had been formed in 1885 to promote independence, because the organization was mostly Hindu. In 1906, the Muslim League was set up in India to protect Muslim interests. The leader of the Muslim League, Muhammad Ali Jinnah, insisted that the Muslims resign from the National Congress party. The Muslim League stated that they would never accept Indian independence if it meant rule by the Hindu-dominated Congress party. At their Lahore Conference in 1904, the Muslim League first officially proposed the partition of India into separate Hindu and Muslim nations. Most Muslims lived in the northwest and northeast of the subcontinent. When World War II ended, the British realized that they could no longer keep India. As independence approached, widespread rioting broke out between Hindus and Muslims in Calcutta, East Bengal, Bihar, and Bombay. In August 1946, four days of rioting left more than 5,000 people dead and 15,000 hurt. In 1947, the British parliament passed the Indian Independence Act. This act ended British rule in India but also provided for the partition or subdivision of the Indian subcontinent into two separate, independent nations. One nation was the Hindu-dominated India and the other was Pakistan, with a Muslim majority. Muhammad Ali Jinnah became Governor-General of Pakistan. This partition led to an explosion of violence between Muslims and Hindus. Although India and Pakistan had promised each other religious toleration, distrust and fears were deep-rooted. Close to 1 million people died in the fighting. To escape death, millions of Muslims fled India to Pakistan, and millions of Hindus left Pakistan. An estimated 15 million people took part in this mass migration that led to the establishment of separate states for the Hindus and Muslims.

WRONG CHOICES EXPLAINED:

(1) Czechoslovakia was reestablished after the end of World War II in 1945. The Slovaks shared a common language with the Czechs and were only 3 percent of the Czech population. However, they wanted their own state. In January 1993, the separate nations of the Czech Republic and Slovakia were created without a mass migration of people across the borders due to religious tensions.

(2) With the collapse of the Soviet Union in 1991, Kazakhstan and Uzbekistan became independent republics. There have been border disputes between the two countries due to ethnic minorities. Uzbeks who live in Kazakhstan and ethnic Kazaks who live in Uzbekistan want to resettle in their respective countries. Although there have been over nineteen border disputes, they are based more on the struggle for regional supremacy rather than any migration due to religious differences.

(3) Libya became independent in 1951, and Egypt achieved independence in 1952. Neither of these two countries experienced any mass migration of people due to religious tensions when they became independent.

48. **4** The reform most closely associated with Turkish leader Kemal Atatürk is the adoption of Western culture. Kemal Atatürk, which means Father of the Turks, was the founder of Turkey and became the first president in 1923. Between 1923 and his death in 1938, he introduced a program of reform designed to modernize Turkey along Western lines

like the United States and other European countries. Kemal required government workers to wear Western-style business suits and banned the fez, a brimless red felt hat that was once part of traditional Turkish clothing. Kemal himself made a point of dressing in the European style. He no longer required women to wear veils in public. Kemal also broke the close connection between church and state that had existed under the sultan. He replaced the religious court with secular law and replaced the Muslim calendar with the Western calendar. He also transformed the lives of Turkish women by giving them equal legal and political rights, including the rights to vote and hold public office. Atatürk's effort to adapt to Western dress as well as his political and social reforms helped to modernize Turkey along Western lines.

WRONG CHOICES EXPLAINED:

(1) Kemal Atatürk did not implement Sharia law. He replaced Islamic, or Sharia, law with a new law code based on Western models. He established a secular state.

(2) Arabic script existed in Turkey prior to Atatürk's reform. He supported the use of the Western alphabet as part of his modernization program.

(3) Atatürk did not establish a communist government. He set up the first republic in the Middle East in 1923.

49. **2** According to Deng Xiaoping, China's economy could be improved by incorporating economic principles of a market economy into a command economy. Deng Xiaoping is credited with reforming China's economy after the death of Mao Zedong. Unlike Mao, Deng was supportive of allowing some privatization and opening free markets to increase production while maintaining control over major industries. In his quote, he states that combining a planned, or "command," economy with a market economy will increase productivity.

WRONG CHOICES EXPLAINED:

(1) Deng Xiaoping sought to reform the Chinese economy by opening some free markets. Prior to his reforms, there were more restrictions.

(3) Deng Xiaoping wanted to combine free markets with elements of socialism. He was not trying to make China a strictly Marxist socialist state.

(4) Deng Xiaoping rose to power after Mao Zedong's death in 1976. From there, he sought to modernize China to make it stronger economically than it had been under Mao's leadership.

50. **4** The British reliance on India as a market for its manufactured goods caused Mohandas Gandhi to refuse to buy British textiles. Gandhi, who came from a middle-class Hindu family and was educated in England, resented British rule in India. During the 1920s and 1930s, he became leader of the Indian Nationalist Movement. He led a series of nonviolent acts against British rule. One effective form of protest was the boycott in which Indians refused to buy British textiles and other manufactured goods. Gandhi urged Indians to begin spinning their own cloth and used the spinning wheel as the symbol of his Nationalist

Movement. He rejected Western-style clothing and dressed in a simple garment traditionally worn by village Indians. He hoped his nonviolent boycotts would undermine British rule in India and lead to independence.

WRONG CHOICES EXPLAINED:

(1) Gandhi did not run for a seat in the British Parliament.

(2) The Sepoy Rebellion was a revolt by native Indians against the British in 1857.

(3) Gandhi did not support the traditional caste system. He wanted to end divisions within Indian society based on the caste system.

51. **1** One social change Mao Zedong instituted in China after 1949 was granting legal equality for men and women. The communists rejected the inequalities of the Confucian order. To point out the break with tradition, Mao said that "women hold up half the sky." He believed that by forcing gender equality, he would make China a world power. Husbands were not allowed to abuse their wives, have concubines, or use prostitutes. Marriages could no longer be arranged. Wives with unbound feet were encouraged, and divorce was easier to obtain. Both sexes were forced to wear the same gender-neutral padded clothing. These changes initially gave females an increased sense of self-confidence, as they were encouraged to join the workforce and pursue educational opportunities. This was in stark contrast to centuries of being considered second-class citizens.

WRONG CHOICES EXPLAINED:

(2) Mao outlawed arranged marriages.

(3) Mao ended the practice of foot binding.

(4) Mao rejected Confucianism and saw it as the biggest threat to the state philosophy of communism. He believed Confucianism had contributed to China's decline during the 19th and 20th centuries.

52. **1** During the Great Leap Forward, Chinese peasants were forced to join communes. In 1949, Mao Zedong and the Communists gained control of China. Mao wanted to transform China from an agricultural society into a modern industrial nation. In 1958, Mao launched the Great Leap Forward. He called on the Chinese people to make superhuman efforts to achieve modernization. To make farms more productive, he divided China into communes, which are groups of people who lived and worked together and who held property in common. Most communes contained about 5,000 families. By the end of 1958, over 700 million people had been placed into 26,000 communes. Each commune was no more than 15,000 acres in size and included about 25,000 people. Each commune had small farms. The Great Leap Forward also encouraged communes to set up backyard production plants. Communists had production quotas for the amount of agricultural or industrial output that they were to produce. The Great Leap Forward was a failure. Local blast furnaces could not produce steel that was usable, and commune-based industries turned out poorly made goods. Agricultural production declined in 1959 and 1960, resulting in famine across China. In 1961, Mao abandoned the Great Leap Forward in favor of less ambitious plans.

WRONG CHOICES EXPLAINED:

(2) The peasants were not forced to move to the cities. Peasants and workers were forced to live on farms, not in cities. Mao hoped to combine the efforts of peasants and workers on collective farms to improve China's economy.

(3) The Great Leap Forward did not force peasants to convert to Christianity. Under Mao's Communist government, all forms of religions were abolished.

(4) The Red Guards were part of Mao's Cultural Revolution that he started in 1966. The Red Guards consisted of young people who left their classrooms to form revolutionary units. The goal of the Red Guards was to travel around China to ensure that the ideals of Communism were being followed. The Red Guards attacked writers, scientists, doctors, and professors for abandoning Communist ideals.

53. **1** Japan's policy of expansion in the early 20th century was motivated by a lack of natural resources. The primary reason for Japan's territorial growth during this period was that Japan wanted to obtain raw materials and food for its people. As a small island nation, Japan lacked many resources to ensure its growth as an industrial nation. Japan's later 19th-century industrialization created the need for raw materials, especially cotton, iron ore, coal, and oil. Japan also wanted to gain secure markets for its manufactured goods. The additional territories would also lead to the increased production of food. This would help feed the peasants who had been forced off the land and had moved to the cities during the Meiji period of modernization. In Korea, Japan took half the country's yearly rice crop to support its people at home, as well as to achieve its goal of territorial expansion in Asia. In the 1920s and 1930s, the Japanese leaders developed the East Asia Co-Prosperity Sphere. Its aim was to conquer East Asia by taking other countries' raw materials.

WRONG CHOICES EXPLAINED:

(2) The Japanese expansion was not designed to end unequal treaties. The imperial countries signed unequal treaties with China, not Japan.

(3) Japan was an insular nation, and its expansion was not designed to spread Japanese culture but rather to gain raw materials for its industrial economy.

(4) The Japanese were not a communist people and had no desire to spread communism.

54. **2** The statement that can best be supported by information on this 2003 map is that several borders are in dispute between India and China. The map clearly illustrates the border disputes. China and India have historically had border disputes. The disputes are related to two specific areas: Aksai Chin in the western Himalayas, which is claimed by India but governed by China, and Arunachal Pradesh, which is governed by India and borders Tibet to the north and Myanmar Burma to the east. India and China have had a long-running disagreement over these areas. In 1962, China and India fought a brief war over Aksai Chin and Arunachal Pradesh. However in 1993 and 1996, the two countries signed an agreement to respect the border between the two countries. Since 2003, though, China and India have held several rounds of negotiations to resolve their differences on their shared Himalayan border. In May of 2013, the two sides were embroiled in a standoff after India alleged that Chinese troops had intruded into Indian territory.

WRONG CHOICES EXPLAINED:

(1) This map shows that there are many disputes about borders between India and Pakistan, not that there is agreement between the two countries.

(3) This map does not deal with Nepal's borders and does not illustrate any border disputes between Nepal and India.

(4) This map is only showing borders, not how much or how little of a voice the inhabitants of the territory have in any conflicts.

55. **1** Joseph Stalin of Russia, Benito Mussolini of Italy, and Saddam Hussein of Iraq were all totalitarian rulers because each controlled all aspects of life within their respective nations and did not share power. For example, Joseph Stalin used his totalitarian power to collectivize farming and institute his five-year plans to turn Russia into an industrial superpower. Mussolini wielded totalitarian power in Italy beginning in 1925, when he became dictator. Members of other political parties were imprisoned, and he centralized his authority by spreading fascist propaganda in schools and through the control of newspapers. Similarly, in the late 20th century in Iraq, Saddam Hussein and the Ba'athist Party ruled through fear and intimidation to maintain control over the country. Those who opposed the regime were imprisoned or killed.

WRONG CHOICES EXPLAINED:

(2) Although Mussolini was considered a fascist, Joseph Stalin was a communist, which is on the opposite end of the political spectrum. Saddam Hussein was never outwardly considered a fascist.

(3) The idea of "westernizing" is associated with the actions of men such as Peter the Great of Russia and Kemal Atatürk of Turkey. These men sought to modernize their respective countries to make them more like the industrialized nations of Western Europe and the United States.

(4) All three became leaders of countries that were already independent.

56. **2** The author of this 2006 passage concludes that though governments change, circumstances often remain the same. Year Zero refers to the 1975 takeover of Cambodia by the Khmer Rouge regime. Year Zero is a symbolic notion that everything under the new regime was "reset"—the customs and ways that came before Year Zero were to be forgotten, and the Khmer Rouge ushered in a new era for the country. The Khmer Rouge was a communist party that arose from the North Vietnamese People's Army. From 1975 to 1979, the Khmer Rouge ruled Cambodia. Their rule was marked by widespread genocide, famine, and outbreaks of diseases such as malaria due to the regime's commitment to "absolute self-sufficiency." The ruler, Pol Pot, was focused on achieving a strictly agrarian society that would strip away all social institutions. In addition, the Khmer Rouge was dedicated to the ethnic cleansing of Chinese and Vietnamese people. The Khmer Rouge also isolated the country from any outside influence, and citizens were forced to evacuate their homes and undergo long marches to farmland, during which many died. Cambodia was essentially set up to be one large-scale labor camp, where everyone was expected to produce crops for the government. Currency was abolished. People worked 12 hours each day in the field, and many became ill. The isolation meant that people didn't have access to medical care. In addition, Pol Pot killed artists, academics, private merchants, and educators. While there has been speculation on the number of fatalities under the Khmer Rouge, it is estimated that more than 20 percent of the country—close to 1.7 million people—died under the Khmer Rouge.

In 1979, the Khmer Rouge fled, and the country was first ruled by the People's Republic of Kampuchea, which was backed by the Vietnamese. In 1991, after the Paris Peace Accords, the UN briefly ruled Cambodia but withdrew after a democratic election. However, a coup installed the Cambodian People's Party in power. As the author of this passage indicates, Cambodia currently faces many of the same problems they did under the Khmer Rouge. There is rampant poverty and corruption, limited political freedom, and hunger. While the Khmer Rouge is long gone, the country has not been able to rebound in a significant way, and life for Cambodian citizens has not vastly improved.

WRONG CHOICES EXPLAINED:

(1) The author does not conclude that as democracy develops circumstances will improve. In fact, the author indicates the exact opposite; democracy in Cambodia has done little to improve circumstances.

(3) New leadership is determined to replace the Khmer Rouge is incorrect because the Khmer Rouge was replaced in 1979.

(4) The author does not conclude that harsh living conditions have caused people to rely extensively on a social net; the author specifically states that there is barely a social net available in Cambodia.

57. **3** The largest number of hectares affected by soil degradation due to overgrazing is located in Africa is a valid conclusion based on the information shown in this chart. The bar representing overgrazing is largest for Africa. In Africa, the region known as the Sahel, which is the zone that separates the North African Saharan Desert from the Sudanese Savannas, south of the Saharan, particularly suffers from overgrazing due to the movement of livestock in the region.

WRONG CHOICES EXPLAINED:

(1) The chart clearly demonstrates that bio-industrial causes are only a minimal cause of degradation. In North America, Australasia, and South America, it is not even a cause and is only a minimal cause in Africa, Asia, and Europe.

(2) The chart clearly indicates that deforestation in Asia is occurring at a much higher rate per hectare than in South America.

(4) The chart shows that the region with the fewest number of hectares affected by soil degradation due to arable farming is actually in Australasia, not in North America.

58. **1** One way in which Miguel Hidalgo, Ho Chi Minh, and Jomo Kenyatta are similar is that they all were leaders of independence movements. Father Miguel Hidalgo, who was born in 1753, was a leader for Mexican independence. He was a parish priest who believed the Spanish misgoverned Mexico and decided to rise in revolt with the townspeople from Dolores. He was poor but well educated and was a firm believer in the Enlightenment ideals. On September 16, 1810, he rang the bells of his village church. When the peasants gathered, he delivered his Grito de Dolores (the cry of Dolores) and issued a call for rebellion against the Spanish. On the next day, Hidalgo and his followers composed of Indians and mestizos marched toward Mexico City, releasing prisoners in towns along the way. Soon his army numbered close to 60,000 men. The Spanish Army and Creoles were alarmed by the uprising of the lower classes. In reaction, they joined forces against Hidalgo's army. Hidalgo was captured, put on trial, and found guilty of treason and heresy. On July 30, 1811, Father Hidalgo was executed. However, after his death, the revolution did continue. On September 27, 1821, Mexico finally became independent.

Ho Chi Minh, which means "He Who Enlightens," was a Vietnamese leader who had gone to the Versailles Peace Conference in 1919 and called upon France to grant Vietnam independence. France refused. Disappointed, Ho Chi Minh was determined to build a communist movement and win independence. During World War II, Ho formed the Viet Minh and used guerrilla warfare against the Japanese. By 1945, he controlled northern Vietnam, including Hanoi. In 1946, France set out to regain control of Vietnam. After eight years of bitter struggle, Ho's forces defeated the French at Dien Bien Phu in 1954, and the French were forced to withdraw. However, the United States continued the struggle because it wanted to prevent the communists from taking over in Vietnam. Ho died in 1969, but the fight for Vietnamese independence continued. In 1975, communist forces captured Saigon, the capital of South

Vietnam, and renamed the city Ho Chi Minh City in his honor. Vietnam became a united communist country in 1975.

Jomo Kenyatta was the nationalist leader of Kenya. After World War II, Kenyatta, who had been educated and had lived in England, became a spokesman for Kenya's independence. In 1947, Kenyatta was chosen as the leader of the Kenya African Union, a political movement for independence. Other Africans formed a group that the Europeans called the Mau Mau. This secret group was made up of Kikuyu farmers who were forced out of the highlands by the British who had passed laws to ensure British domination. The goal of the Mau Mau was to force the British off the land. The Mau Mau began to carry out attacks against European settlers, such as burning farms and destroying livestock. Kenyatta, who was Kikuyu, had no connection to the Mau but refused to condemn these actions. The British took military action against the movement and jailed Kenyatta, whom they accused of leading the movement. More than 10,000 black Kenyans and 100 white Kenyans were killed during the struggle for independence. In 1963, Britain granted Kenya its independence. Kenyatta was elected the first prime minister. He held office until his death in 1978. He worked hard to unite all the different ethnic and language groups in the country.

WRONG CHOICES EXPLAINED:

(2) Ho Chi Minh was a communist dictator. Neither Miguel Hidalgo nor Jomo Kenyatta was a communist.

(3) None of these leaders was an enlightened despot. Enlightened despots were absolute rulers of the 18th century who based their decisions and government on Enlightenment ideas.

(4) These men did not advocate liberation theology. Liberation theology was a movement in the Roman Catholic Church that urged the Church in Latin America to take a more active role in changing the social conditions that contributed to poverty.

59. **4** A goal of the Sepoy Rebellion in India and of the Zulu Resistance in South Africa was to end foreign control. The Sepoys were Indian soldiers serving under British command. These soldiers were protesting the policies of the British East India Company. The British cartridges used by the Sepoys had to be bitten to remove the seal before they could be inserted into their guns. The coverings were greased with pork and beef fat. In 1857, the Sepoy soldiers refused to accept these cartridges. Both Hindus, who considered the cow sacred, and Muslims, who did not eat pork, were angry. The Sepoy Rebellion lasted more than a year. The British government sent troops to help the British East India Company. This was a turning point in Indian history. After 1858, the British government took direct control of India. Eventually, the British began educating and training Indians for a role in their own Indian government. The Zulus had migrated into southern Africa in the 1500s. In the early 1800s, they emerged as a major force under Shaka. He built a powerful empire northeast of the Orange River. Shaka's war disrupted life across southern Africa. Groups defeated by the Zulus fled to safety, forcing others in their paths to move on. While the Zulus were moving southward, the Boers, Dutch farmers, were moving northward from the tip of South Africa. The Dutch had settled at Cape Town in 1652. In the early 1800s, the Cape Colony passed from the Dutch to the British. Many Boers resented British laws that abolished slavery and interfered in their way of life. To escape British rule, the Boers retreated on the "Great Trek" northward. The Boers set up two independent states in the 1850s, the Orange Free States and the Transvaal inlands, which the Zulus had recently conquered. Battles between the Zulus and Boers for control of the area continued for decades. Finally, the British joined the struggle, and the superior firearms of the Europeans enabled them to win key battles. The Zulu land became a part of the British-controlled land in 1857. Both of these rebellions were nationalist attacks against Western imperialism.

WRONG CHOICES EXPLAINED:

(1) The Sepoy Rebellion in India and the Zulu Resistance in South Africa were not designed to divide their respective countries. They were organized to end foreign interference in their countries.

(2) These movements did not want to establish a theocratic government that was ruled by religious leaders. The Sepoy Rebellion and the Zulu Resistance were formed to protect their way of life.

(3) Both of these movements were not opposed to nationalist movements. They promoted nationalism for their country.

60. **1** Since the end of the Cold War, the primary cause of conflicts in Chechnya, Azerbaijan, and Bosnia has been religious and ethnic tensions. When the Soviet Union collapsed in 1991, the southern Republic of Chechnya, a largely Muslim area in the oil-rich Caucasus region, declared its independence. Boris Yeltsin, the Russian president, denied the region's right to secede. In 1994, Yeltsin sent 40,000 troops to crush the independence movement and restore order. Amid the outcry of growing concern over Russian losses and the unpopularity of the war with the Russian people, Yeltsin was forced to accept a face-saving truce. Chechnya was given some autonomy but not full independence. After September 11, 2001, Vladimir Putin, who became Russia's president in 2000, used the war on terror to resume the war against Chechnyan separatists and to destroy opposition to Russian domination. Although the government declared that the situation in Chechnya was normal, by 2009, sporadic fighting continued.

Azerbaijan gained independence from the Soviet Union in 1991. However, the predominantly Armenian population of the Nagorno-Karabakh region stated their intention to secede from Azerbaijan. War broke out. Backed by troops and resources from Armenia, the Armenians of Karabakh took control of the region and surrounding territory. In 1994, a cease-fire was signed.

The breaking up of Yugoslavia in 1991 and 1992 sparked ethnic violence in Bosnia among Serbs, Croatians, and Muslims. Slobodan Milosevic, the Yugoslav president who was Serbian, began a policy of ethnic cleansing to destroy all non-Serbs. The Serbs dominated Yugoslavia. Milosevic forcibly removed other ethnic groups from the areas that Serbia controlled. Hundreds of thousands of Bosnians became refugees living on food sent by the United Nations and charities. Others were brutalized or killed. Milosevic also waged a brutal campaign of ethnic cleansing against Muslim Kosovans. In November 1990, NATO forces started a military campaign against Yugoslavia. Milosevic was forced to retreat and was ousted from power. The International Court of Justice at The Hague put him on trial, but he died of a heart attack after five years in prison in 2006.

WRONG CHOICES EXPLAINED:

(2) and (3) Neither the adoption of capitalism nor the issue of poor health care and starvation has been the primary cause of conflicts in these areas. The transition to capitalism and poor health conditions have created some problems, but they have not been the main source of the problem.

(4) Russification is a policy adopted by the Russian czar Alexander in 1882 to unite the empire's many provinces.

PART II: THEMATIC ESSAY QUESTIONS

Sample Thematic Response for Question 1

Rapid social and economic changes have been experienced by many nations throughout history. Two nations whose social structures and economies were drastically changed within a short period of time were Russia beginning in 1917 and China beginning in the 1940s. Both nations underwent communist revolutions in which the state eventually assumed all means of production. Russia was able to industrialize. In contrast, China remained more agrarian and experienced more hardship and famine. Both Russia and China would forever be affected by these periods of rapid changes.

Russia's 1917 revolution rapidly changed the country's economy and society, which resulted in economic growth in the decades that followed. Prior to 1917, Czarist Russia was rapidly industrializing, despite still lagging behind the countries of Western Europe. The market economic system in place led to the rise of an industrial class of "proletariat," or workers, who were exploited by factory owners. These factory owners offered low wages, imposed grueling working conditions, and employed child labor. The poor economic conditions combined with a lack of power in government and society led to the rise of Marxist ideology. The Bolsheviks, who were the more radical Marxists led by Vladimir Lenin, gained support. They eventually overthrew the czar and the royal family in 1917, which led to some drastic changes in Russia. Initially, Lenin adopted a small-scale capitalist system called the New Economic Policy in which the state assumed control of only banks and major industries. Under Stalin, who was a totalitarian dictator, the state assumed all means of production as Russia's economy went from a market system to a command economic system. Under his five-year plans, Stalin successfully transformed the economy as industrial production increased more than 25 percent. He was also successful to a degree in transforming life for peasants. Under his leadership, 90 percent of peasants lived on collectives and produced twice as much as they had before the collectives.

Similar to Russia, China experienced a rapid change of the economy and society in the mid-20th century. However, the results were less successful. Prior to the Communist Revolution led by Mao Zedong, China lacked heavy industry and was an agrarian society. Despite the focus on agriculture, land was concentrated in the hands of a small percentage of the population. While using Marxist socialist principles, Mao confiscated the land and redistributed it to create more equity. He also assumed control of private companies, creating a command economy in place of the market system that had existed previously. Although Mao's early reforms were met with success, 1958 was a turning point. Mao instituted "The Great Leap Forward," which created large collective farms or communes. As a result, production declined. Within a few years, famine killed almost 20 million people.

Rapid social and economic changes were experienced by both Russia and China in the 20th century. Both nations, guided by Marxist principles, created economies that were controlled by the state. Russia, however, experienced more initial success in industrialization than did China, which experienced greater hardship and famine. For better or worse, these periods of rapid changes altered the future of both of these nations.

Sample Thematic Response for Question 2

Throughout history, technology has been an ever-evolving process. Existing technology is constantly being modified or replaced by new technological inventions. The invention of the printing press in the 15th century and the development of steam-powered machinery in the 18th century changed the existing technology and led to political, economic, and social changes that helped shape the world.

The invention of the printing press greatly affected society. The earliest books were written on scrolls. During the Middle Ages, books were written by monks in a scriptorium. These books took months and even years to complete. As a result, not many books were available, and they were very expensive. The nobles, who were wealthy and made up a small part of the population, were the few who could own them. Thus, the literacy rate was very low in society.

Methods of papermaking and printing reached Europe from China around 1300. The Chinese had invented block printing in the 700s, and the Koreans had experimented with a movable type in the 1200s. In the 1400s, German printers began to use movable type. German printer Johannes Gutenberg invented the printing press. By using this invention, Gutenberg printed the Gutenberg Bible in 1455. It was the first full-size book printed with movable type. By 1500, the invention of the printing press led to an increase in the number of printers in Europe. Eventually, by the 1800s, some motorization of the presses replaced handwork.

The invention of the printing press had a revolutionary impact on European society. It enabled printers to produce hundreds of copies, all exactly alike, of a single work. By 1500, an estimated half-million printed books were in circulation. For the first time, books were cheap enough that many people could buy them. The printing press quickly spread to other cities in Europe. Eventually, presses in over 250 cities had printed between 9 and 10 million books by the end of the 16th century. Since books were cheaper and more readily available, the literacy rate increased.

The increased circulation of books also helped to spread the ideas of the Renaissance. As people began to read, they became more interested in the accomplishments of the classical civilizations of the Greeks and Romans. The people were hungry for new knowledge about science and medicine. They were also curious about the reports by Christopher Columbus about the New World.

Writing in the vernacular (the language of the country) also increased because even people who could not afford a classical education could now buy books. The vernacular replaced Latin as the language of the people. Printers now produced the Bible in the vernacular, which allowed more people to read it. Previously when books were scarce, most Christians had to depend completely on the priests to interpret the Bible. Now people began to interpret the Bible for themselves and became more critical of the clergy and their behavior.

The printing press paved the way for the Protestant Reformation. Martin Luther attacked the abuses of the Catholic Church and did not agree with the Church's interpretation of the Bible. When Luther posted his 95 Theses on the door of the Castle Church in Wittenberg in 1517, the printing press enabled his ideas to spread. Someone copied Luther's words and took them to a printer. Within six months, Luther's name was known all over Germany. Gutenberg's printing press enabled the ideas of the Reformation to spread and eventually ended the religious unity in Europe, which led to a decline in the power of the Catholic Church.

The printing press also enabled new scientific ideas, such as Newton's theory of gravity and Copernicus's heliocentric view of the universe, to spread quickly throughout Europe. These new ideas led to the rise of the Scientific Revolution and the Enlightenment in the 16th and 17th centuries. The ideas of the Enlightenment influenced political revolutions in Europe, North America, and Latin America. Although the printing press bankrupted Gutenberg, his invention contributed to the spread of the Renaissance, the growth of the Protestant Reformation, and the subsequent birth of political revolutions.

Steam-powered machinery was another invention that greatly affected society. In the early 1700s, women produced cotton or wool thread with spinning wheels. By working by hand at their wheels and looms, spinners and weavers made cloth that could be used by the family. Any surplus materials were sold. This domestic or cottage industry at home was dramatically changed when James Watt improved the steam engine. The use of coal rather than water power now meant that mills no longer had to be built near streams or bodies of water. Although the steam engine had first been used to pump water from mines and to forge iron, Watt adopted the steam engine to power machinery in cotton mills. By 1800, almost 500 steam engines were producing goods more efficiently than those produced by the hand-powered machinery of the spinning jenny.

The improved steam-powered engine could also run multiple machines at one time, which led to an increase in the production and consumption of cotton. The shift in production of goods from handmade to machine-made resulted in the Industrial Revolution. The Industrial Revolution brought about many economic and social changes, with the most dramatic being the increased production and availability of goods. The increased purchase of goods brought riches to the factory owners and also led to the growth of more jobs. Families migrated to the cities as the demand for workers increased, and businessmen built factories around small market towns. The population shifted from the rural areas to the urban regions. In 1750, the population of Manchester was 17,000. By 1800, it had over 70,000 inhabitants.

Legislation, such as the Enclosure Acts that fenced off lands formerly shared by the peasants, also contributed to the growth of the cities. The unplanned growth of the cities contributed to deplorable living conditions. The working poor lived in crowded and unhealthy conditions with no running water, no sewage or sanitation systems, and garbage rotting in the city. Industrialization also affected the family structure. Before, entire families had worked together as a unit under the domestic system. Under the factory system, family members held different jobs and did not work together. Women and children frequently worked under horrible conditions and often labored for 12 to 14 hours per day. Factory owners were able to pay low wages because workers could easily be replaced. Furthermore, women and children provided a ready source of cheap labor.

The invention of steam-powered machinery did provide a ray of light for the workers. Goods that were mass produced were cheaper than those in preindustrial Europe. Therefore, more people were able to purchase these items. A new middle class emerged that would change the political and social structure of many countries. Workers began to form unions that led to an improvement in wages and working conditions. In Great Britain, the Sadler Committee was appointed to investigate complaints that children were being beaten and abused by factory owners. This led to legislation to regulate the employment of children in factories.

The steam-powered machines also revolutionized railroad transportation. Thousands of passengers traveled between cities. Freight trains carried more goods than canals and road coaches combined. By 1890, railroad lines crisscrossed Britain. By offering quick and reasonably cheap transportation, the railroads encouraged people to take distant city jobs. Industrialization swept across Great Britain in the 18th century and went to Holland, Belgium, France, and the United States by 1830. By the 1850s, Germany, Italy, and Austria had become industrialized. By the end of the 19th century, industrialization had spread to eastern Europe and Russia. In the 20th century, it spread to Asia, Africa, and Latin America.

Industrialization also led to the rise of imperialism, as countries competed for markets for their manufactured goods, places to invest their excess capital, and raw materials for their economies. The early success of the Industrial Revolution in Great Britain contributed to the country's growth as the dominant power in the 19th century.

The invention of the printing press and steam-powered machines replaced existing technology and changed the historical development of society and the world. Many of these changes were positive. In some cases, though, they were negative, such as the growth of poor living and working conditions created by the abuses of industrialization. As technology continues to grow and change in the future, society will have to confront how the changes will affect people's way of life.

PART IIIA: DOCUMENT-BASED QUESTIONS

Set 1

Document 1

1a) According to the BBC, one economic problem that contributed to the decline of the Ottoman Empire was the competition from the cheap products from India and the Far East.

Note: This response receives full credit because it gives an economic problem that contributed to the Ottoman Empire's decline.

1b) According to the BBC, one political problem that contributed to the decline of the Ottoman Empire was the weakening of the central government. The Sultan ruler did not maintain rigorous standards in the administration of the Empire.

Note: This response receives full credit because it gives a political problem that contributed to the Ottoman Empire's decline.

Document 2

2) According to Richard Hooker, nationalism led the Slavic people in the provinces, who were controlled by the Ottoman Empire, to lead a rebellion to gain their freedom. Their desire was to unite the Slavic people against Ottoman rule.

Note: This response receives full credit because it correctly one role that nationalism played in the decline of the Ottoman Empire.

Document 3

3) According to Peter Mansfield, one change that occurred as the Ottoman Empire declined and a new state of Turkey began to take shape was that Tanzimat reforms laid the foundations of a secular state.

Note: This response receives full credit because it states a change that occurred as the Ottoman Empire declined and as the new state of Turkey began to take shape.

Document 4

4) Based on the information shown on this map, a problem that the British faced that made it difficult to govern its empire was that the empire was spread out and located on many different continents.

Note: This response receives full credit because it identifies a specific problem the British faced in governing their empire.

Document 5

5a) Based on this excerpt from *Indian Independence and the Question of Pakistan*, one factor that made Great Britain more willing to grant India independence was that many British soldiers who returned home from serving in India realized how unpopular their government was among the Indian people.

Note: This response receives full credit because it describes one factor that made Great Britain more willing to grant India independence.

5b) Based on this excerpt from *Indian Independence and the Question of Pakistan*, the independence movement in India became violent as riots broke out, leading to the deaths and injuries of many.

Note: This response receives full credit because it correctly explains one feature of the independence movement in India in 1945.

Document 6

6) According to Clare McHugh, one change Great Britain faced with the breakup of its empire was that Great Britain lost its wealth as well as the industrial advantages it had enjoyed for years.

Note: This response receives full credit because it identifies one change Great Britain faced with the breakup of its empire.

Set 2

Document 1

1) According to Linda Jacobs Altman, the Ukrainian people were a threat to Stalin's power because they ignored directions from Stalin and refused to surrender their farms.

Note: This response receives full credit because it states why the Ukrainian people's actions were a threat to Stalin's power.

Document 2

2) According to this document, one action the Soviet government proposed to enforce its policies of collectivization and grain quotas was to place villages that organized malicious sabotage on the black list.

Note: This response receives full credit because it identifies one action the Soviet government proposed to enforce its policies of collectivization and grain quotas.

Document 3

3) According to Oleh W. Gerus, two consequences of the great famine-genocide in Ukraine were:

1. It destroyed 4 to 10 million innocent people.
2. It slowed the development of Ukrainian nationhood for generations.

Note: This response receives full credit because it gives two specific examples of how the great famine-genocide affected the people in Ukraine.

Document 4

4) According to Ben Kiernan, two problems Cambodia faced during Lon Nol's rule that enabled Pol Pot to rise to power were:

1. Cambodia was invaded by the United States, and its countryside was destroyed by US bombings, causing the displacement of 60 percent of the population.
2. There were simultaneous invasions by Saigon and Vietnamese Communist forces.

Note: This response receives full credit because it cites two problems Cambodia faced during Lon Nol's rule that enabled Pol Pot to rise to power.

Document 5

5) Based on this *History Place* article, one economic action taken by Pol Pot's government that contributed to human rights violations against the Cambodian people was that it forbade the use of money, which hurt the Cambodian people and affected their quality of life.

Note: This response receives full credit because it correctly identifies an economic action taken by the regime under Pol Pot that led to human rights violations against the Cambodian people.

Document 6

6) According to this *Frontline* transcript excerpt, two causes of conflict between the Hutus and the Tutsi in Rwanda were:

1. Discrimination against the Hutus by the Tutsi occurred because the Belgians had used the Tutsi to enforce their rule over the Hutu majority.
2. Hutus oppressed the Tutsi after independence in the late '50s and early '60s.

Note: This response receives full credit because it identifies two causes of conflict between the Hutus and the Tutsi in Rwanda.

Document 7

7) According to Aimable Twagilimana, the Hutus used the government-run radio to encourage the people to kill their enemies, the Tutsis.

Note: This response receives full credit because it correctly identifies one method that the Hutu officials used to organize the murders of the Tutsis.

Documents 8a and 8b

8) Based on these documents, two effects of genocide on Rwanda are:

1. Nearly 1 million people were killed and more than 3 million fled to other countries and were forced to live in refugee camps.
2. The United Nations established the International Criminal Tribunal for Rwanda that tried high-level Hutu officials for crimes against humanity.

Note: This response receives full credit because it identifies two effects of genocide on Rwanda.

PART IIIB: DOCUMENT-BASED ESSAY QUESTIONS

Sample Document-Based Essay Response for Question 1

The Industrial Revolution of the 18th and 19th centuries led to a variety of changes. These changes occurred within Europe as well as within the rest of the world. In the 20th century, the economic developments in China (1976 to the present) and in Mexico (1980 to the present) have resulted in numerous changes that have had both positive and negative effects on these countries and their inhabitants.

China, under the leadership of Mao Zedong, maintained a centrally planned or command economy prior to 1976. A large share of the country's output was controlled by the state. After Mao's death in 1976, the Communist Party began to launch some economic reforms gradually. In the province of Sichuan, the government allowed some business firms to compete for businesses outside the state central planning process (Doc. 1). The central government also initiated price and ownership incentives for farmers. This enabled farmers to sell portions of their crops on the free market. Economic control of industries was turned over to the provincial and local governments rather than the state planning committee.

In 1980, Deng Xiaoping emerged as the leader in China. He survived the Long March with Mao and was the last of the old revolutionary leaders who governed China since 1949. Unlike Mao, Deng stressed economic reform and capitalist ideas, not the class struggle, to help China achieve wealth and power. He named his program the Four Modernizations. It called for modernizing agriculture, expanding industry, developing science and technology, and upgrading the defense industry. Deng wanted to increase mechanization in farming. He replaced Mao's commune system and leased land to peasant households. Each household could grow any crop they wanted. However, farmers had to sell a certain amount of their harvest to the government at a fixed price and then could sell any surplus at a profit. Deng also extended his program to industry. The government permitted entrepreneurs to set up their own businesses. Managers of state-owned factories were allowed more freedom to set production goals.

Under Deng, China ended Mao's policy of isolation and opened the doors to foreign investment for the first time since the communists had come to power in 1949 (Doc. 1). Deng welcomed foreign technology and investment. To attract foreign capital, Deng set up special economic zones in Southeast China. In these zones, foreign companies enjoyed tax benefits, and private free enterprise flourished. Between 1978 and the end of the 1990s, foreign investors from Japan, Hong Kong, Taiwan, and the West poured more than $180 billion into China (Doc. 1). McDonald's, Coca-Cola, Airbus, Toyota, and other major companies also invested in China (Doc. 1).

Although these reforms changed its economy, China did not adopt a capitalist economy. There was a dual system. One was modern and connected to the markets. It thrived on international trade. The other system was dominated by the government. There were still millions of unemployed workers in state-owned enterprises. Deng was a practical reformer who was interested in promoting economic change, not political parity. One of his famous sayings was "I don't care if the cat is black or white as long as it catches the rat." Deng's Four Modernizations program brought about striking changes in Chinese life. As income grew and the standard of living improved, the Chinese began to purchase consumer goods like televisions and refrigerators (Doc. 2). Chinese leaders embraced the market and asserted that only increased consumer spending could enable them to fulfill the goal of Deng's program (Doc. 2). The Chinese consumers, in their quest for material goods, stylish clothes, and Western music, began to resemble Western capitalists (Doc. 2).

Deng's reforms produced a number of unexpected problems. By the late 1980s, students who had traveled and studied abroad in Western countries began to demand more political freedom. In May 1989, they sparked an uprising. Over 100,000 students occupied Tiananmen

Square, a public space in the center of Beijing. The students, calling for democracy and an end to corruption, gained widespread support. Instead of considering political reform, the Chinese government was determined to remain in complete control and crush any sign of dissent or an attempt to gain democracy (Doc. 2). On June 4, 1989, Deng sent troops when the demonstrators refused to disperse. The police arrested over 10,000 demonstrators. Many others were killed or wounded. After the crackdown on student protestors, foreign investment slowed. However, China still kept its doors open and continued Deng's economic and political reforms.

After Deng's death in 1997, his successors continued his policies of liberal economic reforms. From 1978 until 2010, the Chinese economy grew at an average annual rate of over 9 percent and foreign trade at an average rate of 16 percent. One of the economic benefits for the Chinese people was that the average per capital income doubled every 10 years. In March 2011, China replaced Japan as the world's second-largest economy after the United States.

In recent years, China has accounted for 4 percent of the world's economy and maintained a foreign trade worth close to $851 billion. Its economic growth has contributed to its growing influence in Africa and Latin America. In the years following 2011, China replaced the Netherlands in becoming the second-largest investor in Latin America. China's phenomenal economic development contributed to its emergence as a military power. Within approximately 20 years, China is expected to become the world's largest military spender.

One of the reasons for China's growth as an economic giant is because it has become one of the largest exporters of consumer goods to the world. By the end of the 20th century, plants in southern China produced 60 percent of the toys for the international market (Doc. 2). A majority of the millions of workers who were employed in these factories were women who worked for extremely low wages, lower than that of workers in other countries (Doc. 2). In 2000, China's average monthly wages were $94 compared with $311 per month for workers in Mexico. Yet for many of these Chinese workers, it was the first time that they were earning money, enabling them to buy consumer goods. However, China's businesses might be losing this advantage due to rising wages. In 2012, China's average monthly wages were close to 30 percent higher than those in Mexico.

Unfortunately, China's "floating population" has not benefited from the country's economic growth. Most of these workers come from rural areas and provide labor for low-paying manual jobs in the construction and service industries (Doc. 3a). This population has increased from 70 million in 1993 to 140 million in 2003. These individuals exceed 10 percent of the population and account for about 30 percent of the rural labor force. Most of these workers go home in June to do the planting, come back to the farms to do the harvest by the middle of October, and then leave for another three months. They move from countryside to cities, from undeveloped regions to developed regions, throughout the country (Doc. 3a). These temporary workers are not protected by Chinese labor laws. Their prevalent wages are less than 60 cents per hour. This constant migration of workers will undoubtedly have long-term effects on the stability of the family structure of these workers and will likely lead to problems in the future.

The economic impact of the global financial crisis of 2008 also had negative effects on China's industrial development. The crisis accentuated the widening wealth gap between the rich and the poor. Rising unemployment led to protests and strikes across the country (Doc. 3b). In some cities, workers overturned cars and clashed with the police (Doc. 3b). In some rural areas, there has been a revised migration where the floating population is beginning to return from the city to the farmlands for work (Doc. 3b). The global economic crisis of 2008 also forced China to shift some of its priorities.

It was reported in June 2013 that the government was pushing ahead with a plan to move 250 million rural residents into newly constructed towns and cities over the next dozen years.

It is replacing small homes with highrises, paving over vast amounts of farmlands. The government believes that its new source of growth for a slowing economy will increasingly depend on a consuming class of city dwellers.

Like China, the Mexican economy has undergone an economic transformation from 1980 to the present that has drastically affected the country. After the Mexican Revolution, Mexico developed a mixed economy. The government owned key industries such as oil but allowed other businesses to be privately owned. However, foreign investment was limited in any company to less than 50 percent. From the end of World War II until 1986, Mexico followed a policy of economic nationalism (Doc. 4). Mexico had one of the world's most closed economies. The Mexican economic model was guided by a policy of import substitution for the domestic market. Import licensing requirements were also monitored. Commercial ties with other countries, including the United States, were closely regulated (Doc. 4). The discovery of large oil reserves in Mexico in 1974 and rising oil prices spurred an economic boom. The boom allowed the government to continue its policy of protecting the agricultural sector and state-owned factories that were inefficient. Until 1980, both manufacturing and agriculture continued to prosper. In the 1980s, the drop in oil prices and the rising interest rates plunged the country into debt and created a major crisis. To avoid economic collapse, the government cut spending on social and other programs so it could pay off its debt. It also began to reform the economy. The government moved toward free trade or trade that had a low tariff or no restrictions. The government reduced barriers to foreign investment. It eliminated the import license requirements and the official import prices. Some industries were privatized. The goal of trade liberalization was to make Mexican producers more competitive by giving them access to affordable imports.

In 1986, Mexico joined the General Agreement on Tariffs and Trade, which is now the World Trade Organization (WTO). The General Agreement on Tariffs and Trade (GATT) began in 1947 to establish trade policies for all nations. By joining GATT in 1986, the country began an accelerated process of opening up international markets through deregulation and privatization (Doc. 4). As a result, GATT tariff rates were lowered. After years of chronic trade deficits, Mexico achieved a net trade surplus with the United States. Its imports of US goods began to grow.

In 1994, Mexico, Canada, and the United States signed NAFTA (North American Free Trade Agreement). The agreement was a formal recognition of the policy change that Mexico had been following since 1986. Mexico's hope was that free trade would attract foreign investments, create new jobs and technology, and promote and lay the foundation for future growth (Doc. 4). The implementation of NAFTA in 1994 produced some positive results for Mexicans. Mexico's share of trading with the US and Canada tripled. In addition, Mexico has free-trade agreements with over 40 countries, including Guatemala, Honduras, the European free trade area, and Japan (Doc. 5). Close to 90 percent of Mexican trade has been under free-trade agreements.

The Mexican government expanded competition in seaports, natural gas distribution, electricity generators, and telecommunication (Doc. 5). However, the telecommunication and energy industries have been dominated by a few powerful oligarchs and unions. The government has been unwilling to take on these groups and loosen their power in this sector of the economy. NAFTA left many promises unfulfilled for the Mexican people. Many domestic industries have been dismantled. Multinational corporations have imported parts and goods from their own suppliers. Mexico's exports exploded to over 292 billion in 2008.

Growth was also uneven during the period from 1980 to 2008. The industrialized north attracted billions of dollars in investments from the United States's auto industry (Doc. 5). Guadalajara in northern Mexico turned into a manufacturing hub for the information industry. However, southern Mexico lagged behind this economic growth (Doc. 5). The south lacked the highway, ports, and geographic ties that the United States enjoyed with northern Mexico. NAFTA brought a flood of cheap corn imports for livestock. These cheap imports drove down corn prices in Mexico and forced many farmers to seek other jobs. Many of them sought work in urban centers such as Mexico City.

The liberalization of trade under NAFTA was supposed to provide employment opportunities for many Mexican workers. Unfortunately, many multinational corporations set up maquiladora plants along the Mexican border. Northern Mexico had more than 3,000 of these plants as of 2006 (Doc. 6). Many of these plants can be considered sweatshops composed of workers who earned between $1 and $3 per hour, including benefits and bonuses (Doc. 6). Unfortunately, the cost of living in the border towns is high. Many of the workers have been forced to live in shanty towns surrounding the city. These shanty towns often lack electricity and water. Maquiladoras have been quite prevalent in Mexican cities such as Tijuana and Ciudad Juarez. Since many of the maquiladoras were set up on tariff-free zones, these corporations paid low wages, which meant that the local government did not collect enough taxes to try to improve these shanty towns. In 2005, the workers in these maquiladoras produced more than $100 billion in goods. They assembled parts into goods such as appliances and televisions. Over 90 percent of the goods were exported to the United States (Doc. 6). It was anticipated that corporate investments into these maquiladoras was going to produce a Mexican middle class that would become a large market for US goods. These plants failed to live up to their expectations.

Since 1980, China and Mexico have experienced economic developments that have produced both positive and negative results for these countries. China has emerged as a major economic power whose influence has spread in many parts of the world. However, it still limits the personal freedoms of its people in its own country. Although the standard of living has increased for many Chinese people, migrant and factory workers have not benefited from the country's economic success. Mexico has had the second-largest economy in Latin America. It has liberalized its trading policy and allowed greater competition in certain sectors of the economy. However, the country needs to address the extreme poverty in rural and urban areas as well as the problem of global competition and corruption within the government that is limiting the effects of free trade on the country. Both China and Mexico must confront these challenges to ensure further economic development and growth in the 21st century. The governments of both these countries must pursue policies that seek to address these problems and improve the overall economic conditions of all people within their countries.

Sample Document-Based Essay Response for Question 2

Throughout the world, millions of children have been exposed to inexcusable forms of violence and diseases that have resulted in long-term consequences and have destroyed the innocence of childhood. Armed conflicts and the spread of curable diseases have contributed to the suffering of these children. International organizations, government groups, and individuals have sought to improve conditions for these children most affected by these issues.

Throughout history, children have been seriously affected by warfare. In Sparta, children were reared to prepare for war. At birth, mothers washed their children in wine in order to be sure that they were strong. If they were considered weak or unfit for war, they were abandoned on a nearby hillside and left to die. During the Middle Ages, Christian rulers organized the Children's Crusades. The purpose was to expel Muslims from Jerusalem. Over 30,000 children about 12 years or older were involved in this venture. Many of them died or were captured and sold into slavery. During the Holocaust, Jewish children, like adults, were sent to forced labor camps. It is estimated that more than a million children were killed during this tragic era.

Since the 1990s, more than 2 million children have been killed, and more than 6 million have been seriously injured or permanently disabled due to armed conflicts. More than 1 million children have become orphans, been separated from their parents, and suffered psychological and traumatic effects (Doc. 1). Children caught in the midst of critical stages of their own personal development are more adversely affected than adults.

The armed conflict has also resulted in more than 15 million children becoming refugees or internally displaced (Doc. 1). Since 2003, in the Sudan Darfur region, more than 1 million people have been displaced, and about 65 percent of these internally displaced people are younger than age 18. Many of these children have grown up in Darfur displacement camps. They are in danger of becoming a lost generation. Some of the children, deprived of education, separated from their families, and subjected to sexual abuse and exploitation, have become child soldiers younger than age 18 (Doc. 2). Since 1998, there has been armed conflict involving child soldiers in at least 36 countries. Children are deliberately targeted because they are manipulated more easily than adults and can be indoctrinated to perform crimes and atrocities without asking questions (Doc. 2). In the last 20 years, more than 10,000 children have been abducted by the Lord's Resistance Army (LRA) in northern Uganda and forced to become fighters. They have been trained to use AK-47s and M-16s, serve as human mine detectors, and participate in suicide missions. They also act as spies and messengers (Doc. 2).

The Advocates for Human Rights have made an attempt to address the issue of child soldiers. They have supported the international treaty on child soldiers, entitled the *Optional Protocol to the Convention on the Rights of the Child on the involvement of children in armed conflict*, which went into effect in 2002 (Doc. 2). More than 100 countries have signed this international treaty. Other organizations like Amnesty International started a letter writing campaign to draw attention to ways to help child soldiers. UNICEF, as part of the United Nations, has established rehabilitation centers to help child soldiers. The International Criminal Court has also sought to deal with the issue of child soldiers. War charges have been brought against the governments of Uganda, Rwanda, and the Democratic Republic of Congo for children younger than 15 in war-related situations. Despite these efforts, children are still being used as military soldiers in these countries.

Land mines present another danger to children. After the war, land mines, grenades, and other explosives were left in fields of many countries. Children tend to pick up strange objects. Unfortunately, many children are too young to read or illiterate, which means they cannot understand the signs that are posted in these war-torn areas. Many children suffer debilitating physical injuries from these explosives, such as deafness and blindness (Doc. 3). Children are more likely than adults to die from their mine injuries. About 85 percent of child victims die before they can get medical attention (Doc. 3). The few who survive receive prostheses that will not keep up with the continued growth of their stunted limbs. Since 1995, Rwandan children have made up about one-half of the victims of land mines. In Angola, Mozambique, and Sierra Leone, land mines that stay in the ground continue to kill innocent children who walk near them.

In 1999, more than three-quarters of the world's nations ratified the Mine Ban Treaty. It outlawed the production, stockpiling, and use of land mines (Doc. 3). To further protect children, UNICEF has promoted educational programs in over 30 countries to teach children how to live safely in areas contaminated with land mines and other explosives (Doc. 3). International figures, like the late Princess Diana, Paul McCartney, and Angelina Jolie, have worked with organizations to end the use of land mines. They have raised funds for mine clearance and survivor assistance for many victims. The international efforts to address the needs of children affected by armed conflict and land mines have had some success. However, it is an ongoing problem that nations need to watch in order to protect children.

Another problem faced by children in the developing world is that they suffer from a variety of diseases that seriously affect their health and future. UNICEF estimates that about 29,000 children younger than age 5 die every day, about 21 each minute, mainly from preventable diseases. More than 70 percent of the 11 million children's deaths can be attributed to six causes—acute respiratory infection, neonatal (newborn) causes, malaria, HIV/AIDS, measles, and diarrhea (Doc. 4). Most diarrhea is caused by bacterial, viral, and parasitic infection that is transmitted through water, food, and contact with fecal matter (Doc. 5). Many children are blinded or crippled from the parasites in these dirty waters. These children also suffer from malnutrition, which lowers children's immunity and makes them more susceptible to diseases.

It is estimated that 12–15 percent of all babies in developing countries are born with a low birth weight and are seven times more likely to die of respiratory infections and diarrhea. They die within the first month of life. Many of the mothers do not receive skilled care during and immediately after giving birth. A lack of continuity between maternal and child health programs contributes to the high mortality rate of newborns in developing countries in Africa and South Asia.

Organizations like the Bill and Melinda Gates Foundation, the World Health Organization, and the Global Alliance for Vaccines and Immunization have been formed to help children in developing nations who die from these diseases. One in five children worldwide is not fully protected from the basic curable diseases. As a result, more than 1.5 million children die each year from vaccine-preventable diseases such as diarrhea and pneumonia. The Gates Foundation donated over $100 million in 1998 to get underused vaccines to children in these poor countries (Doc. 5). Gates has also worked with the GAVI, a coalition of international public health agencies, philanthropists, and the pharmaceutical industry to improve the delivery of vaccinations to children in these developing countries and make them more affordable (Doc. 5).

Doctors Without Borders/Medicines Sans Frontieres (MSF) is a nonprofit medical organization that was formed in 1971 to help the suffering people of Biafra in southern Nigeria. Their goal has been to provide humanitarian medical help for these people. These doctors soon witnessed how the lack of medicine for many treatable infectious diseases destroyed many lives in other developing countries (Doc. 6). In 1999, Doctors Without Borders launched the Essential Medicines Campaign to increase access to certain medicines and to encourage the import of less expensive drugs that are needed by the children in these countries (Doc. 6).

Although the children are considered the future of the world, many of them are suffering from armed conflict and infectious diseases that have killed millions of young people. Various organizations have been formed to help fight these terrible problems, but children are still suffering in the 21st century. The struggle to improve the lives of children in developing countries must continue until the safety and health of all children are protected.

Regents Examinations, Answers, Self-Analysis Charts, and Regents Specifications Grids

Examination June 2018

Global History and Geography

PART I: MULTIPLE CHOICE

Directions (1–30): For each statement or question, write in the space provided the *number* of the word or expression that, of those given, best completes the statement or answers the question.

Base your answer to question 1 on the time line below and on your knowledge of social studies.

1697	Spain cedes the western third of Hispaniola to France
1791	Toussaint L'Ouverture leads rebellion of slaves and free blacks
1794	Jacobin government in France declares an end to slavery in all French colonies
1797	Toussaint L'Ouverture assumes command of French armies in Saint Domingue (Haiti)
1802	20,000 French troops arrive in Saint Domingue to reclaim French authority
1803	Withdrawal of the last French troops
1804	Haitian Declaration of Independence

1 In the early 1800s, the French government took action in Saint Domingue (Haiti) to

(1) protect investments in French colonies in the Americas
(2) safeguard King Louis XVI's government
(3) return enslaved blacks to Africa
(4) support Toussaint L'Ouverture's rebellion

1 ____

2 Which feature is shown on a political map?

(1) climate
(2) languages spoken
(3) boundaries
(4) mineral deposits

2 _____

3 Which action best represents what a historian should do when considering primary source evidence about a historical event?

(1) reject the use of eyewitness accounts
(2) take into account different points of view
(3) emphasize the importance of religious values
(4) accept summaries written by journalists

3 _____

4 The Scientific Revolution popularized the idea that

(1) understanding is the result of observation and experimentation
(2) Earth is the center of the solar system
(3) church doctrine should be the source of new ideas
(4) scientific research should be supervised by political authorities

4 _____

Base your answer to question 5 on the passage below and on your knowledge of social studies.

. . . The Irish Potato Famine left as its legacy deep and lasting feelings of bitterness and distrust toward the British. Far from being a natural disaster, many Irish were convinced that the famine was a direct outgrowth of British colonial policies. In support of this contention, they noted that during the famine's worst years, many Anglo-Irish estates continued to export grain and livestock to England.

— Digital History, University of Houston

5 Which conclusion about Irish views on the potato famine is best supported by this passage?

(1) The Irish potato famine resulted in several natural disasters.
(2) The exporting of grain overseas was the sole cause of the Irish potato famine.
(3) British colonial policies worsened the effects of the Irish potato famine.
(4) Ireland did not produce any grain and livestock during the Irish potato famine.

5 ____

---

6 Camillo di Cavour is to unification of Italy as Otto von Bismarck is to unification of

(1) Venezuela
(2) Germany
(3) France
(4) Serbia

6 ____

7 Social Darwinism and the ideas expressed in the "White Man's Burden" were used by Europeans to justify their policies of

(1) pacifism
(2) communism
(3) isolationism
(4) imperialism

7 ____

Base your answer to question 8 on the passage below and on your knowledge of social studies.

> . . . As late as the 1870s, only 10% of the continent was under direct European control, with Algeria held by France, the Cape Colony and Natal (both in modern South Africa) by Britain, and Angola by Portugal. And yet by 1900, European nations had added almost 10 million square miles of Africa—one-fifth of the land mass of the globe—to their overseas colonial possessions. Europeans ruled more than 90% of the African continent. . . .
>
> — Saul David, "Slavery and the 'Scramble for Africa,' "
> BBC British History in Depth

8 Which event most directly influenced the change referred to in this passage?

(1) outbreak of the Boxer Rebellion
(2) meeting of the Berlin Conference
(3) signing of the Munich Pact
(4) collapse of the Ottoman Empire

8 ____

---

9 • Building factories and infrastructure
• Outlawing the wearing of veils by women and fezzes by men
• Modernizing education and government
• Replacing Arabic script with Latin alphabet

Under the rule of which leader did these changes occur?

(1) Emperor Meiji
(2) Kemal Atatürk
(3) Jiang Jieshi (Chiang Kai-shek)
(4) Benito Mussolini

9 ____

10 Which heading best completes the partial outline below?

I. ____________________
  A. Alexander Kerensky's provisional government is toppled.
  B. Vladimir Lenin comes to power.
  C. Czar Nicholas II is executed.
  D. Civil war breaks out.

(1) Causes of the Russo-Japanese War
(2) Outcomes of the Congress of Vienna
(3) Results of the Versailles Treaty
(4) Effects of the Bolshevik Revolution

10 ____

Base your answer to question 11 on the chart below and on your knowledge of social studies.

Population Figures for Ukraine	
1926	31,195,000
1939	28,111,000
Change	– 9.9%

11 What is a key reason for the shift in the Ukrainian population between 1926 and 1939?

(1) Stalin's policies of collectivization and forced famine
(2) establishment of a Jewish homeland in British Palestine
(3) spread of influenza throughout the Soviet Union
(4) Russia's involvement in World War I

11 ____

---

12 The term *totalitarianism* can best be defined as the

(1) belief that change and progress are beneficial
(2) practice of using faith and religious doctrine to maintain followers
(3) idea that all aspects of life are controlled by the state
(4) method for privatizing industry and property

12 ____

Base your answer to question 13 on the excerpt below and on your knowledge of social studies.

> . . . It is inevitable, perhaps, that the present activity in Japanese shipping should be linked with the military program and the drive for expansion both on the mainland of Asia and in the waters to the south. Witness the recent statement of the Japanese Minister of Communications, when he characterized the industry as the "vanguard [trailblazers] of advancing Japan," describing its development as important to "national economy, national defense and the improvement of the country's international accounts.". . .
>
> — Catherine Porter, "Shipping the 'Vanguard of Advancing Japan,'" *Far Eastern Survey*, February 3, 1937

13 Based on this excerpt, which conclusion is most valid?

(1) Japanese military and industrial needs were tied to expansion.
(2) Development of shipping was not a high priority for Japan.
(3) Most Japanese needs were being satisfied by existing resources.
(4) Japan's island position promoted the fishing industry. 13 ____

---

14 Neville Chamberlain visited Munich in 1938 to negotiate the fate of Sudetenland. Which policy is most closely associated with Chamberlain's action?

(1) appeasement
(2) nonalignment
(3) reparations
(4) colonialism 14 ____

15 The Truman Doctrine and the Marshall Plan were established to

(1) put down the Hungarian Revolution
(2) contain communism
(3) end the Soviet blockade of Berlin
(4) destroy the North Atlantic Treaty Organization (NATO) 15 ____

16 What is one of the primary differences between a market economy and a command economy?

(1) A command economy has less government control.
(2) A command economy offers more consumer choices.
(3) A market economy has less private ownership.
(4) A market economy has more business competition. 16 ____

17 Which two nations were created as a result of religious tensions?

(1) India and Pakistan
(2) Israel and Egypt
(3) Brazil and Colombia
(4) Vietnam and Burma 17 ____

18 In Cambodia, Pol Pot and the Khmer Rouge modeled their agrarian society on

(1) Mao Zedong's Great Leap Forward in China
(2) Leonid Brezhnev's doctrine of détente
(3) Mohandas Gandhi's Quit India program
(4) Lech Walesa's Solidarity movement in Poland 18 ____

19 One way in which Mikhail Gorbachev of the Soviet Union and F. W. de Klerk of South Africa are similar is that each leader

(1) sought to increase his country's nuclear arsenal
(2) pursued a foreign policy of isolation from the rest of the world
(3) initiated reforms that led to significant political change
(4) opposed the presence of international observers during elections in his country 19 ____

20 Which global problem is best illustrated by the late 20th-century conflicts in Rwanda, Kosovo, and Sudan?

(1) violation of human rights
(2) proliferation of chemical weapons
(3) disagreement over national borders
(4) lack of water resources 20 ____

21 From a Mexican perspective, what was one argument against adopting the North American Free Trade Agreement (NAFTA)?

(1) Mexican industries would be able to increase their exports to the United States.
(2) Greater economic cooperation would enhance democratic reform in Mexico.
(3) The economies of Canada and the United States would grow more slowly than the economy of Mexico.
(4) Mexican farmers might be put out of work because United States farmers would be able to produce food at much lower costs. 21 ____

Base your answer to question 22 on the passage below and on your knowledge of social studies.

> Mention Africa in polite company, and those around you may grimace, shake their heads sadly, and profess sympathy. Oh, all those wars! Those diseases! Those dictators!
>
> Naturally, that attitude infuriates Africans themselves, since the conventional view of Africa as a genocide inside a failed state inside a dictatorship is, in fact, wrong. . . .
>
> The bane [misfortune] of Africa is war, but the number of conflicts has dwindled. Most of the murderous dictators like Idi Amin of Uganda are gone, and we're seeing the rise of skilled technocrats who accept checks on their power and don't regard the treasury as their private piggy bank. The Rwandan cabinet room is far more high-tech than the White House cabinet room, and when you talk to leaders like Ellen Johnson Sirleaf of Liberia, you can't help wondering about investing in Liberian stocks. . . .
>
> — Nicholas D. Kristof, *New York Times, Upfront Magazine*, April 19, 2010 (adapted)

22 Which statement is best supported by this passage?

(1) The number of wars in Africa has grown.
(2) African countries lack skilled technocrats.
(3) Dictatorships are on the rise in Africa.
(4) Some positive political changes are taking place in Africa. 22 ____

Base your answers to questions 23 and 24 on the chart below and on your knowledge of social studies.

Population Trends in China 1990 to 2003

Year	% of Population in Urban Areas	% of Population in Rural Areas
1990	26.41	73.59
1991	26.94	73.06
1992	27.46	72.54
1993	27.99	72.01
1994	28.51	71.49
1995	29.04	70.96
1996	30.48	69.52
1997	31.91	68.09
1998	33.35	66.65
1999	34.78	65.22
2000	36.22	63.78
2001	37.66	62.34
2002	39.09	60.91
2003	40.53	59.47

— Chinese Government's Official Web Portal

23 Which factor in China is the most likely cause of the population trend shown in this chart?

(1) famine due to the establishment of communes
(2) employment opportunities
(3) spread of disease
(4) one-child policy

23 ____

24 Which potential problem is faced by the government of China due to the trend shown in this chart?

(1) a shortage of recruits for the military
(2) declining labor supply in cities
(3) a growing percentage of the population living in rural areas
(4) overcrowding in urban areas

24 ____

Base your answer to question 25 on the map below and on your knowledge of social studies.

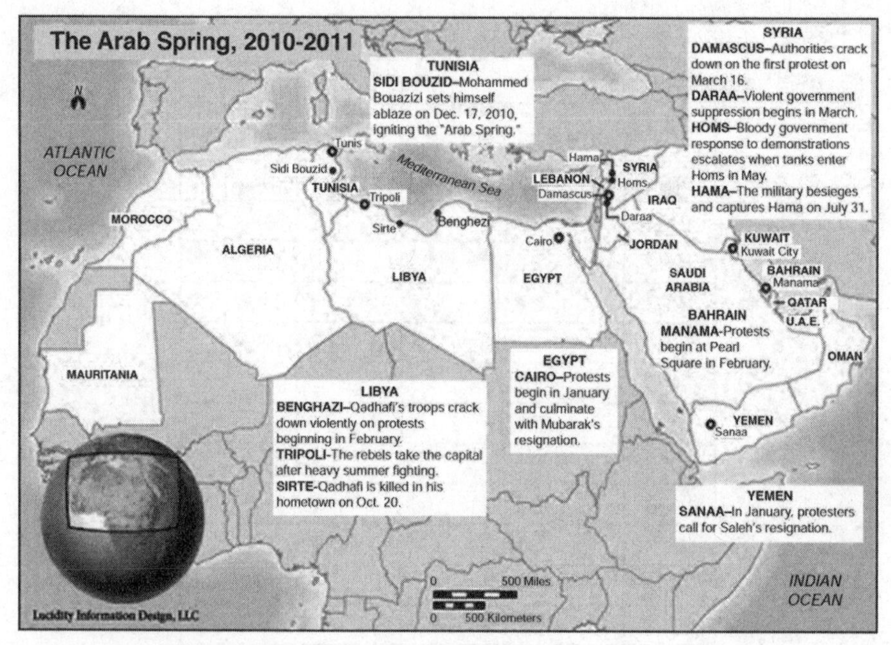

Source: Foreign Policy Association onlin, January 13,2012 (adapted)

25 Based on the information shown on this map, the term *Arab Spring* can be defined as

(1) regional protests against government leaders
(2) a geopolitical alliance for North African and West Asian countries
(3) public support for military crackdowns
(4) terrorist attacks conducted by al-Qaeda

25 _____

26 Locke and Rousseau, as writers during the Enlightenment, expanded the concept of

(1) total war
(2) self-sufficiency
(3) natural law
(4) divine right 26 ____

27 Simón Bolívar, Ho Chi Minh, and Jomo Kenyatta are significant historical figures because they all

(1) instituted theocratic reforms
(2) formed international peacekeeping alliances
(3) established worldwide trade networks
(4) led independence movements 27 ____

28 The purpose of Lenin's New Economic Policy in the Soviet Union and Deng's Four Modernizations in China was to

(1) eliminate elements of a free-market economy
(2) establish isolationist policies
(3) improve agricultural and industrial production
(4) discourage investments by foreigners 28 ____

Base your answers to questions 29 and 30 on the excerpts below and on your knowledge of social studies.

> Immediately after the publication of the present decree, all suspects within the territory of the Republic and still at large, shall be placed in custody.
>
> The following are deemed suspects:
>
> –those who, by their conduct, associations, comments, or writings have shown themselves partisans [supporters] of tyranny or federalism and enemies of liberty; . . .
>
> — Law of Suspects, France, 1793

> Anyone who, by speech, writing, or any other act, uses or exploits the wounds of the National Tragedy to harm the institutions of the Democratic and Popular Republic of Algeria, to weaken the state, or to undermine the good reputation of its agents who honorably served it, or to tarnish the image of Algeria internationally, shall be punished by three to five years in prison and a fine of 250,000 to 500,000 dinars.
>
> — Decree Implementing the Charter for Peace and National Reconciliation, Algeria, 2006

29 Both of these excerpts reflect an intent to

(1) support human rights
(2) limit government's power
(3) eliminate dissent
(4) expand democracy

29 _____

30 According to the Algerian Decree, people may be punished for harming or weakening Algeria's

(1) trade
(2) media
(3) religion
(4) government

30 _____

In developing your answer to Part II, be sure to keep these general definitions in mind:

(a) describe means "to illustrate something in words or tell about it"

(b) discuss means "to make observations about something using facts, reasoning, and argument; to present in some detail"

PART II: THEMATIC ESSAY QUESTION

Directions: Write a well-organized essay that includes an introduction, several paragraphs addressing the task below, and a conclusion.

Theme: Culture and Intellectual Life

Intellectuals, philosophers, and leaders have often recorded their ideas in written works. These ideas have been used throughout history to guide societies and influence the course of national and regional development.

Task:

Select ***two*** intellectuals, philosophers, ***and/or*** leaders and a writing associated with that person and for ***each***

- Describe the historical circumstances surrounding this writing
- Describe a main idea found in this writing
- Discuss how this idea has influenced the development of a nation or region

You may use any intellectuals, philosophers, or leaders from your study of global history and geography. Some suggestions you might wish to consider include:

John Locke—*Two Treatises on Government*
Adam Smith—*Wealth of Nations*
Olympe de Gouges—*The Declaration of the Rights of Woman*
Karl Marx—*Communist Manifesto*
Theodor Herzl—*On the Jewish State*
Adolf Hitler—*Mein Kampf*
Elie Wiesel—*Night*
Mao Zedong—*Little Red Book*
Nelson Mandela—*Long Walk to Freedom*

You are *not* limited to these suggestions.

Do *not* use any intellectual, philosopher, or leader from the United States in your answer.

Guidelines:

In your essay, be sure to:
- Develop all aspects of the task
- Support the theme with relevant facts, examples, and details
- Use a logical and clear plan of organization, including an introduction and a conclusion that are beyond a restatement of the theme

In developing your answers to Part III, be sure to keep these general definitions in mind:

(a) describe means "to illustrate something in words or tell about it"
(b) discuss means "to make observations about something using facts, reasoning, and argument; to present in some detail"

PART III: DOCUMENT-BASED QUESTION

This question is based on the accompanying documents. The question is designed to test your ability to work with historical documents. Some of these documents have been edited for the purposes of this question. As you analyze the documents, take into account the source of each document and any point of view that may be presented in the document. Keep in mind that the language used in a document may reflect the historical context of the time in which it was written.

Historical Context:

Turning points are events that have changed the course of history and had an impact on multiple societies and regions. Some examples of turning points include the ***Opium War***, the ***Industrial Revolution***, and the ***Cold War***.

Task:

Using the information from the documents and your knowledge of global history and geography, answer the questions that follow each document in Part A. Your answers to the questions will help you write the Part B essay in which you will be asked to

Select ***two*** turning points mentioned in the historical context and for ***each***

- Describe the historical circumstances surrounding this turning point
- Discuss the impact of this turning point on societies and/or regions

Part A: Short-Answer Questions

Directions: Analyze the documents and answer the short-answer questions that follow each document in the space provided.

Document 1

> Two things happened in the eighteenth century that made it difficult for England to balance its trade with the East. First, the British became a nation of tea drinkers and the demand for Chinese tea rose astronomically [enormously]. It is estimated that the average London worker spent five percent of his or her total household budget on tea. Second, northern Chinese merchants began to ship Chinese cotton from the interior to the south to compete with the Indian cotton that Britain had used to help pay for its tea consumption habits. To prevent a trade imbalance, the British tried to sell more of their own products to China, but there was not much demand for heavy woolen fabrics in a country accustomed to either cotton padding or silk.
>
> The only solution was to increase the amount of Indian goods to pay for these Chinese luxuries, and increasingly in the seventeenth and eighteenth centuries the item provided to China was Bengal opium. With greater opium supplies had naturally come an increase in demand and usage throughout the country, in spite of repeated prohibitions by the Chinese government and officials. The British did all they could to increase the trade: They bribed officials, helped the Chinese work out elaborate smuggling schemes to get the opium into China's interior, and distributed free samples of the drug to innocent victims. . . .

Source: "The Opium War and Foreign Encroachment," Asia for Educators, Columbia University

1 According to this excerpt from "The Opium War and Foreign Encroachment," what was ***one*** reason England sold opium to China? [1]

____

____

Document 2

Lin Tse-Hsü was appointed imperial commissioner by the Chinese emperor to address the issue of opium trade and consumption.

> This is an instruction to foreigners of all nations:
>
> Foreigners who trade in Canton have realized large profits. They can sell all the goods they have brought to China and purchase on short order any merchandise they wish to buy. Because of this fact, the number of ships that come to China to trade has increased from 50 or 60 in the old days to more than 150 in recent years. His Majesty the Emperor allows all of you to trade in China without discrimination, and his generosity has provided you with the opportunity to realize the profit you desire. If the trade is stopped, where will your profit come from? Moreover, tea and rhubarb are essential to foreigners' livelihood, and we have never begrudged [disapproved] the fact that year after year you have shipped these valuable products to your own countries. The favor we have bestowed upon you is very great indeed.
>
> Feeling grateful for the favor you have received, you should at least observe our law and refrain from enriching yourselves by deliberately inflicting harm upon your benefactors. Why do you choose to ship to China opium which you yourselves do not consume in order not only to swindle people out of their money but also to endanger their very lives? You have used this evil thing to poison the Chinese people for dozens of years, and the amount of profit you have realized from this immoral trade must be very large indeed. This devilish conduct on your part not only stirs the indignation of mankind but is intolerable to Heaven as well. . . .

Source: Lin Tse-Hsü, "A Message to Foreign Traders," March 18, 1839, *China in Transition: 1517–1911*, Van Nostrand Reinhold Company

2 In this letter, what is ***one*** message against the opium trade in China that Lin Tse-Hsü is sending to foreign traders? [1]

___

___

Document 3a

. . . In the spring of 1840 twenty British warships and troop transports appeared off Canton to blockade the port. The Opium War began.

Although the war dragged on for nearly three years, English guns and troops eventually proved too much for the Chinese. Seizing Canton, Shanghai, and other ports, the English sent gunboats up the Yangtze River nearly to Nanking [Nanjing]. Toward the end of 1842, concluding that further fighting was useless, the Emperor Tao-kuang agreed to peace talks. . . .

Source: James I. Clark, *China*, McDougal, Littell & Company, 1982

3*a* According to James I. Clark, what was ***one*** effect of the Opium War on China? [1]

____

____

Document 3b

Excerpts from the Treaty of Nanjing

> . . . *Article 2.* Determined the opening of five Chinese cities—Canton, Fuzhou, Xiamen, Ningbo, and Shanghai—to residence by British subjects and their families "for the purpose of carrying on their mercantile pursuits, without molestation [interference] or restraint." It also permitted the establishment of consulates in each of those cities.
>
> *Article 3.* "The Island of Hong Kong to be possessed in perpetuity [forever]" by Victoria and her successors, and ruled as they "shall see fit."
>
> *Article 4.* Payment of $6 million by the Qing "as the value of the opium which was delivered up in Canton." . . .

Source: Jonathan D. Spence, *The Search for Modern China*, W. W. Norton & Company, 1991

3b What was ***one*** economic impact of the Treaty of Nanjing on China? [1]

____

____

Document 4

Source: Philip Dorf, *Visualized Modern History*, Oxford Book Company, 1947

4 Based on the information in this drawing, state ***one*** way the shift from the domestic system to the factory system changed the way people worked. [1]

____

____

Document 5a

View from Blackfriars Bridge

The Blackfriars Bridge is in Manchester, England, over the Irwell River.

Source: *The Graphic,* October 14, 1876

Document 5b

The State of the Thames [River].

To the Editor of *The Times*.

Sir,—I traversed this day by steamboat the space between London and Hungerford bridges between half-past 1 and 2 o'clock; it was low water, and I think the tide must have been near the turn. The appearance and the smell of the water forced themselves at once on my attention. The whole of the river was an opaque pale brown fluid. In order to test the degree of opacity [cloudiness], I tore up some white cards into pieces, moistened them so as to make them sink easily below the surface, and then dropped some of these pieces into the water at every pier the boat came to; before they had sunk an inch below the surface they were indistinguishable, though the sun shone brightly at the time; and when the pieces fell edgeways the lower part was hidden from sight before the upper part was under water. This happened at St. Paul's-wharf, Blackfriars-bridge, Temple-wharf, Southwark-bridge, and Hungerford; and I have no doubt would have occurred further up and down the river. Near the bridges the feculence [impurities] rolled up in clouds so dense that they were visible at the surface, even in water of this kind. . . .

I am, Sir, your obedient servant,
Royal Institution. July 7.
M. FARADAY.

Source: Michael Faraday, Letter to the Editor, *The Times*, July 9, 1855

5 Based on these documents, what is ***one*** environmental effect industrialization had on English cities? [1]

____

____

Document 6

Cotton Industry

. . . India is a birth-place of cotton manufacture. It probably flourished here before the dawn of authentic history. Indian cotton trade was extensive from the earliest times to the end of the eighteenth century. In the beginning of the nineteenth century, British industry started flourishing while Indian industry declined. Generally attributed causes for the decline of the Indian cotton industry are—the invention of the powerloom and other mechanical appliances, monopoly of trade created by the East India Company in their own favour, the imposition of a heavy tariff on Indian cotton and cotton goods in England, exemption of duty on British staples imported in India, and the raising of duties on Indian goods from time to time. . . .

By 1840, the East India Company ceased to be directly interested in Indian trade. In its new role as an administrator, it presented a petition to British Parliament for the removal of invidious [unfair] duties which discouraged and repressed Indian industries. [The East India] Company's capitalists and Indian capitalists were encouraged to establish industries in India.

The nature and extent of this new industrial awakening in India is well illustrated by the history of cotton mills. By 1850, the European factory system became sufficiently developed and coordinated [enough] to be transplanted to the east. The first cotton mill was started in Bombay in 1854 and by the end of the nineteenth century, their number was increased to 193 of which 82 were in the Bombay area alone. After 1877 several cotton mills were started in a number of other places namely, Nagpur, Ahmedabad, Sholapur, Kanpur, Calcutta and Madras. Jamsetji Tata and Morarji Gokuldas were the first Indian manufacturers who started mills in Nagpur and Sholapur respectively. . . .

Source: Usha Rani Bansal and B. B. Bansal, "Industries in India During 18th and 19th Century," *Indian Journal of History of Science*, April 1984 (adapted)

6*a* According to Bansal and Bansal, what was ***one*** impact British industrialization had on India *before* 1840? [1]

6*b* According to Bansal and Bansal, what was ***one*** impact British industrialization had on India *after* 1840? [1]

Document 7

. . . The war [World War II] produced a redistribution of power more sweeping than in any previous period of history. Among the leading nations in the multipolar prewar international system, Japan, Italy, and Germany were defeated and occupied. Exhausted and nearly bankrupt, once-dominant Britain was reduced to a second-rank power. Defeated at the outset [beginning] of the war and liberated by its allies, France suffered even greater loss of status and power. The Eurocentric world largely through a process of self-destruction came to an inglorious [shameful] end. A new bipolar system replaced the old. Only the United States and the Soviet Union emerged from the war capable of wielding significant influence beyond their borders. . . .

Source: George C. Herring, *From Colony to Superpower: U.S. Foreign Relations Since 1776*, Oxford University Press, 2008

7 According to George C. Herring, what is ***one*** way power was redistributed after World War II? [1]

____

____

Document 8a

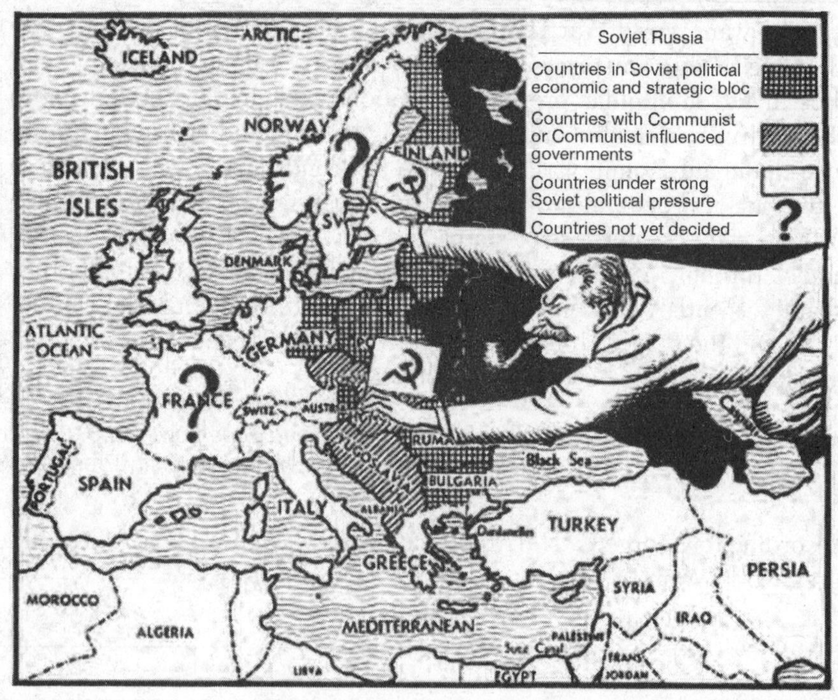

Source: Leslie Illingworth, *Daily Mail*, June 16, 1947 (adapted)

Document 8b

. . . Between the signing of the Yalta treaty, with its promise of free elections in Eastern Europe, and Winston Churchill's "Iron Curtain" speech, which foretold the rise of totalitarianism, a year elapsed. During that year, a great many changes took place. The Red Army brought Moscow-trained secret policemen into every occupied country, put local communists in control of national radio stations, and began dismantling youth groups and other civic organizations. They arrested, murdered, and deported people whom they believed to be anti-Soviet, and they brutally enforced a policy of ethnic cleansing. . . .

Source: Anne Applebaum, *Iron Curtain: The Crushing of Eastern Europe 1944–1956*, Anchor Books, 2013

8 Based on these documents, state ***one*** action the Soviet Union took in Eastern Europe after World War II. [1]

____

____

Document 9a

In the early 1960s, Cuba and the Soviet Union became allies.

Cuba under Castro, 1962

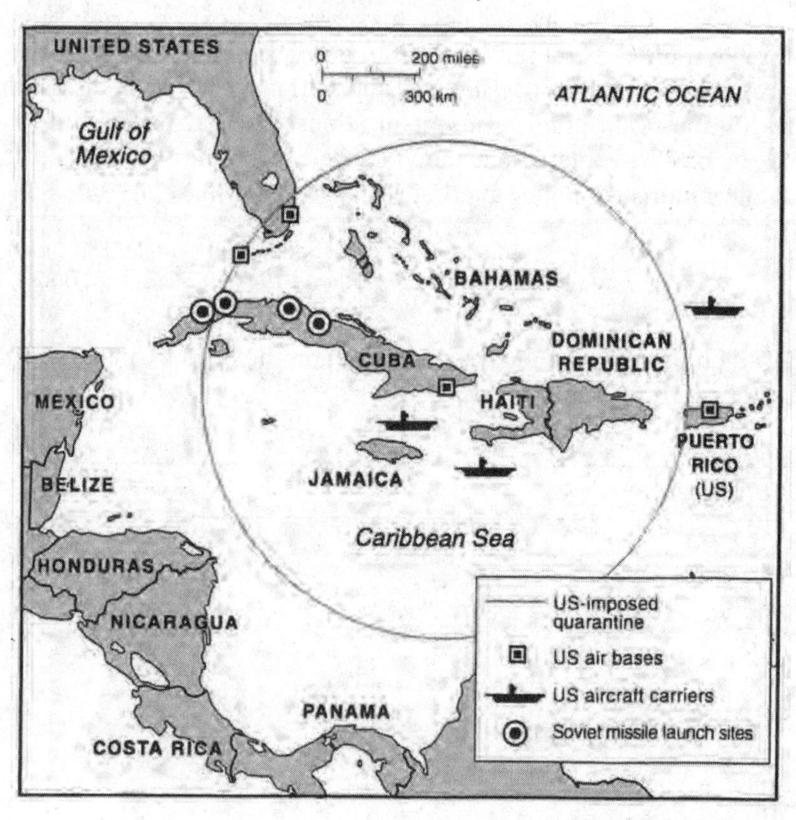

Source: *World History on File, Second Edition, The 20th Century*, Facts on File (adapted)

9*a* Based on the information in this map, state ***one*** way the Cold War affected Cuba as a result of becoming a Soviet ally. [1]

____

____

Document 9b

Excerpt from Nikita Khrushchev's letter to President Kennedy

His Excellency
Mr. John F. Kennedy
President of the United States of America
Washington

You, Mr. President, are not declaring a quarantine, but rather issuing an ultimatum, and you are threatening that if we do not obey your orders, you will then use force. Think about what you are saying! And you want to persuade me to agree to this! What does it mean to agree to these demands? It would mean for us to conduct our relations with other countries not by reason, but by yielding to tyranny. You are not appealing to reason; you want to intimidate us. . . .

Respectfully,
/s/ N. Khrushchev

Moscow
24 October 1962

Source: Library of Congress

9*b* What is ***one*** concern Nikita Khrushchev expressed in his reaction to President Kennedy's communication with the Soviet Union? [1]

____

____

Part B: Essay

Directions: Write a well-organized essay that includes an introduction, several paragraphs, and a conclusion. Use evidence from *at least* ***four*** documents in your essay. Support your response with relevant facts, examples, and details. Include additional outside information.

Historical Context:

> Turning points are events that have changed the course of history and had an impact on multiple societies and regions. Some examples of turning points include the ***Opium War***, the ***Industrial Revolution***, and the ***Cold War***.

Task:

> Using the information from the documents and your knowledge of global history and geography, write an essay in which you
>
> Select ***two*** turning points mentioned in the historical context and for ***each***
>
> - Describe the historical circumstances surrounding this turning point
> - Discuss the impact of this turning point on societies and/or regions

Guidelines:

In your essay, be sure to:
- Develop all aspects of the task
- Incorporate information from *at least* ***four*** documents
- Incorporate relevant outside information
- Support the theme with relevant facts, examples, and details
- Use a logical and clear plan of organization, including an introduction and a conclusion that are beyond a restatement of the theme

Answers June 2018

Global History and Geography

Answer Key

PART I (1–30)

1. 1	**7.** 4	**13.** 1	**19.** 3	**25.** 1
2. 3	**8.** 2	**14.** 1	**20.** 1	**26.** 3
3. 2	**9.** 2	**15.** 2	**21.** 4	**27.** 4
4. 1	**10.** 4	**16.** 4	**22.** 4	**28.** 3
5. 3	**11.** 1	**17.** 1	**23.** 2	**29.** 3
6. 2	**12.** 3	**18.** 1	**24.** 4	**30.** 4

PART II: Thematic Essay See Answers Explained section.

PART III: Document-Based Essay See Answers Explained section.

Answers Explained

PART I

1. **1** The time line shows the events from France's acquisition of Saint Domingue (Haiti) in 1697 to the time when Haiti declared independence in 1804. The question asks why the French government "took action" in Haiti. The time line shows that Toussaint L'Ouverture led a slave rebellion and eventually assumed command of the French army in Saint Domingue (Haiti). At this point, France stood to lose its control over the colony. Thus, France sent 20,000 troops to attempt to reclaim French authority and protect its investments in its American colony, Saint Domingue (Haiti).

WRONG CHOICES EXPLAINED:

(2) Saint Domingue (Haiti) was a French colony in the Americas. While there was a rebellion in Saint Domingue (Haiti), the French government itself was never in danger.

(3) According to the time line, in 1794, the Jacobin government in France ended slavery in all French colonies. Additionally, the time line does not mention returning enslaved blacks to Africa.

(4) Toussaint L'Ouverture led a rebellion for independence against the French government. It would not make sense for France to send troops to aid that rebellion. France wanted to protect its investments in the colony as opposed to helping Saint Domingue (Haiti) achieve independence.

2. **3** A political map is designed to show the boundaries of countries, states, and major cities. In other words, a political map depicts governmental boundaries.

WRONG CHOICES EXPLAINED:

(1) Climate is related to geography and therefore does not appear on a political map. There are maps that are specifically designed to depict climate, but they are not political maps.

(2) A political map does not show the various languages that are spoken in a specific region of the world. Although a political map shows governmental boundaries, many different languages can be spoken within one country or state.

(4) Mineral deposits would most likely be depicted on a resource map and are not directly related to government. Therefore, they do not appear on a political map.

3. **2** When a historian considers primary source evidence (an eyewitness account) about a historical event, he or she must take into account the different points of view of those primary sources. A point of view is how an individual interprets an event based on his or her background, personal experiences, and opinions. Since everyone has a different background, different personal experiences, and different opinions, primary sources tend to contain bias (favor one side of an issue over another). Therefore, historians must watch for bias and take into account different points of view when considering primary source evidence to understand historical events better.

WRONG CHOICES EXPLAINED:

(1) Despite often containing bias, eyewitness accounts are extremely important in the construction of historical events. Without these eyewitness accounts, historians would not have any real understanding of past events.

(3) Emphasizing the importance of religious values would be emphasizing bias. Historians try to avoid emphasizing bias.

(4) Summaries written by journalists are not primary sources. They are secondary sources.

4. **1** Prior to the Scientific Revolution in Europe, understanding of the natural world came from the Bible and the Roman Catholic Church. Beginning in the mid-1500s and fueled both by the knowledge gained from the Middle East as a result of fighting the Crusades and by the questioning spirit of the Renaissance, thinkers began to challenge old assumptions. They replaced these old assumptions with new theories based on the scientific method of observation and experimentation.

WRONG CHOICES EXPLAINED:

(2) During the Scientific Revolution, astronomers like Copernicus and Galileo used observation and experimentation to replace the Earth-centered geocentric model of the solar system with the heliocentric, or sun-centered, theory.

(3) During the Scientific Revolution, church doctrine, or the Roman Catholic Church's interpretation of the natural world, was replaced with the scientific method of observation and experimentation to understand the natural world better.

(4) The government did not have an important role in scientific research during the Scientific Revolution.

5. **3** The passage states that the Irish did not believe that the famine was the result of a natural disaster. Rather, they believed that it was a direct result of British colonial policies. The evidence that the Irish used to support this claim is that during the famine's worst years, many Anglo-Irish estates (English estates in Ireland) continued to export grain and livestock to England.

WRONG CHOICES EXPLAINED:

(1) The passage states that the Irish believed the potato famine was not a natural disaster. In other words, they did not believe that the famine was entirely caused by naturally occurring events. Likewise, there is no evidence to support the idea that the famine resulted in natural disasters.

(2) The passage does not mention exporting grain overseas. It does state that grain was exported back to England. However, this fact was used as evidence to support the claim that the famine was a result of British colonial practices.

(4) The passage states that Anglo-Irish estates were still producing and exporting grain even during the famine's worst years.

6. **2** Prior to Otto von Bismarck's unification of the 39 German states that formed the German Confederation, the German states were dominated by the Austro-Hungarian Empire. United by feelings of nationalism, Otto von Bismarck led Prussia through a series of wars. These included the Seven Weeks' War, in which Prussia gained North Germany, and the Franco-Prussian War. These wars brought southern Germany under Bismarck's control and led to Germany's unification.

WRONG CHOICES EXPLAINED:

(1), (3), and (4) Venezuela, France, and Serbia are not associated with Otto von Bismarck. Otto von Bismarck was the prime minister of Prussia and the unifier of Germany.

7. **4** The term Social Darwinism refers to Charles Darwin's idea of survival of the fittest and applies that idea to society. According to the theory of Social Darwinism, those who were fittest for survival were the ones who were the most successful and enjoyed the most wealth. This concept was used as justification for imperialism in the 19th century and led to the colonization of regions like Africa. Europeans believed non-Europeans to be inferior because they had not developed advanced scientific and technological understanding as the Europeans had. Europeans believed that it was their right and duty to bring European culture, ideas, and progress to non-European nations. Similarly, the "White Man's Burden" was the idea that Europeans had the duty to colonize and care for nonwhite indigenous people.

WRONG CHOICES EXPLAINED:

(1) Pacifism is defined as being opposed to war. This concept is not related to either Social Darwinism or the "White Man's Burden."

(2) Communism is a command economic system in which the state controls all means of production. Communism is in conflict with the ideas of Social Darwinism.

(3) As opposed to isolating Europe, Social Darwinism and the "White Man's Burden" increased European influence in the world and were used to justify imperialism. Isolationism and imperialism are opposing ideas.

8. **2** The Berlin Conference was a meeting of European nations from 1884–1885 to outline rules for dividing up Africa. The conference decided that any nation could claim land in Africa as long as that nation notified other nations of its claim and demonstrated an ability to control the claimed region. By the early 20th century, only Ethiopia and Liberia remained independent of European influence.

WRONG CHOICES EXPLAINED:

(1) The Boxer Rebellion took place in China from 1899–1901. It was a violent uprising against foreigners and Christians. This passage does not mention China.

(3) The Munich Pact, signed in 1938 by British Prime Minister Neville Chamberlain and the Prime Minister of France, Édouard Daladier, allowed Hitler to annex the Sudetenland. This passage does not mention this annexation.

(4) The Ottoman Empire collapsed at the end of World War I. It was officially gone in 1922 when Kemal Atatürk and the nationalists overthrew the last Ottoman sultan. This passage does not mention the Ottoman Empire.

9. **2** Kemal Atatürk helped overthrow the last sultan of the Ottoman Empire and became the president of the newly established Republic of Turkey in 1922. He had the goal of transforming Turkey into a modern nation by "westernizing" Turkey in a similar way that Peter the Great did for Russia. Atatürk forbade the wearing of traditional clothing like fezzes for men and veils for women. He also replaced the Arabic alphabet with the Latin alphabet used in Western countries.

WRONG CHOICES EXPLAINED:

(1) Emperor Meiji was restored to power in Japan in 1868. Although he sought to modernize Japan, the changes listed in the question—such as replacing Arabic script with the Latin alphabet—are associated with Turkey, not Japan.

(3) Jiang Jieshi (Chiang Kai-shek) served as the leader of China from 1928 until he was exiled to Taiwan after the Communist Revolution led by Mao Zedong in 1949. None of the changes listed in the question are associated with China.

(4) Benito Mussolini was the fascist leader of Italy from 1925 until 1945. None of the changes listed in the question are associated with Italy.

10. **4** The Bolshevik Revolution is an appropriate heading for this partial outline because all the events listed are effects of this revolution. After the March Revolution of 1917 led Czar Nicholas II to abdicate (give up) the throne, the leader of the Duma (parliament) established a provisional government led by Alexander Kerensky. This provisional government was eventually toppled by Vladimir Lenin and the Bolsheviks after Lenin's return to Russia. To solidify his power, Lenin ordered Czar Nicholas II and his entire family to be executed. Eventually, a civil war broke out between Lenin's Red Army and the White Army who opposed them.

WRONG CHOICES EXPLAINED:

(1) The Russo-Japanese War was caused by disagreements between Russia and Japan over who would control parts of Korea and Manchuria. This war was not discussed in the partial outline.

(2) The Congress of Vienna was an assembly of European nations that met from 1814–1815 after the Napoleonic Wars. The goal was to prevent further French aggression and to reorganize Europe politically. The Congress of Vienna was not discussed in the partial outline.

(3) The Treaty of Versailles officially ended World War I in 1919 and punished Germany greatly. This treaty is not discussed in the partial outline.

11. **1** In 1928, Stalin began the process of collectivization in which he seized over 25 million privately-owned farms in the Soviet Union. His plan to create large government-owned farms was met with resistance, particularly among the kulaks, a class of relatively wealthy peasants, in Ukraine. To crush the kulak's resistance, Stalin organized mass starvation of the kulaks. This led to the deaths of millions by the early 1930s, which is demonstrated in the chart "Population Figures for Ukraine."

WRONG CHOICES EXPLAINED:

(2) The Jewish homeland was not established until 1948.

(3) Although Eastern Europe has been impacted by various flu pandemics (most notably in 1889, 1918, and 1977), there was no flu epidemic that killed millions from the 1920s to the 1930s.

(4) World War I officially ended in 1919. The population statistics depicted in this chart show changes from 1926–1939.

12. **3** Within the term *totalitarianism* appears the word "total," meaning that the government employs the use of total power. Totalitarian governments are typically dictatorships that control all aspects of life and provide for very little freedom. One of the best examples of a totalitarian dictator is Joseph Stalin, who had total control over the Soviet Union and executed political enemies. Other examples of totalitarian dictators are Benito Mussolini, who was the fascist dictator of Italy from 1925 through World War II, and Adolf Hitler in Germany.

WRONG CHOICES EXPLAINED:

(1) Although many totalitarian dictators did believe that change and progress are beneficial, this is not what defines *totalitarianism*.

(2) Most totalitarian dictatorships rely on fear, intimidation, and the use of the military—as opposed to faith and religious doctrine—to maintain power.

(4) Although not all totalitarian regimes are communist, many have been communist. Communist governments do not allow for privatizing industry and property.

13. **1** This excerpt states that it was inevitable (certain) that the Japanese shipping industry was important to the national economy, should have been linked with the military program, and was the "drive for expansion both on the mainland of Asia and in the waters to the south." Therefore, Japanese military and industrial needs were tied to expansion.

WRONG CHOICES EXPLAINED:

(2) This excerpt begins by stating, "Japanese shipping should be linked with the military program and the drive for expansion." Therefore, shipping was a high priority for Japan.

(3) In the 1930s, when this document was written, Japan's lack of natural resources was the driving force that led the country to invade Manchuria and, later, China. Additionally, this excerpt makes no mention of Japan's satisfaction with its existing resources.

(4) Although the fishing industry in Japan was prominent, as evidenced by the fact that Japan is a series of islands, this excerpt does not mention the fishing industry.

14. **1** Appeasement means to give in to an aggressor to avoid war. After World War I, many European nations, including Britain and France, wanted to avoid war at all costs. When Hitler decided to defy the terms of the Treaty of Versailles, which limited the size of Germany's army, by building up the military, the League of Nations did very little. When Hitler entered the Rhineland, the British adopted the policy of appeasement to avoid war. Then in 1938, at the Munich Conference, British Prime Minister Neville Chamberlain, along with the French Prime Minister Édouard Daladier, appeased Hitler by allowing Hitler to take the Sudetenland.

WRONG CHOICES EXPLAINED:

(2) Nonalignment is a term that is associated with the Cold War. During the Cold War, many nations, particularly new nations in Asia and Africa, did not side with either the communists, led by the Soviet Union, or the Western Bloc, led by the United States.

(3) Reparations are payments made to make amends for doing something wrong. For example, Germany was ordered to pay reparations following World War I for being the major aggressor.

(4) Colonialism is the policy that many European countries adopted to acquire new lands and to control other nations both politically and economically.

15. **2** Both the Truman Doctrine and the Marshall Plan were established with the goal of containing communism following World War II and the start of the Cold War. The Truman Doctrine was the United States's foreign policy of containment. This policy included plans to help weak countries resist influence from the Soviet Union. The Marshall Plan was also part of the United States's policy of containment. According to this plan, the United States would help nations that were devastated by World War II to prevent them from falling to communism.

WRONG CHOICES EXPLAINED:

(1) The Hungarian Revolution was a 1956 uprising in Hungary against the communist government. It is not associated with either the Truman Doctrine or the Marshall Plan.

(3) Both the Truman Doctrine and the Marshall Plan predate the Soviet blockade of Berlin. The Berlin Airlift sought to end the Soviet blockade of Berlin and was successful by 1949.

(4) The United States was part of the NATO alliance and would not have wanted to destroy it.

16. **4** Another name for a market economy is capitalism. A capitalist market system depends on business competition to keep prices competitive and to incentivize the creation of quality products. In a command economy, also called socialism and/or communism, the government controls most means of production. Therefore, there is much less competition.

WRONG CHOICES EXPLAINED:

(1) A command economy has more government control than a market economy, not less. In a command system, the government maintains more control over the means of production.

(2) A command economy offers fewer consumer choices than a market economy because a command economy has less private business and, therefore, less competition.

(3) A market economy has more private ownership than a command economy, not less. A market system relies on private enterprise as a foundation for competition.

17. **1** After the end of World War II, Britain, which had tremendous war debts, was ready to grant India independence to avoid the costs of maintaining overseas colonies. The question, though, was whether Indian Muslims or Indian Hindus should receive political power. Many Muslims resisted attempts to include them in a largely Hindu government. Riots broke out between Hindus and Muslims in many cities throughout India. After thousands were left dead in the riots, Britain decided that the only way to ensure a safe and secure region was to partition India into two separate nations. In 1947, Pakistan was created.

WRONG CHOICES EXPLAINED:

(2) Although Israel was created to provide for a Jewish homeland in Palestine, Egypt was not created as a result of religious tensions.

(3) Brazil gained its independence from Portugal, and Colombia gained its independence from Spain. Neither nation was created as a result of religious tensions.

(4) Neither Vietnam nor Burma was created as a result of religious tensions.

18. **1** Inspired by Mao Zedong's Great Leap Forward in China, Cambodia's communist leader Pol Pot wanted to create an agrarian communist society. Called the Super Great Leap Forward, beginning in 1975, Pol Pot and the Khmer Rouge expelled foreigners, banned foreign languages, banned religion, shut businesses, and forbade the use of money. All Cambodian cities were evacuated, and many residents were forced into peasant slave labor. To ensure that all remnants of Cambodia's capitalist past were abolished, Pol Pot and the Khmer Rouge led mass killings of those who opposed his agrarian communist society, including educated doctors, lawyers, and teachers as well as ethnic groups and minorities.

WRONG CHOICES EXPLAINED:

(2) Leonid Brezhnev's doctrine of détente led to the easing of Cold War tensions between the Soviet Union and the West. The policy of détente led to the signing of the Strategic Arms Limitation Talks (SALT) agreements between the United States and the Soviet Union. The doctrine of détente is not associated with Pol Pot and the Khmer Rouge in Cambodia.

(3) Mohandas Gandhi's Quit India program helped to unite Indian people against British rule in India's quest for independence. This movement is not associated with Pol Pot and the Khmer Rouge in Cambodia.

(4) Lech Walesa's Solidarity movement in Poland led to government recognition of the Solidarity union and helped to defeat communism in Poland. This movement was not an inspiration for Pol Pot and the Khmer Rouge, who wanted to strengthen communism.

19. **3** Both Mikhail Gorbachev of the Soviet Union and F. W. de Klerk of South Africa initiated reforms that led to significant political changes in their nations. Under the totalitarian regimes that preceded Gorbachev's election, change was slow and the economy began to stagnate. Gorbachev believed that economic and social reforms would not occur without the free flow of ideas and information. He therefore issued the policy of glasnost, or openness. Under this policy, churches were reopened, a free press was established, and political dissidents were released from prison. Then in 1985, he introduced the concept of perestroika, or an economic restructuring that allowed for more private businesses. Similarly, F. W. de Klerk initiated reforms in South Africa that led to the end of apartheid and the establishment of the first universal elections in 1994 in which all races of people could vote.

WRONG CHOICES EXPLAINED:

(1) By the 1980s, the Cold War was coming to an end. Nuclear tensions with the Soviet Union under the leadership of Mikhail Gorbachev began to ease. Therefore, the Soviet Union was not concerned with increasing its nuclear arsenal.

(2) Neither country pursued a policy of isolation from the rest of the world. The opposite is true for the Soviet Union under Mikhail Gorbachev. He issued the policy of glasnost, or openness, which led to the free flow of ideas.

(4) Neither leader opposed the presence of international observers during elections in their countries. F. W. de Klerk was the first president to allow all races to participate in elections in South Africa and, therefore, did not oppose the presence of international observers.

20. **1** Human rights violations were prevalent in Rwanda, Kosovo, and the Sudan in the late 20th century. In 1994, genocide took place in Rwanda between the Hutus and the Tutsis. In just a few months, the Hutus massacred over 1 million Tutsis. Similarly in Darfur, the Sudanese government supported Arab militias that attacked African villages. Despite peacekeeping missions, by 2006, over 400,000 people had been killed in the Sudan. Kosovo, a province in southern Serbia made up of mostly ethnic Albanians, erupted into violence in 1998 when an independence movement grew. The Serbian military invaded Kosovo and killed many ethnic Albanians.

WRONG CHOICES EXPLAINED:

(2) Chemical weapons were not used extensively in any of these regions in the late 20th century. The use of chemical weapons by a government against its own people is something that is more associated with places like Syria between 2012 and 2018.

(3) The conflicts in Rwanda, Kosovo, and the Sudan were ethnic and religious conflicts. They were not conflicts over national borders.

(4) A lack of water resources did not lead to conflicts in any of these regions. The conflicts in these regions were mainly ethnic and religious conflicts, not conflicts over natural resources.

21. **4** From a Mexican perspective, the argument against adopting the North American Free Trade Agreement (NAFTA) was that Mexican farmers could be undersold by farmers from the United States who could produce food at a lower cost. This is exactly what happened to many Mexican corn farmers in the decades after NAFTA was adopted. With cheap corn pouring over the border from the United States, many small corn farmers, particularly in southern Mexico, could not compete. Mexico lost close to a million farming jobs.

WRONG CHOICES EXPLAINED:

(1) The ability of Mexican industries to increase their exports (what they sell) to the United States would benefit Mexico and, therefore, would not be an argument against adopting NAFTA.

(2) Greater economic cooperation enhancing democratic reform would benefit Mexico and, therefore, would not be an argument against adopting NAFTA.

(3) The rapid growth of the Mexican economy would benefit Mexico and, therefore, would not be an argument against adopting NAFTA.

22. **4** This passage contains many phrases that lead to the conclusion that positive political changes are taking place in Africa. The passage states that many of the murderous dictators are gone. The author supports that claim with the fact that Idi Amin of Uganda is no longer in power. Additionally, the passage also points to the increased use of technology in the government by stating that the cabinet room of Rwanda's government is more high-tech than the White House cabinet room in the United States.

WRONG CHOICES EXPLAINED:

(1) The passage points to positive changes taking place in Africa. The passage uses the topic of war to demonstrate people's misconceptions about Africa. The passage clearly states that "the number of conflicts has dwindled" or declined.

(2) The passage states that Africa is in fact seeing a rise in the number of skilled technocrats.

(3) The passage states that the number of dictators has declined. It also says that Africa has witnessed the rise of skilled technocrats who understand the importance of receiving checks on their power.

23. **2** This chart shows population trends in China from 1990 to 2003. The chart clearly shows that the percentage of the population living in urban (city) areas has increased while the percentage of the population living in the rural (farming) areas has decreased. When demographic shifts from rural to urban areas like this happen, it is typically due to new job opportunities in cities. Since 1990, China has been industrializing with rapid economic growth. Therefore, cities have grown in population as citizens look for new employment opportunities. Similar demographic shifts occurred in Europe and the United States during the Industrial Revolution.

WRONG CHOICES EXPLAINED:

(1) If famine was a major issue in China between 1990 and 2003, the population would have declined in both rural and urban areas. However, the percentages in each area would have remained stable. Instead, the chart shows a shift in the population from rural to urban areas.

(3) The spread of disease would most likely have caused a population decline in urban areas. Diseases spread rapidly through cities. The chart, on the other hand, shows a population increase in cities (urban areas).

(4) The chart depicts a population shift from rural areas to urban areas as opposed to a decline in the overall population. Therefore, the one-child policy does not explain this shift.

24. **4** This chart, depicting population trends in China from 1990 to 2003, shows a shift in the population from rural (farming) areas to urban (city) areas. As a result, China has seen overcrowding in many urban areas. Many cities in China have populations of over 20 or 30 million people.

WRONG CHOICES EXPLAINED:

(1) A population shift to cities does not cause a shortage in recruits for the military since military recruits can come from urban areas.

(2) Urban areas are places of employment opportunities. The shift in the population to cities would increase the labor supply, not decrease it.

(3) The chart shows an increase in the population in urban areas and a decrease in the population in rural areas. The percentage of the population living in rural areas was 73.59 percent in 1990 and was only 59.47 percent in 2003. Therefore, there is not a growing percentage of the population living in rural areas.

25. **1** Based on the information shown on this map, the term *Arab Spring* refers to regional protests against government leaders. Many clues on the map support this answer. In Libya, the map states that Qadhafi's troops cracked down violently on protests. In Egypt, the map states that protests began in January and ended with the resignation of the country's leader, Hosni Mubarak. In Syria, the map states that authorities began to crack down on protests beginning in March. The entire movement began in Tunisia when Mohammed Bouazizi set himself on fire, igniting the *Arab Spring*.

WRONG CHOICES EXPLAINED:

(2) The map does not depict cooperation in the form of a geopolitical alliance between North African and West Asian countries. Instead, it depicts protests in each of the countries displayed on the map and the reactions from the government in power.

(3) Nothing on the map demonstrates public support for military crackdowns. Although the map does state that military crackdowns took place, particularly in Libya and Syria, nothing on the map states that there was public support for these crackdowns.

(4) Al-Qaeda, the terrorist organization that claimed responsibility for the attacks of September 11th on the World Trade Center and the Pentagon, is not mentioned on the map.

26. **3** Locke and Rousseau were Enlightenment philosophers who emphasized the importance of natural law. According to these philosophers, human beings in their natural state have certain rights that cannot be taken away from them by any government. According to Locke and this theory of natural law, all human beings have the natural rights of life, liberty, and property, and the purpose of government is to protect these natural rights. Rousseau believed that, according to natural law, all men are equal and should be treated equally by the law.

WRONG CHOICES EXPLAINED:

(1) Enlightenment philosophers like Locke and Rousseau concerned themselves with the natural rights of human beings and the role that the government plays in protecting those natural rights. They were not supporters of total war.

(2) Self-sufficiency, or being able to provide everything that is necessary for survival, was not a key idea of Enlightenment philosophers. Locke and Rousseau supported the idea that governments were necessary to protect people's natural rights.

(4) Divine right, or the theory that power comes from God, was the theory used by monarchs (kings and queens) to justify their absolute authority. Enlightenment thinkers like Locke and Rousseau argued against this theory. They instead claimed that a government's power comes from the consent of the governed. In other words, they claimed that the people give the government its power.

27. **4** Simón Bolívar, Ho Chi Minh, and Jomo Kenyatta are significant historical figures because they all led independence movements in their respective regions. Simón Bolívar led

his native country of Venezuela to independence from Spain in 1811. He then went on to join forces with José de San Martín to liberate Bolivia, Colombia, Ecuador, and Peru. In 1945, Ho Chi Minh led Vietnam to independence from France. Jomo Kenyatta led the Kenyan independence movement against British colonial rule in the 1950s and 1960s.

WRONG CHOICES EXPLAINED:

(1) Theocracy is a government ruled by those who claim they are guided by divine forces. None of the people listed in the question established theocracies or are associated with theocratic forms of government.

(2) Simón Bolívar, Ho Chi Minh, and Jomo Kenyatta are all known for independence movements, not international peacekeeping alliances.

(3) None of the people listed in the question are notable in history for establishing worldwide trade networks.

28. **3** Both Lenin's New Economic Policy in the Soviet Union and Deng's Four Modernizations in China were similar in that each leader sought to increase agricultural and industrial production in his nation. After the Bolshevik Revolution in Russia, Lenin did not immediately attempt to install a communist economic system. Instead, he allowed for some private ownership of small farms and industries, but he took control of major industries, banks, and farms. This allowed Russia to recover agriculturally and industrially after World War I. In China after the death of Mao Zedong in 1975, Deng Xiaoping emerged as China's most powerful leader. He supported a set of goals known as the Four Modernizations that hoped to improve China in the areas of agriculture, industry, defense, and science. Deng's policies allowed for foreign investment and ideas. His goals were met with success as China industrialized throughout the 1980s.

WRONG CHOICES EXPLAINED:

(1) Neither Lenin's New Economic Policy nor Deng's Four Modernizations eliminated elements of a free-market economy. Lenin allowed for small farms and industries to remain privately owned. Deng allowed for more free-market ideas in China. For example, in China, farmers could sell their surplus for profit and some private businesses could operate.

(2) Neither Lenin nor Deng sought to establish isolationist policies. The opposite is true, particularly in China where Deng Xiaoping encouraged more Western ideas and foreign investments.

(4) Both Lenin and Deng encouraged foreign investments to increase industrial and agricultural output. Neither leader discouraged investments by foreigners.

29. **3** Both of these excerpts reflect an intent to eliminate dissent, or speaking out against the ideas held by the government. Both documents contain key phrases that demonstrate their intent to eliminate dissent against the government. The *Law of Suspects*, written in France during the Reign of Terror of the French Revolution, states that those who support tyranny or are considered "enemies of liberty" will be placed in custody. The *Decree Implementing the Charter for Peace and National Reconciliation*, written in Algeria in 2006, states that anyone who attempts to weaken the state in speech, writing, or other means will be jailed and fined.

WRONG CHOICES EXPLAINED:

(1) Both excerpts mention imprisoning those who speak out against the commonly held beliefs of the government. This is in direct contrast to human rights.

(2) Neither excerpt mentions limiting the government's power. By discouraging dissent and threatening those who speak out against the government, these governments are increasing their power.

(4) Although the documents might be misinterpreted as attempting to protect freedom and democracy, the intent of each is to warn those who speak out against the government of the penalties they will face for doing so.

30. **4** There are clues in the Algerian Decree that lead to the conclusion that people may be punished for harming or weakening Algeria's government. This document states, "Anyone who . . . exploits the wounds of the National Tragedy to harm the institutions of the Democratic and Popular Republic of Algeria, to weaken the state . . ." will face a penalty. In this case, "state" means government.

WRONG CHOICES EXPLAINED:

(1), (2), and (3) Trade, media, and religion are not mentioned in the decree.

THEMATIC ESSAY: GENERIC SCORING RUBRIC

Score of 5:
- Shows a thorough understanding of the theme or problem
- Addresses all aspects of the task
- Shows an ability to analyze, evaluate, compare and/or contrast issues and events
- Richly supports the theme or problem with relevant facts, examples, and details
- Is a well-developed essay, consistently demonstrating a logical and clear plan of organization
- Introduces the theme or problem by establishing a framework that is beyond a simple restatement of the task and concludes with a summation of the theme or problem

Score of 4:
- Shows a good understanding of the theme or problem
- Addresses all aspects of the task
- Shows an ability to analyze, evaluate, compare and/or contrast issues and events
- Includes relevant facts, examples, and details, but may not support all aspects of the theme or problem evenly
- Is a well-developed essay, demonstrating a logical and clear plan of organization
- Introduces the theme or problem by establishing a framework that is beyond a simple restatement of the task and concludes with a summation of the theme or problem

Score of 3:
- Shows a satisfactory understanding of the theme or problem
- Addresses most aspects of the task or addresses all aspects in a limited way
- Shows an ability to analyze or evaluate issues and events, but not in any depth
- Includes some facts, examples, and details
- Is a satisfactorily developed essay, demonstrating a general plan of organization
- Introduces the theme or problem by repeating the task and concludes by repeating the theme or problem

Score of 2:
- Shows limited understanding of the theme or problem
- Attempts to address the task
- Develops a faulty analysis or evaluation of issues and events
- Includes few facts, examples, and details, and may include information that contains inaccuracies
- Is a poorly organized essay, lacking focus
- Fails to introduce or summarize the theme or problem

Score of 1:
- Shows very limited understanding of the theme or problem
- Lacks an analysis or evaluation of the issues and events
- Includes little or no accurate or relevant facts, examples, or details
- Attempts to complete the task, but demonstrates a major weakness in organization
- Fails to introduce or summarize the theme or problem

Score of 0: Fails to address the task, is illegible, or is a blank paper

PART II: THEMATIC ESSAY QUESTION

Written works have often been the means by which intellectuals, philosophers, and leaders have shared their ideas and have influenced nations throughout history. Two philosophers whose written works influenced the development of nations are John Locke, who wrote *Two Treatises on Government*, and Karl Marx, who wrote *The Communist Manifesto*. Locke's writings had a mainly positive influence on societies, as his writing led to the development of democratic ideas. In contrast, Marx's writings led to the development of a totalitarian communist regime in Russia that had many negative consequences.

John Locke's *Two Treatises on Government* led mainly to positive outcomes, as his ideas were used to establish some of the first democratic governments. In the 17th century during the Enlightenment, the ideas of using logic and reasoning, emphasized during the Scientific Revolution, began to be applied to government and society. This movement began in England with two political philosophers, Thomas Hobbes and John Locke, who disagreed over which government is best. Hobbes believed that people will always act in their own self-interest and, therefore, that the best type of government was an absolute monarchy to maintain control over society. In his written work, Locke argued the opposite. He believed that all people are born free and equal and that they have the same natural rights of life, liberty, and property. Locke stated that the purpose of government is to protect these natural rights. The government is given its power, he believed, by the consent of the governed. He argued that if the government fails to protect people's natural rights, the people have a right to abolish the government and establish a new one. These ideas influenced other Enlightenment thinkers like Rousseau, Voltaire, and Montesquieu. By the 18th century, many of the ideas put forth in Locke's *Two Treatises on Government* began to influence other nations. In the United States, Thomas Jefferson wrote the Declaration of Independence. He was influenced by Locke's idea that a government's purpose is to protect people's natural rights, and when a government fails to do so, the people have a right to abolish it. In the late 18th century, these ideas helped spur the outbreak of the French Revolution of 1789. Locke's ideas that people are born free and equal in rights appeared in the French document the *Declaration of the Rights of Man and of the Citizen*.

While John Locke's ideas were influential in establishing the ideas of democracy, Karl Marx's *The Communist Manifesto* led to the establishment of a totalitarian communist regime in Russia. Many economic philosophies developed during the Industrial Revolution, which took place in the 18th and 19th centuries. Prior to Karl Marx, Adam Smith's *The Wealth of Nations* argued that a free economy with little government interference would guarantee economic progress. By the mid-19th century, however, Marx had witnessed the effects of the free-market system. He believed that it continued to enrich the wealthy and further impoverish the poor. In *The Communist Manifesto*, Marx argued that societies have always been divided into warring classes: the bourgeoisie employers, or the "haves," and the proletariat workers, or the "have nots." In other words, the wealthy exploit the hard labor of the working class, resulting in tension and conflict between the classes. Marx believed that, eventually, the proletariat would revolt and would create communism, or complete socialism. In this system, Marx wrote, private property would cease to exist, the government would no longer be necessary, and all goods and services would be shared equally. By the early 20th century, Marxism inspired the outbreak of revolution in Russia. In 1917, Vladimir Lenin led a successful communist revolution against the Romanov dynasty, bringing czarist rule to an end. Lenin's New Economic Policy still allowed for some private ownership. However, by the time Joseph Stalin came to power, a totalitarian state, where the government controlled every aspect of public and private life, had been established. Like most totalitarian states, Stalin took away all private ownership and personal freedoms. Additionally, he took control over all aspects of the economy and created collectivized farms. Although there were some economic gains that resulted from Stalin's five-year plans, overall the loss of freedom and the eventual economic decline led to the fall of communism in the Soviet Union by the late 20th century.

Written works by intellectuals, philosophers, and leaders have been influential in shaping societies and nations. The ideas in John Locke's *Two Treatises on Government* helped shape Western democracies. The ideas that all people are born free and equal with natural rights and that governments are installed by the people to protect those rights gave rise to free societies in the Western world. On the other hand, the ideas in Karl Marx's *The Communist Manifesto* led to the rise of a totalitarian regime after a successful communist revolution in Russia. Both examples demonstrate that, whether the results are positive or negative, the preserved written works of intellectuals, philosophers, and leaders often have a lasting impact on future societies who are strongly influenced by their powerful rhetoric.

PART III: DOCUMENT-BASED QUESTIONS

Part A: Short Answers

Document 1

1) According to this excerpt from "The Opium War and Foreign Encroachment," one reason why England sold opium to China was to prevent a trade imbalance that resulted from Britain's high demand for tea and Chinese cotton.

Note: This response receives full credit because it correctly identifies England's motivation for selling opium to China, which was to maintain a favorable balance of trade.

Document 2

2) In this letter, one message against the opium trade in China that Lin Tse-Hsü is sending to foreign traders is to stop trading opium to Chinese merchants, who the traders rely on for their livelihoods, simply to take advantage of the merchants and endanger their lives.

Note: This response receives full credit because it correctly identifies one message that the author was trying to send to foreign traders as to why they should stop selling opium. The author was pointing out how immoral selling opium was.

Document 3a

3a) According to James I. Clark, one effect of the Opium War on China was the British seizing several of China's major ports, including Canton and Shanghai.

Note: This response receives full credit because it correctly identifies one effect that the Opium War had on China. By losing their ports to the British, the Chinese realized that fighting was futile. Peace talks then began.

Document 3b

3b) One economic impact of the Treaty of Nanjing on China was that the Chinese had to open five cities and allow British subjects to take up residence there for the purpose of trade without interference by the Chinese.

Note: This response receives full credit because it correctly identifies one economic impact of the Treaty of Nanjing on China. The Chinese could not interfere with British mercantile (trading) pursuits as they were forced to open up cities to the British for their residence.

Document 4

4) Based on the information in this drawing, one way the shift from the domestic system to the factory system changed the way people worked was that prior to the factory system, one person completed an entire task whereas in the factory system, unskilled laborers worked on assembly lines, each completing one individual task.

Note: This response receives full credit because it correctly identifies one change that occurred in the way that people worked as a result of the shift away from the domestic system (manufacturing at home) to the factory system (manufacturing in factories).

Documents 5a and 5b

5) Based on these documents, one environmental effect industrialization had on English cities was the pollution of rivers as they filled with brown fluid.

Note: This response receives full credit because it correctly identifies one environmental effect that industrialization had on English cities. Both documents emphasize the pollution of England's rivers.

Document 6

6a) According to Bansal and Bansal, one impact British industrialization had on India *before* 1840 was the decline of the Indian cotton industry.

Note: This response receives full credit because it correctly identifies one impact that British industrialization had on India before 1840, which was the decline of the cotton industry in India.

6b) According to Bansal and Bansal, one impact that British industrialization had on India *after* 1840 was the increase of manufacturing as cotton mills were built in cities like Bombay.

Note: This response receives full credit because it correctly identifies one impact that British industrialization had on India after 1840, which was an increase in the number of cotton mills built in Indian cities from 1854 through the end of the 19th century.

Document 7

7) According to George C. Herring, one way power was redistributed after World War II was that only the United States and the Soviet Union emerged as superpowers. In contrast, the rest of Europe, particularly Britain and France, lost power beyond their borders.

Note: This response receives full credit because it correctly identifies one way that power was redistributed after World War II by emphasizing the shift in world power from Western Europe to the United States and the Soviet Union.

Documents 8a and 8b

8) Based on these documents, one action the Soviet Union took in Eastern Europe after World War II was to expand communist influence into other countries in Eastern Europe by bringing secret police into every Soviet-occupied country.

Note: This response receives full credit because it correctly identifies one action the Soviet Union took in Eastern Europe after World War II by emphasizing the Soviet Union's desire to spread communism to other countries in Eastern Europe.

Document 9a

9a) Based on the information in this map, one way the Cold War affected Cuba as a result of becoming a Soviet ally was that Cuba became involved in a conflict with the United States during the Cuban Missile Crisis and was affected by the imposition of a US-led quarantine.

Note: This response receives full credit because it correctly identifies one way the Cold War affected Cuba as a result of becoming a Soviet ally by emphasizing that Cuba became entangled in the Soviet Union's conflict with the United States in 1962 during the Cuban Missile Crisis.

Document 9b

9b) One concern Nikita Khrushchev expressed in his reaction to President Kennedy's communication with the Soviet Union was that President Kennedy was trying to give Khrushchev an ultimatum to obey Kennedy's orders or else force would be used.

Note: This response receives full credit because it correctly identifies one concern Nikita Khrushchev expressed in his reaction to President Kennedy's communication with the Soviet Union by emphasizing Khrushchev's discontent with the ultimatum he felt Kennedy was giving him.

DOCUMENT-BASED QUESTION: GENERIC SCORING RUBRIC

Score of 5:

- Thoroughly addresses all aspects of the *Task* by accurately analyzing and interpreting at least **four** documents
- Incorporates information from the documents in the body of the essay
- Incorporates relevant outside information
- Richly supports the theme or problem with relevant facts, examples, and details
- Is a well-developed essay, consistently demonstrating a logical and clear plan of organization
- Introduces the theme or problem by establishing a framework that is beyond a simple restatement of the *Task* or *Historical Context* and concludes with a summation of the theme or problem

Score of 4:

- Addresses all aspects of the *Task* by accurately analyzing and interpreting at least **four** documents
- Incorporates information from the documents in the body of the essay
- Incorporates relevant outside information
- Includes relevant facts, examples, and details, but discussion may be more descriptive than analytical
- Is a well-developed essay, demonstrating a logical and clear plan of organization
- Introduces the theme or problem by establishing a framework that is beyond a simple restatement of the *Task* or *Historical Context* and concludes with a summation of the theme or problem

Score of 3:

- Addresses most aspects of the *Task* or addresses all aspects of the *Task* in a limited way, using some of the documents
- Incorporates some information from the documents in the body of the essay
- Incorporates limited or no relevant outside information
- Includes some facts, examples, and details, but discussion is more descriptive than analytical
- Is a satisfactorily developed essay, demonstrating a general plan of organization
- Introduces the theme or problem by repeating the *Task* or *Historical Context* and concludes by simply repeating the theme or problem

Score of 2:

- Attempts to address some aspects of the *Task*, making limited use of the documents
- Presents no relevant outside information
- Includes few facts, examples, and details; discussion restates contents of the documents
- Is a poorly organized essay, lacking focus
- Fails to introduce or summarize the theme or problem

Score of 1:

- Shows limited understanding of the *Task* with vague, unclear references to the documents
- Presents no relevant outside information
- Includes little or no accurate or relevant facts, details, or examples
- Attempts to complete the *Task*, but demonstrates a major weakness in organization
- Fails to introduce or summarize the theme or problem

Score of 0: Fails to address the *Task*, is illegible, or is a blank paper

Part B: Essay

Pivotal events that have changed the course of history are considered to be turning points. Turning points have impacted a number of societies in both positive and negative ways. Both the Industrial Revolution and the Cold War are considered turning points that have had lasting impacts on societies and regions. They both resulted in negative outcomes, including environmental pollution, as a result of the Industrial Revolution and the threat of nuclear warfare during the Cold War. However, the Industrial Revolution had positive outcomes as well because it resulted in economic growth for nations like Great Britain. Regardless of whether the outcomes were positive or negative, both of these turning points ensured that the nations impacted by these historical events would never be the same.

The Industrial Revolution, which began in Britain in the 18th century, was a turning point with both positive and negative consequences. Britain was the first country to begin the process of industrialization due to its rich supply of natural resources, such as water power and coal to fuel machinery, iron ore, rivers for transportation, and harbors for shipping goods. Additionally, Britain had a growing economy to support industrialization, including an extensive banking system. These conditions made Britain ripe for the Industrial Revolution.

Perhaps the greatest change to occur was the way that goods were produced. Prior to the Industrial Revolution, goods were produced mainly at home by hand or on small machines. After the Industrial Revolution, goods were produced in factories by mainly unskilled workers using a production method called the assembly line (Doc. 4). This changed Britain economically and socially. With the construction of machinery, mills, and factories, Britain experienced a demographic shift from a rural society to an urbanized society. As a result, Britain made major economic gains as the economy grew. However, negative consequences occurred as well. Although the Industrial Revolution generated enormous amounts of wealth, class tensions grew. Most of the money was concentrated in the hands of factory owners. In contrast, the working class made few economic gains while working long hours in often dangerous working conditions. In addition, the growth of mills and factories created environmental problems. In cities like Manchester and London, where factories were built along the rivers, the Irwell River and the Thames River became so polluted that one report claimed that they were flowing with brown fluid (Doc. 5a and Doc. 5b). Eventually, the Industrial Revolution spread to other regions of Western Europe and the United States, which experienced similar positive and negative effects.

Although the Industrial Revolution had both positive and negative outcomes, the Cold War was a much more negative turning point. Tensions increased between communist nations led by the Soviet Union and the free nations of Western Europe and the United States. The Cold War, which was a five-decade long conflict of rising tensions among nations of differing political and economic philosophies, began at the end of World War II. Despite the fact that Great Britain, the United States, and the Soviet Union were allies during the war, the alliance began to unravel toward the end of the war. As the Soviet Union and the United States emerged as superpowers after World War II, they differed greatly in their philosophies and goals. Unlike the United States, the Soviet Union's cities were devastated as a result of the war. Stalin saw the need to create a buffer on the Soviet Union's western border where no natural barriers existed. Ignoring agreements made at the Yalta Conference, where Stalin had agreed to allow free elections in Eastern European countries, he later changed course. Stalin began to use his military forces to spread Soviet influence in countries occupied by the Soviet Union (Doc. 8a and Doc. 8b). In the years that followed, the threat of nuclear war escalated as the Soviet Union became a nuclear power in 1949 when it successfully detonated its first atomic bomb. The threat of nuclear war peaked in 1962 with the Cuban Missile Crisis. After the failed Bay of Pigs Invasion, Soviet chairman Nikita Khrushchev saw an opportunity to expand Soviet influence in Latin America. He began secretly building missile sites in Cuba. The United States responded with a naval blockade and quarantine that almost led to a nuclear war (Doc. 9a). Although a nuclear war was averted, tensions continued to negatively impact the United States and its allies as well as the Soviet Union and its allies until the fall of the Soviet Union in 1991.

Both the Industrial Revolution and the Cold War were turning points that impacted societies negatively, although the Industrial Revolution had positive impacts as well. The Cold War was mainly a negative turning point as it led to escalating tensions between the United States and the Soviet Union and increased the threat of nuclear war. The Industrial Revolution, in contrast, resulted in many positive economic changes as the economy expanded. However, it also led to class tensions, as the wealth became concentrated in the hands of factory owners, and it also caused environmental degradation. Both of these turning points changed the course of history and forever impacted the nations and societies that were affected by these events.

Topic	Question Numbers	Total Number of Questions	Number Wrong	*Reason for Wrong Answer
U.S. AND N.Y. HISTORY				
WORLD HISTORY	3, 4, 6, 7, 9, 10, 18, 19, 20, 22, 27, 30	12		
GEOGRAPHY	2, 5, 8, 11, 14, 15, 17, 23, 24	9		
ECONOMICS	1, 13, 16, 21, 28	5		
CIVICS, CITIZENSHIP, AND GOVERNMENT	12, 25, 26, 29	4		

*Your reason for answering the question incorrectly might be (a) lack of knowledge, (b) misunderstanding of the question, or (c) careless error.

Actual Items by Standard and Unit

	1 U.S. and N.Y. History	2 World History	3 Geography	4 Economics	5 Civics, Citizenship, and Government	Number
Methodology of Global History and Geography		3, 22	2, 5	13		5
UNIT ONE Age of Revolution		4, 6, 7	8	1	26	6
UNIT TWO Crisis and Achievement (1900–1945)		9, 10	11, 14			4
UNIT THREE 20th Century Since 1945		18, 19, 20	15, 17			5
UNIT FOUR Global Connections and Interactions		30	23, 24	21	25	5
Cross-Topical		27		16, 28	12, 29	5
Total # of Questions		12	9	5	4	30
% of Items by Standard		40%	30%	17%	13%	100%

Examination August 2018

Global History and Geography

PART I: MULTIPLE CHOICE

Directions (1–30): For each statement or question, write in the space provided the *number* of the word or expression that, of those given, best completes the statement or answers the question.

Base your answer to question 1 on the map below and on your knowledge of social studies.

5th Arrondissement, Paris, France

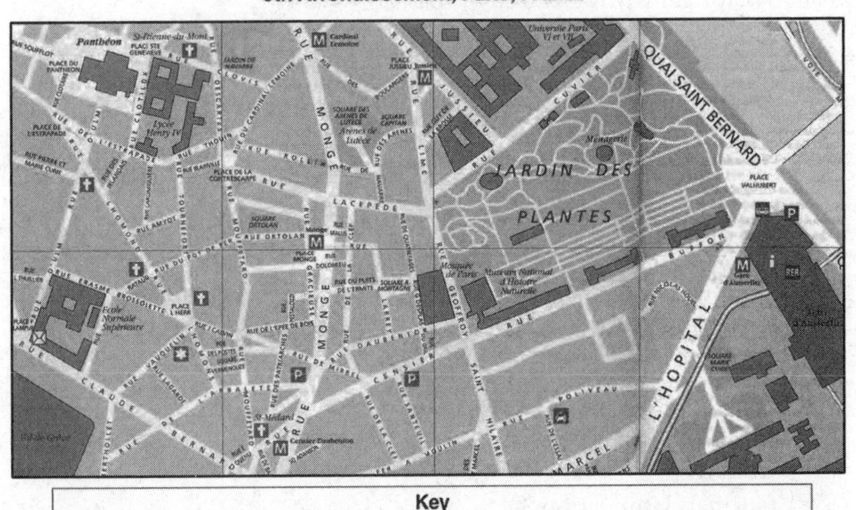

Key				
Church	Synagogue	Parking	Metro	* Mosque of Paris
Gare—Railroad Station	Pont—Bridge	Jardin—Garden	Lycée—High School	

Source: *Eyewitness Travel Guides: Paris*, Dorling Kindersley, 1993 (adapted)

1 Which evidence could best be used to indicate that a diverse population lives in Paris, France?

(1) national government buildings
(2) public gardens
(3) transportation centers
(4) neighborhood places of worship 1 ____

Base your answer to question 2 on the passage below and on your knowledge of social studies.

> There is that great proverb—that until the lions have their own historians, the history of the hunt will always glorify the hunter. That did not come to me until much later. Once I realized that, I had to be a writer. I had to be that historian. It's not one man's job. It's not one person's job. But it is something we have to do, so that the story of the hunt will also reflect the agony, the travail [hardships]—the bravery, even, of the lions.
>
> — Chinua Achebe, "Bravery of Lions,"
> 1994 interview in *The Paris Review*

2 Which idea about history does this passage illustrate?

(1) Historical writing is free of bias.
(2) History is too often written by the victors.
(3) Everyone must be taught to write history.
(4) Using reliable evidence limits historical interpretations. 2 ____

---

3 • Men are born and remain free and equal in rights. Social distinctions may be founded only upon the general good.
• Any law which violates the inalienable rights of man is essentially unjust and tyrannical; it is not a law at all.

Which event was an attempt to implement these ideas?

(1) Berlin Conference
(2) Congress of Vienna
(3) German Unification
(4) French Revolution 3 ____

4 • Prices are determined by supply and demand.
• Governments have little involvement in economic decision making.
• Private ownership is the norm.

Which economic system is best characterized by these statements?

(1) capitalism
(2) socialism
(3) command
(4) traditional 4 ____

5 Which societal issue was examined in the written works of Charles Dickens and Karl Marx?

(1) lack of voting rights in the late 19th century
(2) effects of the worldwide depression in the early 1930s
(3) treatment of indigenous people during the Scramble for Africa
(4) inequities during the Industrial Revolution 5 ____

6 One result of the Treaty of Nanjing was the

(1) establishment of a British sphere of influence in China
(2) creation of a parliamentary democracy in China modeled on Great Britain
(3) granting of Chinese citizenship to the British living in China
(4) formation of a Chinese protectorate in Great Britain 6 ____

7 The Sepoy Rebellion and the Boxer Rebellion are best characterized as responses to

(1) civil conflicts in African colonies
(2) wars of Russian aggression
(3) imperialist practices of European countries
(4) rivalries between Asian nations 7 ____

Base your answer to question 8 on the passage below and on your knowledge of social studies.

> . . . During the five years beginning in 1914, industrial production grew five times; exports, more than three times. The deficit in international accounts, opened in the midnineteenth century, was replaced by a comfortable surplus. The industry that showed the most remarkable growth was shipbuilding; barely started in the latter part of the nineteenth century, in 1919 600,000 tons were built, putting Japan in third place after Great Britain and the United States. . . .
>
> — Masataka Kosaka (adapted)

8 The developments in Japanese history described in this passage are most closely associated with

(1) making reparation payments
(2) implementing modernization
(3) guaranteeing self-sufficiency
(4) enacting economic sanctions

8 _____

---

9 Political boundaries of 19th-century European countries frequently changed due to

(1) social reforms and colonialism
(2) revolutions and nationalism
(3) economic depression and court decisions
(4) diplomacy and suffrage

9 _____

10 Which heading best completes the partial outline below?

1. ______________________________
   A. Austria-Hungary blamed Serbia for encouraging terrorism.
   B. Russia supported the Serbian desire for self-determination.
   C. Great Britain believed it had a duty to protect Belgium from German invasion.

(1) Who Was Responsible for World War I?
(2) Could the Stalemate in World War I Have Been Prevented?
(3) What Was the Role of Imperialism in World War I?
(4) Could an Armistice End World War I?

10 _____

11 One reason Kemal Atatürk faced opposition is that he

(1) attempted ending the nationalist movement of the Young Turks
(2) tried forcing Turkish people to convert to Shia Islam
(3) challenged traditions by modernizing and westernizing Turkey
(4) supported the joint rule of Constantinople by the Greeks and the Turks 11 ____

12 Stalin's forced collectivization in Ukraine in the 1930s resulted in the

(1) elimination of the army's dominance in government decisions
(2) expansion of Soviet agriculture at the expense of industry
(3) starvation and death of millions of people
(4) strong support from Western nations 12 ____

13 Toward the end of the Weimar Republic (1919–1933), many Germans supported fascism because the Nazis

(1) promoted the idea of equality for all citizens
(2) promised to end economic hardships
(3) supported the actions taken by the League of Nations
(4) accepted the provisions of the Treaty of Versailles 13 ____

Base your answers to questions 14 and 15 on the passage below and on your knowledge of social studies.

> NEW YORK — Seventy years ago this month in Munich, the British prime minister, Neville Chamberlain, signed a document that allowed Germany to grab a large chunk of Czechoslovakia. The so-called "Munich Agreement" would come to be seen as an abject [despicable] betrayal of what Chamberlain termed "a far away country of which we know little." But that was not what many people thought at the time. . . .
>
> —Ian Buruma, "The Wrong Lesson of Munich,"
> September 8, 2008

14 Which policy is associated with the historical episode described in this passage?

(1) nonalignment
(2) fundamentalism
(3) containment
(4) appeasement

14 ____

15 What does this passage suggest about Neville Chamberlain's action?

(1) Judgments about events can shift with time.
(2) Ignoring propaganda may result in betraying friends.
(3) War can be avoided by isolating enemies.
(4) History repeats itself.

15 ____

---

16 Which physical feature made the Soviet Union vulnerable to invasion from German forces in World War II?

(1) North European Plain
(2) Arctic Ocean
(3) Aral Sea
(4) Ural Mountains

16 ____

17 Why is D-Day (June 6, 1944) considered a turning point in World War II?

(1) The landing of Allied troops forced Germany to fight on the western front.
(2) A string of Russian victories led to their control over eastern Europe.
(3) The death of Hitler left Germany without clear military leadership.
(4) Dropping the first nuclear bomb quickly led to Japan's surrender. 17 ____

18 A study of organizations like the North Atlantic Treaty Organization (NATO), the European Union (EU), and the United Nations (UN) would show that

(1) international trade functions best without governmental interference
(2) leadership of nonaligned countries is necessary for successful global interaction
(3) decolonization cannot succeed without international coordination
(4) countries can sometimes achieve common goals by joining together 18 ____

19 Which resource makes the Middle East geopolitically important?

(1) gold
(2) diamonds
(3) uranium
(4) oil 19 ____

20 In the 1980s, China's economic growth and reentry into the world economy was most directly the result of the

(1) restoration of dynastic rule
(2) adoption of Deng Xiaoping's Four Modernizations
(3) reestablishment of a regional self-sufficiency plan
(4) implementation of Mao Zedong's Cultural Revolution 20 ____

21 Which heading best completes the partial outline below?

1. ______________________________
   A. Bordered by hostile countries
   B. Limited arable land
   C. Scarce water resources
   D. Intifadas

(1) Reasons for the Pan-Arab Movement
(2) Causes of the Islamic Revolution in Iran
(3) Challenges Facing Israel as a Nation
(4) Factors Leading to Disputes over Tibet 21 ____

Base your answer to question 22 on the passage below and on your knowledge of social studies.

> . . . The scale and the intensity of the conflict, along with the conditions of the use of force against the insurgents [rebels], have focused international attention on Kashmir. Both Indian and international human rights groups have criticized the excessive and unauthorized use of force by the security forces, particularly the BSF [Border Security Force]. Charges have repeatedly been exchanged between Islamabad and New Delhi: the former accusing India of widespread repression in Kashmir, the latter accusing Pakistan of aiding and abetting [supporting] the insurgents. Finally, external powers, principally the United States, have expressed concerns about the potential spillover of the conflict. U.S. officials have articulated fears of an Indo-Pakistani conflict that could escalate to the nuclear level. . . .
>
> —Šumit Ganguly, *The crisis in Kashmir,* 1997 (adapted)

22 According to this author, what is one potential consequence of the Kashmir conflict?

(1) Human rights groups could restore stability to the region.
(2) Local conflict could spread into a major war.
(3) Use of oppression could result in significant territorial losses for both security forces.
(4) The conflict could lead to a refugee crisis in North Africa. 22 ____

Base your answer to question 23 on the cartoon below and on your knowledge of social studies.

Source: David Horsey, *Seattle Post-Intelligencer*, May 23, 2009

23 What is the main idea of this cartoon about global warming?

(1) The developing world has caused the problem.
(2) The industrialized world does not believe this is a serious problem.
(3) Most countries agree that criticizing each other will not solve this problem.
(4) Countries disagree on who should take responsibility for addressing the problem.

23 _____

A. Korean War
B. Communist Revolution in China
C. Cuban missile crisis
D. Fall of the Berlin Wall

24 Which sequence of letters places these Cold War events in the correct chronological order?

(1) $B \rightarrow A \rightarrow C \rightarrow D$
(2) $B \rightarrow D \rightarrow A \rightarrow C$
(3) $D \rightarrow B \rightarrow C \rightarrow A$
(4) $C \rightarrow A \rightarrow D \rightarrow B$ 24 ____

25 The primary goal of Mikhail Gorbachev's policy of perestroika for the Soviet Union was the

(1) restriction of trade
(2) censorship of the press
(3) restructuring of the economy
(4) establishment of five-year plans 25 ____

Base your answers to questions 26 and 27 on the chart below and on your knowledge of social studies.

Reported People's Republic of China (PRC)
Aid by Type and Region, 2002–2007
(Million US $)

Type of Aid	Africa	Latin America	Southeast Asia
Natural Resources Extraction/Production	9,432	18,585	4,788
Infrastructure/Public Works	17,865	7,535	6,438
Not Specified/Other	5,024	608	2,276
Humanitarian	802	32	159
Military	4	0	170
Technical Assistance	10	1	3

Source: NYU Wagner School, *Understanding Chinese Foreign Aid: A Look at China's Development Assistance to Africa, Southeast Asia, and Latin America,* April 25, 2008 (adapted)

Note: Annual totals represent announced loans and other reported aid and economic projects using PRC financing.

26 Between 2002 and 2007, the People's Republic of China spent the most money on which type of foreign aid in Africa?

(1) enhancing the military strength of its allies
(2) providing humanitarian relief
(3) improving infrastructure
(4) obtaining natural resources 26 _____

27 Which inference about China's foreign aid policy can best be made using information from this chart?

(1) China provided technical assistance to decrease its industrial pollution.
(2) China focused on developing regions in order to advance its economic interests.
(3) China used the military to achieve economic advantages for itself.
(4) China sought to enhance its image as the primary protector of human rights. 27 _____

Base your answer to question 28 on the cartoon below and on your knowledge of social studies.

Source: Paresh Nath, *The Khaleej Times*, UAE, June 23, 2009

28 Which action of Kim Jong Il is the subject of this 2009 cartoon?

(1) poorly managing North Korea's economy
(2) polluting North Korea with industrial waste
(3) seeking humanitarian aid for North Korea
(4) proposing the unification of North and South Korea
(5)

28 ____

---

29 Conflicts in Rwanda and Darfur demonstrate the destabilizing effects of

(1) global interdependence
(2) ethnic conflict
(3) satellite countries
(4) natural disasters

29 ____

30 A study of the rule of Czar Nicholas II and the rule of King Louis XVI would show that

(1) overspending on warfare can lead to victory
(2) democratic governments often result from revolution
(3) leaders who ignore the needs of their people are likely to be overthrown
(4) strong advisors usually help monarchs implement successful reforms

30 ____

In developing your answer to Part II, be sure to keep these general definitions in mind:

(a) explain means "to make plain or understandable; to give reasons for or causes of; to show the logical development or relationships of"

(b) discuss means "to make observations about something using facts, reasoning, and argument; to present in some detail"

PART II: THEMATIC ESSAY QUESTION

Directions: Write a well-organized essay that includes an introduction, several paragraphs addressing the task below, and a conclusion.

Theme: Needs and Wants

Societies and leaders have used different methods to obtain resources and products they needed or desired from other societies. These methods have included trading, engaging in imperialism, and waging war. These interactions have had positive and negative effects on the people in different societies and regions.

Task:

Select ***two*** societies or leaders that traded, engaged in imperialism, or waged war to obtain a specific resource or product and for ***each***

- Explain why the society or leader used that method to obtain the resource or product
- Discuss how this method of obtaining the resource or product affected the people in a society or region

You may use any society or leader that used these methods to obtain resources and products from your study of global history and geography. Some suggestions you might wish to consider include Great Britain's need for tea or cotton, King Leopold II of Belgium's desire for rubber or ivory, Japan's need for coal or iron ore, Hitler's desire for more land for the German people, India's desire to control salt production, and Syria's need for water from the Euphrates River.

You are *not* limited to these suggestions.

Do *not* make the United States or a United States leader the focus of your response.

Guidelines:

In your essay, be sure to:

- Develop all aspects of the task
- Support the theme with relevant facts, examples, and details
- Use a logical and clear plan of organization, including an introduction and a conclusion that are beyond a restatement of the theme

In developing your answers to Part III, be sure to keep these general definitions in mind:

(a) explain means "to make plain or understandable; to give reasons for or causes of; to show the logical development or relationships of"
(b) describe means "to illustrate something in words or tell about it"
(c) discuss means "to make observations about something using facts, reasoning, and argument; to present in some detail"

PART III: DOCUMENT-BASED QUESTION

This question is based on the accompanying documents. The question is designed to test your ability to work with historical documents. Some of these documents have been edited for the purposes of this question. As you analyze the documents, take into account the source of each document and any point of view that may be presented in the document. Keep in mind that the language used in a document may reflect the historical context of the time in which it was written.

Historical Context:

Throughout history, there have been individuals who have taken risks in pursuit of what they considered an important goal. These risks have produced varied results. These individuals include ***Galileo Galilei***, ***Mohandas Gandhi***, and ***Nelson Mandela***.

Task:

Using the information from the documents and your knowledge of global history and geography, answer the questions that follow each document in Part A. Your answers to the questions will help you write the Part B essay in which you will be asked to

Select ***two*** individuals mentioned in the historical context and for ***each***

- Explain an important goal of this individual
- Describe a risk this individual took to achieve his goal
- Discuss the extent to which this individual achieved his goal

Part A: Short-Answer Questions

Directions: Analyze the documents and answer the short-answer questions that follow each document in the space provided.

Document 1

This excerpt is from a letter written by Galileo to Johannes Kepler on August 4, 1597.

> . . . "I have as yet read nothing beyond the preface of your book, from which, however, I catch a glimpse of your meaning, and feel great joy on meeting with so powerful an associate in the pursuit of truth, and, consequently, such a friend to truth itself; for it is deplorable that there should be so few who care about truth, and who do not persist in their perverse [improper] mode of philosophising.* But as this is not the fit time for lamenting [complaining about] the melancholy condition of our times, but for congratulating you on your elegant discoveries in confirmation of the truth, I shall only add a promise to peruse [study] your book dispassionately, and with the conviction that I shall find in it much to admire. . . .
>
> *Philosophising is the method used by some to understand the world in which they live.

Source: J. J. Fahie, *Galileo: His Life and Work*, John Murray

1 Based on this 1597 letter excerpt, what goal are both Galileo and Kepler pursuing? [1]

____

____

Document 2

Galileo explains his discoveries to the Pope.

Source: Chris Madden cartoons

2 Based on Chris Madden's cartoon, what risk did Galileo take in presenting his findings to the Church? [1]

____

____

Document 3

Galileo Time Line

August, 1609	Through the connections of his friend Paolo Sarpi, Galileo presents an eight-powered telescope to the Venetian Senate. He is rewarded by a doubling of his salary and life-tenure at the University of Padua. . . .
Fall, 1609	Continues his improvement of the telescope and begins to make celestial observations with the instrument.
April, 1610	Johannes Kepler sends a letter in support of Galileo's discoveries. The letter is published in Prague as *Conversation with the Sidereal Messenger.* It is reprinted in Florence a few months later.
April, 1611	Upon the request of Cardinal Bellarmine, the Jesuit mathematicians of the Collegio Romano certify Galileo's celestial discoveries, although they do not necessarily agree with Galileo's interpretation of these discoveries.
February, 1615	A Dominican friar Niccolo Lorini, who had earlier criticized Galileo's view in private conversations, files a written complaint with the Inquisition against Galileo's Copernican views. He encloses a copy of Galileo's letter to [Galileo's mathematician friend] Castelli.

Source: Al Van Helden, The Galileo Project online, Rice University (adapted)

3*a* Based on the information in this time line, what is ***one*** *positive* response to Galileo's work? [1]

____

____

3*b* Based on the information in this time line, what is ***one*** *negative* response to Galileo's work? [1]

____

____

Document 4

This is an excerpt from a speech given by Mohandas Gandhi at Exhibition Ground, Faizpur, in January 1937.

> . . . Let there be no mistake about my conception of *swaraj*. It is complete independence of alien control and complete economic independence. So at one end you have political independence, at the other the economic. It has two other ends. One of them is moral and social, the corresponding end is *dharma*, i.e., religion in the highest sense of the term. It includes Hinduism, Islam, Christianity, etc., but is superior to them all. You may recognize it by the name of Truth, not the honesty of expedience [benefits] but the living Truth that pervades [spread through] everything and will survive all destruction and all transformation. Moral and social uplift may be recognized by the term we are used to, i.e., non-violence. Let us call this the square of *swaraj*, which will be out of shape if any of its angles is untrue. In the language of the Congress we cannot achieve this political and economic freedom without truth and non-violence, in concrete terms without a living faith in God and hence moral and social elevation. . . .

Source: Raghavan Iyer, ed., *The Moral and Political Writings of Mahatma Gandhi,* Volume III, Clarendon Press

4 Based on this document, what is ***one*** of Gandhi's goals? [1]

____

____

Document 5

Gandhi on March Challenges Arrest
NEW DELHI, March 12 – Mahatma Gandhi's historic "march to the sea" in furtherance of the campaign for civil disobedience began today from the leader's headquarters.
Source: *New York Times*, March 13, 1930

Gandhi Sent to Jail
Special Cable to the *New York Times*, BOMBAY, Monday, January 4, 1932 – Mahatma Gandhi was arrested at his home here at 3 o'clock this morning on the eve of the new civil disobedience campaign which he has predicted will plunge the people of India into "the fires of suffering" once more.
Source: *New York Times*, January 4, 1932

Jail Terms No Curb on Indian Defiance
BOMBAY, January 24 (AP) – Despite jail terms of unprecedented severity, Mahatma Gandhi's army of Nationalist rebels showed no sign of penitence [regret] tonight.
Source: *New York Times*, January 25, 1932

Gandhi Weakening as Fast Continues
RAJKOT, India, March 5 – Mohandas K. Gandhi was cheerful today on the completion of forty-eight hours of his fast, but doctors said he had lost two pounds and that his general weakness was increasing. He has appealed to members of the Congress party not to. . . .
Source: *New York Times*, March 6, 1939

5 Based on these *New York Times* headlines, what are ***two*** risks taken by Gandhi in pursuit of his goal? [2]

(1) ____

____

(2) ____

____

Document 6

. . . Mahatma Gandhi failed to prevent the partition of India because religious divisions were stronger than nationalistic cohesions [bonds]. Demagogues [political agitators] appealed more successfully to the feelings that separated Hindus from Moslems than Gandhi, Nehru and others could to the interests that should have united them. The crystals of Indian nationalism were not yet packed together in a hard enough mass to prevent the axe of religion from cutting it in two. Britain granted national freedom to India before India had become a nation; therefore she became two nations. Of these, Pakistan was a religious community struggling to arrive at nationhood, and the Indian Republic a near-nation troubled by provincial [local] isolationism, linguistic differences, and religious hatreds. Gandhi was really the father of a nation still unborn. . . .

Source: Louis Fischer, *Gandhi: His Life and Message for the World*, Mentor, 1982

6 According to Louis Fischer, what is ***one*** problem British India faced at the time of independence? [1]

____

____

Document 7

This is an excerpt from Nelson Mandela's address to the Court before sentencing at his trial in November 1962.

. . . I hate the practice of race discrimination, and in my hatred I am sustained by the fact that the overwhelming majority of mankind hate it equally. I hate the systematic inculcation [instilling] of children with colour prejudice and I am sustained in that hatred by the fact that the overwhelming majority of mankind, here and abroad, are with me in that. I hate the racial arrogance which decrees that the good things of life shall be retained as the exclusive right of a minority of the population, and which reduces the majority of the population to a position of subservience [submission] and inferiority, and maintains them as voteless chattels [slaves] to work where they are told and behave as they are told by the ruling minority. I am sustained in that hatred by the fact that the overwhelming majority of mankind both in this country and abroad are with me.

Nothing that this Court can do to me will change in any way that hatred in me, which can only be removed by the removal of the injustice and the inhumanity which I have sought to remove from the political, social, and economic life of this country. . . .

Source: Nelson Mandela, *No Easy Walk to Freedom,* Basic Books, 1965

7 Based on this excerpt from Nelson Mandela's address to the Court, what is ***one*** of Nelson Mandela's goals? [1]

____

____

Document 8a

> . . . In secret, underground meetings, the leadership of the ANC [African National Congress] decided in June 1961 to launch sabotage campaigns against the government, one part of a broader strategy that also included mass non-violent action as well as advocating sanctions against the government and diplomatic isolation from the world community. The sabotage campaigns would be organized by a new group, MK, led by Nelson Mandela. MK was the armed wing of the ANC, but that connection was not to be made public in order to protect ANC members from further jeopardy. Additionally, while Luthuli [President-General of the ANC] most likely knew of this shift in ANC policy to include the use of violence as one of the four pillars in the struggle, it is not clear whether he condoned [approved of] it. He, in particular, was shielded from connections to MK. Headquarters for MK were at a secluded house (paid for partly by the Communist Party) in Rivonia, a white suburb of Johannesburg. . . .

Source: *Freedom in Our Lifetime: South Africa's Struggle,* Choices Program, Watson Institute for International Studies, Brown University

8*a* Based on this excerpt, state ***one*** action Nelson Mandela took to achieve his goal. [1]

____

____

Document 8b

Nelson Mandela and Cecil Williams were driving back to Johannesburg on August 5, 1962.

> ... Cecil and I were engrossed in discussions of sabotage plans as we passed through Howick, twenty miles northwest of Pietermaritzburg. At Cedara, a small town just past Howick, I noticed a Ford V-8 filled with white men shoot past us on the right. I instinctively turned round to look behind and I saw two more cars filled with white men. Suddenly, in front of us, the Ford was signaling us to stop. I knew in that instant that my life on the run was over; my seventeen months of "freedom" were about to end. ...
>
> Cecil and I were locked in separate cells. I now had time to ruminate [think] on my situation. I had always known that arrest was a possibility, but even freedom fighters practice denial, and in my cell that night I realized I was not prepared for the reality of capture and confinement. I was upset and agitated. Someone had tipped off the police about my whereabouts; they had known I was in Durban and that I would be returning to Johannesburg. For weeks before my return the police believed that I was already back in the country. In June, newspaper headlines blared "RETURN OF THE BLACK PIMPERNEL"* while I was still in Addis Ababa. Perhaps that had been a bluff ? ...
>
> *The press and the police referred to Nelson Mandela as the "Black Pimpernel." Mandela, as the leader of MK, tried to remain invisible.

Source: Nelson Mandela, *Long Walk to Freedom,* Little, Brown and Company, 1995

8*b* Based on this excerpt, state ***one*** risk taken by Nelson Mandela in pursuit of his goals. [1]

____

____

Document 9

. . . From the moment he was freed, Mandela had used his acumen [insight] to steer the ANC towards racial reconciliation and compromises on issues such as multiracial power sharing (under which Mr de Klerk stayed on as first deputy president for what turned out to be two years). Tactfully but firmly, Mandela outflanked radicals to unite the movement behind this concession. During dangerous moments in the transition, which pushed South Africa to the brink of civil war, Mandela insisted his followers should remain peaceful. They obeyed. He also handled white audiences with a deftness [skillfullness] born of his charm.

Fighting his first general election, Mandela and the ANC won a clear victory. The way was open at last for him to become South Africa's leader. As president, he oversaw his country's efforts to heal old wounds, chief among them the fraught [emotional] hearings of the Truth and Reconciliation Commission. The formula, agreed with Mr de Klerk, allowed the judge-led commission to grant individual amnesties provided those who had perpetrated murder and torture under apartheid admitted the truth of what they had done. . . .

Source: Reed and Cramb, "Nelson Mandela, first president of democratic South Africa," *Financial Times online,* December 5, 2013

9 According to Reed and Cramb, what is ***one*** achievement of Nelson Mandela after he was released from prison? [1]

____

____

Part B: Essay

Directions: Write a well-organized essay that includes an introduction, several paragraphs, and a conclusion. Use evidence from *at least **four*** documents in your essay. Support your response with relevant facts, examples, and details. Include additional outside information.

Historical Context:

Throughout history, there have been individuals who have taken risks in pursuit of what they considered an important goal. These risks have produced varied results. These individuals include ***Galileo Galilei***, ***Mohandas Gandhi***, and ***Nelson Mandela***.

Task:

Using the information from the documents and your knowledge of global history and geography, write an essay in which you

Select ***two*** individuals mentioned in the historical context and for ***each***

- Explain an important goal of this individual
- Describe a risk this individual took to achieve his goal
- Discuss the extent to which this individual achieved his goal

Guidelines:

In your essay, be sure to:

- Develop all aspects of the task
- Incorporate information from *at least **four*** documents
- Incorporate relevant outside information
- Support the theme with relevant facts, examples, and details
- Use a logical and clear plan of organization, including an introduction and a conclusion that are beyond a restatement of the theme

Answers August 2018

Global History and Geography

Answer Key

PART I (1–30)

1. 4	**7.** 3	**13.** 2	**19.** 4	**25.** 3
2. 2	**8.** 2	**14.** 4	**20.** 2	**26.** 3
3. 4	**9.** 2	**15.** 1	**21.** 3	**27.** 2
4. 1	**10.** 1	**16.** 1	**22.** 2	**28.** 1
5. 4	**11.** 3	**17.** 1	**23.** 4	**29.** 2
6. 1	**12.** 3	**18.** 4	**24.** 1	**30.** 3

PART II: Thematic Essay See Answers Explained section.

PART III: Document-Based Essay See Answers Explained section.

Answers Explained

PART I

1. **4** A diverse population is defined as a population that is made up of many distinct groups with varied races, cultures, ethnicities, and/or religions. The map depicts a variety of neighborhood places of worship, including multiple Christian churches, a Jewish synagogue, and a Muslim mosque, which is evidence to support the claim that Paris has a diverse population.

WRONG CHOICES EXPLAINED:

(1) National government buildings are typical of any population with a centralized government. They do not necessarily indicate that the population is diverse or made up of many cultures, races, ethnicities, and/or religions.

(2) While Paris has many public gardens, the existence of public gardens does not indicate that the population is made up of many distinct groups of people.

(3) Transportation centers are used to move people around the city, but their presence in the city does not indicate that the population of Paris is diverse. Therefore, they cannot be used as evidence for diversity.

2. **2** The passage begins with the proverb "that until lions have their own historians, the history of the hunt will always glorify the hunter." This can be interpreted to mean that history is written from the point of view of those who were the victors, and the stories of those who lost or were oppressed have been diminished or ignored altogether. For example, historians have traditionally glorified Christopher Columbus for his discovery of the Americas, but until recently, very little attention was given to the Native American populations that were impacted by the colonization of the Americas in the decades and centuries that followed Columbus's voyages. The author of this passage states that he strived to be a historian who would also tell the story of the oppressed in history rather than focusing solely on the victors.

WRONG CHOICES EXPLAINED:

(1) Historical writing virtually always contains bias to a certain extent because a historian's point of view is shaped by his or her background, which impacts the way in which events are interpreted. Additionally, this passage emphasizes that historical writing is biased in the sense that it glorifies the victors.

(3) While the author of this passage states that he was inspired to become a historian to tell the story of those who have been oppressed throughout history, he doesn't state that everyone must be taught to write history. Instead, he encourages all historians to tell the story of those who have been oppressed.

(4) Using reliable evidence can aid in expanding, not limiting, historical interpretations. Additionally, the author of this passage does not discuss the use of evidence.

3. **4** The ideas stated in this question are ideas that were put forth by philosophers during the period of the Enlightenment, which impacted Europe in the 17th and 18th centuries. This period is thought to be the age of logic and reasoning, when thinkers like John Locke, Baron de Montesquieu, Voltaire, and Jean-Jacques Rousseau began to question the role of government in society and the government's relationship to the people. John Locke theorized that men are born free and equal and have certain natural rights of life, liberty, and property and that governments exist to protect these natural rights. Additionally, these

philosophers emphasized that a government derives its power from the people, and if the people are dissatisfied with their government, they have a right to establish a new one. These ideas challenged the authority of monarchs, who believed their power was absolute and was derived from God. Enlightenment ideas were tested in France in 1789 when the French Revolution broke out. The new government established by the National Assembly drafted *Declaration of the Rights of Man and of the Citizen*, which reflected Enlightenment ideals.

WRONG CHOICES EXPLAINED:

(1) The Berlin Conference (1884–1885) was a meeting of European powers in which formal claims were made on Africa. This event further intensified the colonization of the region in what became known as the Scramble for Africa.

(2) The Congress of Vienna (1814–1815) was a meeting of European nations at the end of the Napoleonic Wars to ensure a peace plan for Europe after years of warfare. It was not an attempt to implement ideas of equality and natural rights.

(3) German Unification occurred as a result of the ideas of nationalism, as opposed to the ideas of the Enlightenment, which emphasized equality, freedom, and natural rights.

4. **1** A capitalist, or market, economic system is one in which prices are based on supply and demand, the government plays a limited role in making economic decisions, and private ownership of property and business is common. The US economy is one example of a capitalist economic system. Private businesses make economic decisions, and government regulation is limited. Adam Smith, political philosopher and author of *The Wealth of Nations*, emphasized the importance of *laissez-faire*, the idea that the government should not intervene in the free market.

WRONG CHOICES EXPLAINED:

(2) Socialism is an economic system that emphasizes community over the individual. Socialism is often described as a less extreme form of communism. In a socialist system, the government imposes more regulations and greater taxation to then distribute resources more evenly to the people.

(3) A command economic system is the opposite of the characteristics stated in the question. In a command, or communist, economic system, the government plays a major role in the regulation of the economy as it controls all factors of production and economic decision-making. Private ownership and business is limited, and prices are set by the state. The former Soviet Union had a command, or communist, economic system.

(4) In a traditional economic system, history, customs, and traditions are considered when making economic decisions. Traditional economic systems are typically found in developing nations in Africa, Asia, and Latin America.

5. **4** Both Charles Dickens and Karl Marx examined the issue of social and economic inequalities during the Industrial Revolution. Dickens's *Oliver Twist* reflected the problems caused by the Industrial Revolution in England, such as child labor, poverty, and pollution. Karl Marx wrote *The Communist Manifesto*, in which he and coauthor Friedrich Engels argued that human societies had been divided into warring classes and that industrialization had created two classes: the "bourgeoisie," or middle class, which controlled all means of production, and the "proletariat," or working class, which did the hard labor.

WRONG CHOICES EXPLAINED:

(1) Both Charles Dickens and Karl Marx wrote in the mid-19th century as opposed to the late 19th century. Neither one addressed the lack of voting rights, but instead wrote about social and economic inequalities in society during the Industrial Revolution.

(2) Both Charles Dickens and Karl Marx were 19th-century authors and wrote their works well before the global economic depression of the 1930s.

(3) Neither Charles Dickens nor Karl Marx were concerned about native Africans during the European scramble and division of Africa during the period of New Imperialism in the late 19th century.

6. **1** The Treaty of Nanjing, signed in 1842, ended the Opium Wars between China and Great Britain. Prior to the Opium Wars, China had little interest in trading with the West, and the balance of trade was mostly in China's favor. That changed when Great Britain found a commodity that Chinese people would buy in large quantities. Opium, a highly addictive narcotic, was being smuggled into China in the first few decades of the 19th century. By 1835, up to 12 million Chinese people were addicted. When Great Britain refused to stop selling opium, a war broke out in 1839. After suffering a loss to the British, the Chinese government was forced to sign the Treaty of Nanjing, which gave the island of Hong Kong to Great Britain and allowed the British and other Western powers to expand their spheres of influence in the region. Foreigners gained extraterritorial rights that allowed them to benefit from trade in East Asia without subjecting them to Chinese laws.

WRONG CHOICES EXPLAINED:

(2) China has never had a British-style parliamentary democracy, and thus the Treaty of Nanjing, which ended the Opium Wars, didn't establish one. Instead, it gave the British more economic influence in the region.

(3) The British did not seek to gain Chinese citizenship. The Treaty of Nanjing allowed for more control of trade and influence in the region, but it did not establish Chinese citizenship for the British.

(4) A protectorate is a country or region that is controlled or protected by another state or region. The Chinese never established a protectorate in Great Britain.

7. **3** Both the Sepoy Rebellion in India and the Boxer Rebellion in China were responses to European imperialism. By the 1850s, the British controlled much of India, which led to Indian nationalism and resentment of imperial policies. Sepoys, or Indian soldiers, revolted in violent clashes against the British in 1857, which ultimately resulted in Great Britain having more direct control over India. In China, a similar situation erupted against a foreign influence. Chinese peasants and workers who resented foreign privilege and influence rebelled against the Chinese government. Despite the failure of the Boxer Rebellion, resentment against foreign influence strengthened feelings of nationalism, and the Chinese people felt an even greater need to resist foreign control.

WRONG CHOICES EXPLAINED:

(1) Neither the Sepoy Rebellion nor the Boxer Rebellion took place in African colonies. The Sepoy Rebellion was a rebellion in India against British control, and the Boxer Rebellion was a rebellion in China against Western influences.

(2) Neither the Sepoy Rebellion nor the Boxer Rebellion involved Russia or had anything to do with Russian aggression.

(4) Although the Sepoy Rebellion took place in India and the Boxer Rebellion took place in China, these were not rebellions that resulted from rivalries between the two nations. Both nations were being hurt economically by foreign influence from Western powers, and, therefore, the rebellions were against foreign powers.

8. **2** The passage describes Japanese industrial growth in the early 20th century, which was a direct result of the implementation of modernization efforts that began during the Meiji Restoration in 1868. During the Meiji period, Japan adopted many Western ideas, including the Western path of industrialization. The Japanese people built railroads, opened communication in telephone and telegraph lines, and increased coal production. Additionally, they developed modern industries, such as shipbuilding, that made them competitive with European powers and the United States, all of which is described in the passage.

WRONG CHOICES EXPLAINED:

(1) Reparation payments are payments made by a defeated country to compensate for damages caused in a war. For example, the Treaty of Versailles required Germany to pay reparations for war damages incurred during World War I. The passage does not mention reparation payments.

(3) Although modernization efforts created a stronger Japan by the early 20th century, Japan was not completely self-sufficient. The passage discusses the need for shipbuilding, which indicates that Japan relied on trade and therefore was not entirely self-sufficient.

(4) Economic sanctions are penalties that include trade barriers, tariffs, and other restrictions placed on one nation by another. The passage does not mention any penalties but instead discusses industrial growth, which is a direct result of modernization efforts.

9. **2** During the 19th century, nationalism swept through Europe, which led to changes in political boundaries throughout the continent. Nationalists were not loyal to the government but instead were loyal to the people who shared a common ancestry. As a result of nationalism, revolutions broke out against monarchies in Italy, Austria, and Germany. Although the revolutions of 1848 were initially unsuccessful, feelings of nationalism were strengthened. Nationalism was then both a force for unity and disunity in Europe. For example, nationalism led to the unification of both Italy and Germany in the mid-19th century, but it also caused the collapse of Europe's largest empires, like the Austrian Empire. Ethnic diversity within the Austrian Empire created resentment and feelings of nationalism, which eventually caused the empire to become the Austro-Hungarian Empire, making Austria and Hungary independent states. Feelings of nationalism persisted, and after World War I, Austria-Hungary broke into several smaller nations.

WRONG CHOICES EXPLAINED:

(1) Although there were social reforms and colonialism that took place in Europe at this time, the main forces behind the change in political boundaries during the 19th century were revolutions and feelings of nationalism.

(3) The 19th century was a period of industrialization and economic growth, not economic depression. Court decisions did not redraw political boundaries during this time period.

(4) Diplomacy and diplomatic relationships did not create new nations or redraw political boundaries. Similarly, suffrage, or the right to vote, did not change political boundaries in Europe during the 19th century.

10. **1** The partial outline describes the events that led to the outbreak of World War I. "Who Was Responsible for World War I?" would be the best heading because each statement in the partial outline places blame on various nations for starting the war. For example, statement A states that Austria-Hungary placed blame on Serbia for encouraging terrorism. This is referring to the assassination of the Archduke Franz Ferdinand of Austria, who was murdered by a Serbian nationalist. Statement B places blame on Russia for supporting Serbia's desire for independence from Austria-Hungary, and statement C places blame on Great Britain for coming to the aid of Belgium to protect it from German invasion.

WRONG CHOICES EXPLAINED:

(2) Stalemates occurred during World War I when armies on both sides had such advanced defenses that neither army could break through defenses. There were many stalemates during World War I, but the most notable ones occurred on the Western Front in Belgium and France. However, nothing in the partial outline addresses these stalemates.

(3) Imperialism, or extending a country's power and influence in other parts of the world, played a significant role in World War I. However, nothing in the partial outline mentions imperialism.

(4) The three statements in the partial outline address the events surrounding the outbreak of World War I, not the end of the war.

11. **3** Kemal Atatürk faced opposition because he challenged traditions by modernizing and westernizing Turkey after World War I. Atatürk became the first president of the new Republic of Turkey after the last sultan of the Ottoman Empire was deposed. He issued sweeping reforms to modernize the nation to make it competitive with Western countries. He separated religious law and national law, abolished religious courts, and based the new legal system on Western laws. He granted suffrage to women and allowed them to hold public office. He also issued reforms to industrialize Turkey and spur economic growth. Although these reforms benefited Turkey in many ways, the sweeping changes were met with some opposition, particularly from religious clerics. Kemal Atatürk's westernization and modernization efforts are often compared to Peter the Great's reforms in Russia. Peter the Great also sought to westernize and modernize his nation in the late 17th century and early 18th century.

WRONG CHOICES EXPLAINED:

(1) The nationalist movement of the Young Turks led to the Young Turk Revolution of 1908, which was fifteen years before Atatürk became the Republic of Turkey's first president. Additionally, Atatürk himself was a nationalist and therefore would not have ended the Young Turks' movement.

(2) Atatürk was a Sunni Muslim who sought to westernize and secularize Turkey by separating religion from government. Therefore, he would not have forced the Turkish people to convert to Shia Islam.

(4) Prior to becoming the Republic of Turkey's first president, Atatürk was a commander who led Turkish nationalists in fighting back against the Greeks. Therefore, he would not have supported the joint rule of Constantinople by the Greeks and the Turks.

12. **3** In 1928, Stalin began to collectivize farms throughout the Soviet Union by seizing control of privately owned farms and turning them into large, state-controlled farms. This action was met with resistance, particularly in Ukraine, where kulaks, or wealthy peasants, fought against collectivization. Stalin responded to the kulaks' resistance by confiscating food, blocking borders, and essentially starving the kulaks to death. Within a few years, millions of kulaks had died as a direct result of Stalin's collectivization efforts.

WRONG CHOICES EXPLAINED:

(1) Collectivization is defined as the seizure and conversion of small privately owned farms into large state-run farms. Therefore, collectivization would not lead to the elimination of the army's dominance in government decisions.

(2) Although collectivization focused on agriculture, the expansion of Soviet agriculture complemented the expansion of industry, which grew as a result of Stalin's five-year plans. The five-year plans were implemented first, but the growth of agriculture was never meant to come at the expense of industry.

(4) Although Western nations were Stalin's allies during World War II, they never supported Stalin's communist policies in the Soviet Union. The Cold War fought between Western nations and the Soviet Union demonstrates the lack of support from Western nations.

13. **2** By the end of the Weimar Republic in Germany (1919–1933), the global economy had collapsed, and the Great Depression had begun. Even before the Great Depression, Germany faced many economic hardships after their defeat in World War I. Faced with reparations and war debts, the Germans printed more money, causing hyperinflation of the German mark. Just as Germany began to recover economically, the collapse of the American stock market and financial systems caused a global depression. Many Germans therefore supported fascism because the Nazis promised to end economic hardships.

WRONG CHOICES EXPLAINED:

(1) The Nazis did not promote equality for all citizens and were instead openly anti-Semitic.

(3) In 1933, Hitler pulled Nazi Germany out of the League of Nations. Therefore, the Nazis did not support the actions taken by the League of Nations.

(4) The Nazis gained support by openly defying the terms of the Treaty of Versailles, not by supporting this treaty. For example, Hitler promised the German people that he would rebuild the military despite the limitations placed on the expansion of the German military as outlined in the Treaty of Versailles.

14. **4** Appeasement is defined as giving in to a foreign nation's demands in order to avoid conflict. In the 1930s, countries like Great Britain and France, recalling the devastation caused by World War I, adopted the policy of appeasement to avoid another major conflict. The passage describes British prime minister Neville Chamberlain and his signing of the Munich Agreement, which allowed Adolf Hitler to take a large piece of Czechoslovakia for Germany in order to avoid the outbreak of war. Both France and Britain had adopted the policy of appeasement in order to avoid the outbreak of World War II, but the more they gave in to Hitler's demands, the more aggressive Hitler became. Thus, the outbreak of war could not be avoided.

WRONG CHOICES EXPLAINED:

(1) Nonalignment refers to the policy of not being allied with other nations and is typically used to describe countries that did not create alliances with either Western or Eastern Blocs during the Cold War. The passage does not mention nonalignment.

(2) Fundamentalism is used to describe a sect of a religion that takes a literal and strict interpretation of a religious text. The passage does not mention fundamentalism.

(3) Containment is used to describe the policy adopted by the United States during the Cold War to keep communism from spreading to other nations. America's involvement in the Vietnam War was a result of its policy of containment.

15. **1** The passage indicates that judgments about events can shift with time. In the passage, it states that the Munich Agreement, which allowed Adolf Hitler to take a large chunk of Czechoslovakia for Germany, would come to be seen as an "abject [despicable] betrayal," and it goes on to state that this is not how many people viewed the agreement at the time that it was signed. This demonstrates that judgments about events can change over time.

WRONG CHOICES EXPLAINED:

(2) Propaganda, or biased, exaggerated, or misleading information designed to garner support for a political cause, is not mentioned in the passage.

(3) The passage describes Neville Chamberlain's signing of the Munich Agreement, which allowed Germany to take a large chunk of Czechoslovakia. Chamberlain was not trying to isolate Germany to avoid war but was instead appeasing Germany to avoid war.

(4) While historical events can often repeat themselves throughout history, there is nothing in the passage that suggests that giving a large chunk of Czechoslovakia to Germany was history repeating itself.

16. **1** The North European Plain, an area of relatively flat land that stretches across northern Germany into parts of Eastern Europe, is a grassland area that has few natural barriers to protect the land from invasions. The North European Plain left the Soviet Union open to an invasion by Germany during World War II.

WRONG CHOICES EXPLAINED:

(2) The Arctic Ocean, the ocean located to the north of Russia, would have acted as a natural barrier to an invasion from the north. It is not the geographic feature that allowed Germany to invade the Soviet Union.

(3) The Aral Sea, which lies between Kazakhstan and Uzbekistan, would have acted as a natural barrier to an invasion and thus did not allow Germany to invade the Soviet Union. Additionally, Germany invaded the Soviet Union on its western border, whereas the Aral Sea lies south of the Soviet Union.

(4) The Ural Mountains, which divide western Russia from eastern Russia, would have acted as a natural barrier to the advancement of Germany.

17. **1** D-Day is considered an important turning point in World War II because it forced Germany to fight on the western front (Western Europe as opposed to Eastern Europe and the Soviet Union). By June of 1944, Allied forces, including troops from the United States, Great Britain, and France, were ready to liberate France from German control and push German forces eastward. On June 6, 1944, the Allies fought their way onto the beaches of Normandy and within a month were able to march on Paris, liberating France from Germany.

WRONG CHOICES EXPLAINED:

(2) Russian forces did not participate in the D-Day invasion on the beaches of Normandy. The Battle of Stalingrad is considered a turning point on the eastern front. This battle prevented German forces from overrunning the Soviet Union.

(3) Hitler committed suicide on April 30, 1945, when Germany's defeat in World War II was certain. This was almost 11 months after D-Day.

(4) D-Day refers to the Allied invasion on the beaches of Normandy with the goal of liberating France from German occupation. The dropping of the atomic bombs on Hiroshima and Nagasaki played a role in ending the war in Japan, but these events had nothing to do with D-Day.

18. **4** The North Atlantic Treaty Organization (NATO), the European Union (EU), and the United Nations (UN) were formed to achieve common goals. NATO, made up of North American and European countries, was formed in 1949 at the start of the Cold War. NATO offered mutual defense to any member nation in the event of an attack. The European Union had the common goal of creating greater political and economic unity throughout Europe. The EU allows for the free movement of people, services, goods, and capital, and it fosters

more political cooperation between member states. The United Nations, a peacekeeping organization created after World War II, is also an example of countries achieving common goals by joining together.

WRONG CHOICES EXPLAINED:

(1) Neither NATO nor the UN focuses on free trade as its ultimate goal. NATO was created as an alliance against the Soviet Union and other communist nations, and the UN was created as an international peacekeeping body after World War II.

(2) Nonaligned countries are countries that have not forged alliances with other nations. This is a term usually used to describe countries that did not take sides in the Cold War. NATO, which was formed to align the United States and many European countries against Soviet aggression, is an organization that consists of aligned members.

(3) None of the organizations described in the question were formed with the goal of decolonization. Additionally, decolonization was successful as a result of nationalism, not international coordination.

19. **4** Oil has given the countries of the Middle East geographic and political importance because of the world's increasing reliance on oil in the latter half of the 20th century and the early 21st century. When the Arab members of the Organization of the Petroleum Exporting Countries (OPEC) declared an oil embargo in the 1970s, many Western countries experienced an economic decline as a result. In the 1990s, when Iraq invaded Kuwait and fears mounted over Iraq invading oil-rich Saudi Arabia, many nations declared war on Iraq, leading to the Persian Gulf War. Foreign policy relations with Saudi Arabia and other oil-producing countries have been shaped by the need for oil from this region.

WRONG CHOICES EXPLAINED:

(1) The Middle East is a producer of oil. Gold is not a natural resource in this region.

(2) Diamonds are not plentiful in the Middle East. South Africa, Botswana, and Angola are the major producers of diamonds on the continent of Africa.

(3) Uranium occurs naturally all over Earth's crust and is necessary to produce nuclear reactions. The Middle East is not a major producer of uranium, but this region is a major producer of oil.

20. **2** In the 1980s, China experienced economic growth and reentered the world economy due to Deng Xiaoping's Four Modernizations. Deng Xiaoping, who had emerged as China's most important leader in 1980, was a communist who was open to using capitalist ideas to promote economic growth. His Four Modernizations focused on growth in the areas of agriculture, industry, defense, and science and technology. For example, he gave farmers the ability to sell crops for a profit, which increased production by 50 percent. In industry, Deng allowed for some private businesses to operate and gave managers of state-run industries more freedom to set goals for production. This policy of openness led to rapid economic growth throughout the 1980s and 1990s.

WRONG CHOICES EXPLAINED:

(1) Dynastic rule in China ended when the Qing dynasty fell in 1912 and was never restored.

(3) Beginning in the 1950s, China began promoting a policy of food self-sufficiency, but for the past four decades, this country has increased its investments in African agriculture. Therefore, a regional self-sufficiency plan was not reestablished.

(4) Mao Zedong's Cultural Revolution took place between 1966 and 1976, during which time Mao's Red Guards attempted to create a society of peasants and workers who were all equal. Artists and intellectuals were considered dangerous, and the Red Guards shut down schools and colleges and imprisoned thousands. The chaos caused by the Cultural Revolution led to an economic decline, not economic growth.

21. **3** There are many clues in the partial outline that suggest that the heading "Challenges Facing Israel as a Nation" is the most appropriate heading. Israel, a Jewish state, is bordered by nations, including Palestine, Syria, Jordan, and Lebanon, which are Muslim-majority countries. Additionally, Israel is a desert nation with a lack of arable land for farming and few freshwater resources. Lastly, Israel has dealt with intifadas, or Palestinian uprisings against Israel's occupation of the Gaza Strip and West Bank. The intifadas began in the 1980s.

WRONG CHOICES EXPLAINED:

(1) The Pan-Arab Movement is an idea that is based on the belief that the Arab countries of North Africa and Southwest Asia should unite to form one state. None of the statements in the partial outline are reasons for the Pan-Arab Movement.

(2) The Islamic Revolution in Iran occurred between 1978 and 1979 when the Shah was overthrown and replaced by the Ayatollah Khomeini. None of the statements in the partial outline are causes of the Islamic Revolution in Iran.

(4) Disputes over Tibet have been caused by China's claim that Tibet is an integral part of China and Tibet's government in exile claiming that it is an independent state. None of the statements in the partial outline are factors that led to disputes over Tibet.

22. **2** The passage discusses the conflict between India and Pakistan over the disputed territory of Kashmir. The conflict began shortly after the partitioning of India in 1947. The passage states that the United States and other external powers were concerned that the conflict could potentially cause a spillover or a larger conflict outside of the region. Therefore, "local conflict could spread into a major war" is one potential consequence of the Kashmir conflict.

WRONG CHOICES EXPLAINED:

(1) The passage does not mention human rights groups' potential to restore stability to the region.

(3) Although the passage discusses use of excessive force on the part of the Border Security Force, it does not mention the potential for territorial loss.

(4) The passage does not mention the potential for a refugee crisis. Additionally, a conflict in South Asia would be unlikely to cause a refugee crisis as far away as North Africa.

23. **4** This cartoon depicts Earth being cooked on the stove, signifying that global warming is causing catastrophic environmental problems throughout the globe. At the kitchen table sits a man who represents "industrialized nations" and a woman who represents the "developing world." The man who represents industrialized nations says to the woman who represents the developing world that she should turn down the stove before something burns. She responds by blaming him, or the industrialized nations, for starting the problem, and states that he should be the one to turn it down. Therefore, this cartoon's main idea is that countries disagree on who should take responsibility for addressing the problem of global warming.

WRONG CHOICES EXPLAINED:

(1) The man who represents industrialized nations does not place blame on the woman who represents the developing world for starting the problem. He simply thinks that she (the developing world) should be the one to solve the problem.

(2) This cartoon demonstrates that the industrialized world *does* believe that global warming is a serious problem. The man who represents industrialized nations wants the burner to be turned off before something burns.

(3) There is nothing in this cartoon to suggest that most countries agree that criticizing each other will not solve the problem of global warming.

24. **1** The first listed event of the Cold War was the Communist Revolution in China led by Mao Zedong in 1949. In 1950, after a successful revolution in China, communist North Korean forces, backed by China and the Soviet Union, invaded the 38th parallel, or the border between North Korea and South Korea. This set off the Korean War. In 1962, the threat of nuclear war escalated during the Cuban missile crisis between the United States and the Soviet Union. Finally, in 1989, the Cold War began its final stages, and the Berlin Wall then fell in 1991.

WRONG CHOICES EXPLAINED:

(2), (3), and (4) These choices all place the events out of order. The earliest event was the Communist Revolution in China in 1949. Thus, choices (3) and (4) are incorrect. Choice (2) is incorrect because it places the fall of the Berlin Wall before the Korean War and the Cuban missile crisis, yet the fall of the Berlin Wall occurred at the end of the Cold War. Therefore, *D* should be placed last.

25. **3** The term *perestroika* means "restructuring" and is used to describe the change in economic policies as enacted by Mikhail Gorbachev and the Communist Party of the Soviet Union during the 1980s and 1990s. Perestroika allowed for more local control over factories and farms and also allowed individuals to open small private businesses instead of leaving all economic matters up to the inefficient central planning agency. Although Gorbachev did not want to abandon communism completely, perestroika was an important step toward the fall of communism in the Soviet Union.

WRONG CHOICES EXPLAINED:

(1) Gorbachev's goal was to increase economic productivity. He would not have wanted to restrict trade.

(2) Gorbachev created a policy of *glasnost*, or openness, in the Soviet Union. After more than 60 years of censorship, the government allowed the free flow of ideas. Books that were banned previously were published again. Churches were opened again. Gorbachev wanted less censorship, not more.

(4) The five-year plans were the Soviet Union's efforts to industrialize under the leadership of Joseph Stalin. Gorbachev never attempted to reinstate these plans, but he did try to restructure the economy to allow for some small business and private ownership.

26. **3** According to the chart, the People's Republic of China spent the most money on improving infrastructure in Africa between 2002 and 2007. Under the Africa column, it states that China gave $17,865,000,000 to Africa for infrastructure and public works. In areas like natural resources extraction and production, the People's Republic of China gave $9,432,000,000 in aid, and in humanitarian aid, it gave $802,000,000.

WRONG CHOICES EXPLAINED:

(1) The People's Republic of China only gave $4,000,000 to Africa in military aid as opposed to over 17 billion dollars in infrastructure aid.

(2) The People's Republic of China only gave $802,000,000 to Africa in humanitarian aid as opposed to over 17 billion dollars in infrastructure aid.

(4) The People's Republic of China only gave $9,432,000,000 to Africa in natural resources extraction and production aid as opposed to over 17 billion dollars in infrastructure aid.

27. **2** Africa, Southeast Asia, and Latin America are all regions of the developing world. It could be inferred that China offered aid to these regions in order to boost its own economic interests in these regions as opposed to giving aid simply to benefit these regions as the sole motivation. In all three regions, infrastructure/public works and natural resources extraction/production were the areas where China spent the most money and were also the areas that could lead to economic benefits for China.

WRONG CHOICES EXPLAINED:

(1) Industrial pollution is one of China's major environmental problems, yet curtailing industrial pollution has not taken priority over economic growth in the nation. Therefore, it would be wrong to infer that China gave aid to these regions with the goal of decreasing pollution in mind.

(3) In all three regions, China gave little to no aid to the military compared to the amount of money devoted to the other types of aid. Therefore, it would be wrong to infer that China was attempting to bolster the local militaries to achieve economic advantages for itself.

(4) In recent years, China has been accused of various human rights violations against various ethnic groups, including Muslims, Tibetan Buddhists, and other minority groups and individuals. The Chinese government's goal has never been to be viewed as the protector of human rights within China itself or within other regions of the developing world.

28. **1** This 2009 cartoon depicts Kim Jong Il, North Korea's leader at the time, showing his son the country he would inherit. Kim Jong Il says, "All this will be yours, son!" but he is standing over a devastated North Korea. The cartoon shows missiles labeled "sanctions," which are economic and financial penalties, such as trade barriers, restrictions, and withholding of aid, that one nation imposes on another. As a result of North Korea's communist government, Western nations have imposed sanctions on North Korea that have devastated that country's economy. The cartoon depicts skulls of the dead and a man who is starving as a result of Kim Jong Il's mismanagement of the economy.

WRONG CHOICES EXPLAINED:

(2) While the image of North Korea depicted in this cartoon makes the country look as though it is a wasteland, it is depicted this way to emphasize the impact that economic sanctions have had. There is nothing in the cartoon that specifically points to industrial waste as the cause for the devastation in North Korea.

(3) Although North Korea applied for humanitarian assistance under the leadership of Kim Jong Il, this cartoon does not reflect this action. There is nothing in the cartoon that suggests that Kim Jong Il sought humanitarian aid.

(4) This cartoon depicts economic devastation, and there is no representation of South Korea in the cartoon. Therefore, this cartoon does not reflect a desire to unify North and South Korea.

29. **2** The conflicts in Rwanda and Darfur are considered genocides and are ethnic conflicts. In Rwanda, conflicts arose between two ethnic groups: the Hutus and the Tutsis. In 1994, the Hutu majority slaughtered the Tutsi minority, killing up to a million people in a three-month period. In Darfur, beginning in 2003, rebel groups began to fight Sudan's government, which they viewed as being oppressive to non-Arabs in the region. The government responded with the ethnic cleansing of the non-Arab population, which led to the deaths of hundreds of thousands. Thus, both conflicts are considered ethnic conflicts.

WRONG CHOICES EXPLAINED:

(1) Global interdependence is defined as the increasing dependence that countries have on each other for various goods and services. Both of these conflicts were fought between ethnic groups and were not a result of global interdependence.

(3) A satellite country is one that is recognized as independent but is under direct influence from a superior power. Neither Rwanda nor Darfur was a satellite country at the time of their conflicts.

(4) The conflicts in Rwanda and Darfur are considered genocides. They were caused by ethnic conflicts, not natural disasters.

30. **3** Czar Nicholas II of Russia and King Louis XVI of France were both leaders who were overthrown and eventually executed by their own people, who felt as though their needs were being ignored. In Russia, Czar Nicholas II was forced to abdicate the throne after growing resentment of the Czar's absolute power and his mismanagement of the economy led to the March Revolution of 1917, in which riots broke out. The following year, he was executed. In France, a revolution broke out in 1789 due to a number of factors, including the spread of Enlightenment ideas of shared power and limited government, economic problems due to mismanagement of the economy, and an unfair tax structure. After being placed under arrest, King Louis XVI was executed in 1793.

WRONG CHOICES EXPLAINED:

(1) Although Czar Nicholas II overspent on warfare, this action did not lead to victory, as Russia lost the Russo-Japanese War. King Louis XVI did not necessarily overspend on warfare.

(2) While both Czar Nicholas II and King Louis XVI were monarchs during revolutions, neither revolution led to the creation of a democratic government.

(4) Neither Czar Nicholas II nor King Louis XVI made successful reforms, which is why both became victims of revolutions within their respective countries.

THEMATIC ESSAY: GENERIC SCORING RUBRIC

Score of 5:
- Shows a thorough understanding of the theme or problem
- Addresses all aspects of the task
- Shows an ability to analyze, evaluate, compare and/or contrast issues and events
- Richly supports the theme or problem with relevant facts, examples, and details
- Is a well-developed essay, consistently demonstrating a logical and clear plan of organization
- Introduces the theme or problem by establishing a framework that is beyond a simple restatement of the task and concludes with a summation of the theme or problem

Score of 4:
- Shows a good understanding of the theme or problem
- Addresses all aspects of the task
- Shows an ability to analyze, evaluate, compare and/or contrast issues and events
- Includes relevant facts, examples, and details, but may not support all aspects of the theme or problem evenly
- Is a well-developed essay, demonstrating a logical and clear plan of organization
- Introduces the theme or problem by establishing a framework that is beyond a simple restatement of the task and concludes with a summation of the theme or problem

Score of 3:
- Shows a satisfactory understanding of the theme or problem
- Addresses most aspects of the task or addresses all aspects in a limited way
- Shows an ability to analyze or evaluate issues and events, but not in any depth
- Includes some facts, examples, and details
- Is a satisfactorily developed essay, demonstrating a general plan of organization
- Introduces the theme or problem by repeating the task and concludes by repeating the theme or problem

Score of 2:
- Shows limited understanding of the theme or problem
- Attempts to address the task
- Develops a faulty analysis or evaluation of issues and events
- Includes few facts, examples, and details, and may include information that contains inaccuracies
- Is a poorly organized essay, lacking focus
- Fails to introduce or summarize the theme or problem

Score of 1:
- Shows very limited understanding of the theme or problem
- Lacks an analysis or evaluation of the issues and events
- Includes little or no accurate or relevant facts, examples, or details
- Attempts to complete the task, but demonstrates a major weakness in organization
- Fails to introduce or summarize the theme or problem

Score of 0: Fails to address the task, is illegible, or is a blank paper

PART II: THEMATIC ESSAY QUESTION

The desire for resources has led to imperialism and warfare in many regions throughout world history. Two societies that attempted to fulfill their desire for resources by engaging in imperialism and waging war were Japan in the early 20th century and Spain during the 16th century. Japan and Spain used both imperialism and warfare to subdue local populations and strip them of their natural resources with the intent to increase their own wealth and power. In both East Asia and Latin America, local populations were exploited and left devastated by imperialism and warfare waged by Japan and Spain in their quests for resources.

Japan's desire to industrialize and become a competing world power led to imperialism and warfare in East Asia. Prior to the mid-19th century, under the Tokugawa Shogunate, Japan was relatively economically isolated from the rest of the world. *Sakoku*, the Tokugawa isolationist foreign policy, restricted trade with other powers. A lack of trade and natural resources left Japan open to foreign economic domination. In 1853, Commodore Matthew Perry of the United States changed Japan economically and politically. Japan was forced to sign the Treaty of Kanagawa, which opened two ports to US ships. This angered many Japanese people, who rebelled against the Tokugawa Shogunate in favor of the restoration of Emperor Meiji to power. In order to compete with Western countries and prevent unwanted foreign influence, Japan began to modernize and industrialize during the Meiji Restoration period. However, Japan, a mountainous archipelago, lacked suitable farmland and metals, such as copper, iron, and coal, which are necessary for industrialization. As a result, Japan began to imperialize and wage war against other nations to expand its influence into other areas of East Asia.

A desire for resources led to imperialism and warfare in other parts of East Asia, reduced China's overall influence in the region, and devastated local populations. In 1876, Japan forced Korea to open ports to trade. Both Japan and China valued trade with Korea, so both signed an agreement claiming they would not send troops to the Korean peninsula. In 1894, China broke this agreement, which led to the First Sino-Japanese War. After a few months of fighting, the Japanese emerged victorious as they drove the Chinese out of Korea and gained a foothold in Manchuria. This was the beginning of Japan's imperial age. By the 1920s, Japan's rising population led to the desire for more land and the establishment of an empire. Additionally, by the early 1930s, the Great Depression in the United States led to the desire for more resources, materials, and markets for Japanese goods. Japan focused its attention on China's northeast province of Manchuria, which was rich in coal and iron. Within a few years, Japan invaded Beijing and then eventually the city of Nanjing. In 1937, in an event described as the "Rape of Nanjing," the Japanese killed tens of thousands of civilians, leading to Japan's involvement in World War II. Japan's need for more resources led to China's loss of power and influence in East Asia and the deaths of many in the regions that Japan attempted to imperialize.

Similar to Japan, Spain conquered local populations in Latin America in an attempt to gain more resources and a world empire. During the Age of Exploration, the economic theory of mercantilism emerged, which stated that a nation's power was derived by increasing its supply of gold and silver and by acquiring natural resources. Spain's desire for these resources led to the conquests of Aztec populations in Mexico and Incan populations in Peru, as well as the establishment of the colonies known throughout Latin America as "New Spain."

Imperialism led to power and prestige for Spain, but it also led to the exploitation and devastation of local populations throughout the region. Many of the Native American populations that did not die in the conquests by Hernán Cortés in Mexico and Francisco Pizarro in Peru died as a result of the spread of diseases like smallpox. The native populations, which were relatively isolated from contact with Europeans, had no immunity to such diseases. Those who did not die of disease were subjugated and enslaved in the encomienda system, in which they were overworked and beaten in mines or on farms, which led to the deaths of many.

Imperialism and warfare throughout history have often been the byproduct of one nation's desire for resources at the expense of another nation. Both Japan and Spain engaged in imperialism and warfare with the intent to secure resources and build a world empire. Japan's desire to modernize, industrialize, and compete with Western powers led to its expansion into Manchuria and other parts of China. As a result of the warfare waged in cities like Nanjing, tens of thousands of civilians lost their lives. Spain's conquests led to the establishment of a world empire, but also to the death and enslavement of many natives in Mexico and South America. In both examples, it is clear that the desire to obtain more resources came at a very high cost.

PART III: DOCUMENT-BASED QUESTIONS

Part A: Short Answers

Document 1

1) Based on this 1597 letter excerpt, both Galileo and Kepler were pursuing the goal of understanding the world in which they lived through the pursuit of scientific truth.

Note: This response receives full credit because it correctly identifies one goal that was pursued by both Galileo and Kepler in 1597 during the Scientific Revolution. Galileo referred to Kepler as a "friend to truth itself" and congratulated him on his "confirmation of the truth."

Document 2

2) Based on Chris Madden's cartoon, one risk that Galileo took in presenting his findings to the Church was being punished by the Church for explaining ideas that challenged the Church's teachings.

Note: This response receives full credit because it correctly identifies one risk that Galileo took by presenting his findings that supported the heliocentric, or sun-centered, model of the solar system. The cartoon depicts the Pope thinking about hitting Galileo on the head with his telescope, demonstrating the Pope's anger with Galileo's ideas.

Document 3

3a) Based on the information in this time line, one *positive* response to Galileo's work was a letter, published in Prague and reprinted in Florence, by Johannes Kepler in support of Galileo's discoveries.

Note: This response receives full credit because it correctly identifies one specific positive response to Galileo's discoveries during the Scientific Revolution. Other acceptable answers include that Galileo was given life tenure at the University of Padua and that Galileo's salary was doubled.

3b) Based on the information in this time line, one *negative* response to Galileo's work was that Dominican friar Niccolo Lorini filed a written complaint with the Inquisition against Galileo's Copernican views.

Note: This response receives full credit because it correctly identifies one specific negative response to Galileo's discoveries during the Scientific Revolution. Another acceptable answer is that Jesuit mathematicians did not agree with Galileo's interpretation of celestial discoveries.

Document 4

4) Based on this document, one of Gandhi's goals was to gain both political and economic independence from British control.

Note: This response receives full credit because it correctly identifies one specific goal that Gandhi had. The excerpt states that his conception of *swaraj,* or self-rule, is "complete independence of alien control and complete economic independence."

Document 5

5) Based on these *New York Times* headlines, one risk taken by Gandhi in pursuit of his goal was being arrested and serving a severe jail sentence for leading a campaign of civil disobedience. A second risk taken by Gandhi in pursuit of his goal was fasting, which caused him to become weak and ill.

Note: This response receives full credit because it correctly identifies two *different* risks taken by Gandhi in pursuit of his goal. If both identified risks focused on his arrest, only partial credit would be awarded. Another acceptable risk is that Gandhi put the army of Nationalist rebels at risk.

Document 6

6) According to Louis Fischer, one problem British India faced at the time of independence was that the population was divided by religion, and religious divisions were stronger than nationalistic bonds.

Note: This response receives full credit because it correctly identifies one problem faced by British India at the time of independence by focusing on Gandhi's failure to prevent a partition of India due to deep religious divisions between Hindus and Muslims. The excerpt opens by emphasizing that "religious divisions were stronger than nationalistic cohesions [bonds]." Other acceptable answers include that India was troubled by provincial isolationism and linguistic differences.

Document 7

7) Based on this excerpt from Nelson Mandela's address to the Court, one of Nelson Mandela's goals was to end racial discrimination and injustice.

Note: This response receives full credit because it correctly identifies one goal that Nelson Mandela states in his address to the Court. In the excerpt, he states that he hates "the practice of race discrimination," and he goes on to state that his hatred "can only be removed by the removal of the injustice and the inhumanity which [he has] sought to remove from the political, social, and economic life of this country."

Document 8a

8a) Based on this excerpt, one action Nelson Mandela took to achieve his goal was leading the armed wing of the African National Congress (ANC), which organized sabotage campaigns against the government.

Note: This response receives full credit because it correctly identifies one action that Nelson Mandela took to achieve his goal of ending apartheid and discrimination in South Africa. The excerpt emphasizes Nelson Mandela's role in the creation of the MK, the armed wing of the ANC, and the organization of sabotage efforts against the government through the use of sanctions and diplomatic isolation from other nations.

Document 8b

8b) Based on this excerpt, one risk taken by Nelson Mandela in pursuit of his goals was returning to Johannesburg, which led to his being captured and jailed when he was caught by police.

Note: This response receives full credit because it correctly identifies one risk that Nelson Mandela took to achieve his goal of ending apartheid and discrimination in South Africa. The primary source excerpt, written by Nelson Mandela, emphasizes his fear of being caught and imprisoned after being on the run for seventeen months of "freedom."

Document 9

9) According to Reed and Cramb, one achievement of Nelson Mandela after he was released from prison was that he steered the African National Congress (ANC) toward peaceful racial reconciliation and compromises, ultimately leading to his becoming president of South Africa.

Note: This response receives full credit because it correctly identifies one achievement of Nelson Mandela upon his release from prison. The excerpt states that Nelson Mandela was responsible for maintaining peace among his followers throughout the period of transition, which could have ended in civil war. The excerpt also emphasizes his achievement of winning a clear victory to become South Africa's first black president.

DOCUMENT-BASED QUESTION: GENERIC SCORING RUBRIC

Score of 5:
- Thoroughly addresses all aspects of the *Task* by accurately analyzing and interpreting at least **four** documents
- Incorporates information from the documents in the body of the essay
- Incorporates relevant outside information
- Richly supports the theme or problem with relevant facts, examples, and details
- Is a well-developed essay, consistently demonstrating a logical and clear plan of organization
- Introduces the theme or problem by establishing a framework that is beyond a simple restatement of the *Task* or *Historical Context* and concludes with a summation of the theme or problem

Score of 4:
- Addresses all aspects of the *Task* by accurately analyzing and interpreting at least **four** documents
- Incorporates information from the documents in the body of the essay
- Incorporates relevant outside information
- Includes relevant facts, examples, and details, but discussion may be more descriptive than analytical
- Is a well-developed essay, demonstrating a logical and clear plan of organization
- Introduces the theme or problem by establishing a framework that is beyond a simple restatement of the *Task* or *Historical Context* and concludes with a summation of the theme or problem

Score of 3:
- Addresses most aspects of the *Task* or addresses all aspects of the *Task* in a limited way, using some of the documents
- Incorporates some information from the documents in the body of the essay
- Incorporates limited or no relevant outside information
- Includes some facts, examples, and details, but discussion is more descriptive than analytical
- Is a satisfactorily developed essay, demonstrating a general plan of organization
- Introduces the theme or problem by repeating the *Task* or *Historical Context* and concludes by simply repeating the theme or problem

Score of 2:
- Attempts to address some aspects of the *Task*, making limited use of the documents
- Presents no relevant outside information
- Includes few facts, examples, and details; discussion restates contents of the documents
- Is a poorly organized essay, lacking focus
- Fails to introduce or summarize the theme or problem

Score of 1:
- Shows limited understanding of the *Task* with vague, unclear references to the documents
- Presents no relevant outside information
- Includes little or no accurate or relevant facts, details, or examples
- Attempts to complete the *Task*, but demonstrates a major weakness in organization
- Fails to introduce or summarize the theme or problem

Score of 0: Fails to address the *Task*, is illegible, or is a blank paper

Part B: Essay

Individuals have changed the course of history by taking risks to achieve important goals. These risks have resulted in varying degrees of success. Two notable individuals who took risks to achieve their goals were Mohandas Gandhi of India and Nelson Mandela of South Africa. While Gandhi's goal was to free India from British colonial rule, both Gandhi and Mandela had the shared goal of creating more unity within their respective nations. Although Gandhi and Mandela achieved their goals to some degree, Mandela was more successful at creating unity among the population in South Africa than Gandhi was in creating unity in India.

Nelson Mandela's goal was to end apartheid, or segregation, in South Africa. As a result of Dutch and British colonial rule, South Africa was racially divided, as the small white minority ruled the black majority. When South Africa gained its independence from Great Britain, the constitutional government granted authority to the white minority, which held the vast majority of political and economic power while denying political and economic opportunities and rights to the black majority. The situation worsened in 1948 when the government passed new laws creating apartheid, in which interracial marriage became illegal and integrated schools were forbidden. In the early 20th century, the black majority of South Africa began to resist the imposed restraints and formed the African National Congress (ANC). When Nelson Mandela joined the ANC, he fought to end the practice of racial discrimination and remove injustice from political, economic, and social life in the nation (Doc. 7).

To achieve his goal of ending racial discrimination and segregation, Mandela took many risks that put his life in danger. In 1961, the ANC began planning sabotage campaigns against the government, which were organized by the MK, the armed wing of the ANC led by Mandela (Doc. 8a). As a result, the government banned the ANC and imprisoned many members, including Mandela, in 1962. In his autobiography, Mandela recounted his arrest, admitting that despite being a freedom fighter, he was not prepared for confinement in a prison cell (Doc. 8b). Nevertheless, Mandela spent the next 27 years in prison after being given a life sentence. Mandela risked his freedom in an attempt to attain racial equality and end apartheid.

Although he spent 27 years in prison, Mandela eventually achieved his goal of ending apartheid, yet some racial discrimination still exists in South Africa today. While Mandela was imprisoned, the fight to end segregation continued. In 1976, riots broke out, leaving approximately 600 students dead. The following year, Bantu Stephen Biko, a popular protest leader, was beaten to death by police. As a result, protests increased, and by the 1980s, there was mounting pressure for change in South Africa. When President Frederik Willem de Klerk was elected, he legalized the ANC and released Mandela from prison. Leading the ANC, Mandela was able to steer South Africa toward a peaceful reconciliation. As the first black president of South Africa, Mandela oversaw the creation of the Truth and Reconciliation Commission, which granted amnesty to those who admitted to the atrocities they had committed under apartheid (Doc. 9). Despite the overall success of establishing a desegregated South Africa, discrimination still lingers there in the 21st century. This is true of many countries with a history of racial segregation.

Like Nelson Mandela in South Africa, Mohandas Gandhi had the goal of creating more social unity in India. Gandhi also sought independence from British colonial rule. He wanted *swaraj*, which is defined as complete political and economic independence from the colonial powers that he believed discriminated against native Indians (Doc. 4). By the 20th century, colonial economic policies had left Indians dependent on British manufactured goods. Politically, the native Indians were treated as inferiors, and laws such as the Rowlatt Acts were passed, which denied Indians legal rights to a trial by jury. In addition to complete freedom from foreign control, Gandhi's goal was to use the concept of *dharma*, or truth, to unite Indians of all faiths and social class backgrounds (Doc. 4). At the time, many Indians had been divided by religious backgrounds (Hindus and Muslims) as well as by social castes within the Hindu faith. *Swaraj* and *dharma* became the goals of many of Gandhi's followers during the independence movement.

In order to achieve his goals, Gandhi took many personal risks. He led the independence movement, utilizing the concept of *ahimsa*, or nonviolence, which was an ideal in many Indian religions, including Hinduism, Buddhism, Jainism, Islam, and Christianity. Gandhi endorsed civil disobedience in that he encouraged Indians to deliberately refuse to obey laws that were considered unjust. He called for boycotts against the purchasing of British goods and urged Indians to weave their own cloth. By the 1930s, the boycotts had hurt the British economy, leading to the passage of the Salt Acts. According to these laws, Indians were forbidden from buying salt from anywhere else but the government. Gandhi led his followers on a peaceful protest called the Salt March, where they walked over 200 miles to the coast to make their own salt. As a result of the Salt March and other planned acts of civil disobedience, he was arrested and jailed in 1932 (Doc. 5). The risks of arrest and serving multiple jail sentences were not deterrents to Gandhi, who was determined to achieve his goals.

Although India eventually gained its independence from British colonial rule, sovereignty created further divisions between Hindus and Muslims. While the shared goal to achieve independence from British rule created some unity between Hindus and Muslims, once the British were ready to hand over power, the question became whether Hindus or Muslims would rule. Gandhi failed to recognize that religious divisions were stronger than the feelings of nationalism expressed during the independence movement (Doc. 6). Muslim resistance to attempts to be included in a Hindu-dominated government led to riots in Calcutta, which ended with the deaths of thousands. The riots convinced British officials that the only way to ensure peace in the region was to "partition" India by dividing the country into separate Hindu and Muslim nations. Gandhi, while successful in his goal of achieving independence, failed in his goal of creating a religiously unified region.

History has been shaped by individuals who took extraordinary risks to achieve their goals. Both Nelson Mandela and Mohandas Gandhi are examples of such individuals. Nelson Mandela risked a sentence of life in prison to end apartheid in South Africa. After serving 27 years of imprisonment, he achieved his goal. Mohandas Gandhi wanted freedom from colonial rule as well as religious unity for India. Although he achieved his goal of independence from British rule, he failed to create religious unity between Hindus and Muslims. Ultimately, India was partitioned into separate countries to maintain peace in the region. Although Gandhi's goal was not fully reached, without the risks taken by both of these individuals, none of their goals would have seen any measure of success.

Topic	Question Numbers	Total Number of Questions	Number Wrong	*Reason for Wrong Answer
U.S. AND N.Y. HISTORY				
WORLD HISTORY	2, 5, 7, 8, 10, 14, 15, 18, 22, 24, 28, 29, 30	13		
GEOGRAPHY	1, 6, 9, 16, 17, 19, 21, 23, 27	9		
ECONOMICS	4, 12, 13, 20, 25, 26	6		
CIVICS, CITIZENSHIP, AND GOVERNMENT	3, 11	2		

*Your reason for answering the question incorrectly might be (a) lack of knowledge, (b) misunderstanding of the question, or (c) careless error.

Actual Items by Standard and Unit

	1 U.S. and N.Y. History	2 World History	3 Geography	4 Economics	5 Civics, Citizenship, and Government	Number
Methodology of Global History and Geography		2	1			2
UNIT ONE Age of Revolution		5, 7, 8	6, 9		3	6
UNIT TWO Crisis and Achievement (1900–1945)		10, 14, 15	16, 17	12, 13	11	8
UNIT THREE 20th Century Since 1945		18, 24		25		3
UNIT FOUR Global Connections and Interactions		22, 28, 29	19, 21, 23, 27	20, 26		9
Cross-Topical		30		4		2
Total # of Questions		13	9	6	2	30
% of Items by Standard		43%	30%	20%	7%	100%

Examination June 2019

Global History and Geography

PART I: MULTIPLE CHOICE

Directions (1–30): For each statement or question, write in the space provided the *number* of the word or expression that, of those given, best completes the statement or answers the question.

1 Which heading best completes the partial outline below?

I. ________________________
- A. The world in spatial terms
- B. Places and regions
- C. Environment and society
- D. Human and physical systems

(1) Elements of Geography
(2) Levels of Technological Development
(3) Classifications of Economic Activities
(4) Models of Government

1 _____

2 Which type of map would be most useful in determining boundaries and capitals of countries?

(1) climate
(2) physical
(3) resource
(4) political

2 _____

3 In which economic system does the government control what to produce, how to produce it, and who shall receive the goods and services produced?

(1) command economy
(2) market economy
(3) traditional economy
(4) mixed economy

3 _____

4 Which area of Japan is most densely settled?

(1) mountains
(2) forests
(3) northern snow zones
(4) coastal plains

4 _____

Base your answer to question 5 on the diagram below and on your knowledge of social studies.

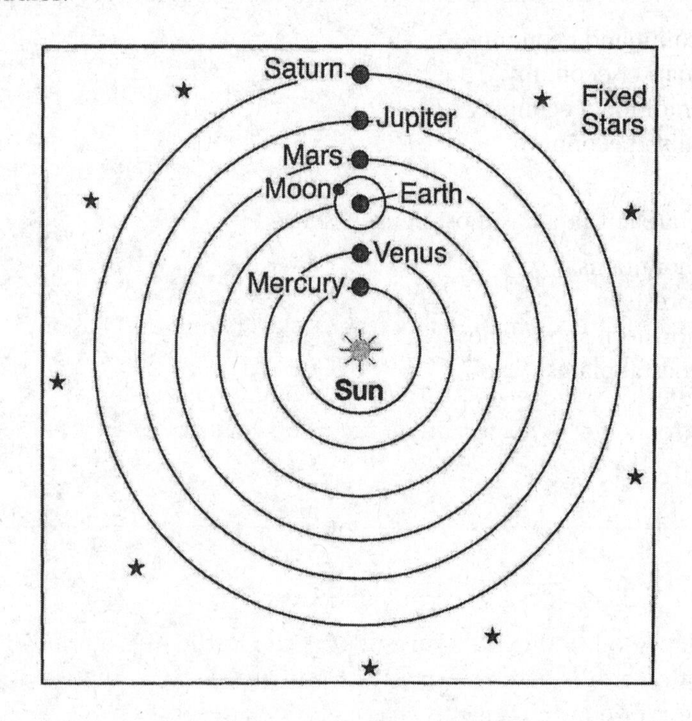

5 Which individual is credited with developing the scientific theory illustrated in this diagram?

(1) Charles Darwin
(2) Nicolaus Copernicus
(3) René Descartes
(4) Isaac Newton 5____

---

6 One way in which the writings of John Locke and of Baron de Montesquieu are similar is that they

(1) supported the idea of governments having limited powers
(2) resulted in the development of mercantile economic systems
(3) promoted the ideas of the Protestant Reformation
(4) strengthened the divine right claims of European monarchs 6____

Base your answer to question 7 on the proclamation below and on your knowledge of social studies.

Article 1. –General Toussaint and General Christophe are outlawed; every good citizen is commanded to seize them, and to treat them as rebels to the French Republic. . . .

— Leclerc Saint-Domingue proclamation (1802)

7 Based on this 1802 French proclamation, the French government reacted to the Haitian Revolution by

(1) accepting Haitian demands to end slavery and oppression
(2) encouraging Haitians to rebel against French rule
(3) ordering the capture of Haitian revolutionary leaders
(4) agreeing to give Haitians all the rights guaranteed to French citizens

7____

---

8 German unification was the immediate result of

(1) Napoleon Bonaparte's surrender at the Battle of Waterloo
(2) Otto von Bismarck's wars with Denmark, Austria, and France
(3) Maria Theresa's reign as an enlightened despot
(4) Archduke Franz Ferdinand's assassination in Sarajevo

8____

9 In the 19th century, a major reason the British wanted to control the Suez Canal region was to

(1) ensure easier access to India
(2) facilitate the slave trade in eastern Africa
(3) promote nationalism in Egypt
(4) improve farming in the Middle East

9____

10 As a result of the growth of Zionism, which region experienced an increase in immigrants from Eastern Europe in the early 20th century?

(1) Chechnya
(2) Kosovo
(3) Kurdistan
(4) Palestine

10 ____

11 • More than 400,000 workers go on strike as a result of Bloody Sunday.
• Czar Nicholas II abdicates the throne.
• Lenin returns from exile and challenges the Kerensky government.

These events are considered causes of the

(1) Russo-Japanese War
(2) Bolshevik Revolution
(3) Great Depression
(4) Treaty of Kanagawa

11 ____

12 An example of self-determination after World War I is the

(1) establishment of the Polish Corridor
(2) demilitarization of the Rhineland
(3) creation of new countries from the Austro-Hungarian Empire
(4) occupation of German colonies by the Allied powers

12 ____

Base your answer to question 13 on the images below and on your knowledge of social studies.

The Rhodes Colossus

Source: *Punch*, 1892 (adapted)

Yoruba Wood Carving

Source: Leon E. Clark, ed., *Through African Eyes*, Praeger, (adapted)

13 These images related to Africa best represent

(1) viewpoints on the nature of imperialism
(2) evidence of traditional art forms
(3) obstacles to developing the Nile River region
(4) efforts to promote travel from Cairo to Capetown

13 ____

Base your answer to question 14 on the map below and on your knowledge of social studies.

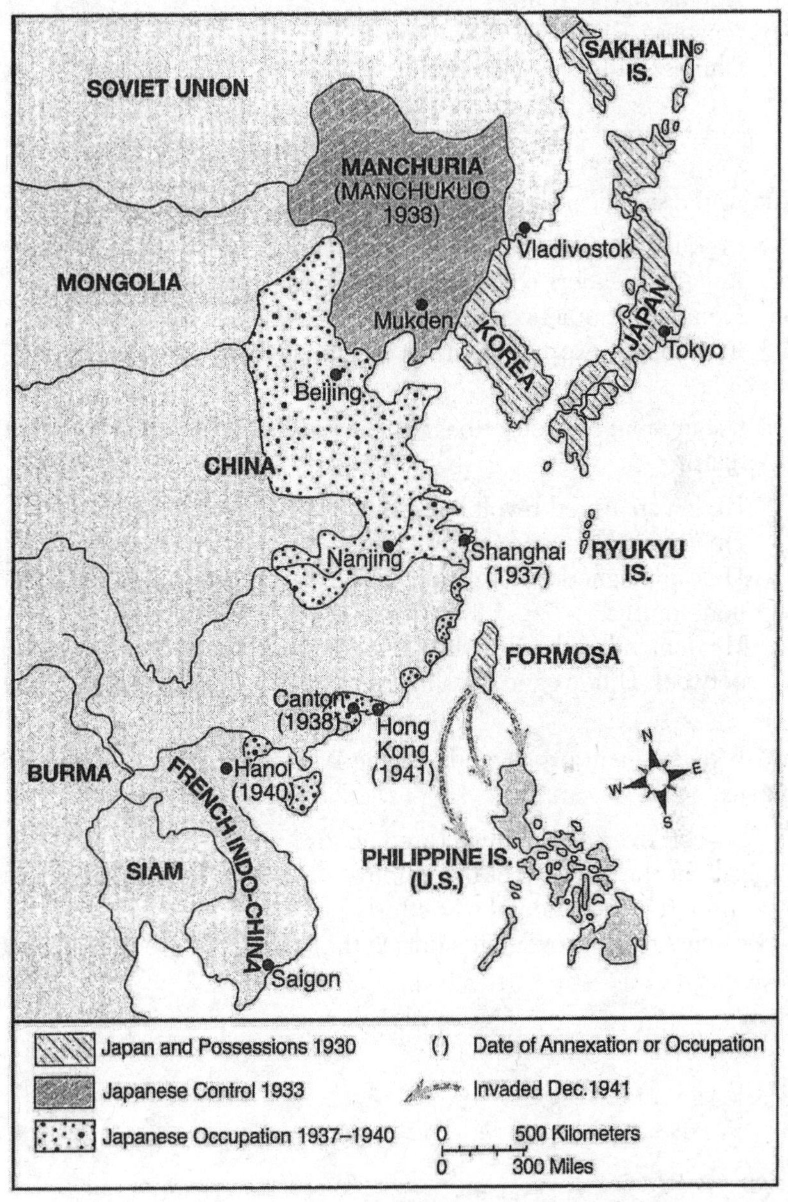

Source: Henry Brun et al., *Global History: The Growth of Civilizations,* AMSCO, 2000 (adapted)

14 What is the best title for this map?

(1) Southeast Asian Independence Efforts
(2) Korean Battlegrounds
(3) Japanese Territorial Expansion
(4) Chinese Military Aggression

14 ____

---

15 What was a significant result of Stalin's five-year plans?

(1) Production in heavy industries increased.
(2) Religious leaders controlled the courts.
(3) Democratic practices spread.
(4) Freedom of expression in the arts flourished.

15 ____

16 Which statement best describes Mohandas Gandhi's response to British imperialism?

(1) He led an armed revolt backed by the Sepoys.
(2) He urged Indians to follow a policy of noncooperation.
(3) He campaigned for the Indians and the British to rule the subcontinent jointly.
(4) He demanded the British Parliament partition the subcontinent between Hindus and Muslims.

16 ____

17 British government propaganda during World War II encouraged British citizens to

(1) boycott overseas manufactured goods
(2) call for the breakup of the empire
(3) support governmental war efforts
(4) discuss troop movements during the war

17 ____

18 How was the conduct of World War II affected by geography?

(1) The Black Sea restricted military activities between Europe and Africa.
(2) Mountain ranges and oceans were effective barriers against aerial bombardment.
(3) North- and south-flowing rivers were primarily used to move troops to battle sites quickly.
(4) The harsh climate and long distances hampered Germany's efforts to succeed on its eastern front. 18 ____

19 One reason the Soviet Union established satellites in Eastern Europe after World War II was to

(1) protect its western border
(2) remove nuclear weapons
(3) assure cultural diversity
(4) provide space for its increasing population 19 ____

Base your answer to question 20 on the passage below and on your knowledge of social studies.

> . . . The UN [United Nations] must be re-founded on the basis of its original principles. The standard for admission should not be a country's mere existence, but its fulfillment of certain criteria of democratic governance. Like the European Union, the UN should possess mechanisms to suspend or even expel members that fail to respect democratic norms [rules]. . . .
>
> — Emma Bonino and Gianfranco Dell'Alba, "Making the UN Fit for Democracy," June 2003

20 According to these authors, which type of criteria should all members of the United Nations meet?

(1) religious
(2) military
(3) economic
(4) political 20 ____

---

21 Which factor strongly contributed to most independence movements in Africa and Asia after World War II?

(1) migrations
(2) industrialization
(3) nationalism
(4) pandemics 21 ____

22 Which statement best explains why the Communists won the Chinese civil war in 1949?

(1) Communist Party membership was promised to businessmen and landlords.
(2) Large numbers of women voted for the Communist Party.
(3) China's peasant population supported the Communists.
(4) Western powers provided arms and advisers to China's Communist army. 22 ____

23 Which term describes India's foreign policy during the Cold War?

(1) militarism
(2) containment
(3) appeasement
(4) nonalignment 23 ____

24 What was the purpose behind the construction of the Berlin Wall?

(1) safeguarding industrial secrets
(2) protecting the power of a regime
(3) discouraging the movement of pastoral herders
(4) testing the viability of technological innovations 24 ____

Base your answer to question 25 on the cartoon below and on your knowledge of social studies.

Source: Danziger, *Times Union*, April 25, 2005 (adapted)

25 The main idea of this cartoon suggests that Russian President Putin

(1) supports a free press
(2) limits dissent
(3) promotes capitalism
(4) distrusts the United States

25 ____

26 **"Chemical Plant at Bhopal, India, Releases Toxic Fumes"**

"Nuclear Reactor Explodes at Chernobyl, USSR; Releases Radiation"

"Oil Tanker *Exxon Valdez* Runs Aground in Alaska"

Which global concern is illustrated in these headlines?

(1) events that pollute the environment
(2) disasters that cause tsunamis
(3) circumstances that contribute to soil erosion
(4) incidents that lead to the depletion of the ozone 26 ____

27 Which situation is a cause of the other three?

(1) Agricultural output increased.
(2) Crops were grown more efficiently.
(3) The Green Revolution was introduced.
(4) Chemical pesticides were used to increase agricultural output. 27 ____

28 Which nation's ongoing efforts to develop nuclear weapons in the early 21st century has caused international concern?

(1) France
(2) China
(3) North Korea
(4) Soviet Union 28 ____

29 One way in which the Congress of Vienna (1814–1815) and the Paris Peace Conference (1919) are similar is that both meetings sought to

(1) protect the rights of ethnic and religious minorities in newly created countries
(2) restore monarchs to power in France, Germany, and Russia
(3) distribute aid to people displaced by conflict
(4) establish stability after a period of war and revolution 29 ____

30 Terrace farming, building bridges, and constructing canals are ways in which various societies have

(1) promoted cultural diversity
(2) reduced the threat of invasion
(3) established permanent boundaries
(4) modified their environment 30 ____

In developing your answer to Part II, be sure to keep these general definitions in mind:

(a) **describe means "to illustrate something in words or tell about it"**

(b) **discuss means "to make observations about something using facts, reasoning, and argument; to present in some detail"**

PART II: THEMATIC ESSAY QUESTION

Directions: Write a well-organized essay that includes an introduction, several paragraphs addressing the task below, and a conclusion.

Theme: Human Rights

At various times in history, the human rights of certain groups have been denied. Individuals and groups have made attempts to resist and oppose these human rights violations.

Task:

Select ***two*** groups whose human rights have been denied and for ***each***

- Describe how the human rights of this group were denied
- Discuss an attempt made by an individual or a group to resist or oppose this violation of human rights

You may use any group whose human rights have been denied from your study of global history and geography. Some suggestions you might wish to consider include untouchables in India, indigenous people in Latin America, Armenians, Ukrainians, Jews, Black South Africans, Cambodians, Chinese students, Rwandans, and Afghani women.

You are *not* limited to these suggestions.
Do *not* write about a group from the United States.

Guidelines:

In your essay, be sure to:

- Develop all aspects of the task
- Support the theme with relevant facts, examples, and details
- Use a logical and clear plan of organization, including an introduction and a conclusion that are beyond a restatement of the theme

In developing your answers to Part III, be sure to keep these general definitions in mind:

(a) describe means "to illustrate something in words or tell about it"
(b) discuss means "to make observations about something using facts, reasoning, and argument; to present in some detail"

PART III: DOCUMENT-BASED QUESTION

This question is based on the accompanying documents. The question is designed to test your ability to work with historical documents. Some of these documents have been edited for the purposes of this question. As you analyze the documents, take into account the source of each document and any point of view that may be presented in the document. Keep in mind that the language and images used in a document may reflect the historical context of the time in which it was created.

Historical Context:

Throughout history, leaders and their governments developed policies in response to specific issues. These policies have had significant impacts on the leader's country or the surrounding region. These leaders and their policies include ***Emperor Meiji and westernization***, ***Kemal Atatürk and westernization***, and ***Deng Xiaoping and the one-child policy***.

Task:

Using the information from the documents and your knowledge of global history and geography, answer the questions that follow each document in Part A. Your answers to the questions will help you write the Part B essay in which you will be asked to

Select ***two*** leaders and the associated policy mentioned in the historical context and for ***each***

- Describe the historical circumstances that influenced this leader and his government to develop this policy
- Discuss the impacts of this policy on the leader's country ***and/or*** on a region

Part A: Short-Answer Questions

Directions: Analyze the documents and answer the short-answer questions that follow each document in the space provided.

Document 1a

In the mid-1800s, the Tokugawa shogunate was weak and faced external threats. This passage explains the situation.

> . . . Most of all the Japanese realists noticed what had happened to China—noticed, and were appalled. China was not just another country but the Middle Kingdom, the Central Country. Its emperor had historically referred to Japan's emperor as "your little king." A new China had been carved up by Westerners, debauched [corrupted] by opium and left totally unprotected by either the Ch'ing dynasty or armed force. If the British and French could polish off China, what hope was there for little Japan—against Britain, France, Russia and the United States? Japan could try to enforce its seclusion law, said one of its very shrewdest leaders after the Biddle affair, but if "the foreigners retaliated, it would be a hopeless contest, and it would be a worse disgrace for Japan.". . .

Source: James Fallows, "When East met West: Perry's mission accomplished," *Smithsonian,* July 1994

Document 1b

Japanese Wood Block Print Depicting One of Perry's Ships

. . . On July 8, 1853 four black ships led by USS *Powhatan* and commanded by Commodore Matthew Perry, anchored at Edo (Tokyo) Bay. Never before had the Japanese seen ships steaming with smoke. They thought the ships were "giant dragons puffing smoke." They did not know that steamboats existed and were shocked by the number and size of the guns on board the ships. . . .

Source: "Commodore Perry and the Opening of Japan,"
U.S. Navy Museum online

1 Based on these documents, what is ***one*** fear Japanese leaders had for their country? [1]

____

____

Document 2a

. . . As the object of modernisation was to obtain equal treatment by the West many of the cultural innovations, besides being more than outward forms to the Japanese themselves, had an important psychological influence on Western diplomats and politicians. Under the [Tokugawa] shogun, members of the first Japanese delegation to the United States in 1860 wore traditional samurai dress with shaved pate [top of the head] and long side hair tied in a bun and carried swords. Under the [new Meiji] emperor, Western-style haircuts were a major symbol of Westernisation. Soldiers and civilian functionaries [officials] wore Western-style uniforms, and politicians often adopted Western clothes and even full beards. In 1872 Western dress was prescribed for all court and official ceremonies. Meat eating, previously frowned on because of Buddhist attitudes, was encouraged, and the beef dish of sukiyaki was developed at this time. Western art and architecture were adopted, producing an array of official portraits of leading statesmen as well as an incongruous [incompatible] Victorian veneer [appearance] in the commercial and government districts of the cities and some rather depressing interiors in the mansions of the wealthy. . . .

Source: Richard Perren, "On the Turn–Japan, 1900,"
History Today, June 1992

Document 2b

Picture of Songs Amid Plum Blossoms

Source: Hashimoto Chikanobu,
December 1887 (adapted)

2*a* According to Richard Perren, what was ***one*** reason the Japanese government adopted Western cultural innovations? [1]

____

____

2*b* Based on these documents, state ***one*** way westernization influenced Japanese culture during the rule of Emperor Meiji. [1]

____

____

Document 3

Growth of Nationalism Under the Meiji

> ... Nationalism also emerged in Japan in the 1880s, but there under [Meiji] government sponsorship after a period of vigorous Westernization. During the 1870s large numbers of Western advisers had poured into Japan, staffing and administering much of the growing school system, among other duties. Conservative officials, including the emperor, worried that Western individualism and other corrosive [destructive] values might damage Japanese culture, and they called on nationalism, supplemented by a revived Shinto religion and other, partially invented traditions, to support more assured loyalty to state and hierarchy. Nationalism began to be used to motivate higher production, economic sacrifices, and other qualities that helped propel rapid development; it soon sparked a new imperialism as well. . . .

Source: Peter N. Stearns, *Cultures in Motion: Mapping Key Contacts and Their Imprints in World History,* Yale University Press

3 According to Peter N. Stearns, what is ***one*** way the conservative Japanese officials attempted to prevent westernization from damaging Japanese traditions? [1]

____

____

Document 4a

1918
- World War I ends; Ottoman lands in southwest Asia divided into European-controlled mandates
- Britain, France, Italy, and Greece occupy Turkish lands in Asia Minor

1920–1922
- Kemal Atatürk forms nationalist government; conflict erupts between Atatürk's government and government of Sultan Mohammed VI
- Sultan Mohammed VI forced to abdicate throne

1923
- Treaty of Lausanne establishes borders of Turkey
- European powers recognize Turkey as a country
- Turkey officially declared a republic with Atatürk as leader

Source: Based on L. E. Snellgrove, *The Modern World Since 1870,* Longman Group

4*a* According to this chart, what was ***one*** problem Turkey faced that convinced Atatürk that Turkey needed to undergo major changes? [1]

____

____

Document 4b

... No nation was ever founded with greater revolutionary zeal than the Turkish Republic, nor has any undergone more sweeping change in such a short time. In a very few years after 1923, Mustafa Kemal Atatürk transformed a shattered and bewildered nation into one obsessed with progress. His was a one-man revolution, imposed and steered from above. Atatürk knew that Turks were not ready to break violently with their past, embrace modernity and turn decisively toward the West. He also knew, however, that doing so would be the only way for them to shape a new destiny for themselves and their nation. So he forced them, often over the howling protests of the old order.

The new nation that Atatürk built on the rubble of the Ottoman Empire never could have been built democratically. Probably not a single one of his sweeping reforms would have been approved in a plebiscite [public vote]. The very idea of a plebiscite, of shaping a political system according to the people's will, would have struck most Turks of that era as not simply alien but ludicrous [ridiculous]. . . .

Source: Stephen Kinzer, *Crescent and Star: Turkey Between Two Worlds,* Farrar, Straus and Giroux, 2001

4*b* According to Stephen Kinzer, what was ***one*** problem Atatürk faced as he forced his country to change? [1]

____

____

Document 5

. . . Powerful leaders used to be called "makers of history"; few so obviously deserve the title as Atatürk. Between 1923 and 1938, the year he died, he made this mostly Muslim country into a largely secular state, modeled on the nations of Western Europe. History has seen no national transformation swifter or more dramatic. In a little more than 15 years, he tried to accomplish the work of centuries.

He abolished the sultanate in 1922 and, a year later, exiled the caliph, took education away from the clerics and closed the religious courts. The effect of these measures was to separate church and state, something that had never happened before in western Asia. He banned the fez [traditional hat], which had become a symbol of Ottoman and Islamic orthodoxy, adopted a modified Latin alphabet, outlawed polygamy and championed equal rights for women. It's largely because of Atatürk that, today, Turkish women have made their mark in medicine, law, even politics. Though her political future is currently in doubt, Tansu Ciller, Turkey's bright, forward-looking prime minister [1993–1996], has been one of only a handful of women to head a government anywhere. . . .

Source: Eric Lawlor, "Isn't modernizing a nation a serious business?", *Smithsonian,* March 1996 (adapted)

5 Based on this excerpt from Eric Lawlor's 1996 article, state ***two*** actions Atatürk took to make his country into a more modern, secular state modeled on the nations of western Europe. [2]

(1) ______________________________

____

(2) ______________________________

____

Document 6

... The dichotomy [between dictatorship and democracy] was built into the new state [of Turkey] by its founder. Atatürk was a soldier; in the heady, early days of revolution the Army could be regarded as its shield, guaranteeing survival against the machinations [conspiracies] of the dictators to the west and north. Atatürk encouraged the formation of an opposition party, the Liberal Republican Party, but it received little support and the ghazi [warrior/Atatürk] reverted to what was essentially one-party rule, that of his own Popular Party.

The machinery of democratic government was left in place by him. But his legacy also included the idea that army leaders, being above politics, could and should intervene to save the country from itself—as when MPs [members of Parliament] broke up sittings of Parliament, brandishing guns and indulging in fisticuffs, or when rival gangs of political gunmen took their quarrels on to the streets, or when inflation began to turn the lira into 'funny money'.

Three times in twenty years the army has taken over Turkey, tearing up the Constitution and invoking the spirit of Atatürk. . . .

Source: John F. Crossland, "Turkey's Fundamental Dilemma," *History Today*, November 1988 (adapted)

6 According to John F. Crossland, what was ***one*** impact of Atatürk's rule on Turkey? [1]

___

___

Document 7

One-Couple-One-Child Policy: Science Becomes Party Policy

. . . In mid-September 1980 the third session of the Fifth National People's Congress [NPC] gave its seal of approval to a new policy designed to keep the population within 1.2 billion by the end of the century by encouraging one child for all. The Government Work Report issued by the NPC was the first general call for one-child families. This policy was then widely publicized in a highly unusual Open Letter dated 25 September from the Central Committee to all members of the party and the Communist Youth League. Packed with numbers of every kind, the Open Letter embodied the new, numerical mode of political reasoning about population. In its formulations of the population problem, the Letter combined the social and natural scientists' formulations into a picture of a grave population-economy-environment crisis. With all scientific uncertainty having been put to rest, the Letter outlined China's severe crisis in grim terms:

> According to the present average of 2.2 children per couple, China's population will reach 1,300 million [1.3 billion] in 20 years and will surpass 1,500 million [1.5 billion] in 40 years. . . . This will aggravate the difficulties for the four modernizations and give rise to a grave situation in which the people's standard of living can hardly be improved. . . . Moreover, too fast a growth of population not only creates difficulties in education and employment but will overtax [make excessive demands on] the energy, water, forest, and other natural resources, aggravate environmental pollution and make the production conditions and living environment downright bad and very hard to be improved. . . .

Source: Susan Greenhalgh, "Science, Modernity, and the Making of China's One-Child Policy," *Population and Development Review,* Vol. 29, No. 2, June 2003 (adapted)

7 According to this article by Susan Greenhalgh, what was ***one*** reason Chinese authorities were concerned about rapid population growth? [1]

____

____

Document 8a

The Internal Debate on Birth Planning

. . . As preparations were being made to launch the propaganda and sterilization campaign in late 1982, special attention was also being given to a profoundly disturbing consequence of the program. With couples limited to only one child, or perhaps two, reports of female infanticide, infant abandonment, and violence against women who gave birth to girls began to rise dramatically. Although many of those reports came from backward rural areas, there were urban cases as well, suggesting a deeply ingrained sex bias. That bias transcended [went beyond] socio-economic and educational status and could not be eliminated by the ongoing propaganda campaign denouncing "feudal" preferences for sons over daughters. . . .

Source: Tyrene White, *China's Longest Campaign: Birth Planning in the People's Republic, 1949–2005*, Cornell University Press, 2006 (adapted)

Document 8b

Billboard in Hebei Province Promoting Girls

The advertisement reads, "There's no difference between having a girl or a boy—girls can also continue the family line."

Source: Therese Hesketh, et al.,
"The Effect of China's One-Child Family Policy after 25 Years,"
The New England Journal of Medicine online, September 15, 2005

8 Based on this excerpt by Tyrene White and on this Chinese advertisement, state ***one*** cultural impact the one-child policy had on Chinese society. [1]

____

____

Document 9

China announced an end to its one-child policy in October 2015.

> BEIJING – The "one child" policy change announced by the Communist Party on Thursday left some economists and investors wondering how the government would address longer-term financial and economic pressures. . . .
>
> Mr. Yao [director of the China Center for Economic Research at Peking University in Beijing], said that an aging population threatened to weigh down China's economic prospects not so much because of a shrinking work force, but because of shrinking consumer demand. He drew comparisons to Japan, saying that its [Japan's] struggle to revive the economy in the 1990s showed that the biggest threat came from stagnating [sluggish] demand as people aged. . . .
>
> China's population has grown increasingly lopsided since the "one child" policy was introduced in 1979. A third of the population is expected to be over age 60 by 2050, up from about a seventh last year, placing significant strains on the government's budget and its benefits programs for older citizens.
>
> At the same time, the size of the labor force has dwindled in recent years and will probably continue to shrink, economists said, raising questions about how China will sustain a historic economic boom and pay for pensions and health insurance programs. The working-age population dropped for the first time in 2012; last year, it totaled 916 million people, down 3.7 million from 2013, according to the government.
>
> In the long term, an increase in the birthrate would likely offset some of the decline in the working-age population. But in the short term, as children remain out of the labor force and in school, it could place new pressure on the economy, as the overall share of the population dependent on the government rises. . . .

Source: Javier C. Hernández, "Experts Weigh Likely Impacts of China's 'One Child' Reversal," *New York Times* online, October 29, 2015

9 According to Javier C. Hernández, what is ***one*** way the discontinued one-child policy will continue to impact China after 2015? [1]

____

____

Part B: Essay

Directions: Write a well-organized essay that includes an introduction, several paragraphs, and a conclusion. Use evidence from *at least **four*** documents in your essay. Support your response with relevant facts, examples, and details. Include additional outside information.

Historical Context:

Throughout history, leaders and their governments developed policies in response to specific issues. These policies have had significant impacts on the leader's country or the surrounding region. These leaders and their policies include ***Emperor Meiji and westernization***, ***Kemal Atatürk and westernization***, and ***Deng Xiaoping and the one-child policy***.

Task:

Using the information from the documents and your knowledge of global history and geography, write an essay in which you

Select ***two*** leaders and the associated policy mentioned in the historical context and for ***each***

- Describe the historical circumstances that influenced this leader and his government to develop this policy
- Discuss the impacts of this policy on the leader's country ***and/or*** on a region

Guidelines:

In your essay, be sure to:

- Develop all aspects of the task
- Incorporate information from *at least **four*** documents
- Incorporate relevant outside information
- Support the theme with relevant facts, examples, and details
- Use a logical and clear plan of organization, including an introduction and a conclusion that are beyond a restatement of the theme

Answers
June 2019
Global History and Geography

Answer Key

PART I (1–30)

1. 1	**7.** 3	**13.** 1	**19.** 1	**25.** 2
2. 4	**8.** 2	**14.** 3	**20.** 4	**26.** 1
3. 1	**9.** 1	**15.** 1	**21.** 3	**27.** 3
4. 4	**10.** 4	**16.** 2	**22.** 3	**28.** 3
5. 2	**11.** 2	**17.** 3	**23.** 4	**29.** 4
6. 1	**12.** 3	**18.** 4	**24.** 2	**30.** 4

PART II: Thematic Essay See Answers Explained section.

PART III: Document-Based Essay See Answers Explained section.

Answers Explained

PART I

1. **1** Geography is defined as the study of the physical features of the world and how these features both affect and are affected by human populations. The partial outline states important subcategories of geography that support the heading "Elements of Geography." These subcategories include the spatial information about the world itself, places of the world, the natural environment and human populations, and human and physical systems.

WRONG CHOICES EXPLAINED:

(2) Technological development is defined as the application of scientific knowledge for practical use to solve problems or to invent useful tools. The subcategories of the partial outline define characteristics of geography as opposed to levels of technological development.

(3) Economics is concerned with the distribution of scarce resources within a society. The subcategories in the partial outline define characteristics of geography as opposed to classifications of economic activities.

(4) Models of government are defined as various methods of creating law and order in nations, states, and communities. Numerous models of government have developed throughout history, including monarchies, democracies, and oligarchies. The partial outline defines characteristics of geography as opposed to models of government.

2. **4** A political map focuses on boundaries of nations as well as boundaries of major cities, including capitals. Unlike physical maps, political maps do not emphasize major geographic features like mountains, deserts, and plateaus. Instead, political maps focus on governmental boundaries.

WRONG CHOICES EXPLAINED:

(1) A climate map emphasizes weather patterns and may depict a variety of colors representing climate zones.

(2) A physical map focuses on the many physical features of an area, including mountains, oceans, deserts, rivers, and plateaus.

(3) A resource map depicts where natural resources are found. These natural resources may include timber, coal, and iron ore.

3. **1** In a command economic system, the factors of production that determine what to produce, how to produce it, and for whom to produce are decided by the central government. The command economy is a key feature of communist societies, including North Korea, Cuba, and the former Soviet Union. Joseph Stalin's five-year plans in the Soviet Union are an example of the command economic system because all industry was nationalized under Stalin's control, and the central government set quotas for industrial output.

WRONG CHOICES EXPLAINED:

(2) A market economic system, like those found in capitalist societies, allows the factors of production to be determined by supply and demand. In a market economic system, the government plays a limited role.

(3) In a traditional economic system, like those found in rural societies, the factors of production are determined by customs and beliefs as opposed to central governments.

(4) A mixed economic system, like the economic system found in China, combines elements of a command economy and a market economy. In a mixed system, the government determines some factors of production while leaving others up to private enterprise.

4. **4** The most densely settled areas of Japan are in the coastal plains. A coastal plain is defined as a relatively flat area of lowlands near the coast. The majority of Japan's topography is comprised of mountains, and therefore the coastal plains became the most settled regions because they were the most suitable for agriculture. Additionally, their location along the coast allows for easy access to the seas and the ports for trade.

WRONG CHOICES EXPLAINED:

(1) Despite the fact that the majority of Japan is mountainous, mountains pose agricultural challenges and therefore are not the most settled areas.

(2) Japan's forests pose agricultural challenges as they are not as conducive to agriculture as are the coastal plains. Therefore, the forests are not the most settled areas.

(3) The northern snow zones pose agricultural challenges due to freezing temperatures and significant snowfall. Therefore, they are not the most populated regions.

5. **2** The diagram depicts the heliocentric, or sun-centered, model of the solar system that was published by Nicolaus Copernicus in the 16th century during the Scientific Revolution. Prior to the heliocentric model, the geocentric (earth-centered) model was the accepted theory by the Roman Catholic Church. Copernicus's heliocentric model placed the sun near the center of the solar system with Earth and the other planets orbiting around it in elliptical paths.

WRONG CHOICES EXPLAINED:

(1) Charles Darwin is notable for presenting the theory of evolution by natural selection.

(3) René Descartes was a French philosopher and mathematician who is notable for his theory of dualism, or the idea that the mind is a separate and immaterial force from the body that engages in rational thought.

(4) Isaac Newton was an English mathematician, physicist, and astronomer who is notable for presenting the theory of gravity.

6. **1** Both John Locke and Baron de Montesquieu were philosophers of the Enlightenment (17th to 18th centuries). The Enlightenment was a period of European history in which great thinkers questioned and challenged absolute monarchies and supported limited power of government. John Locke is notable for believing that people are born with the natural rights of life, liberty, and property and that governments were given their power by the consent of the governed in order to protect those rights. Baron de Montesquieu is notable for supporting the role of limited government by separating government into three branches.

WRONG CHOICES EXPLAINED:

(2) Mercantile economic systems, based on the idea that a nation's power and wealth were increased by maintaining a favorable balance of trade or exporting more than importing, developed as a result of the Commercial Revolution. Neither John Locke nor Baron de Montesquieu is associated with mercantilism. They are Enlightenment thinkers.

(3) The Protestant Reformation of the 16th century was led by Martin Luther, a German monk who wanted to reform the practices of the Roman Catholic Church that he deemed corrupt, such as the selling of indulgences. Neither John Locke nor Baron de Montesquieu is associated with the Protestant Reformation.

(4) The divine right theory claimed by European monarchs was the idea that a monarch's power was given to that monarch by God. John Locke and Baron de Montesquieu were

Enlightenment philosophers who argued against the divine right theory. John Locke argued that a government's power is derived from the consent of the governed, not from God.

7. **3** Based on the 1802 French proclamation, the French government reacted to the Haitian Revolution by ordering the citizens to "seize," or capture, General Toussaint L'Ouverture and General Henri Christophe. Both L'Ouverture and Christophe were key leaders in the Haitian Revolution for independence. By 1793, the spirit of the French Revolution had spread to the colonies, and Haitians began to fight for their own independence against French colonial rule. In 1801, the French attempted to reconquer the colony. However, the Haitians were able to defeat the French and gain their independence.

WRONG CHOICES EXPLAINED:

(1) The French proclamation states that "good citizens" are those who attempt to "seize," or capture, General Toussaint and General Christophe, who were both leaders in the Haitian Revolution against the French. The proclamation does not state anything about accepting Haitian demands to end slavery.

(2) The purpose of the proclamation was to end the rebellion by the Haitians against the French. Therefore, the French were not encouraging Haitians to rebel against them. It wouldn't have made sense for the French to encourage their colonial subjects to rebel.

(4) The proclamation does not state that Haitians will receive any rights. The purpose of the proclamation was to encourage citizens to capture revolutionary leaders.

8. **2** German unification was the immediate result of Otto von Bismarck's wars with Denmark, Austria, and France. Prior to German unification, the German Confederation existed as an association of 39 German-speaking states in central Europe. However, the confederation was weakened over time by rivalries between Austria and Prussia. When Otto von Bismarck became Chancellor of Prussia, his goal was to unite the German states into a strong empire with Prussia at its core. In the mid-19th century, he waged war against Denmark, Austria, and France to unite the German states and create one united Germany.

WRONG CHOICES EXPLAINED:

(1) Napoleon Bonaparte's surrender at the Battle of Waterloo ended the Napoleonic Wars in 1815. At the Congress of Vienna that followed, the German Confederation was created. However, the confederation would not be unified until 1871.

(3) Maria Theresa was the Habsburg ruler of the Holy Roman Empire from 1740 until 1780. She ruled almost 100 years before German unification.

(4) The outbreak of World War I, not German unification, was an immediate result of the assassination of Archduke Franz Ferdinand of Austria in 1914.

9. **1** By the mid-19th century, Great Britain ruled India as a colony. This meant that the British needed easier access to Indian ports. The Suez Canal, a man-made waterway connecting the Mediterranean Sea to the Red Sea, was originally financed by France and Egypt. When the British realized it shortened the distance to India, the need for Britain to remain the dominant power in the Middle East increased. This is due to the fact that India was Britain's most important colony for exports.

WRONG CHOICES EXPLAINED:

(2) The British slave trade ended in 1807, and the Suez Canal was not completed until 1869.

(3) Egyptian nationalism would have threatened Britain's influence in the Middle East at a time when Britain sought to maintain its dominance in the region in order to benefit from the Suez Canal.

(4) The Suez Canal was a man-made waterway that allowed trading vessels to avoid going around the tip of Africa by connecting the Red Sea to the Mediterranean Sea. This would not have a major impact on farming.

10. **4** Zionism is the belief that Judaism is a nationality and that the Jewish people deserve their own state in their ancestral homeland, Palestine (the modern-day state of Israel, the West Bank, and the Gaza Strip). By the early-20th century, Jews throughout Europe, particularly Eastern Europe where Jewish population densities were high, faced growing anti-Semitism. Under the leadership of Theodor Herzl, modern Zionism became a movement as he called for political recognition of a Jewish homeland in the area then known as Palestine. The rise of the modern Zionist movement led to massive Jewish immigration into Israel.

WRONG CHOICES EXPLAINED:

(1) Chechnya is a Muslim-majority region in the Russian Federation that has been fighting Russia for independence for centuries. Zionism was the movement for the reestablishment of a Jewish homeland.

(2) Kosovo is a Muslim region and self-declared independent state of the former Yugoslavia. It is not associated with Zionism or Judaism.

(3) Kurdistan, an autonomous region in northern Iraq, is ethnically Kurdish and is not associated with Zionism or Judaism.

11. **2** The Bolshevik Revolution in 1917 in Russia was precipitated by a number of explosive events. Centuries of imperial rule by the Romanov dynasty began to crumble in 1905 with the Bloody Sunday massacre. Large protests by peasants and workers against the monarchy were met with force by the imperial troops. Hundreds of unarmed protesters were killed by the czar's troops. This sparked the Revolution of 1905 in which tens of thousands of workers launched a series of strikes that crippled the nation. As a result, Czar Nicholas II promised to create representative bodies called Dumas to represent the masses and work toward reform. By 1917, after devastating losses in World War I as well as a worsening economic situation, protesters demanding bread took to the streets of Petrograd, eventually causing Czar Nicholas II to abdicate the throne while leaving the provisional government in place. Eventually, this provisional government, the Kerensky government, was overthrown by communist leader Vladimir Lenin, who gained the support of the people by promising "peace, land, and bread."

WRONG CHOICES EXPLAINED:

(1) The Russo-Japanese War was fought between Russia and Japan from 1904 to 1905 over rival imperial ambitions in Korea and Manchuria. It resulted in a Japanese victory. The Russo-Japanese War did not lead to strikes or to the abdication of the throne by Czar Nicholas II.

(3) The Great Depression began in 1929 with the crash of the stock market. This was over a decade after Czar Nicholas II's abdication of the throne and Lenin's return from exile.

(4) The Treaty of Kanagawa was a mid-19th century treaty between the United States and Japan that opened Japan's ports and effectively ended centuries of relative Japanese isolation from the west.

12. **3** The idea of self-determination is a consequence of nationalism. It is defined as the process by which a group of people within a nation who share a national identity form their own state and choose their own government. In other words, the people of the nation determine their nation's trajectory themselves without foreign imperial influence. Self-determination became an important objective in maintaining peace in Europe after World

War I. As a result, the Austro-Hungarian Empire broke into smaller, independent states, including Poland and Czechoslovakia.

WRONG CHOICES EXPLAINED:

(1) The Polish Corridor was created by the Treaty of Versailles after World War I and gave the Poles a strip of land that allowed for access to the Baltic Sea. This divided East Prussia from the rest of Germany and led to Germany's invasion of Poland during World War II. The creation of the corridor was not a result of the concept of self-determination.

(2) As a result of the Treaty of Versailles that ended World War I, Germany was ordered to demilitarize the region of the Rhineland to maintain peace in the region, but this was not a result of self-determination.

(4) Allied powers occupied German colonies after Germany's defeat in World War I, but this was not a result of self-determination.

13. **1** Imperialism is the policy of expanding a nation's influence or borders through various methods, including warfare and diplomacy. In the 19th and early-20th centuries, many European nations and the United States engaged in imperialism. "The Rhodes Colossus" depicts a British imperialist, Cecil Rhodes, as a giant who is straddling the African continent. This represents Europe's total dominance over Africa during this period. The cartoon is dated from the period of New Imperialism in 1892, during the Scramble for Africa. In this period, European countries divided, occupied, and colonized weaker African nations. Similarly, the Yoruba wood carving depicts the influence that Europe had on African culture from the perspective of the Africans. The African man in the carving is riding a horse, an animal native to Europe. Additionally, he is holding a gun, which was a weapon used by Europeans.

WRONG CHOICES EXPLAINED:

(2) Although the Yoruba wood carving was created by the Yoruba people of Nigeria and is a traditional art form, "The Rhodes Colossus" was a political cartoon created by a British cartoonist and is not considered a traditional art form.

(3) Neither image represents obstacles to developing the Nile River region. "The Rhodes Colossus" depicts Rhodes straddling the entire African continent. It represents the desire to dominate the entire region, not just the Nile River. The Yoruba wood carving was created by the people of Nigeria, which is in West Africa, whereas the Nile River is in Northeast Africa.

(4) Although a misinterpretation of these images may lead to the belief that they were designed to promote travel from Cairo, Egypt, to Cape Town, South Africa, a more accurate interpretation of the images shows viewpoints on the nature of imperialism.

14. **3** Japanese expansion was a major catalyst for warfare in the Pacific during World War II. Japanese expansion during the decade leading up to the war is clearly labeled on the map. It depicts the few possessions Japan had control over in 1930, which included Korea and Formosa. The map also depicts the expansion into Manchuria that occurred by 1933. By 1937, Japan was beginning to expand into parts of China, including the southern city of Nanjing. By 1938, Japan had expanded southward to Canton.

WRONG CHOICES EXPLAINED:

(1) There is no indication that this is a map depicting Southeast Asian independence efforts. Like many other regions that had been imperialized by European nations, independence did not occur until after World War II.

(2) Although Korea is depicted on the map as being a possession of Japan by 1930, there is no other indication on the map that this is a map depicting Korean battlegrounds.

(4) The map clearly shows that China was occupied by Japan by 1937. Therefore, China was not the aggressor. Instead, Japan was clearly the aggressor. It possessed, controlled, and occupied various regions throughout East Asia in the 1930s.

15. **1** Joseph Stalin's five-year plans were developed with the goal of industrializing heavy industries rapidly. Stalin understood that the Soviet Union faced threats externally from the West as well as internally from political dissidents. From 1928 to 1932, during the period in which the first five-year plan was implemented, factories were used to produce weapons for war and to produce tractors and other heavy machinery for increasing agricultural output. Although many of the goals set by the first five-year plan were not met, total industrial output increased over 100 percent, and thus this plan was thought to be a relatively successful plan.

WRONG CHOICES EXPLAINED:

(2) Stalin attempted to completely eliminate all religious practice in the U.S.S.R. and did not put religious leaders in control of the courts.

(3) Stalin was a totalitarian dictator who maintained total control over the U.S.S.R. There were no democratic practices in the U.S.S.R.

(4) Freedom of expression was forbidden under Joseph Stalin. Many political dissidents who spoke out against the government were executed.

16. **2** Mohandas Gandhi responded to British imperialism by urging Indians to follow a policy of noncooperation and civil disobedience. After the 1919 Amritsar massacre in which British troops killed hundreds of unarmed Indian protesters who were attending a political rally, Gandhi advised Indians to resist British rule by boycotting British goods. In addition, he preached nonviolence to achieve the goal of gaining independence from British colonial rule.

WRONG CHOICES EXPLAINED:

(1) Mohandas Gandhi was influenced by the Hindu concept of *ahimsa*, which means nonviolence. He urged Indians to use nonviolent strategies, such as boycotting British goods and organizing a march to the sea to protest the salt tax. Therefore, he would not have led an armed rebellion.

(3) Gandhi's goal was to achieve *swaraj*, or self-rule (independence), not to rule the subcontinent jointly with Britain.

(4) Gandhi was not in favor of the two-nation solution to the conflict between Hindus and Muslims in India.

17. **3** British government propaganda during World War II encouraged British citizens to support governmental war efforts. After the carnage experienced during World War I, support for another war was minimal. Various forms of media were used to influence the people to support the war effort, including the use of movies, newsreels, radio, and posters. Posters were circulated with sayings like "Freedom is in peril, defend it with all your might," and "Your courage, your cheerfulness, and your resolution will bring us victory."

WRONG CHOICES EXPLAINED:

(1) The government's main goal was to gain support for the war not to boycott overseas goods. No such boycotts were encouraged by the British government.

(2) The British had a worldwide empire that they intended on keeping because their colonial possessions brought wealth to the nation.

(4) Citizens discussing troop movements would not have benefited the government in any way during the war and therefore was not encouraged.

18. **4** When German forces invaded the Soviet Union during World War II, many thought that Germany would defeat the Soviets quickly before the extreme cold and frost of the winter set in. Still wearing their summer uniforms when the cold set in, German forces faced extreme frostbite, which weakened them. German tanks and jeeps refused to start in subzero temperatures, and guns and other artillery froze and failed. Additionally, the sheer size of Russia made swift conquest nearly impossible.

WRONG CHOICES EXPLAINED:

(1) The Black Sea did not restrict military activities between Europe and Africa. Instead, a North Africa campaign took place from 1940–1943 and resulted in an Allied victory.

(2) Aerial bombardment, or dropping bombs from planes, was not hindered by oceans or mountains because aircraft could fly over them.

(3) Troops were primarily moved over land as opposed to using riverboats, which were not as efficient.

19. **1** After World War II, Soviet forces occupied Eastern European nations. They were able to implement Stalinist-style governments in nations such as Poland, Romania, Czechoslovakia, Hungary, and others. With growing tensions between the Western nations and the Soviet Union, these satellite nations acted as protection against invasion and influence from the West during the postwar years and the Cold War era.

WRONG CHOICES EXPLAINED:

(2) The satellite countries were not nuclear-capable, and therefore nuclear weapons did not have to be removed.

(3) Cultural diversity was not a goal of the Soviet Union. The Soviet Union favored homogeneity over diversity.

(4) Russia is the largest nation in the world, and thus it did not need space for its population.

20. **4** According to these authors, all members of the United Nations should have to meet the "criteria of democratic governance." This is a political criterion because politics, by definition, relates to the government of a nation. The passage emphasizes that members of the United Nations must demonstrate principles of democracy.

WRONG CHOICES EXPLAINED:

(1) There is no mention of religion in the passage. The purpose of the United Nations is to maintain peace throughout the world. It would be counterproductive to impose a religious criterion on member nations since a variety of religions are practiced throughout the world.

(2) There is no mention in the passage of a military requirement for membership in the United Nations. Instead, the emphasis is on basing the criteria for admission on democratic principles, which is a political emphasis.

(3) There is no mention of resources, scarcity, or trade in the passage. Therefore, the author does not believe that the criteria for admission into the United Nations should be economic in nature.

21. **3** Nationalism is the identification of an individual with his or her own nation. Nationalists reject imperialism and support self-determination. In the post–World War II period, feelings of nationalism in nations throughout Africa and Asia led to the decolonization of the regions. In the postwar period, many European nations were driven out of Asia by the Japanese. After Japan's defeat in 1945, former Asian colonies supported independence rather than returning to colonial rule. Similarly in Africa, nationalistic movements for independence

led to the decolonization of the region. As a result, dozens of new nations were formed throughout Africa and Asia. Nations such as Indonesia, the Philippines, India, and the majority of countries in Africa were formed as a result of nationalist sentiments after World War II.

WRONG CHOICES EXPLAINED:

(1) Although both Asia and Africa had experienced migrations throughout history, including the Indo-European and Bantu migrations, there were no mass migrations in the post–World War II period. Additionally, migrations have not directly led to independence movements throughout history.

(2) Industrialization did not occur in the immediate aftermath of World War II and did not lead to the desire for independence from colonial powers.

(4) Pandemics are diseases that impact entire nations or regions. They typically weaken a nation as opposed to strengthening it and do not often lead to the desire for independence.

22. **3** The Communists' victory in the Chinese civil war of 1949 can be attributed to China's large population of peasants who supported Mao Zedong and the Chinese Communist Party. In the mid-20th century, China was an agrarian nation that depended on a large population of peasants who were often exploited. Poor economic conditions led to the support of the Communist Party. As the party's leader, Mao Zedong was able to mobilize the peasants to fight the Nationalist forces under Chiang Kai-shek.

WRONG CHOICES EXPLAINED:

(1) Businessmen and landlords did not want to be members of the Communist Party. The Communists wanted to nationalize all businesses and create collective farms, which would threaten the way of life of the businessmen and landlords.

(2) China was a highly patriarchal society, and women did not have the right to vote.

(4) Western powers supported democratic ideals and did not support the Communists. Therefore, they would not have provided arms and advisers to China's Communist army.

23. **4** India can be described as a nation that supported the idea of nonalignment during the Cold War. In the years following independence from British colonial rule, the survival of India as an emerging independent power was a top priority. India's Prime Minister, Jawaharlal Nehru, emphasized the importance of maintaining freedom by refusing to align India with any alliance, particularly NATO, which was led by the United States, and the Warsaw Pact, which was led by the Soviet Union.

WRONG CHOICES EXPLAINED:

(1) India's goal was to remain nonaligned, or neutral, by not joining alliances during the Cold War. India's nonalignment movement was in some ways inspired by its nonviolent independence movement and was not focused on militarism.

(2) Containment was a foreign policy of the United States and other Western nations during the Cold War. The goal of containment was to stop communism from spreading to free nations. India wanted to maintain its freedom by remaining neutral.

(3) Appeasement is a term used to describe the foreign policy of many European nations in the period before World War II. Many European powers appeased Adolf Hitler by giving into his demands in the hopes that appeasing him would avoid the outbreak of war. India did not have a part in appeasement.

24. **2** Germany split into free West Germany and communist East Germany in 1949, which led millions of East Germans to flee to West Germany. To prevent this and to protect

the Soviet government's political interests in the region, East Germany constructed a wall in 1961, separating East Berlin from West Berlin. The goal was to keep the East German people in and keep Western ideas out.

WRONG CHOICES EXPLAINED:

(1) Both regions of Germany had industrialized by 1961 when the wall was constructed. Protecting industrial secrets was not the purpose of the wall.

(3) Pastoral herders are people who migrate to graze their animals in areas of large grasslands, like the Eurasian Steppe. The Mongols are examples of pastoralists. Berlin, the capital of Germany, is west of the Eurasian Steppe. Additionally, there weren't mass migrations of pastoral herders in the mid-20th century.

(4) The building of walls for defensive purposes has been occurring since early history. The construction of the Berlin Wall, although an engineering achievement, was not a technological innovation.

25. **2** This political cartoon is titled "Mr. Putin Demonstrates to Secretary Rice that Russia Indeed Has a Free Press." A nation with a free press allows its citizens to publish their opinions about government openly in newspapers and other media sources. The image, however, contradicts the idea that Russia has a free press. Russian officers have their guns pointed at someone out of view, who we can assume is a journalist who wants to publish his or her opinion on the Russian government. Putin is shown telling Rice that this is the editorial process in Russia. Therefore, it can be inferred that Russia limits dissent against the government and is oppressive toward those who attempt to speak out against the regime.

WRONG CHOICES EXPLAINED:

(1) The image depicts the "editorial process" in Russia. According to the cartoon, the process includes officers pointing guns at what is presumed to be a journalist. Therefore, the government does not support a free press.

(3) Capitalism is an economic system based on private ownership of business and industry as opposed to government ownership. There is nothing in the cartoon that suggests anything about Putin promoting a capitalist economy.

(4) When the cartoon was published in 2005, the United States Secretary of State was Condoleezza Rice, who is depicted standing next to Putin. The guns are pointed away from her, not toward her, so there is nothing in the cartoon that suggests a distrust of the United States.

26. **1** The three headlines concerning the release of toxic fumes from a chemical plant, a nuclear explosion in Chernobyl, and the oil spill caused by the oil tanker *Exxon Valdez* all address events that have caused serious pollution in the environment. In 1984, an accident at a pesticide plant in Bhopal, India, led to the releasing of highly toxic gases that poisoned thousands and polluted the environment. In 1986, the Ukrainian city of Chernobyl experienced the worst nuclear disaster in history when an explosion occurred and released deadly radiation, making the city uninhabitable for possibly thousands of years. In 1989, the *Exxon Valdez* oil tanker hit a reef off of the coast of Alaska, releasing millions of gallons of oil into the environment leading to Prince William Sound and destroying the local aquatic environment in the process.

WRONG CHOICES EXPLAINED:

(2) Tsunamis are giant waves typically caused by earthquakes in the ocean off the coast. There is no mention of giant waves in the headlines.

(3) Soil erosion is often caused by the loss of topsoil due to the movement of water. The events mentioned in the headlines did not cause soil erosion.

(4) The major cause of the depletion of the ozone layer in Earth's atmosphere is the release of chlorine and bromine in man-made compounds. The Chernobyl nuclear disaster and the *Exxon Valdez* oil spill did not release these compounds.

27. **3** The Green Revolution of the mid-20th century was a period in which new agricultural methods and technologies led to an increase in crops worldwide. Crops were grown more efficiently using heavy tractors, more efficient irrigation techniques, and fertilizers and pesticides. Therefore, the introduction of the Green Revolution was the cause, whereas the other three answer choices are effects of the Green Revolution.

WRONG CHOICES EXPLAINED:

(1), (2), and (4) This question is asking for the cause of the other three choices given. In other words, which one happened first and led to the other three? The Green Revolution led to the use of chemical pesticides, which led to crops being grown more efficiently, which then led to an increase in agricultural output.

28. **3** North Korea's efforts to develop nuclear weapons in the early-21st century has caused concerns in the international community. In 2003, North Korea withdrew from the Treaty on the Non-Proliferation of Nuclear Weapons. In 2005, it admitted to having nuclear weapons. In the years since, North Korea has attempted to demonstrate its nuclear capability. The goal of leaders in the international community has been to put an end to North Korea's international ballistic missile testing. In 2018, United States President Donald Trump met with North Korea's leader Kim Jong-un to work toward denuclearization of the Korean Peninsula. However, little progress has been made.

WRONG CHOICES EXPLAINED:

(1) Although France developed nuclear weapons in 1960 and is one of the five "nuclear weapon states" under the Treaty on the Non-Proliferation of Nuclear Weapons, it is not known to be an aggressor and has not caused international concern.

(2) China is also one of the five "nuclear weapon states." However, it has also signed the treaty to limit its nuclear capability.

(4) The Soviet Union had collapsed by the early 21st century. However, its successor state, Russia, remains part of the Treaty on the Non-Proliferation of Nuclear Weapons.

29. **4** One way in which the Congress of Vienna (1814–1815) and the Paris Peace Conference (1919) are similar is that both meetings sought to establish stability after a period of war and revolution. The Congress of Vienna took place after Napoleon Bonaparte's defeat in the Napoleonic Wars. It was a meeting led by Great Britain, Prussia, Russia, and Austria, who redrew the map of Europe to prevent France from becoming an aggressor again in the future. Similarly, the Paris Peace Conference of 1919 was held at the end of World War I. The victorious Allied powers signed the Treaty of Versailles and attempted to limit Germany's ability to start another war by disarming the country.

WRONG CHOICES EXPLAINED:

(1) Ethnic and religious minorities were largely ignored when the maps of Europe were redrawn after both the Congress of Vienna and the Paris Peace Conference. This led to future ethnic conflicts and the breakup of empires due to feelings of nationalism.

(2) These meetings did not seek to restore monarchs to power but, instead, sought to maintain peace and stability.

(3) Both the Congress of Vienna and the Paris Peace Conference took place after international wars. Distributing aid to the people displaced by conflict was not a major goal of either meeting.

30. **4** Terrace farming, building bridges, and constructing canals are ways in which various societies have adapted to and modified their environments. Terrace farming is an agricultural technique used in mountainous regions around the world, including in the Andes Mountains of Peru and the Himalayan Mountains in Tibet. Terrace farming is the creation of steps carved into the side of mountain in order to create flat farmland in areas of high altitude. Canals are man-made waterways like the Panama Canal and the Suez Canal. Both of these canals required the environment to be modified to create the waterways through existing land. Likewise, bridges facilitate the movement of people over waterways and other difficult terrain. The construction of bridges requires the modification of the surrounding environment.

WRONG CHOICES EXPLAINED:

(1) Cultural diversity is the presence of a variety of different ethnic, racial, or religious groups within a society. Terrace farming, building bridges, and constructing canals do not directly lead to cultural diversity.

(2) Bridges and canals facilitate the movement of goods and people. Therefore, they do not reduce the threat of invasion.

(3) Terrace farming, building bridges, and constructing canals do not establish boundaries. Additionally, they are not necessarily permanent structures and therefore cannot establish permanent boundaries.

THEMATIC ESSAY: GENERIC SCORING RUBRIC

Score of 5:
- Shows a thorough understanding of the theme or problem
- Addresses all aspects of the task
- Shows an ability to analyze, evaluate, compare and/or contrast issues and events
- Richly supports the theme or problem with relevant facts, examples, and details
- Is a well-developed essay, consistently demonstrating a logical and clear plan of organization
- Introduces the theme or problem by establishing a framework that is beyond a simple restatement of the task and concludes with a summation of the theme or problem

Score of 4:
- Shows a good understanding of the theme or problem
- Addresses all aspects of the task
- Shows an ability to analyze, evaluate, compare and/or contrast issues and events
- Includes relevant facts, examples, and details, but may not support all aspects of the theme or problem evenly
- Is a well-developed essay, demonstrating a logical and clear plan of organization
- Introduces the theme or problem by establishing a framework that is beyond a simple restatement of the task and concludes with a summation of the theme or problem

Score of 3:
- Shows a satisfactory understanding of the theme or problem
- Addresses most aspects of the task or addresses all aspects in a limited way
- Shows an ability to analyze or evaluate issues and events, but not in any depth
- Includes some facts, examples, and details
- Is a satisfactorily developed essay, demonstrating a general plan of organization
- Introduces the theme or problem by repeating the task and concludes by repeating the theme or problem

Score of 2:
- Shows limited understanding of the theme or problem
- Attempts to address the task
- Develops a faulty analysis or evaluation of issues and events
- Includes few facts, examples, and details, and may include information that contains inaccuracies
- Is a poorly organized essay, lacking focus
- Fails to introduce or summarize the theme or problem

Score of 1:
- Shows very limited understanding of the theme or problem
- Lacks an analysis or evaluation of the issues and events
- Includes little or no accurate or relevant facts, examples, or details
- Attempts to complete the task, but demonstrates a major weakness in organization
- Fails to introduce or summarize the theme or problem

Score of 0: Fails to address the task, is illegible, or is a blank paper

PART II: THEMATIC ESSAY QUESTION

In regions throughout the world at various times in history, certain groups have been stripped of their human rights by those who sought to subjugate those who differed from them. Two examples of those who have been denied human rights in history are the untouchables in India, also known as the Dalits, and Black South Africans during the period of apartheid. Both the Dalits of India and the Black South Africans lived under oppressive policies, which caused inequality in society, the economy, and government.

The denial of the Dalits' human rights is deeply ingrained in Indian history and has led to millennia of inequality, oppression, and subjugation. Once called "untouchables" because they were thought to be so polluted, the Dalits were trapped at the bottom of India's rigid caste system since the second millennium B.C. Some historians argue that this system was created by the Indo-European Aryans who subjugated the non-Aryans, forced them into positions of unskilled labor, and limited their economic opportunities. Over the centuries as the caste system was justified by the dominant Hindu belief of karma, Hindus believed that those in the lowest castes were born in a low position in society because they had acquired bad karma in a previous life. The justification of the caste system through Hindu ideas strengthened the caste system. Eventually, the "untouchable" caste emerged, which comprised those who were required to work the worst jobs. For example, they were often forced to handle dead animal carcasses. In more modern times, they have been relegated to cleaning the latrines of upper caste members by hand. Additionally, they have been historically denied the ability to marry those in the upper castes. In many ways, they were segregated from upper caste members in society. By the early-20th century, Dalits were prohibited from eating meals with members of the upper castes and denied entry into upper caste homes. They had to pray in different temples, drink from separate cups in tea stalls, and even had segregated burial grounds. This denial of human rights began at an early age as Dalit children were segregated in schools. Their inability to obtain equal education and the discrimination they experienced in the workforce kept Dalits in the lowest socioeconomic positions within Indian society.

Although the Civil Rights Acts of 1955, 1976, and 1989 progressively protected Dalit interests and made discrimination based on the caste system illegal, the practice of caste discrimination persisted. It forced the Dalits to organize to fight for their civil rights. The support of Hindu religious beliefs, along with the caste system's long history of rigidity, has led to continued discrimination in society and government as many of the laws passed have been largely ignored. Similar to the civil rights movement that began in the 1950s in the United States, the Dalits have been and continue to organize and mobilize using peaceful solutions to gain equality and equal opportunities. They were instrumental in the formation of the International Dalit Solidarity Network, which works to end caste discrimination in India and within regions throughout the world with large Hindu populations. Although they still have many hurdles to overcome, the Dalits continue to fight for their rights. Most recently, in 2014, the Dalits organized marches and protests and used social media to document atrocities they've faced by upper caste members to work toward the end of discrimination and to create a society with equal opportunities for all.

Similar to the Dalits of India, Black South Africans who lived during the period of apartheid were denied their human rights as they experienced discrimination, subjugation, and segregation. When Britain granted South Africa its independence in 1910, it granted power solely to the white minority, which comprised only 20 percent of the total population. When the National Party came to power in 1948, it officially introduced the policy of apartheid with the goal of subjugating and segregating the Black South Africans from those of European descent known as "Afrikaners." Although segregation had existed in South Africa for decades, apartheid made segregation a law. Black South Africans were no longer allowed to marry white people. Hospitals, hotels, and restaurants were segregated, and education was restricted. Over time, more laws were passed to restrict the movement of Black South Africans as they had to carry a passbook and could not enter a city without immediately finding a job. The segregation and discrimination by the Afrikaners and the Nationalist Party kept the Black South Africans in a subjugated socioeconomic position.

As a result of their oppression, Black South Africans began to organize and fight to end apartheid. The African National Congress (ANC) was formed in 1912 after the British handed over all political power to white Afrikaners. Under apartheid, the ANC was led by a new and younger generation whose goal was to end apartheid. By the 1950s, the ANC's leadership under Nelson Mandela broadened its base of support. Inspired by Gandhi, he used principles of nonviolence by organizing boycotts, strikes, and demonstrations. Black South Africans burned their passbooks in protest. In response, the Nationalist Party, which was controlling the government, banned the ANC and imprisoned its leadership. The struggle to end apartheid was now in the hands of student groups who organized the Black Consciousness Movement. In Soweto, students organized an uprising to protest the use of the Afrikaner's language in the education system, leading to the deaths of hundreds. South Africa was facing growing demands to end apartheid, not just from internal pressures but from the international community as well. By 1994, growing internal and external pressures led to the abandonment of apartheid. Nelson Mandela was released from prison after 27 years, and he became the country's first black president. The struggle to end apartheid in South Africa is an example of individuals and groups who have fought to end the denial of human rights.

In many areas of the world, groups have been subjugated, oppressed, and denied their basic human rights. Two examples of regions where human rights were denied are India, where the Dalits were oppressed for millennia, and South Africa, where Black South Africans were denied equality under apartheid. In both regions, the oppressed have fought back using mostly nonviolent strategies to achieve their goals of attaining their civil rights.

PART III: DOCUMENT-BASED QUESTIONS

Part A: Short Answers

Documents 1a and 1b

1) Based on these documents, one fear the Japanese leaders had for their country was being dominated by Western nations in the same way China had been.

Note: This response receives full credit because it correctly identifies one fear Japanese leaders had for their country by focusing on the threat of Western nations.

Documents 2a and 2b

2a) According to Richard Perren, one reason the Japanese government adopted Western cultural innovations was to demonstrate to Western diplomats that they were changing and modernizing and ultimately to receive equal treatment by Western nations.

Note: This response receives full credit because it correctly identifies one reason the Japanese government adopted Western cultural innovations by focusing on the government's desire to show diplomats from Western nations that the Japanese people were attempting to change.

2b) Based on these documents, one way westernization influenced Japanese culture during the rule of Emperor Meiji was that the Japanese people began to wear Western styles, including growing Western-style beards and wearing Western clothing.

Note: This response receives full credit because it correctly states one way westernization influenced Japanese culture during the rule of Emperor Meiji.

Document 3

3) According to Peter N. Stearns, one way the conservative Japanese officials attempted to prevent westernization from damaging Japanese traditions was to revive the Shinto religion and encourage nationalism to propel rapid development.

Note: This response receives full credit because it correctly states one way the conservative Japanese officials attempted to prevent westernization from damaging Japanese traditions. This response emphasizes the officials' desire to create more loyalty to traditional Japanese culture and use nationalism to achieve the goals of modernization.

Document 4a

4a) According to this chart, one problem Turkey faced that convinced Atatürk that Turkey needed to undergo major changes was that Ottoman lands in southwest Asia were divided into European-controlled mandates.

Note: This response receives full credit because it correctly states a problem Turkey faced, according to this chart, that convinced Atatürk that Turkey needed to undergo major changes by emphasizing the fear of losing more territory to the nations of Western Europe.

Document 4b

4b) According to Stephen Kinzer, one problem Atatürk faced as he forced his country to change was that Turks were not ready to embrace modernity.

Note: This response receives full credit because it correctly states one problem Atatürk faced as he forced the country to change by focusing on Atatürk's understanding that he needed to take charge of the efforts to modernize because he would have faced opposition from the people.

Document 5

5) Based on this excerpt from Eric Lawlor's 1996 article, two actions Atatürk took to make his country into a more modern, secular state modeled on the nations of western Europe were:

1. Banning the fez (traditional hat)
2. Adopting a modified Latin alphabet

Note: This response receives full credit because it correctly identifies two different actions Atatürk took to create a more modern, secular state by identifying his actions to prohibit traditional forms of dress and change the alphabet to be more similar to the alphabet used in Western Europe.

Document 6

6) According to John F. Crossland, one impact of Atatürk's rule on Turkey was that he left the machinery of democratic government in place despite ruling through one party.

Note: This response receives full credit because it correctly identifies an impact of Atatürk's rule on Turkey by focusing on the legacy he left behind to make Turkey a more democratic society.

Document 7

7) According to this article by Susan Greenhalgh, one reason Chinese authorities were concerned about rapid population growth was that it would put strains on Chinese resources, including water and energy.

Note: This response receives full credit because it states one reason Chinese authorities were concerned about rapid population growth according to the author. This response focuses on the problems the Chinese people could face with strained resources.

Documents 8a and 8b

8) Based on this excerpt by Tyrene White and on this Chinese advertisement, one cultural impact the one-child policy had on Chinese society was that male children were favored and female infanticide increased.

Note: This response receives full credit because it correctly states one cultural impact the one-child policy had on Chinese society by focusing on the disparity between the desire for male children and female children.

Document 9

9) According to Javier C. Hernández, one way the discontinued one-child policy will continue to impact China after 2015 is that the size of the labor force will continue to shrink.

Note: This response receives full credit because it correctly states one way the discontinued one-child policy will continue to impact China after 2015 by focusing on the economic impact of a dwindling population.

DOCUMENT-BASED QUESTION: GENERIC SCORING RUBRIC

Score of 5:

- Thoroughly addresses all aspects of the *Task* by accurately analyzing and interpreting at least **four** documents
- Incorporates information from the documents in the body of the essay
- Incorporates relevant outside information
- Richly supports the theme or problem with relevant facts, examples, and details
- Is a well-developed essay, consistently demonstrating a logical and clear plan of organization
- Introduces the theme or problem by establishing a framework that is beyond a simple restatement of the *Task* or *Historical Context* and concludes with a summation of the theme or problem

Score of 4:

- Addresses all aspects of the *Task* by accurately analyzing and interpreting at least **four** documents
- Incorporates information from the documents in the body of the essay
- Incorporates relevant outside information
- Includes relevant facts, examples, and details, but discussion may be more descriptive than analytical
- Is a well-developed essay, demonstrating a logical and clear plan of organization
- Introduces the theme or problem by establishing a framework that is beyond a simple restatement of the *Task* or *Historical Context* and concludes with a summation of the theme or problem

Score of 3:

- Addresses most aspects of the *Task* or addresses all aspects of the *Task* in a limited way, using some of the documents
- Incorporates some information from the documents in the body of the essay
- Incorporates limited or no relevant outside information
- Includes some facts, examples, and details, but discussion is more descriptive than analytical
- Is a satisfactorily developed essay, demonstrating a general plan of organization
- Introduces the theme or problem by repeating the *Task* or *Historical Context* and concludes by simply repeating the theme or problem

Score of 2:

- Attempts to address some aspects of the *Task*, making limited use of the documents
- Presents no relevant outside information
- Includes few facts, examples, and details; discussion restates contents of the documents
- Is a poorly organized essay, lacking focus
- Fails to introduce or summarize the theme or problem

Score of 1:

- Shows limited understanding of the *Task* with vague, unclear references to the documents
- Presents no relevant outside information
- Includes little or no accurate or relevant facts, details, or examples
- Attempts to complete the *Task*, but demonstrates a major weakness in organization
- Fails to introduce or summarize the theme or problem

Score of 0: Fails to address the *Task*, is illegible or is a blank paper

Part B: Essay

Significant changes within nations are often a result of the actions of world leaders who recognize the need for change to improve the status of their country. Two world leaders who brought about significant changes to their nations were Emperor Meiji of Japan and Kemal Atatürk of Turkey. Both Emperor Meiji and Kemal Atatürk responded to external threats to their independence, from Western nations, by implementing policies of westernization to modernize their countries and to achieve the ability to compete with Western powers. Emperor Meiji in Japan, however, sought to use nationalism and retain more elements of traditional culture than did Kemal Atatürk in Turkey.

External threats to power posed by Western nations, such as the United States and Britain, led both Emperor Meiji and Kemal Atatürk to implement policies to westernize and modernize their countries. Prior to the Meiji Restoration in 1868, Japan was ruled for over two hundred years by the Tokugawa shogun, or military ruler. The shogun's role was to keep the hundreds of daimyo, or landlords, who had their own loyal samurai, from waging war on each other. In comparison to many Western, modernized, and centralized nations, Japan lacked a central law code, a tax system, a central army, and a unified currency. Foreign intervention led Japan to desire change. Ever since the 17th century when the Japanese expelled Christian missionaries, Japan deliberately limited contact with foreigners. In 1853, Japan was forever changed when Commodore Matthew Perry of the United States sailed into Japan's harbor with his giant steamboats, which were intimidating to the Japanese people, who had never seen such vessels (Doc. 1b). He was sent by the United States government with the purpose of forcing the Japanese to open their ports for trade. Japan immediately surrendered and agreed to sign unequal treaties. However, the humiliating incident led to the erosion of support for the shogun. After a brief civil war, a political coup expelled the last Tokugawa shogun and restored Emperor Meiji to power. Emperor Meiji recognized that Japan needed to gain the natural resources like coal and iron that Japan was lacking so that Japan could industrialize. He understood that modernization was the key to maintaining autonomy and self-rule, and he issued policies to achieve his goals.

Similar to Japan, the fear of the power of Western nations led Kemal Atatürk, leader of Turkey after the collapse of the Ottoman Empire, to westernize and modernize his nation. Prior to the creation of the republic, Turkey was part of the Ottoman Empire, which was ruled by the Sultan Mohammed VI. In fact, Atatürk had been an Ottoman general who fought off Greek, French, Italian, and British efforts to dismember what was left of the old empire. After the war ended, Britain, France, Italy, and Greece still occupied Turkish lands in Asia Minor, which threatened the freedom of the Turks. As a result, Kemal Atatürk formed a nationalist government that forced Sultan Mohammed VI to abdicate the throne (Doc. 4a). By 1923, Kemal Atatürk had officially become the leader of a newly independent Republic of Turkey. His desire to modernize and westernize the new nation led to a series of policies issued by Atatürk's newly formed government.

Both Emperor Meiji and Kemal Atatürk were successful in achieving their goals of modernization and westernization. As the emperor, Meiji raised a national army of members from all classes of society that challenged the old Confucian social order. The new national army used rifles and cannons and wore Western-style uniforms. This resulted in the formerly elite samurai forces being stripped of their titles and being prohibited from carrying swords. Culturally, Japan was significantly westernized as well. The consumption of meat, which was discouraged by Buddhist traditions, was encouraged. In addition, Western styles of dress were used at court and official ceremonies (Doc. 2a). Similar to Emperor Meiji, Kemal Atatürk successfully westernized and modernized the Republic of Turkey and focused on cultural changes to garner support for his policies. Kemal Atatürk ordered Turkish men to abandon the fez, which was a traditional style of headdress, and women were no longer required to wear a veil. Atatürk also restructured the government to secularize it to make it more like the countries of Western Europe (Doc. 5). He adopted new law codes modeled on Western law codes, which replaced Sharia law based on Islamic traditions. Westernization efforts were successful in both Japan and Turkey.

Although both Emperor Meiji and Kemal Atatürk wanted modernization, after the period of westernization, Emperor Meiji had a greater desire to retain elements of traditional culture in Japan than did Kemal Atatürk in Turkey. Under Meiji sponsorship, nationalism began to emerge. As a result, the native traditional religion of Shintoism was revived. Additionally, he began to use nationalism to motivate higher production, economic sacrifices, and rapid development (Doc. 3). Kemal Atatürk, on the other hand, wanted to enter European civilization completely. Although he understood that he needed a single-party political system to achieve his sweeping reforms, Kemal Atatürk left in place the machinery for Turkey to develop into a democratic style of government. He did so by including the idea that army leaders were above politics and could intervene to save the country and rewrite the constitution (Doc. 6). Kemal Atatürk had less of a desire to retain elements of traditional culture than did Emperor Meiji.

Emperor Meiji of Japan and Kemal Atatürk of Turkey are examples of two world leaders who brought about significant changes to their respective nations. Both leaders feared foreign domination and loss of autonomy, and both leaders responded by successfully modernizing and westernizing their nations. Emperor Meiji, however, was committed to retaining elements of Japanese culture while Kemal Atatürk desired to immerse Turkey fully in Western culture.

Topic	Question Numbers	Total Number of Questions	Number Wrong	*Reason for Wrong Answer
U.S. AND N.Y. HISTORY				
WORLD HISTORY	5, 7, 8, 11, 12, 16, 17, 19, 20, 21, 22, 23, 25, 28, 29	15		
GEOGRAPHY	1, 2, 4, 9, 10, 13, 14, 18, 24, 26, 30	11		
ECONOMICS	3, 15, 27	3		
CIVICS, CITIZENSHIP, AND GOVERNMENT	6	1		

*Your reason for answering the question incorrectly might be (a) lack of knowledge, (b) misunderstanding of the question, or (c) careless error.

Actual Items by Standard and Unit

	1 U.S. and N.Y. History	2 World History	3 Geography	4 Economics	5 Civics, Citizenship, and Government	Number
Methodology of Global History and Geography			1, 2, 4	3		4
UNIT ONE Age of Revolution		5, 7, 8	9		6	5
UNIT TWO Crisis and Achievement (1900–1945)		11, 12, 16, 17	10, 13, 14, 18	15		9
UNIT THREE 20th Century Since 1945		19, 20, 22, 23	24, 26	27		7
UNIT FOUR Global Connections and Interactions		21, 25, 28				3
Cross-Topical		29	30			2
Total # of Questions		15	11	3	1	30
% of Items by Standard		50%	37%	10%	3%	100%

Examination August 2019

Global History and Geography

PART I: MULTIPLE CHOICE

Directions (1–30): For each statement or question, write in the space provided the *number* of the word or expression that, of those given, best completes the statement or answers the question.

1 For which application would a physical map be most useful?

(1) showing the distribution of religious groups in Lebanon
(2) identifying regional population densities in China
(3) comparing the elevation of settlements in Peru
(4) examining the historical changes in Middle Eastern political boundaries

1 ____

2 In which political system are both the religious and political authority in the hands of the government?

(1) representative democracy
(2) theocracy
(3) oligarchy
(4) constitutional monarchy

2 ____

3 The rules of evidence used by historians require that a primary source be

(1) authentic
(2) narrative
(3) modern
(4) unbiased

3 ____

4 A significant result of the Scientific Revolution was the development of an understanding of the universe based on

(1) tradition
(2) laws of nature
(3) religious principles
(4) geocentrism 4 ____

5 Which writer is credited with the idea that the powers of government should be separated into three branches with each branch keeping the others in check?

(1) René Descartes
(2) Maximilien Robespierre
(3) Baron de Montesquieu
(4) Bishop Jacques-Bénigne Bossuet 5 ____

6 What was an unintended consequence of Napoleon's conquests?

(1) an increase of nationalism in Europe and Latin America
(2) the beginning of the American Revolution
(3) a reduction of the status of women throughout Europe
(4) the destruction of the British economy 6 ____

7 One reason the Industrial Revolution began in Great Britain was that Great Britain had a

(1) decline in the birth rate
(2) smooth coastline
(3) compulsory education system
(4) plentiful supply of iron ore and coal 7 ____

8 Which 19th-century economic condition was the basis for the ideas of Karl Marx?

(1) Capitalism contributed to a widening gap between the rich and the poor.
(2) The availability of material goods increased.
(3) Access to certain resources changed how goods were produced.
(4) People left farms and moved to the cities in search of work. 8 ____

9 In the 19th century, the idea of Social Darwinism was used by Europeans to justify their policy of

(1) multiculturalism
(2) imperialism
(3) national self-determination
(4) secular humanism 9 ____

10 The Suez Canal has been an important waterway because it

(1) links the Mediterranean Sea and the Red Sea
(2) guarantees protection for Egypt
(3) separates Israel from its neighbors
(4) provides water for irrigating the Sahara Desert 10 ____

11 What was a major goal of the Boxer Rebellion in China and the Sepoy Rebellion in India?

(1) restoring divine right monarchs
(2) obtaining aid from Europe
(3) annexing neighboring territories
(4) reducing foreign influences 11 ____

12 The success of the Meiji Restoration depended on Japan's ability to

(1) borrow military models from China and Korea
(2) strengthen the traditional roles of the samurai
(3) replicate the power and wealth of the industrial West
(4) eliminate the imperial form of government 12 ____

13 Which factor caused many European countries to become involved in World War I?

(1) religious obligations
(2) entangling alliances
(3) communist ideologies
(4) opposition to fascism 13 ____

14 How did the political map of Europe change immediately after World War I?

(1) Newly independent countries were formed from the Austro-Hungarian territory.
(2) Germany's territory expanded to include the Netherlands and Belgium.
(3) Russia gained control of Serbia and Bosnia.
(4) The Ottoman Empire dominated northern Africa. 14 ____

15 • Occupation of Korea—1905
• Seizure of Manchuria—1931
• "Rape of Nanjing"—1937

Which country is responsible for these events?

(1) Soviet Union
(2) China
(3) Great Britain
(4) Japan 15 ____

Base your answer to question 16 on the cartoon below and on your knowledge of social studies.

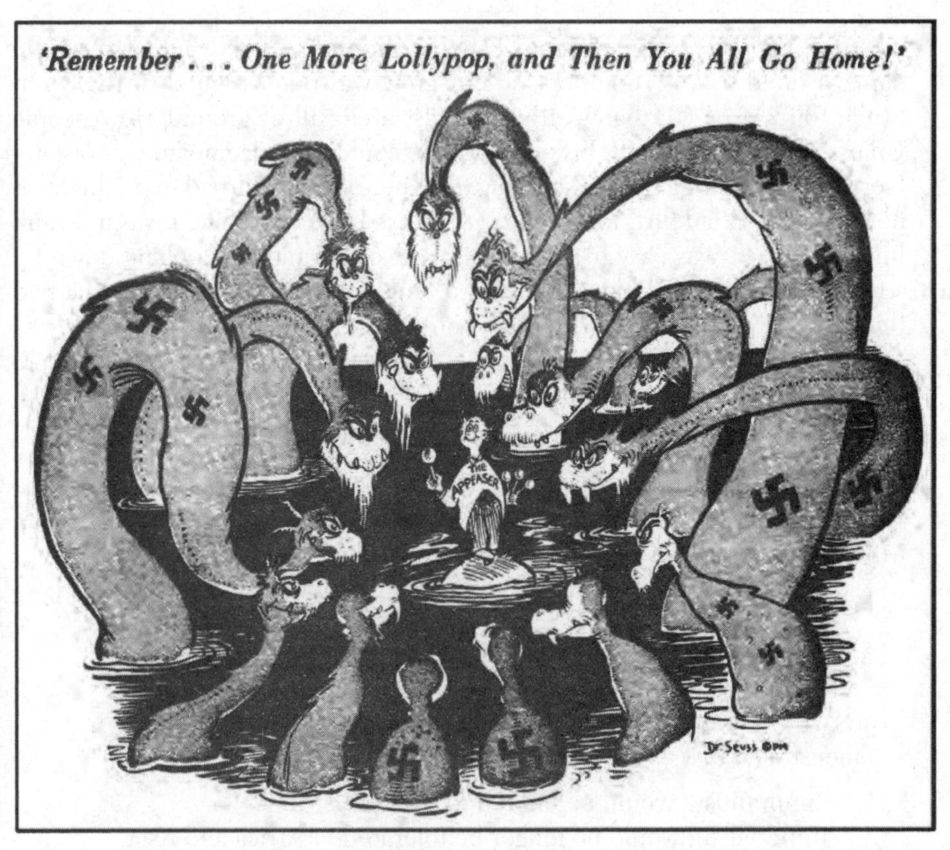

Source: Dr. Seuss, PM Magazine in *Dr. Seuss Goes to War*, August 13, 1941

16 This 1941 cartoon expresses the opinion that the policy of appeasement

(1) poses no threat to peace
(2) will not be tolerated
(3) is costly but necessary
(4) is shortsighted and unwise

16 _____

Base your answer to question 17 on the passage below and on your knowledge of social studies.

> After VE [Victory in Europe] Day the ground people wanted to see the damage done by "us" bombers, so our crew was one assigned to fly low altitude tours over Germany with our waist area full of ground crew people. Unless one could see with his own eyes, he could not imagine how devastated Germany was. Not a bridge standing anywhere, not a railroad, not a highway, not a factory. Frankfurt, for instance, was just a pile of rubble. I was in Frankfurt in 1977. It was easy to distinguish new construction. Looking down the street I could see that about every third building was old, indicating that two-thirds had been completely bombed out. . . .
>
> —Lt. Robert Pepper, U.S. Army Air Force pilot

17 The scene described in this passage is most closely associated with the

(1) policy of nonalignment
(2) doctrine of containment
(3) impact of modern war technology
(4) effects of industrialization on the environment 17 ____

---

18 After World War II, the actions taken by the Nuremberg Tribunal demonstrated that

(1) communism would be limited to Central Europe
(2) imperialism would no longer be tolerated in Africa and Asia
(3) policies of apartheid would be eliminated
(4) persons who committed wartime atrocities would be held accountable 18 ____

19 One way in which the Chinese Communist Revolution and the Cuban Revolution are similar is that both revolutions

(1) embraced capitalist ideals
(2) rejected industrial development
(3) used peaceful methods to achieve their goals
(4) gained strong support from the peasants 19 ____

Base your answers to questions 20 and 21 on the cartoon below and on your knowledge of social studies.

Source: Signe Wilkinson, *Philadelphia Daily News*, Washington Post Writers Group in *NY Times*, December 19, 2010

20 The message to the dove in this cartoon is most likely referring to the tension between

(1) Sikhs and Tamils
(2) Hutus and Tutsis
(3) Palestinians and Israelis
(4) Serbs and Bosnians

20 _____

21 Which factor best explains the message on the screen?

(1) reluctance of governments to market reserves of oil
(2) failure to resolve competing territorial claims
(3) lack of global involvement in the region
(4) absence of traditional belief systems in the region

21 _____

22 The European Union (EU) and the North American Free Trade Agreement (NAFTA) were created to

(1) seek justice for human rights victims
(2) promote nuclear disarmament
(3) encourage economic development
(4) legislate pollution reduction

22 _____

23 South Korea's economic miracle in the late 20th century was modeled after the success of which nation?

(1) Russia
(2) India
(3) Vietnam
(4) Japan

23 _____

24 Which health care issue has most frustrated African governments and health care workers in the early 21st century?

(1) cost of treatment for HIV and AIDS
(2) shortage of smallpox vaccines
(3) overwhelming number of cancer patients
(4) spread of polio to their countries

24 _____

Base your answer to question 25 on the passage below and on your knowledge of social studies.

. . . "Oh, of course. Once there were gardens to the south, to the banks of the Niger, when canals brought the river water here. Now, there is only sand."

"The Niger is at least ten kilometers away from here, isn't it?"

"Yes. It used to be much nearer. But the desert is closing in."

"The poor people were cutting down the few scraggly trees for firewood. They had no other source of fuel and no options; you can't eat goat meat raw. . . ."

—Marq De Villiers, *Water: The Fate of Our Most Precious Resource*

25 According to this passage, what is a valid conclusion concerning the Niger River region?

(1) Irrigation has damaged the region.
(2) Canals are used to conduct trade.
(3) Desertification has altered the landscape.
(4) Fertilization of the sand allowed gardens to flourish. 25 ____

---

26 • Deforestation in Latin America
• Acid rain in Europe
• Pollution in the Mediterranean Sea

Which conclusion can best be drawn from these situations?

(1) Industrialization is slowing down in these areas.
(2) Environmental issues only affect these specific areas.
(3) Environmental problems need international attention.
(4) Technological remedies for waste management are unavailable. 26 ____

27 The success of Otto von Bismarck in Germany and of Mohandas Gandhi in India demonstrate that

(1) imperialism usually acts as a positive force
(2) more than one method can be used to build nationalism
(3) economic prosperity is the key to social change
(4) urbanization strengthens traditional values 27 ____

28 One way in which Kemal Atatürk and Reza Pahlavi are similar is that both supported policies of

(1) promoting membership in the United Nations
(2) denying women the right to vote
(3) modernizing and westernizing their nations
(4) preventing their citizens from traveling overseas 28 ____

Base your answers to questions 29 and 30 on the cartoons below and on your knowledge of social studies.

Ⓐ **MUZZLED?**

Source: *London Opinion*, reprinted in *Literary Digest*, September 13, 1919 (adapted)

Ⓑ **THE RAINBOW.**

Source: *London Evening News*, reprinted in *Literary Digest*, September 13, 1919 (adapted)

29 These cartoons were published immediately after

(1) the Russo-Japanese War
(2) World War I
(3) World War II
(4) the Cold War

29 _____

30 Which ideas best represent the cartoonists' views about the ability of the League of Nations to function?

(1) Cartoonist A is distrustful and Cartoonist B is hopeful.
(2) Cartoonist A is watchful and Cartoonist B is guarded.
(3) Cartoonist A is fearful and Cartoonist B is uneasy.
(4) Cartoonist A is optimistic and Cartoonist B is pessimistic.

30 _____

In developing your answer to Part II, be sure to keep this general definition in mind:

> **discuss means "to make observations about something using facts, reasoning, and argument; to present in some detail"**

PART II: THEMATIC ESSAY QUESTION

Directions: Write a well-organized essay that includes an introduction, several paragraphs addressing the task below, and a conclusion.

Theme: Technology

> Transportation and communication technologies have been used by governments, groups, and individuals to unify and control societies and regions.

Task:

> Select ***two*** governments, groups, ***and/or*** individuals that have used transportation or communication technologies and for ***each***
>
> - Discuss how a specific government, group, or individual used transportation ***or*** communication technologies to unify ***and/or*** control a society or region

You may use any governments, groups, or individuals that have used transportation or communication technologies from your study of global history and geography. Some suggestions you might wish to consider include Great Britain's use of railroads in India/Africa, Germany's use of submarines, Great Britain's use of the Suez Canal, Gandhi's use of mass media, Hitler's use of mass media, Stalin's use of propaganda, Egypt's seizure of the Suez Canal, Mao's use of propaganda, and Arabs' use of social media during the Arab Spring.

You are *not* limited to these suggestions.

Do *not* use an example from the United States in your answer.

Guidelines:

In your essay, be sure to:

- Develop all aspects of the task
- Support the theme with relevant facts, examples, and details
- Use a logical and clear plan of organization, including an introduction and a conclusion that are beyond a restatement of the theme

In developing your answers to Part III, be sure to keep these general definitions in mind:

(a) describe means "to illustrate something in words or tell about it"
(b) discuss means "to make observations about something using facts, reasoning, and argument; to present in some detail"

PART III: DOCUMENT-BASED QUESTION

This question is based on the accompanying documents. The question is designed to test your ability to work with historical documents. Some of these documents have been edited for the purposes of this question. As you analyze the documents, take into account the source of each document and any point of view that may be presented in the document. Keep in mind that the language and images used in a document may reflect the historical context of the time in which it was created.

Historical Context:

Throughout history, the actions of certain individuals have had impacts on societies and regions. These individuals include ***King Leopold II of Belgium***, ***Deng Xiaoping of China***, and ***Desmond Tutu of South Africa***.

Task:

Using the information from the documents and your knowledge of global history and geography, answer the questions that follow each document in Part A. Your answers to the questions will help you write the Part B essay in which you will be asked to

Select ***two*** individuals mentioned in the historical context and for ***each***

- Describe the historical circumstances that led this individual to take action
- Describe an action taken by this individual
- Discuss an impact this individual had on his society and/or on another society

Part A: Short-Answer Questions

Directions: Analyze the documents and answer the short-answer questions that follow each document in the space provided.

Document 1

> . . . In the midst of the rivalries among the Great Powers of Europe, King Leopold II of the tiny nation of Belgium played the most important role in the story of the Congo. This leader of a country overshadowed by its larger, more powerful neighbors wanted desperately to build up an overseas empire in order to secure his position in the world. He thought that a great opportunity existed in Central Africa, a region in which other European countries had not shown interest . . . .

Source: *Colonialism in the Congo: Conquest, Conflict, and Commerce*, Choices Program, Watson Institute for International Studies, Brown University

1 Based on this excerpt, state ***one*** goal of King Leopold II. [1]

____

____

Document 2a

In 1887 and 1888 the Congo Free State was on the brink of bankruptcy. King Leopold II was looking for solutions.

> . . . At this [Brussels] conference [1889–1890], which was devoted to ending the slave trade and liquor and arms trafficking in Africa, Leopold persuaded the European powers to permit him to create a new system of taxation in Congo for the purpose of combating the slave trade and building a stronger infrastructure for governance. In the two years after the conference, the Congo Free State instituted a new tax system in which African chiefs were forced to collect and pay taxes in goods and labor.
>
> Furthermore, in 1891, Leopold arrogated [seized] all "vacant lands" in Congo, as well as the present and future produce of those lands. "Vacant lands" were defined as any lands without a human settlement or crops under cultivation. Leopold thus placed the greatest part of Congo at his disposal, putting an end to free trade in most of the state's territory and enabling him to gain revenue by circumventing the Berlin Act's prohibition against trade duties. . . .

Source: Kevin Grant, *The Congo Free State and the New Imperialism*, Bedford/St. Martin's, 2017 (adapted)

2*a* According to Kevin Grant, what was King Leopold II attempting to do in the Congo Free State? [1]

____

____

Document 2b

Beginning around 1889, the European and American markets demanded more rubber. To produce this rubber, Congolese men, women, and sometimes children harvested sap from rubber vines in forests near their villages instead of tending to their crops.

Rubber Exports from Congo

Year	Value (1000) Belgian Francs	Weight in Tons
1888	260	81.6
1890	556	135.6
1895	2,882	634.9
1900	39,874	5,859.9
1905	43,755	5,358.3

Source: Ch. Didier Gondola, *The History of Congo*, Greenwood Press, 2002 (adapted)

2*b* Based on this document, state ***one*** impact the demand for rubber had on the Congo Free State. [1]

____

____

Document 3

E. D. Morel formed the Congo Reform Association. In 1906, E. D. Morel published his book *Red Rubber* in which he voiced concerns about what was happening to the native peoples in the Congo Free State and to inform the British public. This excerpt is from the book's conclusion.

> . . . Nothing impracticable, nothing unrealisable is being demanded on behalf of the Congo natives. No grandmotherly legislation, no sentimental claims are being urged in their interest. Only justice. They have been robbed of their property. We demand that their property shall be restored to them. They have been robbed of their liberty. We demand that their liberty shall be restored to them. They are bound in chains. We demand that those chains shall be rent asunder [split apart]. For fifteen years they have been degraded, enslaved, exterminated. We demand that this shall stop, not fifteen years, or five years, or one year hence: but now. . . .

Source: E. D. Morel, *Red Rubber*, Haskell House Publishers, 1970, first published 1906

3 According to E. D. Morel, what was ***one*** impact of King Leopold II's control over the Congo Free State? [1]

____

____

Document 4

. . . After the Communists [under Mao Zedong] rose to power in 1949, China's existing market economy was gradually transformed into a socialist economy. Agriculture was collectivized, industry was nationalized, and the private sector was eliminated by 1956. Under the central plan, the state determined the allocation [distribution] of economic inputs and outputs, and maintained a monopoly over production and distribution. As well as the 'Iron Rice Bowl' of lifetime employment, under the *danwei** system, enterprises provided housing and benefits to employees, restricting their ability to live outside of the system. Despite official efforts, however, entrepreneurship was never entirely suppressed and continued to exist on a small scale, particularly in the form of the black market and underground economy. Unfortunately, much of this activity was unproductive rent-seeking [attempt to gain revenue] taking advantage of the inefficiencies in the economy. . . .

Source: Liao and Sohmen, "The Development of Modern Entrepreneurship in China," *Stanford Journal of East Asian Affairs* (adapted)

**danwei* – a government-controlled work unit

4 According to Liao and Sohmen, what were ***two*** characteristics of the socialist economy after the communists rose to power in China in 1949? [2]

(1) ____

____

(2) ____

____

Document 5a

> . . . Deng's reforms abolished the communes and replaced them with a contract system. Though the state continues to own all land, it leases plots, mostly to individual families. Rent is paid by delivery of a set quantity of rice, wheat or whatever to the state at a fixed price. But once that obligation is met, families can grow anything else they wish and sell it in free markets for whatever price they can get (though the state does set limits on how much some prices can fluctuate). . . .

Source: George J. Church, "Person of the Year: Deng Xiaoping," *Time*, January 6, 1986

5*a* According to George J. Church, what is ***one*** action taken by Deng Xiaoping to reform China? [1]

____

____

Document 5b

. . . Yet Deng did not just focus on the economy. He identified other areas where changes had to be made for China to become a world power: there was the need to revamp the educational system, especially universities and research institutes; the military had to be streamlined and professionalized; lawyers had to be trained in the intricacies of commercial and corporate law, and be able to have cases heard in a viable and expanded judicial system; more Chinese had to be permitted to study overseas, and foreign students and tourists to come to China. As a complementary move, Deng ordered far-reaching reviews of the cases of hundreds of thousands of intellectuals, students and professionals who had been sent into internal exile in impoverished rural areas after the Hundred Flowers Movement in 1957, and later during the Cultural Revolution; under Deng, many were allowed to return to their homes and families. . . .

Source: Jonathan Spence, *Time: 60 Years of Asian Heroes, Deng Xiaoping*, 2006

5*b* According to Jonathan Spence, what was ***one*** change Deng Xiaoping thought had to be made in an attempt to transform China into a world power? [1]

____

____

Document 6

This is an excerpt from an obituary for Deng Xiaoping.

> . . . At the end of his life, Mr. Deng seemed unable to chart a clear path to economic success; his economic reforms still faced daunting challenges. China's rise as a great economic power was becoming a race against time as population growth and incomplete reform were adding to the siege of China's straining foundations. Shortages of water and arable land mounted, and unchecked industrial pollution contributed to an overall degradation of the environmental landscape.
>
> Still, in cities and in villages, real incomes more than doubled in the Deng era. Most Chinese who have watched a television or used a washing machine or dialed a telephone have done so only since Mr. Deng came to power. The struggle to survive in the Chinese countryside has greatly eased. . . .

Source: Patrick E. Tyler, "Deng Xiaoping: A Political Wizard Who Put China on the Capitalist Road," *New York Times*, February 20, 1997

6 According to Patrick E. Tyler, what was ***one*** impact of Deng Xiaoping's rule in China? [1]

____

____

Document 7

. . . With the ANC [African National Congress] banned, new opposition forces emerged. Black Consciousness, led by charismatic student leader Steve Biko, took off in the late 1960s. Then in 1972–1973, the black labor movement came to life again in a sudden, massive strike wave. Things were on the boil and with a rigid, inflexible, and intolerant government at the helm of state, the country finally exploded in 1976, ignited by student protests in Soweto.

Although the 1976 protests were quashed [put down] by harsh measures from the state security forces that saw many casualties, popular resistance reemerged in the 1980s. This coalesced [joined forces] around vibrant, new mass organizations. The United Democratic Front (UDF, formed in 1983), was a very wide coalition of more than 600 community, labor, sport, and church organizations. The Congress of South African Trade Unions (COSATU, formed in 1985), with its largest affiliate [associate], the National Union of Mineworkers (1982), led by ex-student activist Cyril Ramaphosa, grew rapidly and challenged the previously monolithic [rigid] economic domination of the apartheid state. Many church leaders, such as Archbishop Desmond Tutu, lent their weight to popular protests. All across the country these diverse groups spoke out loudly and their support grew rapidly, with many people aligning themselves with the ideas of the ANC exemplified [represented] in the Freedom Charter. One of their major demands was the release of [Nelson] Mandela and all political prisoners. . . .

Source: Peter Limb, *Nelson Mandela: A Biography*, Greenwood Press, 2008

7 According to Peter Limb, what was ***one*** problem faced by blacks in South Africa from the 1960s through the 1980s? [1]

____

____

Document 8

This is an excerpt about Desmond Tutu from a biographical dictionary.

> . . . The problem faced by anti-apartheid clergymen was how to simultaneously oppose both violent resistance and apartheid, which was itself increasingly violent. [Desmond] Tutu's opposition was vigorous and unequivocal, and he was outspoken both in South Africa and abroad, often comparing apartheid to Nazism and Communism. As a result the government twice revoked his passport, and he was jailed briefly in 1980 after a protest march. It was thought by many that Tutu's increasing international reputation and his rigorous advocacy of non-violence protected him from harsher penalties. Tutu's view on violence reflected the tension in a Christian approach to resistance: "I will never tell anyone to pick up a gun. But I will pray for the man who picks up a gun, pray that he will be less cruel than he might otherwise have been. . . ."

Source: "Archbishop Desmond Tutu Facts," *Encyclopedia of World Biography*, The Gale Group, 2010

8 Based on this document, state ***one*** action taken by Desmond Tutu to resist South African government policies. [1]

____

____

Document 9

. . . During apartheid in South Africa, Desmond Tutu emerged as a voice for the voiceless; someone who was able to "articulate the aspirations and the anguishes" of marginalised people.

After the 1994 elections and Nelson Mandela's inauguration as the country's first democratically elected president, Archbishop Tutu was asked to preside over a process "to heal a wounded and traumatised nation". The Truth and Reconciliation Commission (TRC) was established to bear witness to apartheid-era crimes, record and in some cases grant amnesty to the perpetrators.

It subsequently became an important model for other commissions of its kind throughout the world. Archbishop Tutu articulates that the main lesson learnt from this process was that "all human beings are fundamentally good". Despite the most horrendous atrocities committed, "people amazed the world with the exhibition of their magnanimity [mercy], their generosity of spirit, their willingness not to seek revenge and retribution [punishment], but to be willing to forgive".

Archbishop Tutu mustered a group of close friends and associates to form the Desmond Tutu Peace Trust in 1998. The Trust administers and oversees the development of the Desmond Tutu Peace Centre.

Source: "How We Began," The Desmond Tutu Peace Centre online

9 According to this statement from the Desmond Tutu Peace Centre website, what is ***one*** impact of Desmond Tutu's leadership? [1]

____

____

Part B: Essay

Directions: Write a well-organized essay that includes an introduction, several paragraphs, and a conclusion. Use evidence from *at least* ***four*** documents in your essay. Support your response with relevant facts, examples, and details. Include additional outside information.

Historical Context:

Throughout history, the actions of certain individuals have had impacts on societies and regions. These individuals include ***King Leopold II of Belgium***, ***Deng Xiaoping of China***, and ***Desmond Tutu of South Africa***.

Task:

Using the information from the documents and your knowledge of global history and geography, write an essay in which you

Select ***two*** individuals mentioned in the historical context and for ***each***

- Describe the historical circumstances that led this individual to take action
- Describe an action taken by this individual
- Discuss an impact this individual had on his society and/or on another society

Guidelines:

In your essay, be sure to:

- Develop all aspects of the task
- Incorporate information from *at least* ***four*** documents
- Incorporate relevant outside information
- Support the theme with relevant facts, examples, and details
- Use a logical and clear plan of organization, including an introduction and a conclusion that are beyond a restatement of the theme

Answers August 2019

Global History and Geography

Answer Key

PART I (1–30)

1. 3	**7.** 4	**13.** 2	**19.** 4	**25.** 3
2. 2	**8.** 1	**14.** 1	**20.** 3	**26.** 3
3. 1	**9.** 2	**15.** 4	**21.** 2	**27.** 2
4. 2	**10.** 1	**16.** 4	**22.** 3	**28.** 3
5. 3	**11.** 4	**17.** 3	**23.** 4	**29.** 2
6. 1	**12.** 3	**18.** 4	**24.** 1	**30.** 1

PART II: Thematic Essay   See Answers Explained section.

PART III: Document-Based Essay   See Answers Explained section.

Answers Explained

PART I

1. **3** A physical map would be most useful in comparing the elevation of settlements in Peru because a physical map focuses on the geography of the region. Physical maps emphasize physical features, including land elevation. Typically, maps use various colors to depict land elevation. Often, darker colors represent areas of higher elevation, and lighter colors depict areas of lower elevation. Rivers, mountain ranges, and lakes are also labeled on a physical map.

WRONG CHOICES EXPLAINED:

(1) The distribution of religious groups in Lebanon would be depicted on a thematic map. A thematic map focuses on a particular theme, such as population distribution, rather than on the physical features of a region, such as elevation.

(2) Regional population densities would also be depicted on a thematic map. Thematic maps do not focus on physical features and topography, such as elevation.

(4) Changes in political boundaries would be depicted on a political map. Political maps focus on the political boundaries between nations, and major cities are usually labeled.

2. **2** A theocracy is a political system in which both the religious and political authority are in the hands of the government. An example of a modern-day theocracy is the Islamic Republic of Iran. In 1979, after the more secular shah was overthrown by the Ayatollah Khomeini, a theocracy was established. The Ayatollah was named supreme leader, and he established a political system based on traditional Islamic beliefs.

WRONG CHOICES EXPLAINED:

(1) A representative democracy is a political system in which elected officials represent the interests of various groups of people as opposed to a direct democracy. The United States of America is an example of a representative democracy because people vote for officials to represent their interests in Congress. Typically, representative democracies are secular, and there is a separation between church and state.

(3) An oligarchy is a political system in which an elite few rule as a group over a nation. Ancient Sparta is an example of an oligarchy. An oligarchy does not necessarily hold both political and religious authority.

(4) A constitutional monarchy is a political system in which a nonelected official is granted the power to serve as a head of state. A constitution limits the role of the monarch in favor of elected officials who serve as representatives of the people. The United Kingdom is an example of a constitutional monarchy.

3. **1** When using a primary source, or a firsthand account of events, historians must be certain that the primary source is authentic. To determine if the information in a source is authentic and accurate, historians will often use other primary sources written in that time period to corroborate the source's information.

WRONG CHOICES EXPLAINED:

(2) Primary sources come in various forms, including maps, charts, political cartoons, and photographs. Therefore, a primary source is not required to be a narrative, which is defined as a spoken or written account.

(3) Primary sources are those that originate in the time period being studied. Primary sources from early civilizations are not modern sources. Therefore, it is not required that a primary source be modern.

(4) Primary sources typically contain some bias because they are firsthand accounts, often created by individuals with various backgrounds and experiences. Although historians must be aware of bias in sources, biased sources can still be valuable in the reconstruction of history.

4. **2** A significant result of the Scientific Revolution of the 16th through 18th centuries was the development of an understanding of the universe based on the laws of nature, or natural laws. The laws of nature are based on the idea that a divine being does not control the forces of nature on Earth in a random way. Instead, occurrences on Earth are orderly and regular, and, therefore, they can be predictable. Thinkers during the Scientific Revolution believed that natural laws could be discovered through the use of logic and reason, which led to the use of the scientific method to test ideas in a scientific way.

WRONG CHOICES EXPLAINED:

(1) Before the Scientific Revolution, the understanding of nature was based on traditional ideas guided by the Bible and the Roman Catholic Church. For example, the Roman Catholic Church supported the geocentric model of the solar system in which Earth is located at the center and all other celestial bodies, including the Sun, planets, and other stars, revolve around it. By studying the natural movements of planets and stars, thinkers during the Scientific Revolution used the laws of nature to develop the heliocentric, or sun-centered, model of the solar system.

(3) Before the Scientific Revolution, the world was understood in the context of religion. Rather than looking for the laws of nature, many believed that God controlled the various forces of nature in a random way. These ideas were reinforced by the dominant religious institution of the time, the Roman Catholic Church.

(4) Geocentrism is the belief that Earth is at the center of the solar system and all of the planets, the Sun, and the stars revolve around it. This was the accepted model of the solar system prior to the Scientific Revolution, a model that was upheld by the Roman Catholic Church. During the Scientific Revolution, observations of the motion of the planets led to the development of heliocentrism, or the sun-centered model of the solar system.

5. **3** Baron de Montesquieu was a French Enlightenment philosopher of the 18th century who emphasized the importance of political balance through the separation of powers within the central government. He believed that Great Britain had the best example of a separation of powers in that the king and his ministers would carry out the laws while the Parliament had legislative power to pass laws and the judges of the courts interpreted the laws as they applied to specific cases. In his book, *The Spirit of Laws*, Montesquieu stated that a separation of powers would keep the balance of power by preventing any one individual or group from gaining total control over the government.

WRONG CHOICES EXPLAINED:

(1) René Descartes was a 17th-century mathematician during the Scientific Revolution and is most famous for saying “I think, therefore I am.” The only thing that Descartes could know with absolute certainty was that he existed, because he could think. Everything else had to be proven by reason and scientific thought.

(2) Maximilien Robespierre was a Jacobin leader during the French Revolution and governed France during the phase of the revolution later known as the Reign of Terror. Although Robespierre was influenced by Enlightenment ideas, such as separating powers into three branches, he is not the writer who is credited with that idea.

(4) Bishop Jacques-Bénigne Bossuet was a 17th-century French bishop who was influential in speaking for the rights of the French church against the power of the pope. He is not associated with the Enlightenment or with the idea that powers in government should be separated.

6. **1** An unintended consequence of Napoleon's conquests was an increase of nationalism in Europe and Latin America. Napoleon used nationalism to make France a great power in Europe during the Napoleonic Wars. His ideas of nationalism spread throughout Europe during his conquests. When Napoleon was defeated, the victorious European powers met at the Congress of Vienna with the goal of eliminating nationalism from Europe. When the political boundaries of European nations were redrawn during the Congress of Vienna, the goal was to prevent the spread of nationalism. The opposite occurred, however. The redrawing of political boundaries with little regard to feelings of nationalism only roused nationalistic feelings, particularly in Germany. This eventually led to the unification of the German states later in the 19th century. Nationalism in Latin America was also influenced by Napoleon's conquests. When Napoleon conquered Spain and deposed the Spanish king, Spanish Creoles in Latin America began to question their allegiance to Spain and began to push for independence.

WRONG CHOICES EXPLAINED:

(2) The American Revolution occurred from 1775 to 1783. Napoleon did not come to power in France until 1799.

(3) Although the code of laws created by Napoleon, the Napoleonic Code, did reduce the status of women within France, it did not reduce the status of women throughout Europe.

(4) Great Britain was a victor in the Napoleonic Wars, and its economy was not greatly affected.

7. **4** One reason the Industrial Revolution began in Great Britain was that Great Britain had a plentiful supply of natural resources, such as iron ore and coal. The Industrial Revolution changed the way goods were produced as machines were developed to produce goods in factories as opposed to being handmade in the home. Iron ore was required to construct the machines, tools, and factories. Coal was necessary to help fuel the machines. Great Britain, although a small nation, was rich in these natural resources. In addition, Great Britain had water power from the River Thames and harbors for merchant ships to dock and set sail.

WRONG CHOICES EXPLAINED:

(1) The Industrial Revolution required a large population of unskilled labor to work in factories. A decline in the birth rate would have been detrimental to the development of the Industrial Revolution in Great Britain.

(2) Although Great Britain had natural harbors, which facilitated trade, the coastline of Great Britain is not considered smooth.

(3) Great Britain did not have a compulsory education system until the late 19th century. In addition, factories required an unskilled labor force, and an education was not necessary to work in factories.

8. **1** The 19th-century economic condition that was the basis for the ideas of Karl Marx was the widening gap between the rich and the poor that resulted from capitalism. Marx believed that the capitalist system, which helped spur the Industrial Revolution, had enriched those who were already wealthy and had impoverished those who were already poor. He believed that factory owners would put small artisans out of business and exploit workers to

the point that they would rise up and revolt to create a society where private ownership and inequality would cease to exist. Karl Marx called this form of complete socialism "communism." Along with Friedrich Engels, Karl Marx published *The Communist Manifesto* in 1848 in which he outlined his ideas.

WRONG CHOICES EXPLAINED:

(2) Although the availability of material goods did increase as a result of the Industrial Revolution, the capitalist economic system created inequalities in society and eventually led to the ideas of communism, as outlined by Karl Marx.

(3) Although industrialization changed how goods were produced, access to certain resources did not change nor did it lead to the ideas of creating a classless society, as outlined by Karl Marx in *The Communist Manifesto*.

(4) Although people did leave farms and move to the cities in search of work during the Industrial Revolution, the capitalist system created greater inequalities, which led to the ideas of communism, as outlined by Karl Marx.

9. **2** In the 19th century, the idea of Social Darwinism was used by Europeans to justify their policy of imperialism. Many Europeans began to apply Charles Darwin's theory of evolution through natural selection to society. They believed that those who were the fittest to survive became the wealthiest and most successful in society. They considered non-Europeans to be physically and culturally inferior because non-Europeans had not made the technological advancements that the Europeans had made. Europeans believed not only that they had the right to bring this technological progress to non-European societies but also that they had a duty to bring their progress to those they deemed inferior. This led to the expansion of imperialism in places like Africa.

WRONG CHOICES EXPLAINED:

(1) Social Darwinism is the belief that the fittest to survive become the most successful in society. Europeans used this idea to promote their ideas of European superiority. They did not believe in creating multicultural societies.

(3) Self-determination is the process in which a country determines its own government. Social Darwinism was used to promote the supremacy of Europeans over developing societies. It was used to justify their right to imperialize "weaker" nations.

(4) Secular humanism is the philosophy that humans are capable of being moral and ethical without the influence of religion. Secular humanism does not relate to the ideas of Social Darwinism.

10. **1** The Suez Canal has been an important waterway because it links the Mediterranean Sea to the Red Sea and eventually to the Indian Ocean. Prior to the opening of the Suez Canal in 1869, the only all-water route linking Europe to India and East Asia was around the continent of Africa. The trip was costly and dangerous for European merchants, who had to travel over 12,000 miles to reach India. The Suez Canal reduced the trip to just over 7,000 miles, making it a faster, less dangerous, and less costly trip for European merchants.

WRONG CHOICES EXPLAINED:

(2) Although Egypt built the Suez Canal, the British were able to conquer Egypt and turn it into a virtual colony after the construction was completed. Therefore, the Suez Canal did not offer Egypt protection from foreign powers.

(3) The Suez Canal does not separate Israel from its neighbors. Despite the construction of the canal, Israel is still bordered by Egypt, Jordan, and Lebanon.

(4) Although canals are sometimes used to transport water for human uses, such as irrigation, canals are constructed for the purpose of linking waterways and facilitating the movement of merchant ships, which is why the Suez Canal is so important.

11. **4** A major goal of the Boxer Rebellion in China and the Sepoy Rebellion in India was to reduce foreign influences. In China, peasants believed the Empress Dowager gave foreigners special privileges. Additionally, they resented Chinese Christians, who they believed had adopted a foreign religion. In 1900, Chinese peasants, known as Boxers, rebelled against this foreign influence by surrounding the European section of Beijing. Although they kept the city under siege for months, the Boxers were eventually defeated by the Europeans. In India, a similar situation occurred against British control of the Indian subcontinent. Economic problems and overt racism led sepoys, or Indian soldiers, to rebel against the British. Although both the Sepoy Rebellion and the Boxer Rebellion failed, they are examples of the desire to reduce foreign influences.

WRONG CHOICES EXPLAINED:

(1) Divine right monarchs are monarchs who justify their power through religion. Divine right monarchs are associated with the kings of Europe during the Age of Absolutism. Neither the Boxers in China nor the sepoys in India sought to restore divine right monarchs to power.

(2) The Boxers in China and the sepoys in India both wanted to reduce foreign influences. Obtaining foreign aid from Europe would have increased European influences.

(3) Both China and India wanted to end foreign influences. Their interests were in expelling foreigners, not in annexing neighboring territories.

12. **3** The success of the Meiji Restoration depended on Japan's ability to replicate the power and wealth of the industrial West. Prior to the mid-19th century, Japan was relatively isolated from foreigners and had not industrialized in the way the West had. When Commodore Matthew Perry of the United States sailed into Tokyo Bay with steamships and cannons, Japan realized that it could not compete with Western industrialized countries unless it modernized. In 1867, the Tokugawa shogun stepped down, and the Emperor Meiji was restored to power. He sent diplomats to Europe and North America to study Western ways.

WRONG CHOICES EXPLAINED:

(1) Japan wanted to modernize so that it could compete with Western industrialized powers. China and Korea had also been subjected to foreign influences by the 19th century, so Japan would not have benefited from borrowing Chinese and Korean military models.

(2) In order to modernize, the imperial government had to adapt Western military styles and the use of firearms. Therefore, the samurai were stripped of their titles and were prohibited from carrying their swords.

(4) An imperial form of government is one that is ruled by an emperor or empress. During the Meiji Restoration, the emperor was restored to power. The government of Japan became imperial with the restoration of Emperor Meiji. Prior to the restoration of the emperor, Japan was ruled though a system of centralized feudalism under the Tokugawa shogunate.

13. **2** Entangling alliances was one factor that caused many European countries to become involved in World War I. The alliance system created in the latter part of the 19th century was designed to maintain peace in Europe, but instead it was one factor that brought about the outbreak of World War I. For example, Otto von Bismarck of Germany viewed France as the greatest threat to peace in Europe, so he formed the Triple Alliance with Austria-Hungary and, later, Italy. By the early 20th century, Great Britain had begun to fear

Germany's militarism, and so it created the Triple Entente with France and Russia. When Archduke Franz Ferdinand of Austria was assassinated by a Serbian nationalist, Russia came to the aid of Serbia, which entangled its allies in a war against Austria and its allies.

WRONG CHOICES EXPLAINED:

(1) Religion was not a motivating factor in causing many European countries to become involved in World War I. Instead, the various alliances caused many countries to become entangled in the conflict, which began with just two nations, Austria-Hungary and Serbia.

(3) Communism did not play a role in the outbreak of World War I in 1914. There were no communist countries at that time. Russia was the first European country to fall to communism, which occurred in 1917, three years after the outbreak of World War I.

(4) Fascism arose in Europe after the devastation of World War I, when people desired national unity and stability through strong leadership.

14. **1** After World War I, the political map of Europe changed as the defeated Central Powers signed peace treaties with Western nations. This led to the creation of new countries in the region formerly controlled by the Austro-Hungarian Empire. Austria, Hungary, Yugoslavia, and Czechoslovakia were all recognized as independent nations as a result of the peace treaties.

WRONG CHOICES EXPLAINED:

(2) The Treaty of Versailles punished Germany after its defeat in World War I. Germany lost a substantial amount of territory as a result of the treaty.

(3) Russia suffered a loss of land after World War I. Finland, Latvia, Estonia, and Lithuania—which had once been part of the Russian Empire—became independent nations. Serbia and Bosnia were part of Yugoslavia.

(4) The Ottoman Empire also lost territories in Southwest Asia after its defeat in World War I.

15. **4** As a result of its modernization efforts during the Meiji Restoration and desire to become a global power, Japan became an aggressor in the late 19th and early 20th centuries. After defeating Russia in the Russo-Japanese War, Japan drove out Russian troops from the Korean Peninsula. In 1905, Japan attacked Korea and made it a protectorate. By 1910, Japan had fully annexed Korea. By the 1920s, Japan's population was growing and a demand for natural resources and land led Japan to seek an empire in Asia. In 1931, Japan invaded Manchuria and seized control over that Chinese province. By 1937, a border dispute with China led to a full-scale war between the two nations. The capital, Nanjing, fell to the Japanese. During their invasion of the city, the Japanese killed tens of thousands of innocent civilians in what became known to the Chinese as the "Rape of Nanjing."

WRONG CHOICES EXPLAINED:

(1) The Soviet Union did not exist in 1905. As a result of Russia's loss in the Russo-Japanese War, the Soviet Union had little influence in East Asia in the early 20th century.

(2) Nanjing was the capital of China in 1937. Japan invaded the city, leading to the "Rape of Nanjing."

(3) Great Britain had little influence in East Asia in the early 20th century.

16. **4** This 1941 cartoon expresses the opinion that the policy of appeasement is shortsighted and unwise. The evil-looking monsters with swastikas on their bodies represent Adolf Hitler and Nazi Germany. In the middle stands an "appeaser," who is trying to fend off the monsters by feeding them lollipops. The appeaser represents Great Britain, which was

attempting to appease Hitler by giving into his demands in order to avoid war. The caption says, "Remember . . . one more lollypop, and then you all go home!" However, the hungry monsters have expressions on their faces that can be interpreted as their being hungry for more than the appeaser is willing to give them. Therefore, the cartoon represents the opinion that appeasement is not the right choice of action but is instead shortsighted and unwise.

WRONG CHOICES EXPLAINED:

(1) The monsters that represent Germany are depicted as hungry for more than the appeaser can give them. Therefore, appeasement threatens to bring war and threatens peace.

(2) The appeaser appears to attempt to fend off the monsters with lollipops. Nothing in the cartoon suggests that appeasement will not be tolerated.

(3) Nothing in the cartoon depicts the financial cost of appeasement.

17. **3** The scene described in this passage is most closely associated with the impact of modern war technology. The passage emphasizes the destruction of Germany seen after the war had ended. The author states that there was not a bridge, highway, or railroad left standing. He also states that two-thirds of the buildings had been destroyed. This destruction was due to modern war technology, including modern bombs and the use of planes to drop those bombs during World War II.

WRONG CHOICES EXPLAINED:

(1) The policy of nonalignment was a policy adopted by India and other newly independent countries during the Cold War that did not align with either NATO or the Warsaw Pact. Nothing in the passage mentions the Cold War.

(2) The doctrine of containment was the doctrine adopted by Western nations to prevent communism from spreading during the Cold War. Nothing in the passage mentions the Cold War.

(4) Industrialization had occurred in Western Europe a century before VE Day. Nothing in the passage discusses industrialization.

18. **4** After World War II, the actions taken by the Nuremberg Tribunal demonstrated that persons who committed wartime atrocities would be held accountable. In 1945, a tribunal representing 23 nations put Nazi criminals on trial in Nuremberg, Germany. They were tried for war crimes committed when waging war in Europe, as well as for "crimes against humanity" committed during the Holocaust, when millions of people were murdered and acts of genocide were committed against Jewish people and members of other groups. High-ranking Nazi officials, such as Hermann Göring, the commander of the German Luftwaffe, were convicted and sentenced to death.

WRONG CHOICES EXPLAINED:

(1) The Nuremberg Tribunal was not established to contain communism. Instead, it was created to put Nazi war criminals on trial.

(2) Although many countries in Africa and Asia gained their independence in the years following World War II, their independence was not caused by the Nuremberg Tribunal.

(3) The Nuremberg Tribunal was not created to end the policies of apartheid in South Africa.

19. **4** One way in which the Chinese Communist Revolution and the Cuban Revolution are similar is that both revolutions gained strong support from the peasants. By the mid-20th century, the majority of China was made up of rural peasants, who were dominated

by landlords and local officials. Mao Zedong, leader of China's Communist Revolution, was able to mobilize the peasants by offering them land reform, which led to Mao's victory in 1949. As in China, the majority of Cuba's population by the mid-20th century was unemployed peasants, many of whom were only employed for low wages and could find work only a few months per year. Fidel Castro was able to win his guerrilla war against Fulgencio Batista in 1959 by mobilizing the peasants in a similar way that Mao did in China.

WRONG CHOICES EXPLAINED:

(1) Both revolutions were communist revolutions that rejected capitalist ideals and promoted ideals of more socioeconomic equality.

(2) Although both Cuba and China were not industrialized nations at the time of their revolutions, neither rejected industrial development. For example, Mao Zedong attempted to industrialize and modernize his country during the Great Leap Forward in the years following the revolution.

(3) Both revolutions were civil wars that led to the deaths of many. Neither revolution was peaceful.

20. **3** The message to the dove in this cartoon is most likely referring to the tension between Palestinians and Israelis. The cartoon depicts a dove with an olive branch in its mouth representing peace. The dove is looking for peace in the Mideast on the computer, but there are "no matches." Jewish Israel has not been able to maintain peace with Muslim Palestine for the majority of the region's history. Both are fighting over the same land and who gets to control it. Despite calls for a two-state solution in the region, no peace agreement has been met. Conflict continues to this day.

WRONG CHOICES EXPLAINED:

(1) Sikhs and Tamils are minority groups in South Asia and do not occupy the Mideast. Additionally, there are no modern tensions between these two groups.

(2) Hutus and Tutsis are the dominant ethnic groups in Rwanda. In 1994, genocide broke out when the Hutu majority began slaughtering the Tutsi minority. They are not still fighting, nor do they occupy the Mideast.

(4) Serbs and Bosnians occupy the Balkan Peninsula in Eastern Europe. During the breakup of the former Yugoslavia, Serbians waged a genocidal war against Bosnian Muslims; however, peace has been restored to the region.

21. **2** Failure to resolve competing territorial claims best explains the message on the screen. Territorial disputes broke out after the establishment of the Israeli state in 1948, when Palestinians were ready to wage war for control over the territory they viewed as rightfully theirs. In 1967, the conflict again escalated during the Six-Day War, in which Israel captured Jerusalem, Gaza, and the West Bank. These territories remain the most contentious territories in the conflict.

WRONG CHOICES EXPLAINED:

(1) Although disputes over oil have occurred in the region because the land sits on major oil reserves that are not currently being exploited, the source of the conflict is territory, not oil.

(3) Israel has been backed by the United States of America as well as other members of the United Nations. The lack of peace in the Mideast is not the result of a lack of global involvement in the region.

(4) The dominant belief systems in the region are Judaism and Islam. An absence of traditional belief systems in the region is not the cause of ongoing conflict.

22. **3** The European Union (EU) and the North American Free Trade Agreement (NAFTA) were created to encourage economic development through free trade. Free trade agreements eliminate trade barriers like tariffs, or taxes on imports, among nations. In 1994, NAFTA was signed by Canada, the United States, and Mexico. NAFTA facilitated economic growth in all three nations, as evidenced by GDP growth. Free trade in Europe dates back to the mid-20th century.

WRONG CHOICES EXPLAINED:

(1), (2), and (4) These three choices are incorrect because the EU and NAFTA were created to encourage economic development. Trade agreements, like NAFTA, do not seek justice for human rights victims, promote nuclear disarmament, or legislate the reduction of pollution.

23. **4** South Korea's economic miracle in the late 20th century was modeled after the success of Japan. Japan's economy rapidly expanded after the country's defeat in World War II as a result of the occupation of the United States, which helped establish a free, democratic society in Japan in the postwar world. Japan began to industrialize rapidly and became a major exporter of cars and electronics. South Korea's miracle was modeled after the success of Japan. South Korea underwent rapid industrialization and maintained exceptionally high economic growth rates between the 1960s and 1990s.

WRONG CHOICES EXPLAINED:

(1) Russia experienced an economic decline in the late 20th century, which eventually led to the collapse of communism.

(2) Although India did experience some economic growth in the late part of the 20th century, India's major economic growth occurred in the early 21st century.

(3) Vietnam has had economic growth, but its growth is not considered an economic miracle. Additionally, Vietnam has a smaller economy than does South Korea.

24. **1** The cost of treatment for HIV and AIDS has been the health care issue that has most frustrated African governments and health care workers in the early 21st century. AIDS has been a worldwide problem since the 1980s, but sub-Saharan Africa has been the region most affected. About 70 percent of all AIDS cases are concentrated in the region. The reason why AIDS is so prevalent in the region is that the developing nations of the region do not have adequate access to treatments as a result of limited economic resources. Additionally, high transmission rates continue because of a lack of education about the disease.

WRONG CHOICES EXPLAINED:

(2) Smallpox was declared eradicated by the World Health Organization in 1980.

(3) Although cancer is a health issue in Africa as it is in the rest of the world, the number of those afflicted with AIDS far exceeds the number afflicted with cancer.

(4) Although polio has not been completely eradicated, the rate of polio around the world has been reduced by over 99 percent.

25. **3** According to this passage, a valid conclusion concerning the Niger River region is that desertification has altered the landscape of the region of West Africa. Desertification is the process by which fertile land becomes infertile and desert-like. Desertification is typically the result of deforestation, poor agricultural techniques, and drought. Many clues in the passage lead to the conclusion that desertification is an issue concerning the Niger River region. The passage states that the river used to be closer and now "the desert is closing in."

WRONG CHOICES EXPLAINED:

(1) Although poor irrigation techniques can lead to desertification, there is nothing in the passage that suggests that poor irrigation techniques are the cause of the desertification in the Niger River region.

(2) Although the passage mentions canals, it does so in the context that canals used to channel water to the region, but now they run dry. No reference to trade is made in the passage.

(4) The passage mentions that the landscape has become barren and infertile. According to the passage, there are only a few scraggly trees to use for firewood.

26. **3** Environmental problems need international attention is the conclusion that can best be drawn from the situations listed. The situations listed describe three different environmental problems in different regions of the world, including Latin America and Europe. These are problems that exist everywhere, and, therefore, international attention is needed to address the issues.

WRONG CHOICES EXPLAINED:

(1) Industrialization causes environmental problems. The situations described indicate that deforestation, acid rain, and pollution are current problems. Therefore, one cannot conclude that industrialization is slowing down in these areas.

(2) Although only environmental issues from these regions of the world are listed, one cannot simply conclude that environmental issues affect only those regions. It should be recognized that a few examples of environmental issues are listed, but the list is not all-inclusive.

(4) Although a lack of waste management technologies can cause pollution and other environmental problems, deforestation has no connection to a lack of waste management technologies.

27. **2** The success of Otto von Bismarck in Germany and of Mohandas Gandhi in India demonstrate that more than one method can be used to build nationalism. Otto von Bismarck relied on the strength of the military to promote nationalism, whereas Mohandas Gandhi relied on nonviolent methods to achieve nationalism. Bismarck, the unifier of Germany, had the goal of creating a strong, unified German state. In the mid-19th century, he made his famous "blood and iron" speech in which he indicated that a unified Germany could only be achieved through military force. Mohandas Gandhi, on the other hand, used nonviolent techniques to unify the Indian people against British colonial rule. Rather than military force, Gandhi promoted peaceful noncooperation with authorities in addition to massive boycotts of British goods.

WRONG CHOICES EXPLAINED:

(1) Germany was not under colonial rule at the time of its unification under Bismarck. Additionally, imperialism is what led Gandhi to lead the Indian independence movement.

(3) Neither region was experiencing a period of major economic prosperity that would have led to the promotion of nationalism.

(4) Cities weaken traditional values as cities become more multicultural than rural areas. Additionally, India did not urbanize under Gandhi.

28. **3** One way in which Kemal Atatürk and Reza Pahlavi are similar is that both supported policies of modernizing and westernizing their nations. When Mustafa Kemal Atatürk overthrew the last Ottoman sultan in 1923, he became the president of the newly established Republic of Turkey. He sought to modernize the nation by making it more like the countries of Western Europe. He separated Islamic law from national law while also abolishing

religious courts and creating a new legal system based on European law. Similarly, in 1926, Reza Pahlavi of Iran began a series of reforms to modernize the country. He focused on Iran's infrastructure by building railways, roads, schools, and universities. Additionally, he emancipated women and forbade them from wearing the traditional veil. Both leaders focused on modernization and westernization.

WRONG CHOICES EXPLAINED:

(1) The United Nations was not established until 1945. Kemal Atatürk died in 1938.

(2) Both Atatürk and Pahlavi promoted women's rights and extended suffrage to women.

(4) Both Atatürk and Pahlavi wanted more connections to the West, not less. They would not have wanted to prevent their citizens from traveling overseas.

29. **2** These cartoons were published immediately after World War I. In 1918, United States president Woodrow Wilson outlined his vision for the League of Nations, the first world peacekeeping body, in his Fourteen Points speech. The cartoons depict differing views about joining the League of Nations. Cartoon A depicts the League of Nations as a muzzle around the "Dog of War" and was published in 1919. Cartoon B, also published in 1919, depicts a man, who represents the world, sailing toward the rainbow, representing the League of Nations.

WRONG CHOICES EXPLAINED:

(1) The Russo-Japanese War was a war fought between Russia and Japan between 1904 and 1905. Both cartoons were published in 1919.

(3) World War II ended in 1945. Both cartoons were published in 1919.

(4) The Cold War ended in 1991 with the collapse of the Soviet Union. Both cartoons were published in 1919.

30. **1** The two cartoons depict differing views about the ability of the League of Nations to function. Cartoonist A depicts the "Dog of War" with a muzzle representing the League of Nations. The caption asks the question "Muzzled?" This can be interpreted to mean that the cartoonist was distrustful that the League of Nations could actually prevent war. Cartoonist B takes the opposite view. The man on the boat representing the world is sailing away from the rain and toward the rainbow representing the League of Nations, which demonstrates a more hopeful view.

WRONG CHOICES EXPLAINED:

(2) Cartoonist B depicts a man smiling as he sails out of the rain and toward the rainbow, which represents the League of Nations. This cartoon has a positive outlook about the League's ability to function. Being guarded is another way of saying distrustful, and there is nothing to indicate that feeling in cartoon B.

(3) Cartoonist A doesn't depict fear of the League of Nations as much as he or she questions the League's ability to maintain peace.

(4) The opposite is true. Cartoonist A is pessimistic as he or she depicts distrust of the League's ability to maintain peace. Cartoonist B is optimistic because he or she depicts the League of Nations as a rainbow.

THEMATIC ESSAY: GENERIC SCORING RUBRIC

Score of 5:
- Shows a thorough understanding of the theme or problem
- Addresses all aspects of the task
- Shows an ability to analyze, evaluate, compare and/or contrast issues and events
- Richly supports the theme or problem with relevant facts, examples, and details
- Is a well-developed essay, consistently demonstrating a logical and clear plan of organization
- Introduces the theme or problem by establishing a framework that is beyond a simple restatement of the task and concludes with a summation of the theme or problem

Score of 4:
- Shows a good understanding of the theme or problem
- Addresses all aspects of the task
- Shows an ability to analyze, evaluate, compare and/or contrast issues and events
- Includes relevant facts, examples, and details, but may not support all aspects of the theme or problem evenly
- Is a well-developed essay, demonstrating a logical and clear plan of organization
- Introduces the theme or problem by establishing a framework that is beyond a simple restatement of the task and concludes with a summation of the theme or problem

Score of 3:
- Shows a satisfactory understanding of the theme or problem
- Addresses most aspects of the task or addresses all aspects in a limited way
- Shows an ability to analyze or evaluate issues and events, but not in any depth
- Includes some facts, examples, and details
- Is a satisfactorily developed essay, demonstrating a general plan of organization
- Introduces the theme or problem by repeating the task and concludes by repeating the theme or problem

Score of 2:
- Shows limited understanding of the theme or problem
- Attempts to address the task
- Develops a faulty analysis or evaluation of issues and events
- Includes few facts, examples, and details, and may include information that contains inaccuracies
- Is a poorly organized essay, lacking focus
- Fails to introduce or summarize the theme or problem

Score of 1:
- Shows very limited understanding of the theme or problem
- Lacks an analysis or evaluation of the issues and events
- Includes little or no accurate or relevant facts, examples, or details
- Attempts to complete the task, but demonstrates a major weakness in organization
- Fails to introduce or summarize the theme or problem

Score of 0: Fails to address the task, is illegible, or is a blank paper

PART II: THEMATIC ESSAY QUESTION

Communication technologies, such as propaganda, have been used by world leaders throughout history to control societies. Two world leaders who used propaganda to control the masses were Joseph Stalin of the Soviet Union and Mao Zedong of the People's Republic of China. Both Joseph Stalin and Mao Zedong used propaganda that contained exaggerated or false information to create a totalitarian state in their communist nations, which provided these men with the opportunity to control every aspect of public and private life.

When Joseph Stalin assumed power as dictator of the Soviet Union in 1922, he sought to create a perfect communist society through the creation of a totalitarian state and control of mass media. All publications, music, art, and film were censored and restricted unless given permission by the state. If an individual suggested that the information he or she was being given was incorrect in any way, the statement was considered treasonous, and the individual was harshly punished. Under Stalin, Soviet radio broadcasts, newspapers, and all other media forms were used to glorify the achievements of Stalin and communism, as well as all economic achievements in general. Mass-produced posters placed in visible areas throughout the Soviet Union glorified the Communist Party and its economic achievements. Artists were used to create paintings and portraits that glorified Stalin and implied that he had broad support from the masses. Additionally, Stalin relied on alterations of photographs to rid them of those who had fallen out of his favor and were executed. His control of all forms of media, art, and communications helped Stalin create a state that had total control over public and private life.

Similarly to Joseph Stalin, when Mao Zedong won the Chinese Civil War, he sought to create a totalitarian state and foster support for his regime through the use of propaganda and control of mass media. Like Stalin, Mao used posters placed in highly visible areas to glorify his economic reforms, particularly the period of the Great Leap Forward. In 1958, Mao sought to industrialize China. However, his reforms turned out to be disastrous for the Chinese economy. These reforms caused mass famine and the deaths of millions. Despite the failure, propaganda posters predicting that China's economy would soon surpass Great Britain's economy were used to overshadow the atrocities that took place during the period of industrialization. After the failure of the Great Leap Forward, Mao wanted China to return to the ideals of communism under which the People's Republic of China was founded. He urged young students to learn the ideas of the revolution by making revolution. They responded by forming the militia known as the Red Guards, who became the enforcers of Mao's propaganda machine during the period of the Cultural Revolution. The heroes were the peasants and the workers; all intellectual and artistic life was considered useless and even dangerous. In response, the Red Guards shut down schools and universities. Intellectuals were forced into hard labor to purify themselves. The propaganda used under Mao helped control the masses and promote his communist ideals.

Propaganda has been a communications method used by world leaders to control all aspects of public and private life, particularly in totalitarian states. Both Joseph Stalin and Mao Zedong controlled mass media and used propaganda in the form of posters, newspapers, and artwork to maintain their control over the masses and promote the support of their communist ideals. Any ideas that were considered threatening to their ideology and power were stamped out. Their use of propaganda allowed these world leaders to maintain the appearance of strong support for their leadership and communist ideology.

PART III: DOCUMENT-BASED QUESTIONS

Part A: Short Answers

Document 1

1) Based on this excerpt, one goal of King Leopold II was to build an overseas empire to secure his position in the world.

Note: This response receives full credit because it correctly identifies one goal of King Leopold II by emphasizing his desire to compete with other countries of Western Europe by acquiring a new colony in Central Africa.

Document 2a

2a) According to Kevin Grant, King Leopold II was attempting to create a new system of taxation in which African chiefs were required to collect and pay taxes in goods and labor.

Note: This response receives full credit because it correctly identifies what King Leopold II was attempting to do in the Congo Free State by focusing on his desire to exploit the region for Belgium's gain.

Document 2b

2b) Based on this document, one impact the demand for rubber had on the Congo Free State was that the Congolese neglected their crops to harvest sap from rubber vines to meet the demands of European and American markets.

Note: This response receives full credit because it correctly identifies one impact the demand for rubber had on the Congo Free State by focusing on the Congolese people's disregard for their own crops to meet the demand for rubber.

Document 3

3) According to E. D. Morel, one impact of King Leopold II's control over the Congo Free State was that the Congo natives essentially lost their freedom and became slaves.

Note: This response receives full credit because it correctly identifies one impact of King Leopold II's control over the Congo Free State by focusing on the loss of the natives' freedom.

Document 4

4) According to Liao and Sohmen, the following are two characteristics of the socialist economy after the communists rose to power in China in 1949:

1. Industry was nationalized.
2. Agriculture was collectivized.

Note: This response receives full credit because it correctly identifies two characteristics of the socialist economy after the communists rose to power in China in 1949 by emphasizing the seizure of industry and agriculture on the part of the Chinese government.

Document 5a

5a) According to George J. Church, one action taken by Deng Xiaoping to reform China was to abolish the communes and replace them with a contract system where individual families could lease plots. After paying the rents, these individual families could grow whatever they wanted to sell in a free-market system.

Note: This response receives full credit because it correctly identifies one action taken by Deng Xiaoping to reform China by emphasizing the abolishment of communes.

Document 5b

5b) According to Jonathan Spence, one change Deng Xiaoping thought had to be made in an attempt to transform China into a world power was to revamp the educational system, particularly in universities and research institutes.

Note: This response receives full credit because it correctly identifies one change Deng Xiaoping thought had to be made in an attempt to transform China into a world power by focusing on the need to modernize education, particularly at the postsecondary level.

Document 6

6) According to Patrick E. Tyler, one impact of Deng Xiaoping's rule in China was that real incomes more than doubled in cities and in villages.

Note: This response receives full credit because it correctly identifies one impact of Deng Xiaoping's rule in China by focusing on a positive impact like income increases despite some negative outcomes, such as environmental pollution.

Document 7

7) According to Peter Limb, one problem faced by blacks in South Africa from the 1960s through the 1980s was being ruled by a rigid, inflexible, and intolerant government.

Note: This response receives full credit because it correctly identifies one problem blacks in South Africa faced from the 1960s through the 1980s by focusing on the harsh rule of the dominant minority government.

Document 8

8) Based on this document, one action taken by Desmond Tutu to resist South African government policies was to oppose a violent resistance to apartheid.

Note: This response receives full credit because it correctly identifies one action taken by Desmond Tutu to resist South African government policies by focusing on his advocacy of nonviolence.

Document 9

9) According to this statement from the Desmond Tutu Peace Centre website, one impact of Desmond Tutu's leadership was that he helped heal the nation after the end of apartheid by overseeing the Truth and Reconciliation Commission.

Note: This response receives full credit because it correctly identifies one impact of Desmond Tutu's leadership by emphasizing the importance of the Truth and Reconciliation Commission in helping to heal the nation after the end of apartheid.

DOCUMENT-BASED QUESTION: GENERIC SCORING RUBRIC

Score of 5:
- Thoroughly addresses all aspects of the *Task* by accurately analyzing and interpreting at least **four** documents
- Incorporates information from the documents in the body of the essay
- Incorporates relevant outside information
- Richly supports the theme or problem with relevant facts, examples, and details
- Is a well-developed essay, consistently demonstrating a logical and clear plan of organization
- Introduces the theme or problem by establishing a framework that is beyond a simple restatement of the *Task* or *Historical Context* and concludes with a summation of the theme or problem

Score of 4:
- Addresses all aspects of the *Task* by accurately analyzing and interpreting at least **four** documents
- Incorporates information from the documents in the body of the essay
- Incorporates relevant outside information
- Includes relevant facts, examples, and details, but discussion may be more descriptive than analytical
- Is a well-developed essay, demonstrating a logical and clear plan of organization
- Introduces the theme or problem by establishing a framework that is beyond a simple restatement of the *Task* or *Historical Context* and concludes with a summation of the theme or problem

Score of 3:
- Addresses most aspects of the *Task* or addresses all aspects of the *Task* in a limited way, using some of the documents
- Incorporates some information from the documents in the body of the essay
- Incorporates limited or no relevant outside information
- Includes some facts, examples, and details, but discussion is more descriptive than analytical
- Is a satisfactorily developed essay, demonstrating a general plan of organization
- Introduces the theme or problem by repeating the *Task* or *Historical Context* and concludes by simply repeating the theme or problem

Score of 2:
- Attempts to address some aspects of the *Task*, making limited use of the documents
- Presents no relevant outside information
- Includes few facts, examples, and details; discussion restates contents of the documents
- Is a poorly organized essay, lacking focus
- Fails to introduce or summarize the theme or problem

Score of 1:
- Shows limited understanding of the *Task* with vague, unclear references to the documents
- Presents no relevant outside information
- Includes little or no accurate or relevant facts, details, or examples
- Attempts to complete the *Task*, but demonstrates a major weakness in organization
- Fails to introduce or summarize the theme or problem

Score of 0: Fails to address the Task, is illegible, or is a blank paper

Part B: Essay

The actions of individuals have shaped the history of societies and regions. Although some individuals have impacted societies and regions in a negative way, many have had a positive impact. Two individuals who had a positive impact are Deng Xiaoping of China and Desmond Tutu of South Africa. Both Deng Xiaoping and Desmond Tutu brought positive changes to society. Deng Xiaoping helped bring about positive social changes in China through the implementation of economic reforms, while Desmond Tutu helped heal South Africa after decades of apartheid by presiding over an amnesty tribunal to promote reconciliation.

Prior to Deng's reforms, the economic structure under the Chinese socialist economic system led to economic hardships. When Mao Zedong won the Chinese Civil War in 1949, he transformed the economy into a system of communes where agriculture was collectivized and control of industry was seized by the state. All private ownership was eliminated in the first decade after Mao Zedong's victory (Doc. 4). Agricultural collectivization and the nationalization of industry brought about economic hardships in China. During the Great Leap Forward, Mao attempted to rapidly industrialize China. In doing so, much-needed resources were diverted to industry rather than to agriculture. This resulted in a famine that caused the deaths by starvation of tens of millions. China's economy was in need of reform.

After Mao's death, Deng Xiaoping came to power. He instituted economic reforms that provided more opportunities for social mobility and put China on the path to becoming a major world power. Deng's reforms abolished the communes that were established in the 1950s, when agriculture was collectivized. He replaced them with a system in which plots were leased to families where they would pay rents in grain or rice at a fixed price. Once the families paid rents, they were allowed to grow what they wanted and sell it on the free market (Doc. 5a). This reform transformed China's economy from a command economy to a mixed economy, resulting in economic growth and an increase in the GDP.

Deng's reforms had many positive impacts on the Chinese people. As a result of opening up markets, real incomes more than doubled. In fact, access to free market conveniences such as televisions and washing machines was possible (Doc. 6). Additionally, Deng revamped the educational system, particularly in the area of postsecondary education. In addition to opening up free markets, he encouraged the movement of foreigners to study in or tour China (Doc. 5b). China was modernizing. Deng Xiaoping's reforms benefited China as a whole. The people living within its borders no longer had to worry about famine but could prosper economically for the first time since the People's Republic of China was established in 1949.

While China focused on economic reforms to bring social change to the Chinese people, South Africa was in need of healing and unifying after decades of apartheid. When the Nationalist Party came to power in 1948, the policy of apartheid was officially put into place by the white minority government. Black South Africans, who made up the majority of the population, were marginalized and segregated in every way. Black South Africans were confined to specified areas called Bantustans, separate from white Afrikaners. Similar to Jim Crow laws in the American South, Black South Africans could not frequent the same restaurants as whites nor could they share the same public transportation carriages. Economic opportunities were limited, as Black South Africans could only get unskilled labor jobs. By 1976, after the banning of the African National Congress, a new opposition force called the Black Consciousness emerged under the student leader Steve Biko. The Black Consciousness supported the protests against apartheid that eventually led to the Soweto uprising by students. These protests were eventually put down by the government using harsh measures. As a result, many students were killed or injured (Doc. 7). Although apartheid eventually came to an end in 1994, the nation was in great need of healing after decades of racism, discrimination, and state-supported policies of segregation.

Archbishop Desmond Tutu, who took a nonviolent approach to resisting apartheid, presided over the Truth and Reconciliation Commission to help heal the nation. In the process, Desmond Tutu heard revelations of past apartheid-era crimes and offered amnesty to many who committed the crimes rather than reacting punitively (Doc. 9). Over two thousand victims' and perpetrators' stories were heard by the Truth and Reconciliation Commission. In many cases, the perpetrators expressed remorse and sorrow for their actions. As a result, they were granted amnesty. This forgiveness helped heal the nation to an extent.

Although racism still exists in South Africa, the Truth and Reconciliation Commission did put South Africa onto a path to healing and became the model for other nations whose societies experienced human rights violations. It opened up a pathway to openly discuss the atrocities that both Black South Africans and Afrikaners experienced under apartheid. Their testimonies were broadcasted nationwide for everyone to hear. These broadcasts did help to open the minds of some and help the country to heal. Additionally, South Africa's Truth and Reconciliation Commission, led by Tutu, became a model for other nations, including the Solomon Islands and Sri Lanka.

The actions of individuals have impacted societies and regions in positive and negative ways. Both Deng Xiaoping of China and Desmond Tutu of South Africa had a positive impact on their respective nations. Deng Xiaoping put China on a path to becoming a global power by ridding China of the commune system and allowing for the opening of free markets after decades of communism. In South Africa, Desmond Tutu took a nonviolent approach to ending apartheid. He oversaw the Truth and Reconciliation Commission, which helped South Africa heal after decades of segregation and human rights violations. Both leaders influenced the futures of their nations as well as that of other nations that followed their example.

Topic	Question Numbers	Total Number of Questions	Number Wrong	*Reason for Wrong Answer
U.S. AND N.Y. HISTORY				
WORLD HISTORY	3, 4, 6, 9, 11, 12, 13, 15, 16, 17, 19, 20, 21, 24, 27, 28, 29, 30	18		
GEOGRAPHY	1, 7, 10, 14, 25, 26	6		
ECONOMICS	8, 22, 23	3		
CIVICS, CITIZENSHIP, AND GOVERNMENT	2, 5, 18	3		

*Your reason for answering the question incorrectly might be (a) lack of knowledge, (b) misunderstanding of the question, or (c) careless error.

Actual Items by Standard and Unit

	1 U.S. and N.Y. History	2 World History	3 Geography	4 Economics	5 Civics, Citizenship, and Government	Number
Methodology of Global History and Geography		3	1		2	3
UNIT ONE Age of Revolution		4, 6, 9, 12	7, 10	8	5	8
UNIT TWO Crisis and Achievement (1900–1945)		13, 15, 16, 29, 30	14			6
UNIT THREE 20th Century Since 1945		17, 19		22, 23	18	5
UNIT FOUR Global Connections and Interactions		20, 21, 24, 28	25, 26			6
Cross-Topical		11, 27				2
Total # of Questions		18	6	3	3	30
% of Items by Standard		60%	20%	10%	10%	100%

Notes

Notes

Notes

Notes

Notes

Notes

Notes

Notes

Notes

Notes

Notes